GENDER AND NATIONAL IDENTITY

IN TWENTIETH-CENTURY

RUSSIAN CULTURE

GENDER

AND NATIONAL IDENTITY

IN TWENTIETH-CENTURY

RUSSIAN CULTURE

EDITED BY

HELENA GOSCILO AND ANDREA LANOUX

NORTHERN

ILLINOIS

UNIVERSITY

PRESS

DeKalb

Library of Congress Cataloging-in-Publication Data

Gender and national identity in twentieth-century Russian culture / edited by Helena Goscilo and Andrea Lanoux.— 1st ed.

p. cm.

Includes bibliographical references and index.

ISBN-13: 978-0-87580-354-8 (clothbound : alk. paper)

ISBN-10: 0-87580-354-7 (clothbound : alk. paper)

ISBN-13: 978-0-87580-609-9 (pbk. : alk. paper)

ISBN-10: 0-87580-609-0 (pbk. : alk. paper)

1. Sex role—Soviet Union 2. Sex role—Russia (Federation) 3. National characteristics, Russian. 4. Soviet Union—Civilization. 5. Russia (Federation)—Civilization.

I. Goscilo, Helena, 1945– II. Lanoux, Andrea.

HQ1075.5.S65G45 2006

305.4'0947—dc22

2005020692

FOR MALEN'KAIA DARIA

Contents

Preface

Books, like nations, appear as living entities to those near to them, hence the habit of reaching for organic metaphors to tell their stories. This book was a bastard from the start. The brainchild of Laurel Schultz and Petra Rethmann, it grew out of a session of the women's group at the University of Illinois Summer Research Lab in 2000. Without the initiative and input of the scholars attending that summer, it would never have come into being.

Like the evolution of all projects too long in the making, this one was circuitous and repeatedly thwarted. I am grateful for the unflagging commitment, hard work, and inspiring creativity of the contributors, who, like eager parents expecting a child several years overdue, waited silently and patiently for a birth that was to come "any minute now."

I am likewise grateful to Helena Goscilo, who literally brought this book to life. It has been a dream and a true privilege to work with Helena; far from demystifying one of my longtime idols, the experience of working with her has left me in even greater awe of her talents.

Finally, I am grateful to Connecticut College for supporting my work on this book and to Frank Fulchiero for his indispensable help with visuals. I would also like to thank Nathan MacBrien for his candor and comments on an earlier version of this manuscript; the two anonymous reviewers for Northern Illinois University Press, whose careful readings and thoughtful suggestions shaped the final version; and especially our editor, Mary Lincoln, whose professionalism, diligence, and support brought it all to fruition.

A.L.

I enthusiastically echo the words of gratitude to Mary Lincoln, whose frankness, grace, and flexibility throughout the "contracting" stage have been remarkable.

Andrea's modesty has led to an overestimation of my part in this project. Our collaboration has involved genuine sharing: we edited together, wrote together, and for several hours in Moscow (2004) laughed together about the customary "trials and tribs" of combining production with reproduction: as this volume goes to press, Andrea is nursing a newborn girl who, one hopes, will inherit her mother's intelligence, generosity of spirit, and love of ideas. It is to her that we dedicate this collection, which (to introduce a pedestrian note) relies on the Library of Congress system of transliteration.

H.G.

GENDER AND NATIONAL IDENTITY

IN TWENTIETH-CENTURY

RUSSIAN CULTURE

Lost in the Myths

HELENA GOSCILO AND ANDREA LANOUX

The happiest women, like the happiest nations, have no history.

—George Eliot, *The Mill on the Floss*

Binaries and Revolution

Sigmund Freud's notorious characterization of women's sexuality as the Dark Continent, framed in the threadbare rhetoric of light and darkness that contrasts male lucidity and enlightenment to female hysteria and gross mater/iality, reprises the ancient myth of a gendered cosmic division that cast the sky as male and the earth as female.[1] Entrenched in prehistoric lore and artifacts, folktales, and literature, this essentialist dyad was reinforced in medieval Russia by the widespread veneration of Mat' Syra Zemlia (Moist Mother Earth),[2] the "vivifying" soil that doubled as both womb and tomb—a quasi-synonym central to Dostoevsky's concept of resurrection and the philosophy of Village Prose during the Soviet era.[3]

While the earth's fecundity naturalized its feminization, language itself seems to have facilitated the gendering of nation. With Deutschland as notable exception, La France, España, Italia, and virtually all Slavic countries—Polska, Rossiia, Slovakia, Ukraina—have feminine grammatical endings that enable reference to each country as "she" in a gendered allegory of nationhood.[4] England's Britannia, France's Marianne, Matka Boska Polska, Mother India, and Russia's Rodina-Mat' testify to the ubiquitous imagery of embodiment that erases empirical female identity by trope.[5] The antithesis between woman as metaphor and man as individualized agent neatly slotted into the binary model that Iurii Lotman has ascribed to Russia culture[6] and that proved particularly hospitable to the dichotomized gender stereotypes recently deconstructed by Hélène Cixous, Luce Irigaray, and a host of appropriately skeptical feminists.[7]

In the period leading up to the Russian revolutions of 1905 and 1917, the topos of masculine-feminine duality played a central role in national mythology as articulated by members of the Russian intelligentsia. In a classic example, Vasilii Rozanov contended:

> There are two Russias: one is a *visible* Russia, a mass of external forms with proper features that please the eye, and a series of events that had definite beginnings and determinate ends—the "Empire," the history of which Karamzin "depicted," Solov'ev "developed," and the laws of which Speranskii "codified." And there is the other [Other?]: "Holy Russia," "Mother Russia" [*Matushka-Rus'*], whose laws no one knows, with unclear forms, with uncertain tendencies, the conclusion of which cannot be predicted, whose origins are unknown—a Russia of essences, of living blood, of unshakable faith. . . . (Rozanov, "Psikhologiia russkogo raskola" 47; qtd. in Riabov 107–8)

Rozanov's formulation displays the gendered oppositions at work in the fin-de-siècle Russian idea: identified here through its "visible," "external" qualities, the state is associated with historical temporality and events, the code of law, Empire, and the great men (Karamzin, Solov'ev, Speranskii—i.e., the historians and statesmen) who gave it form, all under the aegis of "the Russian Empire." By contrast, the nation is of mysterious origins, located outside historical time, and characterized by the amorphous, sacred, essential, life-giving force that is "Mother Russia." Rozanov's emphasis on "her" unpredictability foregrounds an element that would figure prominently in the apocalyptic rhetoric preceding the revolutions: Russian femininity as *stikhiia* (elemental force—a fundamental trait of Mat' Syra Zemlia) [Fig. I-1].[8]

While the distinction between nation and state may seem too self-evident to warrant commentary, it poses certain problems by virtue of its false transparency, especially when the state is overthrown and a national sensibility continues to function and organize social life. Provisionally defined, the state is a recognizable, "relatively centralized organizational structure with claims to sovereignty over a territory"; its existence depends on various forms of legitimacy and coercion (recall Max Weber's famous formulation of the state as "a human community that [successfully] claims a monopoly on the legitimate use of physical force" over its citizens).[9] The subjective component that distinguishes nations—as "symbolic constructs, categories of identity or systems of social classification that can be used to create horizontal solidarities or 'imagined communities'"—renders them elusive and inseparable from idea or myth.[10] Although both nation and state are grounded in social practices, traditions, institutions, and symbols, the latter possesses an objective dimension that the former lacks: whereas one can visit a country and meet its head of state, one cannot go to a nation, which combines ubiquity with a "capacity for nearly infinite self-differentiation" (Parker 3). That contrast found popular articulation in Russians' long-standing

I-1   "Russia for Truth" (1914). (From Victoria Bonnell, *Iconography of Power: Soviet Political Posters under Lenin and Stalin* [Los Angeles and Berkeley: University of California Press, 1997])

rhetoric of family, which designated the "visible" patriarchal ruler Batiushka-Tsar' and the indefinable nation Matushka-Rus'.

While the Bolshevik Revolution of 1917 brought political turmoil, mass starvation, and civil war in its wake, it also promised social justice, sexual equality, and an end to centuries of patriarchal rule. The cataclysmic demise of the monarchy and the imperial phase of Russian history inevitably transformed Russians' perception of their national legacy and profoundly complicated their sense of national identity. Wholesale disavowal of the past and systemic endeavors to forge the New Man and New Woman in the purportedly classless, gender-equitable order, however, failed to eradicate or to camouflage concepts that had ruled gender disposition from time immemorial. As Elizabeth Hemenway's examination of late-tsarist and early-Soviet sociopolitical activists reveals (Chapter 3), the traditional feminine attributes of maternity, nurture, modesty, and self-sacrifice persisted as uncontested desiderata among female revolutionaries and especially among those who wrote them into Soviet history, partly structuring the behavior of the former and overwhelming the discourse of the latter. In short, the early period of transition trapped Russians in limbo, between remnants of a discredited past, with its values and hierarchies, and a "radiant future" in the making, inspired by untested theories and faith in perfectibility.

Programmatic Emancipation

Even before the USSR adopted its official name on December 30, 1922, a Soviet sensibility was growing out of and grafting onto a Russian national identity in crisis. Whatever the weaknesses of the Bolsheviks' hastily assembled program, its dramatic reversals in ideology and policy had immediate and lasting consequences for relations between men and women, as well as their relation to the new state. Leaders of the freshly constituted regime fostered the development of a Soviet identity not only through relentless attacks on the past and its allegedly retrograde traditions, but also through radically progressive legislation and the creation of new institutions by accelerated decree. Among the most consequential measures intended to safeguard women's rights was the 1918 Family Code concerning the civil registration of births, marriages, and deaths. It established gender equality under the law, legalized divorce, granted all children equal rights, and guaranteed women full control over their property and income after marriage (Ashwin 7). The creation of the Communist Party's Women's Section (Zhenotdel) the following year further advanced an emancipatory agenda by launching initiatives to improve literacy, provide child and orphan care, distribute food and other necessities, and promote public health among women and children. Clearly intended to draw women into the Party and to consolidate their allegiance to the new regime, the institutionalization of Zhenotdel on the state level marked a historic turning point by formally integrating many Russian women into public life—an unprecedented step.

However admirable the state's program for wresting women from the circumscribed niche that had defined their social status under the old regime, the subsequent course of Soviet history unambiguously reflects three irresoluble and interrelated contradictions that thwarted the utopian plan: (1) the official, ideologically motivated drive to incorporate women into society on an equal footing with men versus the knee-jerk, habitual assumption of women's subservience, rooted in the age-old binary of Man as (hu)mankind and Woman as the antithetical complement in, and thus enabler of, that dualistic mode of thought; (2) paper rights—laws promulgated to enfranchise women—versus their empirical reality as second-class citizens; and (3) the discursive habit of troping women as Nation and Ideal versus the reluctance to acknowledge their existence as humans struggling to cope with everyday circumstances in a male-dominated society. In short, the professed remained at odds with experience, discourse at odds with life.

Sarah Ashwin's introduction to *Gender, State, and Society in Soviet and Post-Soviet Russia* (2000) summarizes some of the salient problems inhering in Soviet policies and social practices concerning gender—"always a key organizing principle in the Soviet system. As the regime strengthened its position, gender became the basis on which the duties of citizens to the new polity were defined: men and women had distinctive roles to play in the building of communism." As "worker-mothers," women were expected to supervise the household, and in return received "'protection' from the state in their capacity as mothers, as well as independence through their access to paid work." Male roles not only carried more influence and prestige, but operated on a larger scale, occupying a vastly different space.[11] Men "were to serve as leaders, managers, soldiers, workers—in effect, they were to manage and build the communist system—while the state assumed the responsibility for the fulfillment of the traditional masculine roles of father and provider, becoming, in effect, a universal patriarch to which both men and women were subject" (Ashwin 1).

Bifurcated in its radically progressive yet traditional-essentialist allegiances, the Bolshevik conception of gender derived from medieval notions of masculinity and femininity, valorizing women's domestic function while entrusting to men the leadership that vouchsafed them virtual monopoly over public life. Ashwin astutely interprets attacks on the traditional family in the first decades of the Soviet era "as a means of legitimizing intervention in the private sphere," with the aim of eventually reconstituting the family under Stalin as master patriarch (5, 9). As a consequence of the inner split in the governmental agenda, women confronted the double burden of full-time employment and responsibility for all domestic duties, as well as insistent exhortations, sweetened by incentives, to bear children and to educate them as model citizens of the new order (14). Prodigious feats of reproduction merited military decorations, awarded to mothers of five or more offspring. Indeed, the checkered history of Soviet legislation on abortion exposed the inconsistencies in a system that simultaneously called upon women to join the workforce and to reproduce on a regular basis. Legalized in 1920, abortion became outlawed under Stalin in 1936, only to be officially reinstated in 1955.[12] The state's investment in an ever-expanding labor pool far outweighed any commitment to women's health and freedom of choice; even as late as perestroika Russian women resorted to abortion as the major available means of "contraception."

Citing the regime's inability to realize its declared goal of gender parity as testimony to the complete failure of the Soviet project leaves scant interpretive room for assessing women's gains in the areas of reproductive rights, child and family protection laws, employment, and economic independence. Analyzing how and why the new laws and institutions failed to eradicate gender discrimination is an incomparably more difficult task—one compounded, moreover, by a temptation to offer the "persistence of patriarchy" as the sole explanation for unfulfilled promises and practices that manifestly violated proclamations. A more nuanced analysis leads us beyond the category of policy and political actors, into the realm of culture—that is, beyond the observable sphere of the state and into the mythological space of the nation.

En/gendering Nation

That is precisely the domain under investigation in the present volume, which parallels *Gender, State, and Society in Soviet and Post-Soviet Russia* in its inquiries, but places emphasis on the twinned categories of gender and national identity during the same period. Sundry aspects of this complex interrelation have been scrutinized throughout the last decade by Eliot Borenstein, Barbara Clements, Rebecca Friedman, Dan Healey, Susan Larsen, Eric Naiman, Daniel Rancour-LaFerriere, Oleg Riabov, Thomas Schrand, and Ewa Thompson.[13] Obviously, no single narrative can pretend to grapple adequately with all the ambiguities, paradoxes, vicissitudes, and silences that characterized the seventy-plus years of Soviet rule in order to tell "the whole story" of a national identity crisis after the October Revolution. With that awareness, contributors to our collection have chosen to examine select moments in Soviet and post-Soviet cultural history from a variety of disciplinary perspectives. Scholars from the fields of anthropology, history, literature, linguistics, film studies, and the history of music explore diverse expressions of Russo-Soviet and post-Soviet identities, paying particular attention to how gender informed the processes of state-building and nation-building in the Soviet Union and the Russian Federation.

The ten chapters in this volume analyze both the value-freighted division between the sexes that flourished in Soviet Russia despite strenuous efforts at gender-democracy, and the responses of intellectuals, political leaders, and average citizens of both sexes to tensions between official Soviet ideology and an enduring but unacknowledged imperial legacy. Our collection addresses such questions as: How have categories of gender and national identity constituted each other in Russian, Soviet, and post-Soviet history? Under what social conditions has Russian national identity been articulated as masculine or feminine? What impact do gendered representations of nationhood exert on the lives of real men and women?

Quite puzzlingly, in light not only of far-reaching intellectual developments over the last three decades, but also of the parallelism between gender and nationality as "relational term[s] whose identity derives from [. . . their] inherence in a system of differences" (Parker 5), many recent studies of Russian nationalism and state formation make no mention of gender, let alone treat it as a vital component of national identity.[14] Such inexplicable omissions, which presuppose nation and gender as discrete and autonomous entities, imply that national identity is gender-neutral and that women's experience of citizenship and national affiliations fully accords with men's. Yet Russianness, like all national identities, is historically grounded in notions of masculinity and femininity so pervasive that until the advent of feminism they appeared both natural and incontrovertible.

Feminist scholars outside Slavic Studies have documented a persistent gender demarcation between state and nation that equates state with masculinity and nation with femininity. As Rick Wilford remarks, women "are commonly constructed as the symbolic form of the nation whereas men are invariably represented as its chief agents and, with statehood achieved, emerge as its major beneficiaries" (Wilford 3).[15] With some notable exceptions,[16] this distinction has thrived in Russia. For the greater part of three centuries, Russian and Soviet heads of state have fostered a cult of masculinity, epitomized by imperial Russia's all-male cadre of bureaucrats, military schools, and exclusive institutions for nobles, and subsequently by the Soviet Union's ideological founding fathers, New Men, and Stakhanovite workers. By contrast, Russian nationhood historically has assumed female form, whether in the image of Mother Russia (*Matushka-Rus'*, *rodina-mat'*), the Russian literary heroine, or the foreign currency prostitute—all endowed with the traits of irrationality, passion, enigma, submissiveness, and suffering invariably imputed to women.

The Power of Language and Loss

Unlike subsequent chapters in our chronologically arranged volume, the first two range over several centuries so as to trace the tenaciousness and immutability of specific phenomena amidst evolution and radical change. On the basis of copious materials and genres encompassing informal conversation, proverbs, fiction, posters, and caricatures, Valentina Zaitseva (Chapter 1) demonstrates the extent to which language itself accounts for the feminization of nation. Contrasting the feminine noun *"rodina"* to the neuter *"otechestvo,"* Zaitseva argues that the root of the former [birth, clan] not only denotes motherland and birthplace, but also conjures up the emotive, familial, and ethnic aspects of nationhood. By contrast, *"otechestvo,"* with its root signifying "father," evokes masculine qualities, continuous with the political, historical, and ideological features of state. As Zaitseva observes, the pervasiveness of the generic "unmarked" masculine gender in Russian, especially in professions and politics, automatically relegates women to alterity in the public sphere, confining their experience to the domains of love, sex, family, home, and—when the need arises—collapses them into an allegory of nationhood.

If nation is feminine, then its losses translate all too readily into the trope of widowhood, as Helena Goscilo (Chapter 2) illustrates, through collective rituals of mourning, war imagery, and such genres as lamentations and retrospective hagiographies of Great Men penned by their wives. Russia's embrace of kenoticism informs its self-presentation as a nation of stoic sufferers for the sake of humankind (especially during the Napoleonic campaign and World War II), but the major dramatis personae in Russia's scripted heroic tragedy are men, with women as witnesses, archivists, and modern hagiographers. That distribution of roles feeds into cultural discourse: widowers constitute a non-category, and the infrequency of the Russian word *"vdovets"* (masc.) as opposed to the omnipresent *"vdova"* (fem.)—in a ratio of one to twenty-eight, according to scholarly studies—evidences the asymmetry in the gendered perception of and responses to death on both personal and national fronts (Zasorina 80).

Other gendered asymmetries proliferated during the immediate pre- and postrevolutionary years, when female activists encountered firsthand the dilemma of fulfilling state expectations of the New Woman according to the priorities mandated by Leninist dicta. Heeding the imperative to place the common cause before personal considerations, women separated from their biological families for the sake of full-time revolutionary agitation and education within the metaphorical "big family." Yet, as Hemenway contends (Chapter 3), the irresistible pull of tradition and the incipient familial rhetoric that troped Lenin as the "father" paradoxically colluded in published reports that subsumed women's political engagement and treatment of fellow revolutionaries into surrogate motherhood. Both the Soviet press and the beneficiaries of their "model" behavior fell back on musty stereotypes, lauding the women as virtuous, nurturing, self-abnegating maternal figures, though their very actions countered traditional gender roles.

The Soviet model hardly stood out as an exception. Feminist scholars have amassed evidence attesting a universal pattern of women's co-optation into revolutionary movements with promises to ameliorate women's social status in the new society. Yet, as Cynthia Enloe points out, throughout history the national cause has taken precedence over women's rights, perpetually deferring a solution to the "woman question": "Women who have called for more genuine equality between the sexes . . . have been told that now is not the time, the nation is too fragile. . . . Women must be patient, they must wait until the nationalist goal is achieved; *then* relations between women and men can be addressed" (62).[17] Or, as Anne McClintock

I-2   Gustav Klutis, "Vyshe znamia Marksa Engel'sa Lenina i Stalina!" [Raise higher the banner of Marx, Engels, Lenin, and Stalin!], (1933). (From Victoria Bonnell, *Iconography of Power: Soviet Political Posters under Lenin and Stalin* [Los Angeles and Berkeley: University of California Press, 1997])

formulates it, "To ask women to wait until after the revolution serves merely as a strategic tactic to defer women's demands . . . women who are not empowered to organize during the struggle will not be empowered to organize after the struggle" (122). Indeed, as Goscilo argues, waiting became Soviet women's specialty, in a spirit of trusting optimism derided by ensuing events. The recurrent narrative in official Soviet encomia to women revolutionaries, Hemenway shows, was exclusively one of revolution, not of women's emancipation, despite the female revolutionaries' own commitment to and investment in women's rights.[18] And the Soviet state never succeeded in genuinely enfranchising its female population, which voluntarily surrendered negotiable political terrain during "the struggle."

Masculinity as Tempered Steel

The very possibility of women's bona fide emancipation posed a serious threat to the patriarchal order and contributed to the reassertion of masculinity in the first decades of the Soviet state. The New Man and all that he stood for exemplified the cult of masculinity: progress, industry, technology, and military power. Prerevolutionary images of Mother Russia as elemental force ceded to ubiquitous placards of the "founding fathers" of Communism, who also embodied the quintessentially male sphere of ideology

[Fig. I-2]. Efforts to promote women's equality in this context, in fact, rendered gender-neutrality commensurate with masculinity, forcing women either to cross-dress and adopt traditionally masculine roles in the industrial workforce, or to retain their traditional roles as mothers and homemakers in the private domain. The wholesale masculinization of society during this period of reconstruction leaps out from Soviet political posters featuring "emancipated women" in bomber jackets, overalls, and lab coats, marked as women only by captions, bustlines, or conspicuously straying locks of hair.

The homocentric orientation of Communist ideology emerges most forcefully, perhaps, in its presentation of "ideological enemies," including proponents of the New Economic Policy (1921–1928). Thomas Schrand's commentary on this brief reinstatement of modified capitalism dovetails with Western scholarship's conclusions about the widespread tendency throughout Europe and the United States to associate consumerism with women. Schrand remarks that "the NEP was often gendered and criticized as feminine, characterized by demoralizing (and emasculating?) ideological compromises that the virile pursuit of 'socialism in one country' promised to sweep away" (Schrand 198). The gendered portrayal of ideological hypocrisy finds eloquent incarnation in Iurii Olesha's *Envy* [*Zavist'*, 1927], in the persona of Andrei Babichev, an illustrious NEP-man who opens a communal kitchen as a business venture. His alleged superiority to the socially marginalized narrator-protagonist, Nikolai Kavalerov—a throwback to pre-Soviet values—is consistently subverted though Babichev's emphasized femininity: his jiggling breasts as he descends the stairs, his desire to "give birth to food," and the domestic ("kitchen") arena over which he presides. His very name evokes the retrograde *"baba"* (on the evolving connotations of this term, see Zaitseva in this volume), amplifying in gendered terms his status as a transitional figure, to be superseded by his protégé Volodia Makarov—athlete, comrade extraordinaire, and "the personification of hope," whose determination to become a human machine anticipates the specifications of Stalinist machismo.

Gendered archetypes of power, social intercourse, and ideological correctness likewise overran early Soviet-era film, which visually documented the interplay between gender and national identity under communism. Examining constructions of masculinity in Nikolai Ekk's 1931 film, *The Road to Life* [*Putevka v zhizn'*], Lilya Kaganovsky (Chapter 4) spotlights the paucity of on-screen female images and the strategies for their elimination. Rites of initiation into Soviet manhood required rationalized abrogation of the feminine as a troublesome category that Ekk reduces to grotesque or deified figures, such as the mother, whose purely symbolic function in the national body politic rendered her expendable in the context of homosocial politicking and the metamorphosis of the adolescent into the New Man. Initially universal in its accessibility, with the advent of sound, cinema became increasingly nationalized, eventually functioning as a potential export of Russia's self-image to foreign audiences. Kaganovsky's analysis of "the first Soviet sound film" therefore sheds light on the broader problem of how visual media served to construct and disseminate national identities in the twentieth century.

By the mid-1930s and the definitive consolidation of Stalin's power, the Strong Hand's hypertrophied vision dictated the requisites of Soviet masculinity, articulated through monumentalism, the cult of the machine, and the imperative of imposing control over nature. While the ace flyer Valerii Chkalov and Stalin's "daredevil" young pilots ("*orliata*") commandeered the skies through unparalleled exploits of courage and skill, male prisoners and citizens defied all norms in constructing dams and canals in record time under deplorable conditions. The grandiose "General Plan for the Reconstruction of Moscow" Stalin launched in 1935 required that male "hard bodies" conquer time and space (along both horizontal and vertical axes) to transform the city at accelerated speed into a modern metropolis. The subterranean feats of the coalminer Aleksei Stakhanov paled beside the superhuman tenacity of the men working underground on the spectacular Moscow metro, conceived as an efficient means of transportation and a visual paradise for the masses in the nation's symbolic center, lavishly displayed in screen documentaries of the era. The metro not only demanded indefatigable male labor, but also showcased impressive physiques of Soviet masculinity in the mosaics and sculptures decorating its stations. These sculptures of Herculean beauty and brawn illustrated the dominant role of the male body as the incarnation of Soviet ideals, while the even more massive sculptures of and monuments to Stalin throughout the Soviet Union reminded the population that the Father of All Peoples was the wise architect of these ideals and the epic endeavors vouchsafing the nation's glory. Like the seven skyscrapers ("*vysotki*") built with forced labor from 1947 to 1955, these soaring structures indexed the megalomaniacal proportions of Stalin's ambitions and the public image of state and nation he envisioned. Himself the unrivaled personification of masculine omnipotence and omnipresence, Stalin institutionalized a militaristic machismo that consigned women to their traditional roles of domestic caretakers and reproducers. Abortion became criminalized in 1936 so that women could expand the "small family" according to the blueprint devised by the patriarch of the "Big Family."

Vera Mukhina's famous stainless-steel statue *Male Worker and Female Collective Farm Laborer* [Rabotnik i kolkhoznitsa], featured aloft the Soviet pavilion at the international exhibit in Paris in 1937 as a symbol of the Soviet Union's industrial advances in the modern world, belies the official rhetoric of the Stalinist era through the contrasting forms. In an iconography that testifies to the gendered concept of Soviet progress, the woman, grasping the sickle emblematic of agricultural work in the countryside, stands slightly behind the heroic male laborer, who brandishes the hammer symbolizing urban achievements. In short, Stalinism returned women to Nature and the imaginary, men to Culture and the symbolic order.

The competing ideologies of Soviet masculinity and gender parity were challenged further in the 1940s, when the uncertainties of war and the German threat inspired a concerted revival of Russian national sentiment anchored in traditional attitudes toward gender. Propaganda during the Great Fatherland War (*Velikaia Otechestvennaia Voina*)—the very epithet *otechestvennaia* proleptically invoking a masculine victory—replaced the iconography of men and women building communism side by side with countless images of suffering, vulnerable women and valiant men fighting to protect the once again feminized nation [Fig. I-3]. Age-old gender stereotypes preponderated in songs, poems, and films exalting feminine loyalty and masculine agency, even as thousands of women participated in frontline combat alongside men. Suzanne Ament (Chapter 5) documents how in its campaign to promote patriotism the Party consciously appealed to "bourgeois" emotions and concerns as it solicited the public's input into songs intended to bolster the morale of the troops and those maintaining the home front. Directives encouraged the composition of sentimental songs with a pre-Soviet sensibility that foregrounded personal attachment to the Russian land—frequently indivisible from the faithful women awaiting soldiers' eventual return.

In the aftermath of a victory attained at the cost of countless lives and incalculable material loss, the exigencies of rebuilding a devastated country became the state's paramount priority. This period of gradual, painful recovery was dominated by national images of Soviet victory, on the one hand, and of Russian martyrdom, on the other, which created a highly ambivalent picture of masculine success and feminine sacrifice. Men and women who had united as Russians against the enemy returned to a profoundly changed society that now had to reconstruct an entire way of life. With the male population decimated by both war and Stalin's terror, Russia had transmogrified into a nation of widows—of living memorials to the personal sacrifices made for the country. Accordingly, Russian widowhood renewed in full force its function as national allegory, whereby the bereavement of Russian widows (unlike their European and American counterparts') was generalized, unobtrusively displaced onto the nation itself. Individual and especially collective mourning adopted ritualistic forms of commemoration that provided a means of uniting the living casualties of war.

In the atmosphere of elegy and hope permeating the late 1940s and early 1950s, paintings depicting lonely women, such as Iurii Pimenov's *Night Station* and Maks Birshtein's *Spring* (1945), implied the destruction of Soviet manhood, while the brigade sculpture *We Demand Peace* (1950), executed under Mukhina's direction, captured the dualism of postwar Russia's gendered self-perception (Bown 160, 210) [Fig. I-4]. The group design juxtaposes three stoic men, one in uniform, his arm assertively out-flung, with a woman on a slightly lower, adjacent ledge, her face contorted in anguish, holding an infant's corpse in her outstretched arms. Leading the group as a symbol of the nation's future is the dynamic figure of a woman in mid-

I-3 D. Shmarinov, "Avenge!" (1942).

stride, gazing firmly into the distance, a waving child clasped in one hand and the traditional dove of peace in her upraised right palm. The work, in which the two women embody the standard maternal allegory of nation, eloquently poises Russia in a spatialized temporality, between the claims of a grim past and credence in a brighter future.[19]

I-4   Vera Mukhina, Zinaida Ivanova, Nina Zelenskaya, Aleksandr Sergeev, Sergei Kasakov, "We Demand Peace" (1950).

Melting Masculinity and Surrogate Maternity

That future seemed to arrive with Stalin's death in 1953. The ensuing Thaw allowed for moderate tolerance of comparably moderate dissent and deviation from prescriptions, and the slight easing of authoritarian restraints revealed the discrepancies between official culture and daily experience. Instead of overturning Stalinist principles, the Thaw merely reworked and modified them.[20] Although Khrushchev's denunciation of Stalin's crimes at the Twentieth Party Congress in 1956 intimated a repudiation of the previous era, which five years later culminated in the removal of Stalin's body from the mausoleum in Red Square, his concurrent validation of the Soviet political system ushered in a decade of increasing duplicity, moral ambiguity, and impending political unrest—the Hungarian uprising, the rebellion in Poland, and the Cuban Missile Crisis. Nonetheless, with steel no longer the matrix metaphor for the state's leader as the icon of universal emulation, monumentalism and the compulsion to master nature through indomitable will, muscle, and technology gradually ceded to the new values of small-scale endeavors, emotion, and human bonds—precisely the elements tentatively endorsed in the Il'ia Erenburg novel (1954) whose title supplied the metaphorical label for the Khrushchev era.

Not only the label, which evokes the fabled fluids of the female imaginary, but also the rehabilitated qualities of smallness and interiority (i.e., sentiment and domesticity) pointed to the nation's embrace of femininity. Everyday issues—of personal morality, romance, family life, and children—invaded literature, film, and song, while lyric poetry became the most popular genre. Younger generations flocked to stadiums where Bella Akhmadulina, Evgenii Evtushenko, and Andrei Voznesenskii recited their verses; Bulat Okudzhava, the soft-spoken bard who sang of the seemingly mundane, likewise attracted numerous listeners weary of hyperbole and bombast, just as the unexceptional protagonist of Grigorii Chukhrai's *Ballad of a Solider* [*Ballada o soldate*, 1959] found sympathy with viewers at home and abroad. Not homegrown military heroes welded to a state-sanctioned teleology, but reflective, self-questioning idealists appeared on the screen in Grigorii Kozintsev's adaptation of *Don Quixote* (1957) and his acclaimed *Hamlet* (1964)—"translations" of foreign imports inconceivable under Stalin's xenophobic militaristic regime but magnets for record-breaking Thaw audiences.

Indeed, the Thaw witnessed the feminization of males, or, more precisely, their co-optation of refurbished values "with a human face." Literature and film focused on the sensitive, caring man who now could legitimately indulge in hesitation and uncertainty, pen passionate lyrics about his private world and his affinity for nature, and shed tears of ecstasy or despair—a protagonist most fully realized in Boris Pasternak's *Doctor Zhivago* (wr. 1955, pd. in Italy in 1957), which quite explicitly contrasts the indecisive, apolitical poet favorably with the inflexible revolutionary Strel'nikov and the politicized entrepreneur and pseudo-NEPman Komarovskii. Not leather-clad, bulldozing action, but reaction motivated from within—above all, by sincerity, compassion, and integrity—reigned as the sociocultural dominant among the Thaw's liberal faction.

In tune with these reversals, an overt exchange of gender roles structured narratives sympathetic to a major persona of Thaw culture: the child, who not only metonymized the reconstituted "small family" but also represented authenticity and the nation's future. Such works as Andrei Tarkovskii's *My Name Is Ivan* [*Ivanovo detstvo*, 1962], Vera Panova's *Serezha* (1955), and Georgii Daneliia's prize-winning celluloid version of the novella (1960) feature men as voluntary surrogate mothers to orphan boys. Many "mother"/son constellations generated doubles, in plots that mirrored the nurturing veteran in the solitary male child—both victims of war trauma: for example, Mikhail Sholokhov's story "Man's Fate" ["Sud'ba cheloveka," 1956] and its screen adaptation by Alla Surikova (1959), and *The*

Two Fedors [*Dva Fedors,* 1958], directed by Marlen Khutsiev. Male appropriation of women's traditional identity as compassionate nurturers resulted in the Thaw's portrayal of absent or unfeeling mothers and "incidental," unattached women more invested in personal self-fulfillment than self-abnegation for the sake of family and nation. Clearly, the war had destroyed not only lives, but also a reliable model of implacable masculinity. Projecting men's sense of diminishment and impotence after the horrors of WWII onto little boys whom they saved, sheltered, and treated as "young comrades" may have assuaged ex-soldiers' guilt at having survived their fallen compatriots and reassured men racked by fears of appearing emasculated. By 1964, when Khrushchev's dismissal curtailed the cautious liberalization synonymous with the Thaw, formerly ironclad gender boundaries had destabilized enough to imperil masculinity as a recognizable paradigm.

Division without Conquest

The Brezhnev years inherited the outfall from the Thaw's permeability of gender, lack of direction, and decrease in productivity on all fronts. Elena Prokhorova (Chapter 6) analyzes how television during the 1970s became a perfect medium for shoring up the crumbling edifice of Soviet ideology and for reasserting the virility of bygone eras, especially the mythologized "glorious days" of the October Revolution and the Second World War. Popular television miniseries rearticulated the masculinist, patriarchal paradigm of official ideology, most notably in the genres of the spy thriller and the historical melodrama. Male fantasy reigned supreme in the former, which showcased the protagonist's formidable powers of ratiocination, imperturbable self-discipline, and imperviousness to sex, all crystallized in the cult series *Seventeen Moments of Spring* [*Semnadtsat' mgnovenii vesny,* 1973]. The few female characters that occasionally disrupted the man-to-man game of international intrigue consistently emerged as nonentities or treacherous, demonized threats, whose inevitable demise freed the hero to redirect his attention exclusively to matters of state. The historical melodrama, by contrast, sexualized national struggle across the board, reenacting historical moments as battles of the sexes, with no apparent victor or resolution.

As Prokhorova's contribution suggests, the last two decades of the Soviet Union's existence were appreciably more complex than usually inferred from the dismissive tag of Stagnation—one that blatantly disfavored the era's perceived inertness vis-à-vis the vaunted dynamism of postrevolutionary and Stalinist Russia. Yet, however low-key and circumscribed, diversity and isolated instances of subversion countered the superficial impression of homogeneity and stasis in an empire nearing its twilight.[21] In the ongoing battle between centripetal and centrifugal forces that, according to Mikhail Bakhtin, propel both language and culture, what energy Stagnation possessed sooner aligned itself with the centrifugal variant. Dispersal from the Stalinist center resulted in the "peaceful coexistence" of contradictory tendencies that carried the seeds of what perestroika brought to fruition.

Western Cold War coverage of the trials of Andrei Siniavskii, Iulii Daniel', and Iosif Brodskii, the exile of Andrei Sakharov, and the defection, expulsion, and emigration of dissidents, ballet dancers, bards, and writers (Vasilii Aksenov, Iuz Aleshkovskii, Sergei Dovlatov, Aleksandr Galich, Eduard Limonov, Viktor Nekrasov, Vladimir Voinovich, et al.) dwelled on male figures as heroes of principled resistance against the Soviet establishment. By and large men's prose during this period likewise occupied the cultural and moral high ground insofar as it addressed Big Ideas and dramatized the philosophical and psychological deprivations exacted by a state predicated upon coercion and repression as justifiable means of ensuring conformity and the semblance of loyalty. These publications overshadowed fiction with the more modest goal of creatively documenting everyday life (*byt*)—authored primarily by Iurii Trifonov and an expanding contingent of women writers: Natal'ia Baranskaia, I. Grekova, Maiia Ganina, Nina Katerli, Liudmila Petrushevskaia, Galina Shcherbakova, Viktoriia Tokareva, Irina Velembovskaia, and a host of lesser-known talents. Given the state's general indifference to such mundane issues and to women's cultural production in general, these publications, as well as first-class films exploring female experiences in heavily masculinized professions (Larisa Shepit'ko's *Wings* [*Kryl'ia*, 1966], Kira Muratova's *Brief Encounters* [*Korotkie vstrechi*, 1967] and *Long Farewells* [*Dolgie provody*, 1971], and the Georgian Lana Gogoberidze's *Several Interviews about Personal Questions* [*Neskol'ko interv'iu o lichnykh voprosakh*, 1978]), met with silence or condescension and exerted little or no impact on cultural processes. Significance and public recognition on a nationwide scale remained male prerogatives.

Perhaps nothing more vividly dramatizes the disparity between Soviet ideals of masculinity and femininity during Stagnation than a comparison of the era's two most colorful cultural icons: Vladimir Vysotskii and Alla Pugacheva. A poet, bard, and stage and screen actor adulated for his riveting performances at the prestigious Taganka Theater and for his dynamic guitar-accompanied concerts, which fans illicitly recorded in *magnitizdat*, Vysotskii apotheosized machismo in multiple roles and genres: as the cool, tough Gleb Zheglov in Stanislav Govorukhin's cult TV police series *The Meeting Place Cannot Be Changed* [*Mesto vstrechi izmenit' nel'zia*, 1979]; as the craggy, gravelly voiced alter ego of the intrepid pilots, soldiers, mountain climbers, and prisoners in his songs; and as the hard-drinking, uncompromising iconoclast married to the Russian-French actress Marina Vlady. Vysotskii himself noted that his musical repertory targeted and appealed largely to men—across all social classes and professions, for even the KGB, which kept surveillance over him as a "subversive element," clandestinely listened to his underground recordings and numbered among his legions of fans. Despite the ambiguity of Vysotskii's official status (state publishing houses and Melodiia never released his verses or songs), the thousands of inconsolable mourners at his funeral in 1980 recalled the traumatized masses tearfully escorting Stalin to eternal rest in 1953. Both incarnated the Soviet ideal of the Real Man.

If Vysotskii projected masculinity to the nth power, Alla Pugacheva ruled the world of pop entertainment as a symbol of flamboyant femininity bordering on parody. Whereas he prowled the stage as a brooding Hamlet beleaguered by existential dilemmas, she sang of love and Harlequin in outfits intended to flaunt or disguise the fluctuating dimensions of her figure.[22] He was high tragedy; she was middlebrow, kitschy *estrada* (variety). Prolific and indefatigable performers famed for their emotional intensity, they nonetheless occupied discrete—indeed, antipodal—sociocultural spheres, in congruence with the Soviet binary model of gender.[23]

Post-Soviet Gender and Its Malcontents

National identity in Russia suffered its rudest shock with the demise of the Soviet Union, promptly followed by a deluge of foreign capital and culture, as well as domestic crime. Not surprisingly, many of the gendered features of past national discourses resurfaced in the post-Soviet era, often resulting in confusing non sequiturs between social phenomena and their representation in Russian media and culture. Whereas the Soviet establishment habitually suppressed information about accidents, failures, and losses in favor of self-congratulatory reports on alleged achievements, post-Soviet self-commentary has adopted an apocalyptic rhetoric of doom and self-flagellation.

Perhaps the most frequently cited cause for vocal, widespread alarm has been the dramatic drop in fertility rates, with the decrease in net population emblematizing national crisis. As feminist scholars repeatedly maintain, issues related to reproduction, sexual relations, and marriage—ostensibly "private" matters—often come under public scrutiny and state control because they are fundamental to the maintenance of national boundaries.[24] Michele Rivkin-Fish (Chapter 7) examines how nationalist demagogues who persistently placed fertility issues at the top of their domestic agenda finally (2003) succeeded in limiting abortion rights for the first time since the Stalin era. The insistence on yoking pronatalist discourse to nationalist rhetoric (a connection underlying the announcement of an alleged "demographic crisis" in the 1970s) likewise has occasioned attacks on sex education and the demonization of reproductive rights advocates as sinister Western agents intent on annihilating the Russian people. National-historical context, however, elucidates the inordinate hostility to feminism. Russians harbor deep suspicions regarding any and all aspects of its contemporary instantiation because of its Western provenance and because the unrealized promises of emancipation under socialism remain sedimented in collective memory.

Feminism had the misfortune to infiltrate Russia during perestroika, thus coinciding with a veritable boom in pornography and a formidable rise in prostitution—the latter not only as a social phenomenon but also as a discursive metaphor for national crisis.[25] Eliot Borenstein (Chapter 8) traces the development of Russian discourse on prostitution from perestroika through the late 1990s in the context of its literary heritage. Leaning on the "authoritative cultural precedent" of mainstream texts by Nikolai Nekrasov and Dostoevsky that sentimentalize the Russian prostitute, contemporary Russian authors continue to mythologize and romanticize her as a symbol of suffering and redemption, or a symptom of Western capitalism's evils. In so doing they overlook the bona fide social problems of prostitution, sex-trafficking, and the mail-order bride industry—all multibillion dollar industries. Tellingly, Russian lawmakers declared sex-trafficking illegal and punishable by law only in 2003, the government's delayed reaction to the often involuntary, forced engagement of women in these activities confirming yet again how the institutionalized habit of troping women facilitates the perennial deferral of issues vital to their very survival.

While many foreign and domestic observers deplore the sudden influx of pornography, strip clubs, sex shops, and sexually explicit talk shows as indicators of rampant immorality in a society out of control, others salute the political significance of Russia's untrammeled, ubiquitous sexuality. Indeed, during perestroika, "freedom of political expression became almost synonymous with sexual freedom" (Borenstein, "'About That'" 64). In a self-promoting *profession de foi* in the inaugural issue of *Andrei*—Russia's leading pornographic magazine in the early 1990s—its editors take credit for bolstering democracy and human rights in Russia through their milestone victory in the struggle for "porn liberation": "We're certain that *Andrei* and its battle helped strengthen democratic tendencies in the area of social awareness and rights." Such claims of "democratic tendencies," however, may act as a "fig leaf" for concealing male chauvinism, sexual exploitation, and violence against women (Goscilo, *Dehexing Sex* 136).

As a number of the essays in this volume establish, declining fertility rates, the abduction of Russian women into the global sex trade, and the mass exodus of Russian sex workers to countries with stronger economies have been interpreted, paradoxically, as signs of Russian *male* humiliation, inasmuch as they imply that Russian men cannot impregnate, protect, or economically sustain their own women. Film perhaps more thoroughly than literature has narrativized this crisis in Russian masculinity, which Yana Hashamova (Chapter 9) discusses as the castration complex replayed in contemporary screen offerings. According to Hashamova, recent celluloid images of women as powerful figures, whether positive or negative (such as the Bad Mother, lesbian man-hater, and ace female detective), mark an important relinquishment of Soviet-era gender stereotypes. Yet as Susan Larsen reminds us, recent Russian cinema also continues to scapegoat women, whom retrospective films anathematize as the "principal agents and symbolic representatives of Stalinist power," thus answerable for a dwindling of masculine authority, honor, and sexual potency (Larsen, "Melodramatic Masculinity" 90).

Post-Soviet Gender Bending, or Queering One's Pitch

The increased visibility of gay culture following the 1994 repeal of the Stalin-era ban on homosexuality has provoked criticism by sundry groups and publications in Russia as yet another example of nefarious Western influence rather than a welcome end to the persecution of sexual minorities. National identity, as Luc Beaudoin points out (Chapter 10), plays a decisive role in Russian gay discourse. Many gay Russians are quick to decry American gay consumerist culture, particularly such Western (and especially American) cultural imports as gay discos, bathhouses, and establishments. The acute homophobia of Russian mainstream society and the desire among Russian practitioners of same-sex love to carve out an alternative, non-Western cultural space has left many gays and lesbians suspended between national and sexual identities. Commentators on Russian queer culture, especially Laurie Essig and David Tuller, fancifully attribute this phenomenon to a "fluidity" of sexual identity in Russia that resists the Western categories of hetero-, homo-, and bi- (Essig 125; Tuller 64–65). Such utopian and ahistorical characterizations of Russian sexual identity as less boundary-determined than its Western counterpart actually serve to strengthen the boundaries between Russia and the West. Insistence on geographically based sexual difference—in this case, Russia's unique queer culture, which Tuller rhapsodizes as an extension of the irrational "Russian soul"—hardly squares with an expressed desire for queer solidarity across national lines. In short, such overly personalized and under-theorized accounts highlight a historically unsubstantiated absence of sexual boundaries in Russia under the assumption that national boundaries (Russian, Western) are firmly fixed. Beaudoin proposes an alternative, more coherent scenario, which posits the Russian gay community's unwillingness or inability to conform either to nationalist, gendered models of consumer capitalism or to consumerist models of gender.

Gendered culture has undergone numerous, fundamental changes in post-Soviet society, which have enabled, for instance, the phenomenal success of Liudmila Ulitskaia—the first female recipient of the Booker Award and a favorite with a huge, cross-sectional readership—and Dar'ia Dontsova's enviable status as *the* best-selling author in the traditionally masculine genre of crime novels.[26] Moreover, young women working as models have amassed fortunes, as have a small number of female entrepreneurs (for example, Elena Andreeva, head of the security firm Bastion), though women tend to prefer small and medium-sized businesses, which, while lucrative, do not yield fabulous profits.

Such manifest transformations in the new market economy notwith-standing, gendered national icons from the imperial and Soviet periods are flourishing, evoking a form of "brand recognition" in a broad range of con-temporary ads that relentlessly bombard the public on the streets, in the metro, in cinemas, and at home via television and glossy magazines. Pushkin continues to sell everything from notebooks and candy to potholders; Stalin's image, plus his exhortations to push forward at all costs, presumably guarantees the quality of a new vodka (Stalinskaia) aimed at male clients. Yet, as terrorist attacks by desperate Chechens escalate, the most frequently reproduced "classics" throughout Moscow are Viktor Vas-netsov's paintings *The Warrior at the Crossroads* [*Vitiaz' na rasput'e,* 1892] and *Bogatyri* [*Bogatyrs,* 1898]: hyperbolic incarnations of a divinely or-dained, valorous masculinity entrusted with protecting national borders. Enlisted in the People's Party solemn campaign posters plastered on bill-boards (2003) and in Efim Tsvik's ironic art poster (2000), in Aleksandr Bal-abanov's blockbuster *Brat* [*Brother,* 1997], in the TV commercial for Three Bogatyrs beer and in ads for Roxena men's deodorant, these images of in-vincible virility quicken memory of impregnable empire through reinscrip-tion. Whether ironic or reverent, they provide continuity in a fragmented nation in search of a stable identity.

A historic female image of arguably comparable fame also has become recontextualized, and transvalued in the process. The sturdy peasant woman holding a military recruitment form with the caption "The Mother-land Calls!" [*"Rodina-mat' zovet!"*]—in probably the best-known World War II poster—returns in a post-Soviet advertisement for Tide, brandishing a bottle of liquid detergent in one hand and a box of powder detergent in the other, under the caption "Cleanliness—purely Tide!" [*"Chistota—chisto Taid!"*] [Fig. I-5]. As in countless ads, the key word here is a pun: *"chistota"* denotes both cleanliness and purity, which permits the alternate transla-tion, "Purity—purely Tide!" But the true eye-catcher is the blasphemous use of a formerly sacrosanct, nationally charged image that at once transforms Mother Russia into a common laundress and marketing whore for a West-ern multinational corporation. The double irony is cinched with the word *"chistota,"* the cleanliness and purity Mother Russia *used to* represent before she sold out to the West—values that speak to the loyal Russian addressed by the ad. Though nationalist rhetoric always attempts to "sell" something, here the product is of a different order. At first glance, such a hyperbolic representa-tion of Russian femininity seems wildly out of sync with the present, when an increasing number of young and middle-aged women are gaining economic in-dependence. Just as in earlier eras, however, radical social change is tempered by nostalgia for times past, when men were men and women did laundry.

Russia's position at the geographic and discursive crossroads between East and West has allowed for a dizzying wealth of subject positions—Western, striving to be Western, redeemer of the West, non-Western—which intellectu-als, political leaders, writers, filmmakers, and more recently, pornographers

I-5   *"Chistota—chisto Taid!"*
[Cleanliness—purely Tide!].

have employed at will in the name of national interests. Cultural memory has preserved a corresponding arsenal of gendered representations of·Russianness for the rhetorical needs of the moment: a strong patriarchy (*otechestvo*) for times of imperial expansion; a vulnerable, defenseless female victim for occasions of foreign invasion or threat (*Rodina-Mat'*); ideals of loyal, pure, hardworking men and women in times of (real or projected) social stability; emasculated, degenerate men and untrustworthy, promiscuous women in times of social decline. These archetypes have proven remarkably flexible and productive throughout the ages, causing scholars and statesmen alike to marvel at their apparent contradiction yet harmonious coexistence. If we cannot escape these discursive patterns, then we must at least acknowledge the staggering force of tradition in shaping national narratives and expose the fictions that pass as history lest we become lost in the myths.

Notes

1. Freud's ideas about "femininity," the topic of several lectures and publications that queried, "What do women want?" and attempted to unravel the enigma of womanhood, should be read in the context of Freud's desires, repressions, and status as a bourgeois Jewish intellectual in fin-de-siècle Vienna. Without resorting to crude simplification, one has no difficulty detecting Freud's relegation of women to the status of a "second" sex, limited by both body and "feminine" psychology (i.e., proclivity to masochism, greater vanity and jealousy, etc.). See "Femininity" in Freud 112–35.

2. Tellingly, according to folk belief, she was the spouse of Svarog, god of the sky. Shaparova 350.

3. On the mythology of Mother Russia, see Hubbs.

4. Daniel Rancour-Laferriere in his study devoted to Russian nationalism sifts through the myriad factors implicated in this regrettable practice. See Rancour-Laferriere, *Russian Nationalism*, passim.

5. Monuments such as America's Statue of Liberty in New York and The Motherland in Volgograd (formerly Stalingrad), as well as the iconography of war (Georges Scott's poster "For the Flag! For Victory!" [1917] and I. M. Toidze's famous "The Motherland Calls!" [*"Rodina-Mat' zovet!"* 1941]), epitomize this ironclad habit. On the erasure of women's empirical identity through trope, see Goscilo, "Negotiating Gendered Rhetoric." See also the superb monograph by Marina Warner, *Monuments and Maidens.*

6. Lotman's article treats medieval Russian culture, but the model also obtains for later periods.

7. See Cixous, Irigaray, Moi, and a wealth of publications by Slavists such as Barker, Forrester, Goscilo, Heldt, Holmgren, Kelly, Kolchesvka, and others.

8. Speaking of the violence during 1905–1907, Rozanov resorted to analogous gendered discourse for historical developments: "V revoliutsii russkaia baba poshla na muzhika. . . . Baba-revoliutsiia poshla na muzhika-gosudarstvo [In the revolution the Russian baba attacked the man. . . . The baba-revolution attacked the man-state.]" Rozanov, vol. I, 261; qtd. in Riabov 23.

9. Weber's formulation as cited in Dronberger 279. Originally in Max Weber, "Politics as a Vocation" ["Politik als Beruf"], a lecture delivered at Munich University in 1918.

10. Our definitions of state and nation borrow from Gal and Kligman 24.

11. Ewa Thompson eloquently documents the discrepant spatial proportions of imperial masculine ambitions and practical feminine requirements. See Thompson, passim.

12. For Soviet legislation on abortion, divorce, marriage, and related issues, see the excellent article by Peter H. Juviler, "Women and Sex in Soviet Law."

13. See especially Daniel Rancour-LaFerriere, *Russian Nationalism;* Ewa Thompson, *Imperial Knowledge;* Eric Naiman, *Sex in Public;* Eliot Borenstein, *Men without Women;* Susan Larsen, "Melodramatic Masculinity" and "National Identity, Cultural Authority, and the Post-Soviet Blockbuster"; Oleg Riabov, *Matushka-Rus'* (Riabov's first-rate monograph contains copious well-chosen visuals, 153–68); Thomas Schrand, "Socialism in One Gender"; Dan Healey, *Homosexual Desire in Revolutionary Russia;* and Barbara Evans Clements, Rebecca Friedman, and Dan Healey, eds., *Russian Masculinities in History and Culture.*

14. See, for example, Theodore Weeks, *Nation and State in Late Imperial Russia;* Geoffrey Hosking, ed., *Russian Nationalism Past and Present;* and Dominic Lievan, *Empire: The Russian Empire and Its Rivals.*

15. Jan Pettman states, "[I]n a complex play, the state in often gendered male and the nation gendered female—the mother country—and the citizens/children become kin" (49). Rada Ivekovic and Julie Mostov likewise note, "Practices of nation-building employ social constructions of masculinity and femininity that support a division of labor in which women reproduce the nation physically and symbolically, and men protect, defend, and avenge the nation" (9–10).

16. The phenomenon of women rulers for two-thirds of the eighteenth century (Catherine I [Tsaritsa and Empress, 1725–1727], Empress Anna [1730–1740], Empress Elizabeth [1741–1762], and Empress Catherine II [The Great, 1762–1796]) is

a clear exception to this rule. According to Riabov, these developments likewise led to a process of "autofeminization," in which attributes generally associated with the Other (marginality, femininity) were projected back upon the national self. Riabov argues that in cases of autofeminization, the intellectual potential contained in the concept of the feminine (the peripheral, Other) allows for the construction of a national identity based on the thesis of its own femininity, with an accentuated attention to the suffering, sacrificial nature of its own community (Riabov 54).

17. Pettman adduces as examples the cases of Israel, Nicaragua, and South Africa, demonstrating how "stories from different revolutionary and nationalist struggles suggest an uneven but very widespread pattern of regression in terms of women's claims and participation, after the state is won" (136–37).

18. Similarly, Halina Filipowicz examines the historical reception of Polish national heroine Emilia Plater (1806–1831), showing how "her patriotic self-sacrifice has been readily accepted, but . . . the feminist content of her story has disappeared under the edifying image of a national heroine" (35).

19. For an insightful study of the imagined nation as mapped in spatial terms, see Widdis.

20. For an elaboration of this thesis see the sophisticated analysis of Thaw values and the period's cultural production in Prokhorov. Conversations sustained over several years with Prokhorov revised and refined my view of the Thaw, for which I express warm gratitude [HG]. A more comprehensive study of Thaw cinema, which also treats gender reversals, is the monograph by Woll.

21. See N. N. Schneidman's notion, contained in the title of his book: *Soviet Literature in the 1970s: Artistic Diversity and Ideological Conformity*.

22. Her personal rendition of "Harlequin," composed by the Bulgarian E. Dimitrov, marked Pugacheva's debut at an international variety festival in 1975, where she won the Grand Prix.

23. That model ensured the trivialization of women's writing and relegated it to second-tier literature. Indeed, the Soviet tradition of employing the adjective "*zhenskaia*" as a tacit synonym for "inferior" in the realm of culture accounts for women writers' impassioned self-dissociation from the term.

24. Ivekovic and Mostov write, for example: "[R]eproduction and sexual relations are political acts and must be put firmly under the control of the state and its moral and cultural institutions (church and family). This is the naturalized hierarchy of patriarchy. The instrumentalization of national body politics facilitates the consolidation of the nation-state through regulatory practices rooted in the sexualization of women and their vulnerability to sexual assault" (11). See also Ranchod-Nilsson and Tétreault 1–17.

25. Partly because of their contemporaneous arrival in Russia during perestroika, feminism is often bracketed with both pornography and prostitution by uncomprehending conservatives, pronatalists, and moralists.

26. With market demand rather than patriarchal institutions defining publication patterns, women have made an unprecedentedly strong showing in crime fiction, thereby drawing considerable resentment from male writers. In spring 2004, during an episode of the television talk show *Apokryf* hosted by Viktor Erofeev, the host, who himself resorts to all available means of self-advertisement in the interests of fame and finances, insulted both his guest, Polina Dashkova, and Dontsova, who sat in the audience, by equating the current devaluation of literature with the rise of women's *detektivy*. In response to Erofeev's misogynistic tactlessness, Dashkova

maintained a stoic, but clearly hard-won silence, while Dontsova modestly riposted that she had no pretensions to High Culture and found readers' pleasure in her potboilers gratifying.

References

Anderson, Benedict. *Imagined Communities: Reflections on the Origin and Spread of Nationalism.* London: Verso, 1983.

Ashwin, Sarah, ed. *Gender, State, and Society in Soviet and Post-Soviet Russia.* London and New York: Routledge, 2000.

Borenstein, Eliot. "'About That': Deploying and Deploring Sex in Post-Soviet Russia." *Studies in Twentieth-Century Literature* 24 (Winter 2000): 51–83. Guest ed. Helena Goscilo. Special Issue on Russian Culture of the 1990s.

———. *Men without Women: Masculinity and Revolution in Russian Fiction, 1917–1929.* Durham and London: Duke UP, 2000.

Bown, Matthew Cullerne. *Art Under Stalin.* New York: Holmes and Meier, 1991.

Cixous, Hélène, and Catherine Clément. *The Newly Born Woman.* Trans. Betsy Wing. Minneapolis: U of Minnesota P, 1988.

Clements, Barbara Evans, Rebecca Friedman, and Dan Healey, eds. *Russian Masculinities in History and Culture.* New York: Palgrave, 2002.

Dronberger, Ilse. *The Political Thought of Max Weber: In Quest of Statesmanship.* New York: Appleton-Century-Crofts, 1971.

Enloe, Cynthia. *Bananas, Beaches and Bases: Making Feminist Sense of International Politics.* Berkeley and Los Angeles: U of California P, 1990.

Essig, Laurie. *Queer in Russia: A Story of Sex, Self and Other.* Durham and London: Duke UP, 1999.

Filipowicz, Halina. "The Daughters of Emilia Plater." *Engendering Slavic Literatures.* Ed. Pamela Chester and Sibelan Forrester. Bloomington and Indianapolis: Indiana UP, 1996.

Freud, Sigmund. *New Introductory Lectures on Psychoanalysis.* Trans. and ed. James Strachey. New York: W. W. Norton., 1964/1965.

Gal, Susan, and Gail Kligman. *The Politics of Gender after Socialism: A Comparative-Historical Essay.* Princeton: Princeton UP, 2000.

Goscilo, Helena. *Dehexing Sex: Russian Womanhood During and After Glasnost.* Ann Arbor: U of Michigan P, 1996.

———. "Negotiating Gendered Rhetoric: Between Scylla and Charybdis." *Representing Gender in Cultures.* Ed. Elżbieta Olesky and Joanna Rydzewska. Frankfurt am Main: Peter Lang, 2004. 19–37.

Healey, Dan. *Homosexual Desire in Revolutionary Russia: The Regulation of Sexual and Gender Dissent.* Chicago: U of Chicago P, 2001.

Hosking, Geoffrey, and Robert Service, eds. *Russian Nationalism, Past and Present.* Basingstoke: MacMillan, 1998.

Hubbs, Joanna. *Mother Russia: The Feminine Myth in Russian Culture.* Bloomington and Indianapolis: Indiana UP, 1988/1993.

Irigaray, Luce. *This Sex Which Is Not One.* Trans. Catherine Porter. Ithaca: Cornell UP, 1985.

Ivekovic, Rada, and Julie Mostov. "Introduction: From Gender to Nation." *From Gender to Nation.* Ed. Rada Ivekovic and Julie Mostov. Ravenna, Italy: Longo Editore, 2002.

Juviler, Peter H. "Women and Sex in Soviet Law." *Women in Russia*. Ed. Dorothy Atkinson, Alexander Dallin, and Gail Warshofsky Lapidus. Stanford: Stanford UP, 1977. 243–66.

Larsen, Susan. "Melodramatic Masculinity, National Identity, and the Stalinist Past in Postsoviet Cinema." *Studies in Twentieth-Century Literature* 24 (Winter 2000): 85–120. Guest ed. Helena Goscilo. Special Issue on Russian Culture of the 1990s.

———. "National Identity, Cultural Authority, and the Post-Soviet Blockbuster: Nikita Mikhalkov and Aleksei Balabanov." *Slavic Review* 62.3 (Fall 2003): 491–511.

Lievan, Dominic. *Empire: The Russian Empire and Its Rivals*. New Haven: Yale UP, 2000.

Lotman, Ju. M. "The Role of Dual Models in the Dynamics of Russian Culture (Up to the End of the Eighteenth Century)." Trans. N. F. C. Owen. In Ju. M. Lotman and B. A. Uspenskij, *The Semiotics of Russian Culture*. Ed. Ann Shukman. Ann Arbor: U of Michigan, 1984.

McClintock, Anne. "No Longer in a Future Heaven: Women and Nationalism in South Africa," *Transitions* 51 (1991).

Moi, Toril. *Sexual/Textual Politics: Feminist Literary Theory*. London and New York: Routledge, 1988.

Naiman, Eric. *Sex in Public: The Incarnation of Early Soviet Ideology*. Princeton: Princeton UP, 1997.

Parker, Andrew, Mary Russo, Doris Sommer, and Patricia Yaeger, eds. *Nationalities and Sexualities*. New York and London: Routledge, 1992.

Pettman, Jan Jindy. *Worlding Women: A Feminist International Politics*. London and New York: Routledge, 1996.

Prokhorov, Alexander. *Inherited Discourse: Stalinist Tropes in Thaw Culture*. Ph.D. Diss. University of Pittsburgh, 2002.

Ranchod-Nilsson, Sita, and Mary Ann Tétreault. "Gender and Nationalism: Moving Beyond Fragmented Conversations." *Women, States, and Nationalism: At Home in the Nation?* Ed. Sita Ranchod-Nilsson and Mary Ann Tétreault. London and New York: Routledge, 2000. 1–17.

Rancour-Laferriere, Daniel. *Russian Nationalism from an Interdisciplinary Perspective*. Lewiston: Edwin Mellen Press, 2000.

———. *The Slave Soul of Russia: Moral Masochism and the Cult of Suffering*. New York and London: New York UP, 1995.

Riabov, Oleg. *Matushka-Rus': Opyt gendernogo analiza poiskov natsional'noi identichnosti Rossii v otechestvennoi i zapadnoi istoriosofii*. Moscow: Ladomir, 2001.

Rozanov, V. V. *Sochineniia v dvukh tomakh*. Moscow, 1990.

Schneidman, N. N. *Soviet Literature in the 1970s: Artistic Diversity and Ideological Conformity*. Toronto, Buffalo, London: U of Toronto P, 1979.

Schrand, Thomas. "Socialism in One Gender: Masculine Values in the Stalin Revolution." *Russian Masculinities in History and Culture*. New York: Palgrave, 2002. 194–209.

Shaparova, N. S. *Kratkaia entsiklopediia slavianskoi mifologii*. Moscow: AST/Astrel' Russkie slovari, 2001.

Thompson, Ewa. *Imperial Knowledge: Russian Literature and Colonialism*. Westport: Greenwood Press, 2000.

Tuller, David. *Cracks in the Iron Closet: Travels in Gay and Lesbian Russia*. Boston and London: Faber and Faber, 1996.

Weeks, Theodore. *Nation and State in Late Imperial Russia: Nationalism and Russification on the Western Frontier, 1863–1914*. DeKalb: Northern Illinois UP, 1996.

Widdis, Emma. *Visions of a New Land: Soviet Film from the Revolution to the Second World War*. New Haven and London: Yale UP, 2003.

Wilford, Rick. "Women, Ethnicity and Nationalism: Surveying the Ground." *Women, Ethnicity and Nationalism: The Politics of Transition*. Ed. Rick Wilford and Robert L. Miller. New York: Routledge, 1998.

Woll, Josephine. *Real Images: Soviet Cinema and the Thaw*. London and New York: I. B. Tauris, 2000.

Zasorina, L. N. *Chastotnyi slovar' russkogo iazyka*. Moscow: Russkii iazyk, 1977.

ONE | National, Cultural, and Gender Identity in the Russian Language

VALENTINA ZAITSEVA

The concepts of gender and national identity intersect in Russian culture in a number of important and intricate ways. One reason for this phenomenon is that gender itself belongs simultaneously to grammatical, biological, and sociocultural categories. Intimately related to biological sex, gender is nonetheless distinguished from it as a complex set of "socially and culturally produced ideas about male-female difference, power, and inequality that structure the reproduction of these differences in the institutionalized practices of society" (Gal and Kligman 4). How much can we learn about gender and national identity from the Russian language itself? The answer may depend to a large extent on our view (tacit or explicit) of what constitutes language. Within the field of linguistics, many formal approaches to language as a context-independent system question the existence of links between language and social practices. At the same time, a wealth of research points to a connection between linguistic systems, worldviews, and the sociocultural status of language users. The nature of this interconnection is still far from clear, however, and is surrounded by theoretical and even political controversies.[1]

This chapter presents an overview of some facts of the Russian language related to gender and national identity within a framework that allows us to see some of the indirect and subtle ways in which cultural, cognitive, linguistic, and social categories interact, and how language users express views of Russian women. Specifically, I examine how the grammatical category of gender operates on various linguistic levels to contribute to both a unifying sense of national identity and a deep social divide between Russian men and women. This divide is especially profound in the face of a glaring absence of public debates about sexist uses of language that were so prevalent in the United States and Europe and that brought changes in official language policies.[2] Regardless of their sex, class, and education, most Russians dismiss Western feminists' concern with sexist language or find it mildly amusing.[3] As we shall see, the lack of national awareness of links between social injustice and use of language is not accidental. In some ways it is determined by certain features of the Russian language itself and by its covert relation to cognitive and interpretive discourse strategies. In other ways, it issues from cognitive links between the subordinate role of women, language, and society, which when examined reveal certain mechanisms for the systematic cognitive exclusion of women from domains beyond their traditional "place."

As a grammatical category, gender stands for certain classes of nouns. Thus, almost all Russian nouns belong to one of the three grammatical classes (genders) and most of them obligatorily carry a gender marker (masculine: "-ø" [zero], feminine: "-a," neuter: "-o"). There is nothing inherently masculine about the grammatical gender of the noun "*stul-ø*" (chair), which belongs to the masculine gender in Russian but to the feminine in French ("*la chaise*"). Yet, even in its purely grammatical role, gender in Russian bears on cultural imagery: metaphors and personifications in folklore, poetry, and everyday language use are often motivated by the grammatical gender of a noun. Thus, in his article "On Linguistic Aspects of Translation," Roman Jakobson notes, "Widespread Russian superstition that a dropped knife presages a male guest and a dropped fork a female one is determined by the masculine gender of knife (*nozh*) and the feminine gender of fork (*vilka*) in Russian." Since nouns for "life" and "death" belong to the feminine gender, Russians see their personified images as female (260–66).

What to a large extent motivates the looming image of Russia as a female figure in Russian national collective consciousness is the grammatical gender of such feminine nouns as "*rodina*" (motherland), "*strana*" (country, nation), "*zemlia*" (land, country), and above all the proper noun for its name, "*Rus'*," "*Rossiia*."[4] One of the more famous examples of this gendered phenomenon is Aleksandr Blok's 1908 poem "On Kulikovo Field" ["Na pole Kulikovom": "O, my Russia! My wife!" ("*O Rus' moia! Zhena moia!*")].[5] The female image of a personified sacred Russia draws on the feminine gender of "*dusha*" (soul), whose centrality in the construction of Russian national identity Anna Wierzbicka describes in *Semantics, Culture and Cognition* (1992) and whose status as the generative center of the Russian universe Dale Pesman treats in *Russia and Soul: An Exploration* (2000).

Gendered imagery as suggested by the most prominent nouns related to national identity also finds reflection in their roots: the feminine noun "*rodina*," a word for "motherland" (literally, "birthplace") has the root "*rod-*" (birth), while two nouns for "fatherland," "*otechestvo*" and "*otchizna*," are related to the root "*ots-*" (father). Interestingly, neither of the words for "fatherland" belongs to the masculine gender: the archaic and solemn "*otchizna*" combines a masculine root with a feminine ending, and "*otechestvo*" is a neuter noun. The "birth" root of "*rodina*" (motherland) is related to the adjective "*rodnoi*," an important cultural concept that denotes such combined meanings as "native," "blood relation," "close, one's own," "dear," and "beloved." This adjective, firmly associated with maternity, as in the fixed expression "*rodnaia mat'"* (one's own mother), reinforces the concept of mother not only in the word for "motherland" (*"rodina"*), but also in a range of nouns with which it frequently combines, marking them as building blocks for constructing national identity. Thus, in a number of fixed idiomatic expressions, *"rodnaia"* combines with the feminine nouns for "nature" (*"priroda"*), speech (*"rech'"*), land (*"zemlia"*), "country" (*"strana"*), and "soul" (*"dusha"*). While the noun for "people" or "nation" (*"narod"*) is masculine, it has the same root (*"rod-"*) as *"rodina"* and as the adjective *"rodnoi,"* which denotes something that is "native," "dear," or "one's own." This adjective has been skillfully used by Soviet politicians, who coined such expressions as *"rodnoi kolkhoz"* (our dear collective farm), *"rodnaia partiia"* (our dear Communist Party), and the like to instill a sense of national unity and personal identification with ideological concepts.

The three near-synonyms for motherland and fatherland differ not only in frequency of use (*"rodina"* is used five times more frequently than *"otechestvo"* and eighty times more frequently than *"otchizna"*), but also in their contextual distribution and their range of sociocultural associations.[6] The words for "fatherland" belong to a higher stylistic register and are associated with the westernization of Russia. They connote a sense of civic responsibility to Russia as the state-nation, as poeticized and personalized in the archaic feminine noun *"otchizna"* (fatherland).[7] The feminine noun for "motherland" (*"rodina"*), however, may be used in both lofty and mundane styles. In its mundane usage, *"rodina"* may advert to one's birthplace without referring to the entire nation, signifying an intimate connection to one's home. When used in the high style, *"rodina"* stands both for the country as a whole and for the idea of one's personal closeness to the nation. This secret pull of the umbilical cord embodied in the root *"rod-"* (birth) reveals itself in a traditional description of homesickness or nostalgia often expressed by Russians outside of Russia: In such contexts the emotionally loaded formulation is always "yearning for the motherland" (*"toska po rodine"*), never "yearning for the fatherland" (*"toska po otechestvu"*).

The grammatical gender of the names for the two rival Russian capitals, Moscow (*"Moskva,"* f.) and Saint Petersburg (*"Sankt-Peterburg,"* m.), is consistent with the use of "motherland" (*"rodina"*) vs. "fatherland" (*"otechestvo"*) and with a gendered cultural perception of two aspects of Russian national identity. Saint Petersburg embodies Russians' striving to assimilate the best of Western values and to enter the European family of nations, while Moscow is associated with the uniqueness of the Russian nation and its messianic mission. Furthermore, the opposing categories in the associative line of Saint Petersburg—fatherland—masculine vs. Moscow—motherland—feminine are also linked to the opposing cultural categories of *chuzhoi* (alien, someone else's, distant) for Saint Petersburg, vs. *svoi* (one's own, close) for Moscow.[8]

Thus, the important difference between the nouns for "motherland" (*"rodina"*) and "fatherland" (*"otechestvo,"* *"otchizna"*) as regards the meaning of their gendered roots and usage pertains to the opposition of the concepts "closeness" vs. "distance." The concept of closeness, however, does not always

1-1   Poster by I. Toidze, "The Motherland Calls!" (1941).

convey a positive attitude; after all, one needs proximity not only for kissing but also for hitting someone. Thus, a whole range of Russian obscenities related to the noun "mother" marks that negative closeness, which is absent from words related to "father." While closeness vs. distance ("we" vs. "they") may well be universal cultural concepts, further analysis demonstrates that their connection to grammatical and social gender affects all levels of the Russian language, Russian culture, and discourse strategies in a unique, culturally specific way.

A visual image of Mother Russia ("*rodina-mat'*," literally "homeland-mother") acquires its definition as much from the feminine gender of nouns for "mother," "motherland," and "Russia," as from a famous patriotic poster from the World War II period bearing the slogan "The Motherland Calls!"

("*Rodina-mat' zovet!*"). The poster depicts Mother Russia as a powerful, stout woman, her left hand raised high in the air, her right hand holding the text of a pledge of military allegiance.[9] As a female type representing the *narod* (or Russian people), she certainly is closer to a prototypical image of a Russian *baba* (originally, a peasant woman) than a genteel westernized lady.[10] This image mirrors the verbal portrait drawn earlier by Nikolai Nekrasov's poems: A peasant woman of stately proportions with a regal walk, a Russian beauty with an infinite capacity for hard work, selfless love, and courage: "She would stop a galloping steed, she would walk into a burning hut."[11]

In addition to its original meaning, the word "*baba*" carries a range of negative associations, including that of a vulgar woman with petty domestic concerns. A *baba* not only engages in shameful reproductive activities (for which the Russian language had no neutral terms until recent borrowings from English), but also has the power to make a man forget his high aspirations and honor (as in the lyrics of a popular song about Sten'ka Razin: "He's traded us for a woman, / He spent just one night with her, / And the next morning he himself was like a woman" ("*Nas na babu promenial, / Tol'ko noch' s nei provozzhalsia, / Sam na utro baboi stal*"). The verb "*obabit'sia*" (to become *baba*-like, to forget what a real man should be), the adjective "*babskii*" (referring to the trifling concerns of a *baba*), or even "*babii*" (pertaining to the external appearance of a *baba*: her heavy and ridiculously protruding form and her shrill voice) are all derogatory, as opposed to such positive words as "*muzhestvo*" (courage), whose root, "*muzh-*," denotes "man, male." What is the relevance of such an opposition to national identity?

Susan Gal and Gale Kligman's definition of national identity helps us to answer this question preliminarily: "National identities (civic or ethnic) are made through a semiotic process that classically relies on oppositions and exclusions. National identity is most often created against other categories: against imperial forms of political loyalty; against 'natives' already living in a newly claimed territory; against other categories of nationhood understood to be cohabitating in one state" (24). When Russia is equated to a "*baba*" in the negative sense of the word, such as in Aleksandr Blok's poem "The Twelve" ["*Dvenadtsat'*," 1918], the formerly holy image of Russia acquires the symbolic association of old, regressive traditions, one that revolutionary soldiers are justified in attacking. In Vladimir Maiakovskii's poem "About a *Baba* and the All-Russian Scale" ["*O babe i vserossiiskom masshtabe*"], the word "*baba*" stands for a kind of ideological disloyalty. Falling into the mud, a *baba* curses the Soviet regime for not taking better care of Miasnitskaia Street; her inability to think about the rest of Russia's problems (i.e., to think on an "all-Russian scale") is treated as a stubborn fact of life that the Soviet government must confront (on the opposition between universal/male and local/female categories, see Goscilo in this volume). In this poem, Maiakovskii extends the "petty domestic concerns" associated with the word "*baba*" to the "petty bourgeois concerns" that are hostile to the revolutionary spirit of Soviet Russia.

1-2   Poster by Kukryniksy depicting Hitler in a *baba's* lament posture.

Such examples opposing *"baba"* to national interests are not unique or exceptional.[12] There is always something *baba*-like in representations of a defeated national enemy, as in Leo Tolstoy's depiction in *War and Peace* of the wretched retreat of Napoleon's soldiers, ridiculously wrapped in whatever rags they could procure during the severe Russian winter: "Morel, the stocky little Frenchman with inflamed and streaming eyes, was wearing a woman's cloak and had a kerchief tied over his cap after the fashion of peasant women" [in the original, *po-bab'i,* i.e., in a *baba*-like fashion] (1310).[13] Caricatures from the World War II period were produced by the famous group of artists working under the name of "Kukryniksy."[14] One of their posters, *I've Lost My Little Ring* [*Poteriala ia kolechko*], depicts Hitler after the battle of Stalingrad. Hitler laments his defeat, standing near a map showing the area between the Volga and the Don, while the remnants of his army crawl helplessly within a ring. Hitler's head is covered with a scarf wrapped in unmistakably *baba*-like fashion, and his likeness to a *baba* is underscored by his posture and facial expression, typical of a Russian *baba* performing a ritual lament, as he adds, "and that ring contained twenty-two divisions" (*a v kolechke 22 divizii*).[15]

Clearly, terms such as *"baba"* and "Mother Russia" contribute to cognitive associations feeding a "gendered" sense of national identity. While the sources of such associations are multiple and diverse (language, mythology, history, literature, art, school textbooks, and so on), they meet and interact within one and the same cognitive space: the individual mind of a real person. Real persons, it goes without saying, are equipped with gender identities. The following examples illustrating some well-known but seldom noticed facts of Russian language demonstrate a surprisingly direct interaction of the linguistic system with the gender identity of a real speaker. At first glance, this statement may seem contradictory: As a grammatical category, gender seems to have little to do with who the speaker is. Indeed, the Russian noun for "chair" will remain masculine no matter who is using it or to which chair it refers. Adjectives and other adjectival modifiers lack a gender of their own and must assume the gender of the noun they modify. Verbs in the past tense also show agreement copying the gender of the subject-noun.

A drastically different picture is found in Russian personal pronouns. Although the third-person pronouns *"on/ona"* (he/she) have constant syntactic agreement (m. for "he," f. for "she"), the pronouns *"ia"* (I) and *"ty"* (you) denoting the speaker and the addressee have an extralinguistic basis for assigning gender, i.e., the sex of the speech participant. An obligatory syntactic agreement with the sex of the real participant is apparent in the gender of the verb in sentences such as "I stood there" and "You stood there," depending upon who is talking and to whom: for a male speaker/addressee, *"ia/ty stoial-ø tam"* (I/you stood [m.] there); for a female speaker/addressee, *"ia/ty stoial-a tam"* (I/you stood [f.] there).

The same basis for gender assignment holds for adjectival agreement with *"ia/ty"* (I/you) in appositions, modifiers, predicates, and forms of address like "yes, dear" (m./f.). While gender distinctions in Russian usually occur only in singular number, normative adjectival agreement overrides this rule and reveals the sex of the addressee despite the "polite" plural number of the subject pronoun: speaking to a female, *"vy tak-aia mil-aia"* (you [pl.] [are] so [f.] sweet [f.]); speaking to a male, *"vy tak-oi mil-yi"* (you [pl.] [are] so [m.] sweet [m]). How significant are these facts? Statistically, a lexical group of personal pronouns denoting the speaker and the addressee is but a tiny drop in the ocean of nouns whose gender does not depend on the language users. It is hardly surprising that most studies of grammatical gender have focused on syntactic agreement with nouns rather than on pronouns, treating the facts illustrated by these examples as exceptions to the rule or overlooking them altogether. Thus, Roman Jakobson includes the category of person in a list of categories directly dependent on the speech situation, but places gender in a speech-independent category.[16]

In terms of frequency of use, however, the first and second personal pronouns surpass any nouns. Thus, according to L. N. Zasorina, in a corpus of texts with a million words, "*ia*" (I) occurs 13,839 times, i.e., six times more often than the occurrence of the most frequent noun, "*god*" (year), which occurs 2,167 times; similarly, the personal pronoun "*vy*" (you pl.) occurs 6,547 times, and "*ty*" (you sg.) 6,475 times (Zasorina 115, 724, 802). It is clear that these numbers would be even higher if one considered contextual inferences of pronouns. There are no statistics to account for the speaker's constant presence "behind the lines" when the text is presented in the third person. Such presence, nevertheless, is evident in numerous expressions encoding the speaker's point of view.

As these examples demonstrate, grammatical gender in Russian translates into the speaker's awareness of his or her own sex and the sex of the addressee as part of linguistic coding.[17] In fact, this process is not very different from the interaction of grammatical gender with cultural imagery discussed earlier: both take place within the same cognitive space—the speakers' minds. A pre-linguistic mental operation translating speakers' awareness (conceptualization) of one another's identities into a language form emerges as a constant and rule-governed process in a line of research based on Olga Yokoyama's (1986) theory of communicative competence and extended to studies of gender by Chapman (2001), Yokoyama (1999), and Zaitseva (1999). The theory treats language as the speakers' knowledge of a code able to interact with other kinds of associative knowledge (from cultural to personal) within the same cognitive space. The theory is built around a Transactional Discourse Model designed to capture the stages of information that flow in conversation.[18] Elaborating on the model, I have shown in earlier studies that prior to conversation, a speaker not only defines his or her discourse role (e.g., I speak to you as your mother, as your doctor, etc.), but also imposes a corresponding role on the addressee (I speak to you as a mother to a daughter, as a doctor to a patient).[19] Discourse cannot proceed further unless the addressee accepts the speaker's definition of {I, YOU}, or else successfully negotiates his or her version of {I, YOU}. Below I briefly illustrate the effect of such role categorization on a passage taken from El'dar Riazanov's film *A Forgotten Tune for a Flute* [*Zabytaia melodiia dlia fleity*, 1987].

In this episode, a high-ranking official is courting a medical nurse, whom he gives a ride home. At one point he says that his heart aches. Which of two meanings of the word "heart" ("*serdtse*") does he have in mind: "Heart" as a center of emotion (love, concern) or as a bodily organ? The interpretation of the meaning of this word directly depends on the set of roles implied by the speaker. The nurse reacts professionally: "What, you don't feel well?" treating the heart as an anatomical organ. He answers, "No, it aches in a different way, pleasantly," revealing that he views their {I, YOU} roles as [I am a MAN] and [you are a WOMAN]. These roles evoke the meaning of "heart" as a symbolic repository of lovesickness. After realizing her mistake, she says, nevertheless: "Do you have any heart medicine on you? Nitroglycerin? Validol?" thereby intentionally keeping to her original role [I am a NURSE] and thus imposing [you are a PATIENT] on her addressee. Note that she uses her intentional choice of roles for {I, YOU} to block his confession. Shared referential knowledge of {HERE}, being his car rather than her medical office, however, helps him to return her to his—also intentional—choice of their roles.

This example demonstrates that there indeed exists a dynamic interdependence between referential knowledge (who the person is), propositional knowledge (what the person does), the way the message is coded, and the code itself. Thus, the model provides a perfect tool for analysis of such extralinguistic concepts as national identity with culture-specific communicative strategies, linguistic inventory, and language use. In terms of linguistic inventory we may mention the appearance and instant spread of the new meaning for the plural pronoun "*vy*" (you [pl.]) as a term of polite address to a person of importance, a change that occurred during Petrine reforms and the westernization of Russia, clearly, under the influence of French "*tu*" vs. "*vous*." A native Russian pronoun for "you (sg.)" ("*ty*") that before the seventeenth century used to operate much as the modern English "you," without additional information about the status of the addressee, became a mark of {I} including {YOU} into "our" social group, among other things.

As shown in a classic study of Russian pronominal usage by Paul Friedrich (1979), in addition to conceptualization of Russian national identity as similar to "civilized" Western ways, "polite you (pl.)," this newly acquired item entered a complex picture of social interaction affecting all social strata. Friedrich's analysis of nineteenth- to twentieth-century literary usage demonstrated that the speakers' choice of the second person pronoun functions as a sign of closeness ("*ty*," "you [sg.]") vs. distance ("*vy*," "you [pl.]"), marking a complex web of symmetrical/asymmetrical relations between speakers (from emotional attitudes to social hierarchy, age, and gender).[20] The amazing speed with which this foreign, "Western" "*ty/vy*" distinction was adopted as an inalienable part of the Russian language may be explained by the following two factors. The first one has to do with Russia's embracing its new westernized national identity under the pressure of social changes introduced by Peter the Great. The second factor was the ancient distinction between the Slavic cultural concepts of *svoi* vs. *chuzhoi* ("ours, our own" vs. "alien, somebody else's"). The existence of *svoi/chuzhoi* as a conceptualization dovetailed with the "*ty/vy*" distinction and allowed this new meaning of polite "*vy*" (you [pl.]) to flourish and spread across all social groups. As suggested by Yokoyama (1994), the *svoi/chuzhoi* distinction is still active and underlies much of present-day Russian language and communicative strategies.[21]

While categorization in terms of "we" vs. "others" seems to be universal, the way *svoi/chuzhoi* concepts operate in Russian reveals culture- and language-specific strategies related to both gender and national identity. Let us begin with a look at the most noticeable linguistic items, serving as terms of address to strangers. After the Revolution of 1917, marking the birth of the new Soviet society and the new national identity in Communist Russia, the old prerevolutionary terms of address based on class distinction, such as *"damy i gospoda"* (ladies and gentlemen) and *"sudar',," "sudarynia"* (roughly corresponding to Mister/Sir or Madam/Ma'am) were outlawed. "Comrade" (*"tovarishch"*), a noun of masculine gender, became the required official term of address. It applied without grammatical changes to both women and men: *"tovarishch Ivanov"* (comrade Ivanov [m.]) or *"tovarishch Ivanova"* (comrade Ivanova [f.]). The feminine counterpart, *"tovarka,"* became obsolete in the nineteenth century and has never been available as the new form of address for women. A slightly less official term, "citizen" (modeled after terms used during the French Revolution) had both feminine and masculine variations: *"grazhdanka"* (citizen [f.]) or *"grazhdanin"* (citizen [m.]). Of these, only *"grazhdanka"* (citizen [f.]) could form an even less official term of address with the aid of an endearing/diminutive suffix: *"grazhdanochka."*

The new national identity offered to a Soviet citizen in a supposedly classless society was expressed in the official slogan, "One person to another is a friend, comrade, and brother" (*"Chelovek cheloveku—drug, tovarishch i brat"*), modeled after but challenging the Latin saying *"Homo homini lupus est"* ("One person to another is a wolf"). The term "comrade" did not extend to those who transgressed the law of the socialist society: Those under arrest were forbidden to use it until they had served their term. Instead of the generic masculine "comrade," inmates were required to use "citizen" (in male or female form according to the sex of the addressee). Despite its egalitarian etymology, *"tovarishch"* (comrade) acquired a highly official ring to it, not only through the elevated status of the ruling "comrades," but also through the rigidity of this generic masculine term, which ignores the gender/sex of the real human referent.

When the Communist ideology representing the official "face" of Russia collapsed, so did the ideologically charged terms of address. The official return to prerevolutionary forms such as *"damy i gospoda"* (ladies and gentlemen) first sounded like a playful anachronism or a masquerade with the obligatory nineteenth-century literary costumes, but their continuous use in official media gradually smoothed the stylistic roughness, so that nowadays "Mr. Putin," or "Mr. President" (*"Gospodin Putin,"* or *"Gospodin Prezident"*) sounds completely normal. At the level of mundane interaction, however, the colloquial Russian language (much to the dismay of language purists) opted for new nonofficial and starkly gendered terms: *"Muzhchina"*! (Man!) *"Zhenshchina"*! (Woman!).

The nonliterary "masses" bumping into each other in the unofficial mundane {HERE} of buses or stores refused to wear empty historical masks imposed by nineteenth-century terms of address. It seems that in the absence of new mass ideology, conceptualization of {I, YOU} in colloquial Russian has cut down to the core of basic distinctions: the biological sex of the addressee. Nevertheless, from the standpoint of standard Russian, these colloquial Russian terms ("man," "woman") are perceived as shockingly rude. In terms of the opposition of mundane vs. official discourse settings, it is important to note, however, that the same "uncultured" speaker who uses these terms to address strangers when {HERE} is the street, would never use them when {HERE} is an office of any kind, simply avoiding address terms altogether. "Official" usually requires *chuzhoi* mode.

Thus, with respect to *svoi/chuzhoi* concepts as related to language, culture, gender, and national identity there emerged the following intersecting linguistic/cultural lines:

*   The appearance of "you" (pl.) (*"vy"*) as a term of address coincided with the time when Russia was acquiring a new—westernized—identity, marking distant ("Western") politeness in *chuzhoi,* distant mode, as opposed to "you" (sg.) (*"ty"*) in *svoi,* close mode of communication.

*   Disintegration of the system of address terms ("comrade," "citizen") in the post-perestroika period—when Russia experienced the painful loss of national identity—coincided with the appearance of apolitical, highly unofficial, colloquial terms of address for strangers: "man" or "woman."

Hidden from direct observation are a great number of other subtle and diverse factors related to discourse properties of {I, YOU, HERE, NOW} that influence the way Russian men and women view themselves and one another. Among such covert factors is the speaker's perspective concerning third-person referential terms used for female referents.[22]

When referring to women, masculine nouns denoting professions may cause a disparity in syntactic agreement if used with the past tense verb (as in "the doctor [m.] came [f.]," *"vrach prishla"*), or with the feminine form of the modifier ("our [f.] doctor [m.]," *"nasha vrach"*). A. M. Peshkovskii was among the first scholars to discuss the correlation between the massive influx of women into traditionally male professions and the rise of what he called an "independent feminine gender in verbs" (Peshkovskii 189–91). Judging by his examples, even in the first decade after the October Revolution, this "independent feminine gender" penetrated the media and spoken language: "The graduate student (m.) P. S. Lifshits was (f.) on assignment to study permafrost in Siberia for two months" (*Dzerzhinets* 67 [May 22, 1927], qtd. in Peshkovskii 190). Peshkovskii points out that it would have been better to use the feminine form of the word, *"aspirantka"* (female graduate student), to avoid conflict in grammatical gender, and advocates the use of the rich repertoire of feminine suffixation.[23] Indeed, his solution would have been perfect if not for the uncomfortable fact that "feminized" nouns often sound either less respectful or downright denigrating to the referent (similar to the effect produced by "poet" vs. "poetess," "adventurer" vs. "adventuress" in English).[24] In terms of emotional and evaluative connotations, Russian feminine animate nouns fall into three groups:

1. **Always neutral, respectful: masculine correlates, even if they exist, are not used**: *"mat'," "sestra," "zhena," "boginia," "rabynia," "tsaritsa," "krest'ianka," "tkachikha"* (mother, sister, wife, goddess, slave [f.], czarina, peasant [f.], textile worker or weaver [f.])

2. **Either neutral or less respectful: in official settings, these are usually substituted by masculine correlates:** *"uchitel'nitsa," "prepodavatel'nitsa," "khudozhnitsa," "aspirantka," "pionerka," "pisatel'nitsa"* (schoolteacher [f.], college teacher [f.], artist [f.], graduate student [f.], pioneer [f.], writer [f.])

3. **Always pejorative: masculine substitutes are required for polite style:** *"doktorsha," "vrachikha," "direktrisa," "zavsha," "sud'ikha," "prokurorsha," "filologinia"* (physician [f.], doctor [f.], director [f.], boss [f.], judge [f.], prosecutor [f.], philologist [f.])

Alongside the widespread compound agreement and its prominence in post-Soviet mass media, the use of generic masculine is not only considered normative but is also often preferred by women.[25] A striking example is the recently coined term *"zhenskie pisateli"* (female writers [m. pl.]), an innovation clearly acknowledging the established status of a new wave of Russian female writers. Despite its clumsiness, this term sounds more respectful than the more established *"zhenshchiny-pisateli"* (women writers [m. pl.]) or the traditional feminized *"pisatel'nitsa"* (writer [f.]) that was used as a neutral term throughout the Soviet era. There is no doubt that such masculinization of a feminine referent has to do with social prestige, as argued by Barbara Mozdzierz (165–81). This argument, however, does not explain the lack of uniform usage of terms in references to women professionals. Why, for example, would a neutral term such as "teacher" (*"uchitel'nitsa," "prepodavatel'nitsa"*) suddenly acquire a demeaning connotation when used in official settings (such as an official announcement that a certain teacher received a national award)? The variance in connotations is displayed even by the terms with distinctly pejorative connotations. Both Russian men and women use such terms freely in colloquial speech, mainly with reference to a third party and in a humorous and nonoffensive manner (Zemskaia and Shmelev 126; Yokoyama, "Russian Genderlects" 422).

The traditional, authoritative explanation maintains that the masculine gender of a noun represents the category of "person" and is "sex-neutral" in reference to both men and women.[26] Since a specific reference obligatorily implies the sex of the referent, specificity is indicated by "analytic means," i.e., the feminine form of the verb (as in the case "the doctor [m.] arrived [f.]," "*vrach prishla*"). This view fails to explain, however, why the same specific referent regularly uses the generic masculine in official settings (such as "the teacher [m.] Petrova [f.]," "*prepodavatel' Petrova*," rather than "the teacher [f.] Petrova [f.]," "*prepodavatel'nitsa Petrova*").[27]

In her description of Russian female genderlect as a subcode of Russian, Yokoyama proposes an explanation that relates the use of gender to the ancient cultural opposition of *svoi* vs. *chuzhoi* (one's own vs. somebody else's) and the pragmatic category of "interlocutor distance."[28] When the speaker defines {I, YOU} as {I and you are *svoi*}, the closeness obligatorily evokes a proposition [I am male/female] and the associated lexicon in CODE. The long interlocutor distance obligatorily suppresses the proposition [I am male/female]. This strong connection between short distance and the necessity to choose a gendered term for a specific referent explains why Russian men and women frequently use pejorative terms such as "*zavsha*" (boss [f.]) in informal conversations. It happens when the speakers define their discourse roles as {I and you are *svoi*} implying "closeness"—at the expense of the third person spoken about.

Russian speakers, notes Yokoyama, face a difficult choice of either being disrespectful to the female referent while remaining *svoi* with the addressee, or of being respectful to others but distant with the addressee. The following examples demonstrate the complex operation of the category of "interlocutor distance" in context. The first passage is from Dina Kaminskaia's memoirs, *Zapiski advokata* [*Notes of a Lawyer*]; it describes a court trial in which she is a member of the defense, at odds with the unprofessional Soviet judge, who repeatedly bullies her witness.[29] The word for "witness" is used both in the regular masculine form and its feminized, nonoffensive equivalent. As the {I} of the narration, the author maintains a closeness with {YOU} of the reader, assuming that the reader is sympathetic to her cause. Presenting her own perspective, marked by a positive attitude to the witness, Kaminskaia uses the term "witness" (f.) ("*svidetel'nitsa*"). But the hostile and intimidating judge quoted by Kaminskaia uses "witness" (m.) ("*svidetel'*") so as to emphasize the interlocutor distance and thereby keep the witness "in line":

> And how does Kareva [the judge] cross-examine *the witness* (f.)? What are her questions about? She asks why Galia decided to go out so late at night with a man she did not know: "And how often do you take rides with strange men at night?" Galia stands pale, her eyes full of tears. "You found me, you asked me to come here. You told me to tell everything I know. Why are you attacking me like this now?" "No one is attacking you, *witness* [m.]! You are in court. A court does not attack—a court explains your behavior to you" (117–18).

The second example illustrates the use of an offensive feminized referential term, also in the context of a courtroom. In his memoir *And the Wind Returns . . .* the noted dissident Vladimir Bukovskii describes his trial and his accusatory speech against the torture of political prisoners in Soviet psychological clinics. Despite the female judge's protestations, he keeps "pouring on . . . the nauseating details of tortures." All of his hatred for the Soviet regime shows in one word he uses to describe the reaction of the corrupt female judge: "*Sud'ikhu krivilo*" (the judge [f.] cringed). Bukovskii uses a feminizing suffix "*-ikha*," which per se is not offensive when employed to convey its original meaning of "a female animal." Its use to refer to female human beings, however, is akin to using the English word for a female dog in reference to a woman. Note that Bukovskii's highly negative attitude to this woman does not constitute the distant (*chuzhoi*) mode. The term he uses to describe the past event to the {YOU} of a provisional sympathetic reader is in the close (*svoi*) mode (notice that he did not pronounce this word in his courtroom speech). Thus, for the choice of the form, the speaker's attitude to the third person matters less than the category "distance" operating at the {I, YOU} level. Whether emotionally negative (as in the use of "*sud'ikha*" [judge, f.]) or positive (as in the use of "*svidetel'nitsa*" [witness, f.]), the closeness to the addressee is what dictates feminization.

Let us note that most characteristically "Russian" features, such as "exaggerated emotionality," "nonrationality," and various other spirited splashes of personality—perceived and described as extremes by many foreigners from Marquis Astolphe de Custine to Yale Richmond—as a rule, operate in the *svoi* mode.[30] Linguistically, this mode is expressed through a rich inventory of emotionally colored suffixes, non-neutral word order, interjections, elliptic structures, and other markers of subjectivity. It is noteworthy that feminization and gender distinction operate at the culture-specific level of "Russianness." The exact opposite of this style is the language of bureaucracy—deadly dry, complicated with mistrustful syntax (no ellipses, nothing is left out as "understood" between {I, YOU}, hence a high level of redundancy), no emotional interjections or other hints at subjectivity. This is a final frontier of the *chuzhoi* mode and the absolute domain of generic masculine gender.

The choice between respect and intimacy that the Russian language imposes on its speakers involves grammatical, biological, and socially constructed gender in a number of ways.[31] The fact that the categories of animacy, gender, and person are interrelated in the Russian language greatly contributes to insensitivity to sexism in Russian society. The role of these categories in cognitive and psychological associations is complex and not immediately apparent. Thus, direct object markers distinguish animacy only for masculine nouns denoting men or animals.[32] In singular feminine nouns, animacy manifests itself grammatically only through the fact that they answer the question "who?" ("*kto?*") rather than "what?" ("*chto?*"). But the question-word for "who" in Russian itself belongs to the masculine gender and requires masculine verb agreement even when the question is addressed to a group of women.

The fact that Russian does not have a pronoun to refer to inanimate objects (the way the English "it" does) also contributes to the overall nondistinction among gender, sex, and animacy. The personal pronouns for "he" and "she" are used as substitutes for feminine and masculine nouns to mean "it," as in the exchange: "Where is my pen (f.)?" "Here it (f.) is" (literally, "Here she is"). For this reason, Russian resists such pronominal innovations as the strategies of "s/he, he/she, he or she" used successfully in the United States for raising public awareness about the social inequality of women; instead, Russia retains the purportedly generic "he." To generalize one's personal experience, Russians use *"ty"* (you [sg.]) with masculine verbal agreement even when the speaker generalizing her experience is a woman.

The pervasiveness of the generic "unmarked" masculine gender in Russian is also reflected in extremely frequent substantivized adjectives and participles. These convey animacy/person either through the generic plural (*"bogatye,"* the rich), or the generic masculine singular (*"bogatyi,"* the rich one, one who is rich). Animate substantivized feminine adjectives are rare; as a rule, they are used in opposition to masculine ones and imply a sexual or love relationship:

a.   *Kakoi exal, takuiu i vstretil.* (proverb)
     "The one (m.) riding meets another (f.) like himself." (It takes one to know one.)

b.   *Poliubil bogatyi bednuiu.* (Marina Tsvetaeva)
     "A rich man fell in love with a poor woman."

A corpus of fifty proverbs containing substantivized adjectives and participles, selected from Dal' on the basis of frequency of key words, has very few feminine substantives. Those that do exist are related to women's appearance (*"Moloden'ka, zubki belen'ki"* [A young lass, (with) white teeth]), love and sex (*"Ne pil by, ne pel, vse b na miluiu gliadel!"* [I want no drink or song, I'd rather look at my sweetheart (f.)]), virginity and marriage (*"Posle Pokrova ne budet takova"* [After Pokrov (the church festival of the Virgin) she'll not be the same (f.)], "because she'll be married," comments Dal'), and the household.

The generalized wisdom of proverbs makes extensive use of generic masculine forms in substantives. Experimental switching of gender in proverbs with masculine substantives reveals some interesting facts about cultural expectations with regard to women and the domain associated with them. As a rule, feminized proverbs "do not sound right." This strangeness cannot be ascribed only to a change in a well-known form, since many of the proverbs cited by Dal' fell out of use and are recognized as proverbs exclusively through their "proverbial" poetics. As shown in the set of examples below, the feminization of proverbs drastically changes their meanings. Those new meanings range from ridiculous to impossible, or else lose "the wisdom" conveyed by generalization:

a. *Kazhdomu svoe.*
"To each (m.) his own."

b. *Kazhdoi svoe.*
"To each (f.) her own."

While the first example states a familiar generalization, the second is not a proverb but rather an elliptic statement about the distribution of goods to a specific group of women.

a. *Utopaiushchii khvataetsia*
za solominku.
"A drowning man
grasps at a straw."

b. *Utopaiushchaia khvataetsia*
za solominku.
"A drowning woman
grasps at a straw."

The well-known proverb in example (a) universalizes the human tendency to grab at the smallest hope in a moment of desperation, with "drowning" as a metaphor for desperation and the futility of hope. The feminized version, by contrast, depicts a scene of a specific drowning woman. The straw she grabs at is a specific and ridiculously inadequate tool for salvation, in effect portraying the woman as silly or the narration illogical. Metaphors or generalizations present in the masculine variant disappear in the feminine one. Feminization not only individuates the scene, but also adds to it concepts and connotations totally absent from the masculine version. The following example is a case in point:

a. *Berezhenogo bog berezhet.*
"God protects one
who is protected (m.)."

b. *Berezhenuiu bog berezhet.*
"God protects one
who is protected (f.)."

While "one who is protected (m.)" implies careful and responsible behavior in any area of human life, "one who is protected (f.)" has sexual connotations and suggests protecting one's virginity, protecting against pregnancy, or protecting one's reproductive organs (such as by not sitting on the ground, a common superstition among Russians).

a. *Lezhachego ne b'iut.*
"Don't hit a man
when he's down."

b. *Lezhachuiu ne b'iut.*
"Don't hit a woman
when she's down."

c. *Zhivi vsiak svoim umom.*
"Each lives according
to his own mind."

d. *Zhivi vsiaka svoim umom.*
"Each lives according to her
own mind."

e. *Molod letami da star delami.*   f. *Moloda letami, da stara delami.*
    "Young (m.) in years, old   "Young (f.) in years, old (f.).
    (m.) in deeds."   in deeds."

g. *Svoi svoemu lezha pomogaet.*   h. *Svoia svoei lezha pomogaet.*
    "One (m.) helps one's own   "One (f.) helps one's
    (m.) lying down."   own (f.) lying down."

(A less literal and more meaningful translation would be: "It's no effort to help one's own.")

The meaning conveyed in example (a) depicts the Russian national character as compassionate and merciful: "Be merciful to a fallen enemy." The feminized version (b) presents a picture of a woman lying down and implies taking sexual advantage of her position. While Russian and Slavic folklore abounds in woman-beating scenes,[33] this proverb in a feminized form does not suggest fighting or beating. Although not immediately apparent, the chilling absence of the beating scene from the feminized variant of the proverb indicates a complete exclusion of women from mercy: the meaning "show mercy for a fallen enemy" simply does not apply to women. Even if a woman resists and fights back, her falling down is not a signal for a man to stop. While a man who has been beaten to the ground may shout *"Lezhachego ne b'iut!"* evoking the rule for merciful behavior, no woman in the same situation would ever use this proverb—either in its generic masculine form or in its specifically feminine variant. The traditional masculine form of the proverb would sound baffling, humorous, and just inappropriate ("There's no such a rule for woman, who does she think she is?"). In its feminized form, the proverb sounds both funny and slightly obscene.[34]

The second example (c) tells you to use your own mind and be independent, while its feminized version (d) is strangely vacuous, resembling a line from an overheard conversation. If anything, it advises women not to listen to their female friends, or else not to mind their husbands' authority, at their own risk.

Consider the transformations in the feminized versions of the last two examples: the feminine gender renders them completely meaningless. While the proverb "Young in years, old in deed" is not a generalization, but, rather, a formula to refer to a deserving young man who despite his youth has managed to distinguish himself, its feminine twin is simply devoid of meaning. There is no ready set of associations concerning deeds that may distinguish a young woman above others (except perhaps having many babies early in life, but that would not qualify as "deeds," *"dela"*). Even less clear is the feminized version of the proverb, "One (f.) helps one's own (f.) lying down"/ "It's no effort to help one's own"). While the masculine "lying down" suggests a minimal effort that nevertheless effects valuable mutual support, in the feminized version "lying down" merely denotes a bodily position in space, hence the notion of "supporting" or "helping" cannot be imagined as a meaningful act.

Finally, there are several proverbs with the masculine substantive *"golyi"* (naked) to connote poverty, which convey a range of moral and religious associations, such as *"Golyi—chto sviatoi, bedy ne boitsia"* ("A naked person (m.) is like a saint, [he] is not afraid of poverty/trouble"). The simple operation of changing this substantive's grammatical gender brings a dramatic change in its meaning: A naked woman suggests but one thing—sex, which is absent in the masculine variant; the notion of poverty vanishes altogether, as do all moral and religious associations.

These examples demonstrate that even when used in a generic manner, the category of "woman" is associated with human experience in the severely limited domains of love, sex, family, and the home. There are no cultural associations relating "woman" to "mind"—unless used pejoratively: *"Volos dolog, da um korotok"* ("Long of hair, short on brains")—or to socially valued deeds. "She" emerges as a non-prototypical instance of a human, just as in the Russian proverbs *"Kuritsa ne ptitsa, baba ne chelovek"* ("A hen is not a bird, a wench is not a person") and *"Kobyla ne loshad', baba ne chelovek"* ("A mare is not a horse, a wench is not a person"). Note also that a non-prototypical instance of a category is always specific. Thus, the general category of "person" remains a strong semantic component within the category of "man," both in its generic and individuated use, while in the category of "woman" it is weak and unstable.

Given the long history of the subjugation of women, it comes as no surprise that the basic cognitive domain of operation for the concept of "woman" in Russian is delineated by sex, the family, and the household, and is associated with all the mundane activities presupposed by this domain. What is surprising, however, is the automatic loss of cognitive associations with *any* link beyond that domain: it appears that grammatical feminization not only reflects the traditional place of women, but also effectively reproduces and ensures it. The ability of a domain or scope to change the meaning and perception of an event may be illustrated by the changes in the meaning of the noun "tempest" when its physical scope is designated as a "glass of water," as in the Russian expression "a tempest in a glass of water" (*"buria v stakane vody"*) or its English equivalent, "a tempest in a teapot." The change in scope alters not only the magnitude and the destructive power of possible components of events, as in a "tempest at sea"; the limited scope also cuts off some of the propositions associated with "tempest" and eliminates links to other concepts (e.g., wind, waves hitting the shore or ship, and possible shipwreck). In the same way, the feminization of the substantive *"golyi"* (naked [m.]) and the subsequent limitation to women's traditional domain cut off propositions related to poverty and religious virtue: *"golaia"* (naked [f.]) is primarily associated with sex. Note that the change in scope also codes the speaker's irony: just as a "tempest in a teapot" is not a real storm, so a "poetess" is not a real poet.

The analysis above casts light on several reasons for the negative and positive connotations attached to the respective terms *"baba"* and *"rodina-mat'"* (Mother Russia), so frequently used to articulate a sense of Russian national identity. *"Baba,"* originally a nonoffensive term denoting "a peasant woman"—i.e., a member of the *narod* (the Russian people), which in the Romantic period represented the apotheosis of Russian national identity—came to acquire negative connotations in all contexts beyond woman's domain (as evinced by the expression, "This is not a matter for a *baba's* mind" (*"Ne bab'ego uma delo"*). "Mother" (*"mat'"*), of course, is central to women's domain, and produces a perfectly consistent epithet when combined with the term *"rodina"* (which literally means "birthplace") for conveying the closeness associated with the nation. Hence, the positive connotations of beauty, care, compassion, and courage in protecting her children are all present in the culturally construed image of Mother Russia: a female figure with a Russian *baba* face.

The complex interconnections among grammatical gender, person, and the sociocultural categories of "closeness" vs. "distance" and "one's own" (*svoi*) vs. "alien" (*chuzhoi*) inevitably involve a covert but cognitively active notion of women's domain and are reflected in other key expressions for articulating Russian national identity. Thus, "fatherland" (*"otechestvo"*) connotes civic duties, honor, and ardent service to the country—i.e., concepts beyond women's cognitive domain. It follows that the Russian fatherland (*"otechestvo"*) would linguistically produce only sons, as in the solemn and slightly archaic but common expression, "sons of the Fatherland" (*"syny otechestva"*). As an idiomatic expression, "daughters of the Fatherland" simply do/es not exist.

Notes

I would like to express my gratitude for comments about the substance and/or form of earlier versions of this chapter to Eliot Borenstein, Catherine Chvany, Mark Elson, Alina Israeli, Natalie Kononenko, and Olga Yokoyama, as well as to participants of conferences and talks at which shorter variants of this paper were presented and discussed (AAASS Gender panel 2001, UVA Linguistic/Anthropology seminar 2003, guest lecture at Washington and Lee University, 2004). Special thanks to Eugene and Rebecca Beshenkovsky, Maria Gitlin, and Scott Scullion for their aid with the numerous drafts, and to the anonymous reviewers and the ever-inspiring editors of this volume for helping me to sharpen my arguments.

1. The problem with choosing a theoretical stance is aptly described by Sally McConnell-Ginet in her article "Language and Gender": "In fields like anthropology and literature . . . many leading non-feminist scholars soon saw gender studies as of great potential theoretical significance, whereas linguistic theoreticians (correctly) saw gender as irrelevant to the questions of formal grammar that have been center stage in mainstream linguistics. Many linguists do not see how to combine their linguistic interests and their feminism. Can sex and gender function as central analytical categories in linguistic thought? Can a feminist linguistics profitably interact with mainstream linguistic traditions? Must we swim against that mainstream to explain the language component of gender phenomena?" (75).

2. See the overview of language reform in the United States and Europe in Suzanne Romaine's book *Communicating Gender* 291–321. She states that the U.S. Department of Labor revised the titles of approximately 3,500 jobs to make them gender-neutral; thus "steward" and "stewardess" are officially out and "flight attendant" is in (311).

3. O. V. Shnyreva provides an excellent illustration of the problem, demonstrating that even in Russian educational institutions with well-established gender studies programs, the general attitude to feminism is highly negative (60–63).

4. For a fascinating investigation of the "humanization" of narrative in post-Soviet textbooks of Russian history (revising the formerly dry, impersonal style), see Galina Zvereva's article, "Formy reprezentatsii russkoi istorii." Zvereva shows the transformation of grammatical gender of these and other nouns into personified female images of Russia and Russian history: "Russia is the beautiful, proud, majestic, suffering heroine who is subjected to humiliation and assaults, but invariably is reborn and seeks her own path in life . . . 'National History' looks like the personal path followed by the personified woman—Russia" (174).

5. Aleksandr Blok's poem *On Kulikovo Field* [*Na pole Kulikovom,* 1908] evokes the glorious battle in which the Russians, led by Prince Dmitrii Donskoi, defeated the Mongols. The poem begins, "O, my Russia! My wife! How painfully clearly we see our long path! Our path pierced our hearts with / like an arrow of the ancient Tartar will." ("*O Rus' moia! Zhena moia! Do boli / Nam iasen dolgii put'! / Nash put' streloi tatarskoi drevnei voli pronzil nam grud'.*")

6. According to the frequency dictionary, *Chastotnyi slovar',* the distribution of these terms is as follows: "motherland" ("*rodina*") 172; "fatherland" ("*otechestvo*") 30; "fatherland" ("*otchizna*") 2. An internet database search of 179 contemporary media sources from November 2000 to November 2002 shows slightly different but comparable results: "motherland" ("*rodina*") 97,896; "fatherland" ("*otechestvo*") 42,289; and "fatherland" ("*otchizna*") 3,130.

7. For a discussion of the meaning and political uses of words for "motherland" and "fatherland," see Khan-Pira.

8. For a comprehensive description of the cultural perception of the two capitals, see Figes.

9. This poster by I. Toidze (1941) is reproduced in the volume *Russia: The 20th Century. A History of the Country in Posters* (130).

10. For a description of the meaning of "*baba,*" see Jarintzov 126–31.

11. Among Nekrasov's poems about women, "*Moroz kraznyi nos*" ["Father Frost the Red Nose"] is especially famous for the section depicting peasant women. As required reading in secondary literature programs during the Soviet period, these lines were memorized by several generations of Russian youth and are widely quoted in the media to this day. See my chapter, "Quoting Russian Poetry," in *The Russian Context* 85–202.

12. In their semiotic analysis of male-female oppositions in the ancient Slavic world, V. V. Ivanov and V. N. Toporov list a number of superstitions, omens, and rituals in which woman emerges as a personification of evil, misfortune, and sorcery (178).

13. Leo Tolstoy, *War and Peace,* trans. Ann Dunnigan (London: New English Library, 1968), 1310. The Russian original reads: "*Morel', malen'kii korenastyi frantsuz, s vospalennymi, slezivshimisia glazami, obviazannyi po-bab'i platkom sverkh furazhki, byl odet v zhenskuiu shubenku.*" The image of the French army in female coats and shawls retreating from Russia is also fixed in the Russian national memory through a famous painting by V. Vereshchagin (1842–1904), *On the Smolensk Highway. Retreat*

[*Na bol'shoi Smolenskoi doroge. Otstuplenie*], which during the Soviet period was reproduced in most school textbooks of Russian history.

14. "Kukryniksy" is the collective name of a group of artists (an acronym for their last names): M. V. Kupriianov (1903–1991), P. N. Krylov (1902–1990), and N. A. Sokolov (1903–2000). They worked together beginning in 1927, mainly in satire. Their World War II posters with satirical depictions of the enemy are available on the Web site *Russia and Germany: From the Image of an Enemy to the Image of a Partner,* by E. I. Gotovtseva. See also the Web sites with lyrics of the song used by Kukryniksy, as well as the poster.

15. An actual scarf need not be present to evoke the image of a *baba* in descriptions of a defeated enemy. In his recollection of the Nurenburg trials in 1945, Il'ia Erenburg describes Goering as follows: "Goering's clothes suggested that he had lost some weight, and yet he looked fat; his face had something baba-like about it, his earphones resembled a kerchief" ("*Po odezhde Geringa bylo vidno, chto on pokhudel, i vse zhe on vygliadel tuchnym; v ego litse bylo nechto bab'e, naushniki kazalis' platochkom*"). Erenburg 27.

16. Jakobson's statement from his 1984 *Russian and Slavic Grammar,* "Person and gender are mutually exclusive," is true only in part (53). Indeed, Russian present tense verbal endings signal only person and number, never gender. The past tense forms are also the same for all persons within masculine sg.: "I/you/he said (m.)" ("*ia/ty/on skazal*") and within feminine sg.: "I/you/she said (f.)" ("*ia/ty/ona skazala*"). The basis for gender assignment is language-internal only for third person pronouns: "*ona*" (she) must always agree with the feminine past-tense verb and "*on*" (he) with the masculine. Since the first and the second singular pronouns have no grammatical gender of their own, they regularly imply the sex of the speaker and the addressee, as indicated in the form of the past tense verb. Thus, the patterning of gender and person in Russian operates in ways that are not immediately obvious.

17. Beginning students of Russian as a foreign language have trouble for quite some time with coding gender correctly in first and second person past-tense verbs. Even in the acquisition of a first language, this process may be confused by social context: after spending seven weeks in an exclusively female household, my two-year-old son (whose first language is Russian) began referring to himself in the feminine gender: "*Ia skazala*" ("I said [f.]").

18. For details, see Olga Yokoyama, *Discourse and Word Order.* A word on notation: words in capitals enclosed in curly brackets are so-called deixis, i.e., words whose full meaning can be defined only in a real context setting: {I, YOU, HERE, NOW}. These are the connectors between language and real life: while the meaning of "I" or "here" can be found in a dictionary, a message like "I will meet you here" would make little sense if you didn't know *who* wrote the note and *what place* is referred to as "here." According to Yokoyama, both participants must have shared knowledge of the specific real-life meaning for {I, YOU, HERE, NOW} as a necessary condition for initiating and continuing any discourse.

19. This framework is presented in a number of my earlier studies, including Valentina Zaitseva, "Particles and Subtext," "*RR i KLIA,*" "Referential Knowledge," and "Jakobson's Shifters."

20. In his chapter "Structural Implication of Russian Pronominal Usage," Friedrich examines the second person pronouns "*ty/vy*" in their "interrelation with kinship terms, proper names and official ranks." Among factors governing their use, Friedrich names the speakers' sex (83).

21. See details in footnote 28.

22. Discussions of this problem may be found in Vinogradov; Panov; Rothstein; Bulygina and Shmelev; Mozdzierz; and Yokoyama, "Russian Genderlects," among others.

23. See descriptions of the array of Russian agentive suffixes denoting animacy, person, and gender in Zemskaia's *Slovoobrazovanie kak deiatel'nost'* and in Mozdzierz's study describing the complex semantics and function of feminizing suffixes.

24. The same problem in other languages has been extensively discussed by students of gender. For a comprehensive account see Romaine.

25. Examples may be found in Sirotinina; Il'ina; Rothstein; and Zemskaia and Shmelev 90–136.

26. This traditional view is represented in standard handbooks of Russian grammar by Vinogradov and Shvedova, and is supported in Bulygina and Shmelev.

27. On the occasion of Women's Day on March 8, 2004, and in recognition of their outstanding services, President Putin presented awards to sixteen Russian women. A description of the official award ceremony uses generic masculine forms naming all the professions of the awarded women, except for two: weaver and nurse (*priadil'shchitsa, medsestra*). Some of the terms do not exist in feminine forms ("captain of police," "Chief Police Officer," "control panel operator" [*"kapitan militsii," "nachal'nik Otdeleniia GUVD," "operator pul'ta upravleniia"*]). Generic masculine was also used for such nonoffensive referential terms, regularly used in the feminized form, as in "kindergarten teacher" (*"vospitatel'"* [m.]) and "private school teacher" (*"uchitel' gimnazii"* [m.]). See <http://www.interfax.ru/r/B/0/2.html?id_issue=9678005>

28. Yokoyama, "Russian Genderlects." The significance of the cultural opposition of *svoi* vs. *chuzhoi* for Slavic languages in the premodern period was first described by V. V. Ivanov and V. N. Toporov in *Slavianskie iazykovye modeliruiushchie sistemy*. In her article "Iconic Manifestation of Interlocutor Distance in Russian," Yokoyama suggests that the same opposition still operates in modern Russian (83–102).

29. Dina Vasilievna Kaminskaia belongs to a handful of courageous independent lawyers who dared to defend dissidents during the Brezhnev era.

30. See Marquis Astolphe de Custine, *Letters from Russia* (1843/2002). Comments about the Russian national character may also be found in Richmond.

31. An example of authoritative discourse to that effect could be taken from President Putin's speech at the above-mentioned Award Ceremony on March 8, 2004: "[A]lthough the main privilege of women is to guard the family hearth, bring up the children and fill the home with warmth and coziness, they know how to combine all of this with successful work [at work-places] and social activism." <http://www.interfax.ru/r/B/0/2.html?id_issue=9678005>

32. The case is different in Polish, where the category of animacy excludes nouns denoting animals. For a description of the category of animacy in Russian and other Slavic languages, see Klenin and also Janda.

33. See, for example, Afanas'ev's *Russian Fairy Tales:* "The Cossack gave her a good thrashing and left" (141); "the good woman was laid down and lashed" (227); "the husband jumped out, snatched the whip and began to belabor his wife" (370). See also Kononenko.

34. I thank Helena Goscilo for bringing to my attention "the history of Russian men applying their fists to women." Without her comment I would simply have failed to notice the glaring absence of a beating scene in the feminized variant of the proverb (in itself interesting indirect testimony to the lack of an associative link in native speakers' consciousness).

References

Afanas'ev, Aleksandr. *Russian Fairy Tales*. Trans. Norbert Guterman. New York: Pantheon Books, 1945.

Boyle, Eloise, and Generva Gerhert, eds. *The Russian Context: Language behind the Culture*. Slavica: Bloomington, Indiana, 2002.

Bulygina, T. V., and A. D. Shmelev. *Iazykovaia kontseptualizatsiia mira*. Moscow: Iazyki russkoi kul'tury, 1997.

de Custine, Astolphe. *Letters from Russia*. Ed. and intro. Anka Muhlstein. New York: New York Review of Books, 2002.

Dzerzhinets 22 May 1927.

Erenburg, Il'ia. *Liudi, gody, zhizn'. Vospominaniia v trekh tomakh*. Vol. 3. Moscow: Sovetskii pisatel', 1990.

Figes, Orlando. *Natasha's Dance: A Cultural History of Russia*. New York: Metropolitan Books, Henry Holt, 2002.

Friedrich, Paul. *Language, Context, and the Imagination. Essays by Paul Friedrich*. Selected with an introduction by Anwar S. Dil. Stanford: Stanford UP, 1979.

Gal, Susan, and Gail Kligman. *The Politics of Gender after Socialism: A Comparative-Historical Essay*. Princeton: Princeton UP, 2000.

Gotovtseva, E. I. *Rossiia i Germaniia: Ot obraza vraga k obrazu pertnera* [*Russia and Germany: From Image of an Enemy to Image of a Partner*]. 5 Mar. 2005. <http://vrn.fio.ru/works/30/3/309/index.htm>

Il'ina, N. I. "Glava VIII. Rost analitizma v morfologii." *Ruskii iazyk kontsa XX stoletiia (1985–1995)*. Ed. E. A. Zemskaia. Moscow: "Iazyki russkoi kul'tury," 1996. 326–44.

Interfaks. Politika. Novosti dnia. 1991–2005. Captured 8 Mar. 2004. <http://www.interfax.ru/r/B/0/2.html?id_issue=9678005>

Ivanov, V. V., and V. N. Toporov, eds. *Slavianskie iazykovye modeliruiushchie sistemy (Drevnii period)*. Moscow: Nauka, 1965.

Jakobson, Roman. "On Linguistic Aspects of Translation." *Selected Writings II*. The Hague-Paris: Mouton, 1971.

———. *Russian and Slavic Grammar. Studies 1931–1981*. Ed. Linda R. Waugh and Morris Halle. Berlin and New York: Mouton, 1984.

Janda, Laura. "Whence Virility? The Rise of a New Gender Distinction in the History of Slavic." *Slavic Gender Linguistics*. Pragmatics and Beyond. *New Series 61*. Ed. Margaret H. Mills. Amsterdam-Philadelphia: John Benjamins, 1999. 201–28.

Jarintzov, Madame N. *The Russians and Their Language*. Oxford: B. H. Blackwell, 1916.

Kaminskaia, Dina. *Zapiski advokata*. Benson, VT: Khronika-Press, 1984.

Khan-Pira, R. "Lukavaia sinonimiia." *Znamia* 1 (2001). <http://magazines.russ.ru/znamia/2001/1/hanpir.html>

Klenin, Emily. *Animacy in Russian*. Columbus: Slavica, 1983.

"Kolechko." Online poster. 5 Mar. 2005.<http://a-pesni.narod.ru/ww2/placat/koletchko.jpg>

"Kolechko" (1896). Slova M. N. Ozhegova. Rpt. from *Russkie pesni i romansy*. Comp. and intro. V. Guseva. Moscow: Khudozhestvennaia literatura, 1989. 5 Mar. 2005. <http://a-pesni.narod.ru/popular20/koletchko.htm>

Kononenko, Natalie. "Strike Now and Ask Questions Later: Witchcraft Stories in Ukraine." *Ethnologes* 20.1 (1998): 67–89.

McConnell-Ginet, Sally. "Language and Gender." *Linguistics: The Cambridge Survey*. Vol. 4.

Ed. Frederick J. Nemeyer. Cambridge UK and New York: Cambridge UP, 1988. 75–99.

Mozdzierz, Barbara. "The Rule of Feminization in Russian." *Slavic Gender Linguistics.* Ed. Margaret H. Mills. Amsterdam and Philadelphia: John Benjamins, 1999. 165–81.

Newmeyer, Frederick J., ed. *Language: The Socio-cultural Context.* Cambridge: Cambridge UP, 1988.

Panov, M. V. *Russkii iazyk i sovetskoe obshchestvo: Morfologiia i sintaksis sovremennogo russkogo literaturnogo iazyka.* Moscow: Nauka, 1968.

Peshkovskii, A. M. *Russkii sintaksis v nauchnom osveshchenii.* 7th ed. Moscow: Gosudarstvennoe uchebno-pedagogicheskoe izdatel'stvo Ministerstva Prosveshcheniia RSFSR, 1956/57.

Pesman, Dale. *Russia and Soul: An Exploration.* Ithaca and London: Cornell UP, 2000.

Richmond, Yale. *From Net to Da: Understanding the Russians.* Third edition. London and Yarmouth, ME: Yale Richmond and Intercultural Press, 2003.

Romaine, Suzanne. *Communicating Gender.* Mahwah, NJ: Erlbaum Associates, 1999.

Rothstein, Robert. "Sex, Gender and the October Revolution." *Festschrift for Morris Halle.* Ed. Stephen A. Anderson and Paul Kiparsky. New York: Holt, Rinehart and Winston, 1973. 460–66.

Russia: The 20th Century. A History of the Country in Posters. Moscow: Panorama, 2000.

Shnyreva, O. V. "Rol' gendernykh issledovanii v formirovanii kul'turnykh i mirovozzrencheskikh ustanovok studentov." *Sotsiokul'turnyi analiz gendernykh otnoshenii. Sbornik nauchnykh trudov.* Ed. E. R. Iarskaia-Smirnova. Saratov: Izdatel'stvo Saratovskogo Universiteta, 1998.

Shvedova, Iu. *Russkaia grammatika.* Moscow: Nauka, 1982.

Sirotinina, O. B. "Iazykovoi oblik goroda Saratova." *Raznovidnosti gorodskoi ustnoi rechi.* Ed. D. N. Shmelev and E. A. Zemskaia. Moscow: Nauka, 1988. 247–53.

Tolstoy, Leo. *War and Peace.* Trans. Ann Dunnigan. London: New English Library, 1968.

Vinogradov, V. V. *Russkii iazyk.* Moscow: "Uchpedgiz," 1947.

Wierzbicka, Anna. *Semantics, Culture and Cognition.* Oxford UP: Oxford, 1992.

Yokoyama, Olga. *Discourse and Word Order. Pragmatics & Beyond Companion Series 6* Amsterdam and Philadelphia: John Benjamins, 1987.

———. "Iconic Manifestation of Interlocutor Distance in Russian." *Journal of Pragmatics* 22 (1994): 83–102.

———. "Russian Genderlects and Referential Expressions." *Language in Society* 28 (1999): 401–29.

Zaitseva, Valentina. "Jakobson's Shifters in Speech Act Verbs." *Roman Jakobson: Texts, Documents, Studies.* Ed. Henrik Baran, et al. Moscow: RGGU, 1999. 508–18.

———. "Particles and Subtext: Coding Referential Portraits of the Interlocutor." *Harvard Studies in Slavic Linguistics.* Vol. 3. Ed. Olga Yokoyama. Cambridge: Harvard UP, 1995. 213–33.

———. "Referential Knowledge in Discourse: Interpretation of {I, YOU} in Male and Female Speech." *Slavic Gender Linguistics.* Ed. Margaret Mills. Pragmatics & Beyond New Series 61. Amsterdam and Philadelphia: John Benjamins, 1999. 1–26.

———. *"RR (russkaia razgovornaia rech') i KLIA (kodifitsirovannyi literaturnyi iazyk) v teorii kommunikativnoi kompetentsii. Liki iazyka. Nasledie."* Ed. M. Ja. Glovinskaja. Moscow: Institute of Russian Language, 1998. 104–30.

Zasorina, L. N., ed. *Chastotnyi slovar'.* Moscow: Russkii iazyk, 1977.

Zemskaia, E. A. *Slovoobrazovanie kak deiatel'nost'*. Moscow: Nauka, 1992.

Zemskaia, Elena A., and Dmitrii N. Shmelev, eds. *Russkii iazyk v ego funktsionirovanii: Kommunikativno-pragmaticheskii aspekt*. Moscow: Nauka, 1993.

Zvereva, Galina. "Formy reprezentatsii russkoi istorii v uchebnoi literature 1990-kh godov: Opyt gendernogo analiza." *Pol, gender, kul'tura*. Ed. Elizabet Shore and Karolin Khaider. Moscow: Fraiburgskii Universitet and Rossiiskii Gosudarstvennyi Gumanitarnyi Universitet [RGGU], 1999. 155–80.

TWO | Widowhood as Genre and Profession à la Russe Nation, Shadow, Curator, and Publicity Agent

HELENA GOSCILO

Zaplakannaia osen', kak vdova

V odezhdakh chernykh, vse serdtsa tumanit . . .

[Tear-stained autumn, like a widow in

Black, clouds all hearts . . .]

—Anna Akhmatova (1921)

The comfortable estate of widowhood is the only hope that

keeps up a wife's spirits.

—John Gay, *The Beggar's Opera*

There are inconsolable widows, and then there are widows to whom any

adult male would be delighted to provide the appropriate consolation.

—Arturo Pérez-Reverte, *The Club Dumas*

Both bane and boon, widowhood represents different things for different women, inasmuch as its potential and significance are culture-specific, historically circumscribed, and individually determined. As attested by a massive literature, the West conceives of widowhood primarily as a social and psychological estate, one requiring economic subsistence from official institutions and emotional support from professional or personal do-gooders intent on reintegrating the widow into the life-affirming, financially sound collectives that our societies purport to be. England, for instance, boasts not only a national cricket team, but also a National

Association of Widows, founded by June Hemer (1971), coauthor of *Handbook for Widows* (1978), which teaches one how to be if not a merry widow, then at least an efficiently functioning one.[1]

The brisk practicality of the British finds its complement in the more psychologically oriented, narrative-driven American *Widow's Guide* (1991) by Isabella Taves. Taves subordinates counsel on finances and unemployment to her dominant goal of exhorting widows to overcome grief, "pick up the pieces, and move on," while simultaneously reassuring them that the blend of terror and agony occasioned by a husband's death eventually dissipates.[2] Not only organizations, primers, and self-help tomes, but also a mushrooming Western scholarship have transformed widowhood into a popular TV topic, a sociopsychological rite of passage, and an object of ever-expanding research. As a consequence, categories of and stages in widowhood now slot quite neatly into identifiable, ready-made paradigms of behavior and rely on a by now familiar discourse for their analysis.

No counterpart to this phenomenon exists in Russian scholarship on popular literature.[3] Yet, paradoxically, Russia's habit of troping national identity as female has rendered Russian widowhood an infinitely richer, more complex, and more rhetoric-swathed genre than in the West. Indeed, in Andrei Bitov's novel *Pushkinskii Dom* [*Pushkin House,* 1978], a camp returnee maintains that all wives are widows ("'vse zheny—vdovy,' kak skazal odnazhdy diadia Mitia" (E 179/R212). The construction of the building called Vdovii Dom (Widows' House/Home) on Moscow's Ring Road in 1809–1811, which functioned as a sanctuary-cum-hospital for wounded soldiers during the Napoleonic campaign (Berton 145, 152), recognized widowhood as a distinct social category. And the identification of Zhukova, the dacha settlement outside Moscow, with a "widows' village" (Vasilieva 203) implies a taxonomic normalization, however unreflexive, of Russian wives' outliving their Kremlin husbands.[4] A recent article by a journalist, in fact, observes that "Russia continues to be a 'country of widows'" (Hoffman). And Russia's traditional proclivity to conceive its role in world history in terms of kenosis ultimately equates the nation with widowhood.

In exploring the sociocultural construction of widowhood, one immediately realizes the differences in cultural markings of war widows[5] and "average" peacetime widows, both of which contrast appreciably with the *sui generis* cultural space accorded widows of "famous men." One also inevitably confronts a series of pointed questions: If a man's status in life shapes his widow's fate, how does the widow's activity affect *his* posthumous history? Is widowhood solely synonymous with bereavement or does it also potentially vouchsafe forms of empowerment? What are the terms, consequences, and possible rewards of such an empowerment?

During the mid-1970s, the ratio of widows to widowers in the United States reportedly was 5:1 (Hyman 3). Throughout Europe, too, women have overwhelmingly tended to outlive men and, according to medical predictions, will continue to do so. A study conducted during the 1990s projected a fourteen-year differential in female as opposed to male life expectancy in Russia, men's earlier deaths being partially ascribable to their heavy smoking and Stakhanovite alcohol consumption (see Rivkin-Fish in this volume).[6] According to the Health Ministry, an estimated 70 percent of Russian men smoke, up from approximately 53 percent in 1985. In contrast, 30 percent of women are smokers, whereas in 1985 the figure approximated 10 percent.[7] So the habit of gendering the irretrievable loss of spouse has an empirical basis.

Accordingly, a marriage made in heaven, which culminates in the hagiographic formula, "And they died peacefully on the same day," would match a woman with someone at least ten years her junior, whereas European and American traditions have conventionalized a reverse pairing.[8] Yet the ego-stroking male penchant for wedding younger brides accounts for the widespread phenomenon of widowhood no less than does women's biologically grounded comparative longevity.[9] Statistics suggest that the majority of men exchanging conjugal vows with younger women are putting rings on the fingers of their future widows—not a cheerful thought to pack away in one's honeymoon luggage, for it draws the virginal white of the wedding gown under the black shadow of the widow's weeds.[10] Whatever its bourgeois banality, then, such a marriage may arguably be perceived as utopian, fueled by the male Imaginary, and thus singularly seductive for both Soviet and New Russian men.

Widow as Nation

Russia's immemorial personification of nationhood as mother[11] unavoidably shaped both the projection and the perception of widowhood within Russian culture. As early as the sixteenth century Maksim Grek troped Holy Rus' as "a widow [sitting] by a desolate road in a cursed age"—with the populace presumably cast in the role of bereaved semi-orphans (Billington 94). Contemporary Russian prose likewise has displaced widowhood onto nationhood or vice versa. Although the wholesale decimation of Russia's male population during World War II[12] literalized Grek's metaphor,[13] texts such as I. Grekova's *Vdovii parokhod* [*Ship of Widows*, 1979] continue to sustain its tropological aspects, even as they document women's concrete loss of spouse. *Den' pominoveniia* [*Commemoration Day*, 1989], one of the latest novel-length pieces of fiction published by the then octogenarian Natal'ia Baranskaia, rather than confronting the author's own mortality, erects a monument to the memory of her husband, who perished in World War II, and to the courageous nation that withstood a militarily stronger but *morally* weaker enemy.[14] As Boris Polevoi's exemplary Socialist Realist World War II novel, *Povest' o nastoiashchem cheloveke* [*Story about a Real Man*, 1950], resurrecting the Napoleonic precedent, proclaims, Russia's "fatal riddle" is the Soviet people's unique "character" of "courage and self-sacrifice," hence its "real war potential."[15] It is no accident that "fatal," "riddle," and "self-sacrifice" (if not "war potential") evoke traits conventionally imputed to women, as does the "virtue" of patiently waiting for happier times. Thus the multiple temporal associations built into the gendered concept of widowhood render it a particularly apt self-image for Russia.

As a society, Soviet Russia invested tremendous energy in carefully eliminating attention to, and experience of, the present. Its programmatic focus on the "radiant future" (*svetloe budushchee*) in a spirit of empirically unfounded optimism has its wartime micro-equivalent in the famous gender-specific World War II exhortation, "Wait for me" [*"Zhdi menia"*], now inseparable from Konstantin Simonov's poem by that title (see Ament in this volume),[16] and from the numerous films of the 1950s depicting wives who had waited (either patiently or with consequence-ridden lapses) for their returning hero-husbands (Zorkaya 198–200).[17]

Yet, as the strategies informing its WWII posters illustrate, Soviet Russia also valorized the past in a patriotically sentimental, elegiac spirit.[18] That retrospective stance resulted in the massive incorporation of the dead into Russian society through the ubiquitous genre of the monument, which perpetuated memory by mythologizing not only writers and political leaders, but also generalized symbolic figures of heroism, materialized in the Monuments to the Unknown Soldier scattered throughout the country.[19] Indeed, Svetlana Aleksievich's *Zacharovannye smert'iu* [*Enchanted with Death,* 1993] hypothesizes a national love of death among Russians at all social and intellectual levels. Suspended between history (the tragic but heroic past) and utopia (the ideal but ever remote future), post-WWII Russians bonded in quintessential widowhood, their condition defined by felt loss, experience-denying hope, and expectant endurance—that is, the stoic passivity traditionally attributed to women.[20] And when the Father of All Peoples died, Mother Russia became a collective widow whose orphans keened in despair.

Widow as Shadow

Whereas national pride in withstanding the German invasion lent luster and symbolic weight to women widowed by war (in other words, to Russia's wounded but ideologically revitalized identity), until perestroika, widows of male camp victims ("enemies of the people") remained *personae non gratae*. In either case, they lived not *their* lives, but their dead husbands', at one remove. Insofar as the dead husband determined the texture and trajectory of the surviving wife's daily existence, these widows were little more than posthumous shadows cast by their spouses. Some wives slipped more comfortably into the role of shadow than others. Reading the insipid hagiographic reminiscences of A. N. Pirozhkova, Isaak Babel''s last widow, alongside the "disobedient," "scandalous" volumes by Nadezhda Mandel'shtam gives us an appreciation of how dramatically widows-as-shadows could vary.[21] Pirozhkova's admission that "Babel' . . . was like a cult figure in our home throughout the years following his arrest" testifies to the knee-

jerk submission by self-abnegating Soviet widows to the Stalinist cult mentality, if in political reverse (Pirozhkova 167).

Pirozhkova's memoirs typify the bad faith that inheres in the genre of
widow-writing, which brims with circular contradictions. Morally obliged
to write reminiscences in order to ensure her spouse's immaculate passage
into the nation's mythology, the grieving widow is empowered *solely* by her
involuntarily terminated relationship to a man whose *already* existent reputation validates her efforts (reminiscences of Mr. X, after all, lack an immediate readership). In this mutual conferral of power, which illustrates
Mauss's concept of gift exchange, whereby unreciprocated gifts become
burdens,[22] the widow must negotiate skillfully between her role as "authoritative source," on the one hand, and her reverential subordination to the
subject she must glorify, on the other. The inability to balance these tricky
goals—a skill that the indefatigably devoted Véra Nabokov, startlingly, mastered to perfection not after Nabokov's death, but during their life together
(Schiff)—produces memoirs like Pirozhkova's, which beg for a double-
voiced reading. As on the surface the reader follows her claims about Babel''s kindness, generosity, and human empathy, a contrasting Babel' keeps
peering out from behind the propagandistic screen: the dogmatic, smug
egotist whose letters to his wives resemble a master's orders to his servants
(Proffer, *Widows* 93–94). During her marriage and widowhood, Pirozhkova,
unlike Tamara Ivanova[23] and Nadezhda Mandel'shtam, seemed only too eager for humble service and self-deprecation. In that sense she exemplified
the widow's shadow syndrome, which, debatably, one might sooner expect
from spouses of "famous men" than of "nameless" camp victims. In post-
Soviet Russia, that tradition continues to thrive, as instanced by the case of
Vladislav List'ev, the assassinated managing director of Ostankino TV and
the driving force behind the new self-proclaimed "male chauvinist publication" *Medved'* [*Bear,* 1995]. Now on the magazine's board of directors, his
widow, Albina, has expressed the fervent hope that the unabashedly misogynistic project "has turned out as Vlad would have wanted it" (Matthews
24). The unrelievedly sexist *Medved',* in short, functions as a verbal monument to List'ev, with his shadow/widow as one of its curators.

Perhaps that relegation to secondariness, to a phantom identity, explains
why widowhood is a female profession in Russia, having no counterpart
among males.[24] No one refers to the film director Elem Klimov, for example, as Larisa Shepitko's widower; rather, she was his spouse, who died pre-
maturely. After all, from the perspective of gender, Russian society may be
said to consist of mothers and wives, on the one hand, and simply men, on
the other. Male identity is existential (*an Sich*), whereas females' is exclusively relational. Groups agitating against the war in Chechnya included,
tellingly, the Committee of Soldiers' Mothers, whose members picketed the
Defense Ministry in Moscow, protesting a ban on their peace march. This
activity follows the bleak, long-standing tradition of countless women patiently waiting with letters or food outside prison—memorialized in

Akhmatova's *Rekviem* [*Requiem,* 1961] and Lidiia Chukovskaia's *Sof'ia Petrovna* (1939–1940)—a gender-specific ritual that picks up where the widows of the Strel'tsy and the Decembrists' wives left off, as Akhmatova herself recognized (Nayman 71).

What of women incarcerated during the Tsarist and Soviet eras? No narratives of "conjugal support and supplies" in their cause exists. It is no coincidence, of course, that in the ritual of public mourning enacted in parts of rural Russia, the oral genre of formulaic lament is performed solely by women.[25] This folk tradition of the female mourner inscribed in the funerary ritual, which continued to be observed even in the tsar's family despite the ban imposed on it in 1551 (Pushkareva 104), animates the governing trope in Dziga Vertov's film *Tri pesni o Lenine* [*Three Songs about Lenin,* 1934], as Annette Michelson has argued (114, 125). It likewise marks a key moment in Maiia Ganina's novella *Uslysh' svoi chas* [*Seize Your Moment,* 1975], when the actress protagonist instinctively reverts to the ritualistic lament of village women upon the death of her male colleague and friend—a character based on the writer/actor Vasilii Shukshin (483).

Widowhood may be synonymous with bereavement and loss, but just as Russia has lovingly embraced its pseudo-kenotic identity, portraying itself as the self-sacrificing border between an insufficiently Christian West and a heathen East, so may widowhood confer unexpected blessings. Documents corroborate that in medieval Europe widows generally enjoyed more options than single or married women (Mirrer 2), and during the Renaissance wealthy widows thrived when their husbands expired (Hufton 42–43). In medieval Russia, as long as a widow refrained from marrying, she not only kept guardianship of minor children but often retained control of her late husband's estate (Levin 113). If unmarried women provoked pity or scorn (hence the derogatory terms "spinster," "old maid," and "on the shelf," like moldy provisions), the state of widowhood rescued women not only from the stigma of perceived undesirability, but also from the possible burden of an unsatisfying marriage partner. Mme de Sévigné, in fact, wished to replace her biological birth date with the date on which she was widowed, "which was quite a nice and quite a fortunate thing" (Desaive 281), for, as she subsequently phrased it, "Young widows are scarcely to be pitied. They will be quite happy to be their own mistresses or to change masters" (Desaive 280–81). As a widow, Praskov'ia Saltykova, the wife of Peter the Great's co-tsar, Ivan V, "enjoyed much greater independence, more freedom of action, and an enormous inheritance," as well as an illicit but tolerated intimacy with the boyar Vasilii Iushkov (Pushkareva 125–26). Ekaterina Dashkova's career in scholarship and education flourished when her spouse, whom she outlived by thirty-five years, died in 1765 (Pushkareva 147).

A husband's death was and remains the ultimate divorce granted by an unappealable authority. And as a consequence the widow is *par excellence* an ambiguous human sign (Mirrer 8); neither chaste virgin nor sexually experienced domestic partner, an object potentially of both sympathy and envy or even fear, she is haloed with sorrow yet endowed with a degree of freedom and independence—a combination that may breed unease in both men and other women.

Akhmatova, with her genius for self-promotion, perceived the benefits of assuming the attractive role of Nikolai Gumilev's brave, dedicated, and above all *poetic* widow when his bona fide widow apparently abrogated those generic obligations. Emphasizing her unique bond with Gumilev ("that special, exceptional relationship, that incomprehensible union"), which compelled her "to devote [her]self to the collection and organization of materials related to Gumilev's legacy," Akhmatova found it "astounding that nobody else took it on," and implicitly rebuked Gumilev's official, but, in her eyes, clearly "false" widow for her shocking neglect and irresponsibility. Purportedly in response to the mystic significance of Gumilev's appearance in three consecutive dreams of hers in 1924, Akhmatova accepted the "sacred duty" of a "true widow": "I've done everything possible to preserve his memory" (Akhmatova 117). Gumilev's posthumous fate thus served as a useful prop in the complex staging of Akhmatova's skillful self-dramatization,[26] which eventually extended her widowhood to encompass the entire nation. As Solomon Volkov points out in admiring tones, "In the popular imagination Akhmatova turned into a symbolic 'poetic widow,' the keeper of the sacred flame, the mourner for the victim of the revolution, for Petersburg's lost grandeur" (Volkov xvii).

Given the widespread extramarital sexual activity cited in a 1990s Russian edition of *Cosmopolitan*,[27] the copiously documented dearth of mutual understanding between spouses and the astronomical current divorce rate in Russia, widowhood (its financial drawbacks aside)[28] may well be Russian middle-aged and older women's optimal life genre. Western research reveals that American women find the bereavement of widowhood less traumatic than that of divorce (Hyman 94), apparently preferring to surrender their husbands to the embrace of non-being rather than of another woman. Several literary texts seem to confirm that such a choice obtains in Russia, too. For example, in Iurii Trifonov's *Drugaia zhizn'* [*Another Life*, 1975] the widowed Ol'ga strives to keep a controlling hold on the memory of a husband whom she never understood and jealously tried to manipulate during their marriage. Tatyana Tolstaya's ["Poet i muza" ["The Poet and the Muse"] ironically depicts a widow who rejoices in her husband's death because it frees up space for showcasing wooden spoons and other handicrafts in her two-room apartment. Crass though the latter instance may be, at a minimum widowhood may afford women a greater measure of freedom and an opportunity to forge a new and better life. Indeed, Russian widows have proved impressively resilient in marshaling forces for self-affirmation by drawing on their deceased spouses' lives after years of subordination within the marriage. That vampiric self-abnegation especially holds true for widows of "famous men," and above all of literati and artists.

As noted in a spate of articles on the multimillion-dollar Pablo Picasso industry—articles prompted by the publication of his granddaughter Marina's unforgiving memoirs—a dead artist's widow and offspring, whatever their profession, acquire generally recognized authority to pronounce on the authenticity of his works. In France, for example, that authority derives from the highly assumptive notion that an artist's widow and descendants "are spiritually akin to him and the way he worked" (Waxman and Decker 116). So a writer's or artist's death, in fact, may bring the widow as shadow figure into a limelight inconceivable during her husband's life, transforming her into a key cultural agent, with the power to dispose of his legacy and mold his reputation as she sees fit. Elena Bonner has assumed that role, with mixed results, as dramatized by the conflict over the monument dedicated to Andrei Sakharov. As she declares, "It is not easy to manage the legacy of a great man" (Bonner). Despite Bonner's sharply worded rejection of a $600,000 monument to Sakharov as a human rights activist proposed by the Moscow city government on the grounds that the current corruption, social intolerance, and resurgent authoritarianism in Russia violate Sakharov's ideals, on May 5, 2003, as part of its anniversary celebrations, Saint Petersburg unveiled a bronze monument on the square that carries Sakharov's name (Interfax-Northwest). Nor are all Muscovites prepared to share the deference of the city's monument committee, headed by Boris Nemtsov, to the widow's wishes. Maverick historian Roy Medvedev has argued against Russia's traditional proscriptive Widow's Word, maintaining, "Sakharov was a scientist and a public figure; he belongs to history. It is up to the society and the state to define the ways to pay tribute to him" (Weir). The diversity of responses to Bonner's protests indexes the unstable, and partly diminished, status of the widow in post-Soviet Russia, whose ideology may conflict with that of a larger social body.

Widow as Curator and Publicity Agent

The eleventh-century chronicle *Povest' vremennykh let* [*The Tale of Bygone Years*] contains a model of widowly self-empowerment in the person of Ol'ga, whose resourcefulness enabled her not only to wreak vengeance on the murderers of her hapless spouse, Igor', but also to execute her duties as regent to her son Sviatoslav with such wisdom and strength that her subsequent reputation far surpassed her husband's.[29] Ol'ga's case corroborates some scholars' claims that, in the medieval period, filling a husband's position substantially enhanced "the public stature of medieval widows" (Mirrer 4).[30] Since World War II propaganda relied heavily on past glories,[31] it came as no surprise when Ol'ga's act of "just revenge" was reprised by the *kolkhoznitsa* heroine of Fridrich Ermler's quite improbable film, *Ona zashchishchaet rodinu* [*She Defends the Nation*, 1943]. Transformed into a partisan leader by the death of her husband and son, Praskov'ia—as widowed mother—contrives to kill the Nazi whose tank demolished her boy by subjecting him to an identical mode of bone-crushing extinction.[32] While Ol'ga's gruesome revenge apparently inspired workers' imagination at the kolkhoz (or directors in the studio), the self-empowering aspects of Ol'ga's precedent provided a blueprint for female rulers. Yet its lesson seems sooner to have been imbibed by writerly widows—a state of affairs that lends unexpected plausibility to Solzhenitsyn's notion of literature as an alternative government, with the pen replacing the sword or tank.

In Russia, countless literary widows have employed identifiable strategies for acquiring authority. The nation's cultural psychology enables, and often promotes, that acquisition, while concurrently harboring stringent expectations of the "great writer's widow." Natal'ia Goncharova's exceptional case makes the most eloquent argument for widowhood as a sociocultural genre. The desiderata governing the genre may be inferred from her unwitting infraction of them. As a widow of Russia's sovereign cultural idol, Goncharova was an unparalleled failure, held in almost universal contempt until the relatively recent endeavors to rehabilitate her image.[33] Her presumed failure consists, first, of culpability, however mediated and unwitting, for Pushkin's death; and, second, of apostasy from the code of widowly conduct. Namely, she remarried instead of immolating herself on the altar of perpetual widowhood; she made no effort to preserve every word Pushkin ever penned, let alone to consecrate the remainder of her life to safeguarding the immaculateness of his reputation; and she never parlayed her unique role of the "great man's" wife into memoirs detailing the "private aspects" of the genius presumably entrusted only to his spouse and not to the other women he bedded. What revelations she could have left to posterity are dubious, for in general, Pushkin seems to have favored table talk over pillow talk, or perhaps shared his pillow in a more discreet age.[34]

Unlike later widows—say, those of Dostoevsky and Tolstoy—who painstakingly chronicled instances of their dear departeds' "spiritual" depths, Goncharova was both consolable and mute. Thereby she failed Pushkin, herself, and the country, for she transgressed against the nation's received wisdom that after a genius's death the consolidation of his status becomes his widow's sacred duty. Its fulfillment exonerates her from blame (however irrational) for his death, and ultimately elevates her in the public eye. Goncharova's singular silence is at unorthodox odds, then, with what a recent reviewer called "the peculiar obsessiveness of the literary widow" (Walton). That muteness is sardonically echoed in Liudmila Petrushevskaia's story "Kozel Vania" ["Vania the Old Goat"], in which a dead writer's "venomously sweet widow," abandoned by him and saddled with two repellent offspring, remains uncommunicative about her dear departed.[35] And lest anyone doubt that writers expect their future widows to pen hagiographic memoirs of their genius spouses, Thomas Hardy's example illustrates in extreme form the latter's overweening concern that the image be correctly constructed. To obviate any unwitting errors, Hardy helpfully penned his second wife's "widow's memoir" for her.

Vladimir Vysotskii's widows likewise illustrate both the psychology structuring the requirements of widowhood as social practice and the myths widows are expected to propagate and enhance. Marina Vlady, Vysotskii's celebrity wife, proved an ideal widow for public consumption and discharged two of the genre's classic obligations: Frequently photographed in "memorializing" articles, and widely quoted and thanked in posthumous volumes of his work, she penned memoirs of the standard "I knew him as a man" variety. Furthermore, in the autographed foreword to the collection titled *"Ia, konechno, vernus'"* [*"Of Course I'll Return,"* 1988],[36] Vlady exhorts specialists to assemble a complete scholarly edition of his oeuvre, and she establishes her widowly credentials by assuring all readers that she has donated his manuscripts to TsGALI so as to facilitate that vital undertaking.[37] As an enthusiast of combat songs, Vysotskii not only knew the Simonov poem bidding women to wait for their war-bound lovers and husbands, but in a breathtakingly presumptuous gesture that illustrates how immovably the widowly topos was cemented into the national ethos, he composed and performed a song titled "My vas zhdem/Tak sluchilos', muzhchiny ushli" ["We're waiting for you./It so happened, the men have gone"] from the perspective of a desolate, waiting collective womanhood.

For a long while none of the standard books containing material on Vysotskii's biography even alluded to his *other* widow, Liudmila Vadimirovna Abramova, mother of his sons. The only acknowledgment of her existence until recently occurred in a song by Veronika Dolina, which eloquently opens with the line "Byla eshche odna vdova. O nei zabyli" ("There was another widow. They forget about her").[38] Indeed, everyone did, and with good reason. For, by comparison with a media star—moreover, a French resident and cult figure in her own right—what could an average middle-aged Russian woman contribute to the luster of Vysotskii's larger-than-life image?

In that respect, the widows of Mikhail Bulgakov and Osip Mandel'shtam were exemplars of the widowly genre. According to Bulgakov's first wife, he once cited (and, apparently, took to heart) Aleksei N. Tolstoi's pseudo-witticism that to attain literary fame, a man must marry three times (E. Proffer 19). Whether apocryphal or not, in retrospect the *bon mot* appears like a set of behavioral instructions for Russian writers of the 1920s. Like Babel', Bulgakov left behind *three* widows who could mold his literary legacy— chronologically, Tat'iana Nikolaevna Lappa, Liubov' Evgenievna Belozorskaia, and Elena Sergeevna.[39] They divided among them the widowly tasks mandated by their culture: To the last, official widow, who had acquired stature among Moscow's intelligentsia by "seeing Bulgakov through" the writing of *Master i Margarita* and serving as the prototype of the cult novel's heroine, fell the lot of the power-wielding archivist who preserved Bulgakov's manuscripts and his public reputation. And the convention of aligning the beloved author-husband's posthumous profile with hagiographic models informed her cautious guardianship of Bulgakov's papers and explains her reluctance to familiarize readers with Bulgakov's play about Stalin, *Batum.* Her death permitted Belozerskaia's emergence as Bulgakov's sole *remaining* widow in the nation's capital, who, accordingly, produced bland memoirs detailing an earlier phase of Bulgakov's life (1924/1925–1932),[40] as did the ill-treated but obliging Lappa, who had wisely remarried and returned to the provinces (Proffer, *Widows* 63–78). Both accounts gloss over less attractive features of Bulgakov's personality and behavior—hypochondria, condescension toward Jews—revealed in his own, appreciably more candid, diaries.[41] Thus authorial confession sounds an occasionally discordant note when juxtaposed with uxorial scriptures. Vasily Kandinsky's third wife, Nina, twenty-seven years his junior, likewise propagated the myth of the great man as loving spouse ("We fell in love at first sight, and for that reason we were never apart for one day") after his death in 1944, and, as the sole heiress to his considerable fortune, founded the Kandinsky Fund for studying, exhibiting, and preserving his works (Olga's Gallery).[42]

In such a context Nadezhda Mandel'shtam's widowly accomplishments occupy an anomalous position, for they combine tradition and revolution in unprecedented ways.[43] On the one hand, Nadezhda Iakovlevna heeded the widow's iconic imperative: She had verbatim recall of her late husband's texts, ensured their preservation and transmission, and, with her second volume of memoirs, *Vtoraia kniga* [*The Second Book,* translated as *Hope Abandoned,* 1972], succeeded in exacting a *verbal* Ol'ga-like revenge on Mandel'shtam's perceived enemies. On the other hand, Nadezhda Iakovlevna's widowhood released her from secondariness and allowed her to enter the annals of Russian culture as one of its most uncompromising, clear-sighted, and biliously articulate commentators. Although she spoke openly of her self-effacement (6), in discovering and exercising her own "creative" voice she redefined the possibilities of the widow's genre.[44] Despite her awe at the "great poet's" gifts, her iterated declarations of undying commitment to his posthumous renown, and her expressed sense of guilt (at not having memorized all of Mandel'shtam's verses, at not having done "more" to save him, and so forth), Nadedzda Iakovlevna made little attempt either to camouflage the warts in Mandel'shtam's temperament or self-servingly to magnify her own significance and influence on him.[45] Her primary allegiances were to history and truth as she understood them rather than to monument building and the reinforcement of national mythologies.

Unlike other memoirizing widows, who either sink into the reassuring softness of domestic revelation and emotional confidences or purvey uninspired shopping lists of events (Sergei Dovlatov's widow, Elena, for instance, is more bookkeeper than soul-keeper of his legacy),[46] Nadezhda Iakovlevna boldly adopts the stance of cultural historian who arrogates to herself the power of moral and esthetic judgment. While cognizant of the subjectivity inherent in any perspective, she indubitably was astute enough to realize that her relational role of "great poet's widow" buttressed her existential function of eyewitness and participant, lending her viewpoint a certain "authority by association" that, as one reads, becomes authority by courageous self-confrontation. Perhaps her own awareness of that modulation accounts for the increased frankness of the utterly unsparing second volume.[47] Few authors harbor the dedication to history and concomitant trust in time that emanate from the pages of her controversial memoirs.

The masterpiece of male hysteria that is Veniamin Kaverin's incensed letter to her, demanding by what moral and professional right she dare sit in judgment of her betters (Proffer, *Widows* 36–37), betrays his misogynistic outrage at her violation of gender genre premises. Soviet ideology dictated, after all, that widows in memoirs, like women in government, operate only on a local level. Nadezhda Iakovlevna's crime was "going international." Appealing to the tacit but hallowed proprieties regulating widows' memoirs, Kaverin revealingly maintains that Nadezhda Iakovlevna is Mandel'shtam's "shadow," and a shadow "should know its place" (Proffer, *Widows* 38). That Kaverin should emphasize Nadezhda Iakovlevna's purportedly insulting treatment of Tynianov in *Vtoraia kniga* is marvelously ironic, inasmuch as her evolution as a writer bears out Tynianov's thesis in *Arkhaisty i novatory* [*Archaists and Innovators*] that in the dialectic process, genuine innovators revolutionize the concept of any genre by breaking down the boundaries automated by conservative forces.[48]

Beyond Widowhood

Spotlighting the infractory, transgressive features of Nadezhda Iakovlevna's writings, Beth Holmgren incisively summarizes the process of her maturation and her achievement: "Although she begins writing in the roles of conservator and gatekeeper . . . , she develops into a revisionist cultural critic who begins to acknowledge gender Differences" (172). Indeed, Nadezhda Iakovlevna's sense of gender difference, her observation to Carl Proffer that "women don't have to do whatever they are asked to" (*Widows* 24), and her refusal to conform to the niceties of a "woman's genre" qualify her as an unwitting feminist *avant la lettre*. In its scurrilous, impassioned impotence, the intelligentsia's widespread condemnation of *Vtoraia kniga* in the 1970s bears a striking resemblance to its current animus against the women's movement. Why? Because while Russians habitually showcase their sufferings and heroic endurance during the German invasion of WWII, they find it easier to ignore a ceaseless civil war waged for decades on a less dramatic front: The gender war of prosaically brutal everyday oppression by the minority (men) of the country's majority (women). This is not *otechestvennaia voina* (Fatherland War), crowned by a masculine rhetoric of "honor, pride, and glory," but *patriarkhal'naia repressiia* (patriarchal repression) in a muted key that encourages silence. And its veterans, who in more sustained fashion display the extraordinary fortitude and resilience that optimize chances for survival, are Russian widows. Typically, when the battle subsides, men don medals and make florid speeches, whereas women brew tea, tuck the children into bed, and iron their spouses' pants.

Long life carries certain advantages, among them the chance to have the last word, if not the final say. In Russia, where the facts of life proved more illusory than, and were subordinated to, the fictions and dogmas of verbal formulae, longevity has vouchsafed incalculable power for those capable of seizing it. Among Russian widows of recent memory, Nadezhda Iakovlevna alone was equal to the opportunity, transforming the modest, compliant mythmaking of "old widows' tales" into the wide-ranging, subversive assessment of an independently minded cultural critic—a Cassandra in reverse. Were Tynianov alive today and in possession of his faculties, he might, by analogy with Maksim Gor'kii's "Dvadtsat' shest' i odna" ["Twenty-Six Men and a Woman"], rename his volume *Arkhaisty i novatorka*. And he might dedicate that work to the self-professed "crazy old woman" who, against all odds, outlived her husband by more than forty years, and in her seventies entered the annals of Russian culture not as his shadow, but as a writer of formidable power. In so doing she bequeathed to subsequent widows a heritage inscribed in her name, Nadezhda—hope for their liberating autonomy and indifference to the coercive strictures of a genre rooted in chronicle and hagiography. Logic suggests that since throughout Russia's turbulent history widowhood has repeatedly symbolized nation, the promise of a new concept of widowhood may augur a kindred promise of a refurbished national identity.

Notes

Collegial gratitude to the following groups and individuals, whose responses and input contributed to the final form of this essay: the participants in the lively conference on gender orchestrated by Linda Edmondson at Birmingham University in July 1996; Natal'ia Kamenetskaia and the faculty and graduate students at RGGU who attended the conference on "Gender/Culture: Shifting Paradigms" in May 1995; Mark Lipovetsky and the graduate students at the Ekaterinburg Pedagogical University who took part in the conference on World War II in May 1995; IREX, which funded the research trip that enabled my participation in both conferences; Alexander Prokhorov, who provided a pertinent article, in addition to unfailingly stimulating conversations about Russian culture; and David Birnbaum, whose shared appreciation for the champagne widow expressed itself in generous material (bubbly) aid. Since my commentary treats typologies, it focuses on high-frequency patterns of behavior rather than exhaustively surveying individual cases of widowhood. Exceptions to the paradigms under discussion abound, supplementing (without erasing) them.

1. This 55-page primer, to which the Widows Advisory Trust has copyright, teems with useful advice and information about funeral arrangements, child benefits, taxes, and much else.

2. Taves's signature combination of "touchy-feely" reassurances and practical tips emerges in her own list of the six categories that structure her volume: "[T]he

grieving process, health, money, children, and, finally, recovery, the re-building of your life." Taves xii.

3. Indeed, scholarly investigations of bereaved Russian womanhood have been conducted chiefly in the West and until a few years ago tended to focus on peasant widows of earlier periods. See, for instance, Bohac, and the items listed in the first footnote, 95–112. The only extended commentary on contemporary Russian widows remains Carl Proffer's moving *Widows of Russia*. Proffer completed his monograph, poignantly, as he was slowly dying of cancer. *His* widow compiled the various articles that, together with the monograph on widows, make up the volume.

4. Though devoid of insights, profound analysis, and solid scholarship, Larissa Vasilieva's vapid volume about *Kremlin Wives* nonetheless conveys not only a palpable sense of the secondariness to which Kremlin "wives" are relegated ("pale shadows [sic] of frighteningly powerful men" [233]), but also Soviet Russians' misogynistic insistence on such relegation, especially vocal in the case of Raisa Gorbacheva.

5. In her study of Israeli war widows, Lea Shamgar-Handelman calls them "the lesser known casualties of war," and speaks of widowhood as a "master status," i.e., a condition that spills into every area of the person's life. Like most studies, hers operates within the conceptual framework of an idealized widowhood—one of unalloyed loving grief. My assumption throughout is that (1) countless women's reactions to their spouses' deaths are extremely mixed and (2) those reactions fall willy-nilly into a paradigmatic structure limned partly by social expectations. Shamgar-Handelman xi–xii.

6. Amid a general decline in Russians' life expectancy, which for males fell from 63.9 years in 1990 to 58.9 in 1993. The drop for women, from 74.3 years in 1990 to 71.9 in 1993, charts a smaller decrease (OMRI Daily Digest, 11 Jan. 1995, Vol. 22, No. 8). Statistics for 1994 show male life expectancy at 57.3 years, female at 71.1 (OMRI Daily Digest, 30 Mar. 1995, No. 64).

7. See Sachs, 5 June 1997; Thompson 9–15 June 1997.

8. Masculine preference for younger brides may be traced to the Middle Ages (and, doubtless, beyond). On this, see Labarge 27–28. In recent years, Hollywood has popularized spring/winter matings, the late-season cases of Clint Eastwood, Anthony Quinn, Luciano Pavarotti, and Tony Randall evidencing famous aging males' predilection for Ms X brides anywhere from two to five decades their junior.

9. The marriages of Russian rulers evidence the male propensity to wed women one or two decades younger. Natal'ia Naryshkina was twenty years old, to Tsar Aleksei's forty-one; at seventeen, the future Empress Anna was married off to Friedrich Wilhelm, the Duke of Courland, a man more than twice her age; Count N. P. Sheremet'ev was over fifty when he secretly married the "star" of his theater, the peasant actress Praskov'ia Zhemchugova, two decades his junior (see Pushkareva 122, 133, 150–51). Such literati as Karamzin (in his second marriage), Pushkin, and Dostoevskii (likewise in his second marriage) indicated similar preferences for younger brides.

10. The temporal proximity of the two is exploited boldly, with intriguing implications, in the signally titled films *The Bride Wore Black* and *Black Widow*. In the latter, the bride dispatches each of her husbands so as to acquire their fortunes and enjoy the comforts of merry and affluent widowhood. Recently the term "black widow" has acquired another referent: the widows of Chechens killed in the protracted Russia/Chechen war who, after the loss of their husbands, join suicide squads, strapping explosives to their bodies and perishing along with the enemies targeted for elimination. See Weir, 12 June 2003.

11. On this phenomenon, see Hubbs and, more recently, Goscilo 68–92.

12. It should be kept in mind that 800,000 women actually served in the armed forces (see Green and Reeves 381). Since the military is a supremely male domain, however, during wartime "Matushka Russiia"/Mat'-Rodina (the soft, comforting bosom of origins, forbearance, and warm-heart[h]ed welcome) becomes defended in what Soviet Russians, revealingly, called the "Velikaia Otechestvennaia Voina." In short, steel-and-iron warrior-fathers protected Her borders.

13. By 1946, owing to the colossal scale of fatalities in the war, women outnumbered men by almost 26 million. On this and women's participation in the war, see Buckley 133.

14. On the role of gender in Baranskaia's perception of the wartime dynamic, see Lahusen 205–24.

15. In translation, Polevoi 570.

16. Simonov's "Zhdi menia, i ia vernus'" (1941) became a national mantra for Russian soldiers during the war. See *Antologiia* 141–42. Viktoriia Tokareva's story "Nichego osobennogo" ["Nothing Special"] sounds an ironic variation on that exhortation within a romantic context, in which the doctor Korolev pleads with Margarita, whom he allegedly loves, to wait for him, and while supposedly leaving her for just a day, rejoins his official family and never returns. Such a scenario, in fact, was played out repeatedly during World War II, so that by war's end many of its surviving male participants had two families.

17. Failure to wait for the "beloved male" was deemed tantamount to collusion in his death. See, for example, Kalatozov's film *Letiat zhuravli* [*Cranes Are Flying*]. For an excellent analysis of this phenomenon, see Alexander Prokhorov's doctoral dissertation, *Continuity and Rupture: Cultural Tropes of Stalinism in Thaw Literature and Film*.

18. Many of these posters offered modernized images of epic heroes such as Il'ia Muromets, and they cast the battle against the Germans as a knightly defense of honor and nation. See Paret et al.

19. On monuments in general and in Russia specifically, see Yampolsky 93–112.

20. On women's fabled passivity, see Ellmann 78–82; for a discussion of that trait in the heroines of Harlequin Romances, see Modleski 53–54.

21. Soviets likewise subjected foreign widows to shadow treatment, but to a silent, decorative, and decorous version of it, as evident in an article on Martin Luther King's assassination that appeared in *Ogonek* in 1980. Though eliminated entirely from the verbal text of the fictionalized report ("*povest'-khronika*"), Coretta King in her widow's weeds appears in one of the two photographs accompanying the narrative and is identified, of course, as King's widow (Borovik 20).

22. Vladimir Padunov pointed out to me the possible relevance here of Mauss's discoveries about gift exchanges in archaic societies.

23. Ivanova, pregnant by Babel' when she married Vsevolod Ivanov, offers a remarkably more thoughtful portrait of Babel' in her memoirs. Yet her recollections of her own husband fit snugly into the idealizing widowly mold. See Ivanova 271–301 and 9–247.

24. In a sense, that secondariness likewise marks wives and mistresses, as attested by such eloquently titled volumes as A. Trofimov, *Sviatye zheny Rusi* (1993), M. Dubinskii, *Zhenshchina v zhizni velikikh i znamenitykh liudei* (1990), and Vasilieva's *Kremlin Wives*. Needless to say, we have yet to see parallel surveys of husbands and lovers of famous women.

25. In the twelfth-century lyric epic *Slovo o polku Igoreve* [*Lay of Igor's Campaign*], the lament of Prince Igor''s wife, Iaroslava (recreated in Borodin's opera *Kniaz' Igor'*) illustrates the ritualistic nature of this widely developed genre, which permits improvisation within the framework of well-established oral conventions. On the genre and on the skill of Irina Fedosova, a famous practitioner of the lament (*plach*), see Sokolov 225–34.

26. For a brief, perspicacious glance at Akhmatova's autobiographical and pseudo-widowly maneuverings, see Kelly 209–23; for a vastly more detailed treatment of the same topic, see Zholkovsky.

27. According to the May 1995 issue, "big majorities" [sic] of the 2,500 women from Moscow and Saint Petersburg polled by the magazine "had extramarital affairs." Fifty-five percent of those polled "cheated on their partners."

28. Formerly, and to some extent even today, in rural areas, where the family unit was essential to survival, widowhood threatened severe economic hardship. On this factor, see Bohac and also Goldman 177.

29. True to Russian habit, Ol'ga's ability to eclipse her husband has not prevented scholars from including her in a recent gallery of "holy women," titled, quite amazingly, *Sviatye zheny Rusi,* thereby misleadingly implying that her chief significance in Russian history is uxorial.

30. In the early nineteenth century, Nicole-Barbe Ponsardin, widow of the vintner François Clicquot, far surpassed her husband's skill in manufacturing and exporting champagne. In addition to pioneering the now universally adopted process of clarifying wines, she built the formidable Veuve Clicquot champagne empire and by the time of her death at age 89 (in 1866) was renowned as the Grande Dame of Champagne. Literati devoted to Veuve Clicquot champagne included Pushkin, Gogol', Chekhov, Apollinaire, Proust, and . . . Agatha Christie. Contencin, passim.

31. Russian posters for both world wars, and especially the first, resorted to visuals of medieval *bogatyri* as defenders of the homeland.

32. On this episode and on war films in general, see Kenez 196–97.

33. On Goncharova's reputation in Russia, see the fine essay by Sandler 209–20.

34. As my colleague Mark Altshuller maintained during a conversation about Russian widows, "intimate" revelations by women during the early nineteenth century would have violated that period's strict notions of propriety.

35. See Liudmila Petrushevskaia, *Po doroge boga Erosa: povesti, rasskazy* [*Along Eros Way: Tales and Stories*], 65–69; for the English translation, by Sally Laird, see Ludmilla Petrushevskaya, *Immortal Love* 28–34.

36. The title resonates with the Simonov war poem "Zhdi menia" ["Wait for me"]. In general, Vysotskii's songs regularly repeat scenarios of men going off to prove themselves in battle, mountain climbing, and analogous modes of macho heroism.

37. The volume contains not only selections from Vysotskii's lyrics, but also reminiscences by various fellow poets, prosaists, critics, and film and theater personnel. Until relatively recently, neither Vlady nor anyone familiar with Vysotskii's habits alluded in print to his drug addiction, for Russia favors sanitized posthumous portraits of its "great men." For a sampling of such disinfected views, see *V. Vysotskii: Vse ne tak.* For a less rosy glimpse of relations between Vlady and the bard, see the morose, often sour diaries of the late Nagibin (350).

38. On the recording titled *Moi dom letaet* [*My House Is Flying*], Moscow, 1987. In the 1981 edition of Vysotskii's *Pesni i stikhi* [*Songs and Verses*], the publisher thanks his

widow Vlady for her assistance, without mention of Abramova. In 1997, however, the ignored widow also penned some memoirs.

39. On writers for whom marriage (and, in Babel''s case, fathering of illegitimate children) bordered on a hobby, see Proffer, especially 92–93.

40. L. E. Belozerskaia, *Bulgakov. O med vospominanii.* See Belozerskaia-Bulgakova. A resourceful and, unquestionably, clever woman, Belozerskaia nonetheless adhered to traditional Russian conventions of self-censorship to avoid tarnishing Bulgakov's reputation and to supply a backdrop of conjugal trust and happiness against which to project their shared travails.

41. On this issue, see Curtis, especially 30–33. See also E. Proffer, passim.

42. Though he lived with the artist Gabriele Münter as husband and wife, Kandinsky never married her. She remained his long-term mistress, for whom he left his first, legal wife, Anna Chimiakina. For more information on Kandinsky's trio of wives, see Olga's Gallery.

43. See Proffer's *Widows* and, more recently, the superlative study by Holmgren, especially 97–179.

44. By the epithet *creative* I do not mean to imply that she consciously relies on fiction in her memoirs, but that her choice of structure and style bear the imprint of her aesthetic values. If the memoirs of Pasternak's last (?) mistress, Ol'ga Ivinskaia, tend to the vague exaltation of the Romantics and Symbolists, the concrete, down-to-earth clarity of Nadezhda Mandel'shtam's writing sooner has affinities, unsurprisingly, with the unadorned if heavily freighted surface simplicity of Acmeism. See Ivinskaia (in English translation, Ivinskaya).

45. For instance, how many widows would be capable of a statement that in frankness matches the following disclaimer: "I never had the slightest influence on M., and he would have thrown me over rather than his city" (*Hope Abandoned* 97).

46. At an exchange before the screening of *Komediia strogogo rezhima* [*Comedy of a Strict Regime,* 1991], a film based on Dovlatov's stories of the camps, Elena Dovlatova emphasized the imaginative nature of Dovlatov's fictionalized memoirs, but she, in fact, emerged as the remarkably accurate incarnation of the alienated spouse sardonically portrayed in Dovlatov's witty *Nashi* [*Ours,* 1983].

47. For reactions to the publication of *Vrotaia kniga* see Proffer's *Widows* 34–46.

48. Similarly, Tynianov's notion that literature and *byt* overlap or cross-fertilize, whereby a document may be raised to the status of literature, is not without relevance to Nadezhda Mandel'shtam's memoirs. See especially the first two chapters in Tynianov, "Literaturnyi fakt" [Literary Fact"] and "O literaturnoi evoliutsii" ["On Literary Evolution"].

References

Akhmatova, Anna. *My Half Century. Selected Prose.* Ed. Ronald Meyer. Ann Arbor: Ardis, 1992.

Antologiia russkoi sovetskoi poezii 1917–1957. Vol. 2. Moscow: Gosizkhudlit, 1957.

Belozerskaya-Bulgakova, Lyubov. *My Life with Mikhail Bulgakov.* Ann Arbor: Ardis, 1983.

Berton, Kathleen. *Moscow. An Architectural History.* London: I. B. Tauris, 1990.

Billington, James H. *The Icon and the Axe.* New York: Vintage Books, 1966/1970.

Bitov, Andrei. *Pushkin House.* Trans. Susan Brownsberger. Ann Arbor: Ardis, 1987.

———. *Pushkinskii Dom.* Ann Arbor: Ardis, 1978.

Bohac, Rodney D. "Widows and the Russian Serf Community." *Russia's Women: Accommodation, Resistance, Transformation.* Ed. Barbara Evans Clements, Barbara Alpern Engel, and Christine D. Worobec. Berkeley/Los Angeles: California UP, 1991.

Bonner, Elena. "Vladimir Potemkin." *Wall Street Journal.* 17 June 2003.

Borovik, Genrikh. "Istoriia odnogo ubiistva." *Ogonek* 2 (1980): 18–20.

Buckley, Mary. *Women and Ideology in the Soviet Union.* Ann Arbor: Michigan UP, 1989.

Clements, Barbara Evans, Barbara Alpern Engel, and Christine D. Worobec, eds. *Russia's Women: Accommodation, Resistance, Transformation.* Berkeley/Los Angeles: California UP, 1991.

Contencin, Nicole. *In Search of Perfection.* Reims: Veuve Clocquot Ponsardin, 1995.

Curtis, J. A. *Manuscripts Don't Burn. Mikhail Bulgakov: A Life in Letters and Diaries.* London: Bloomsbury, 1991.

Desaive, Jean-Paul. "The Ambiguities of Literature." *A History of Women in the West,* vol. 3, *Renaissance and Enlightenment Paradoxes.* Ed. Natalie Zemon Davis and Arlette Farge. Cambridge, MA: Belknap Press of Harvard UP, 1993.

Dubinskii, M. (M. Poltavskii). *Zhenshchina v zhizni velikikh i znamenitykh liudei.* Tbilisi: Soiuz teatral'nykh deiatelei, 1990. Rpt. of the work originally published in Saint Petersburg, 1900.

Ellmann, Mary. *Thnking about Women.* New York: Harcourt Brace Jovanovich, 1968.

Goldman, Wendy. *Women, the State and Revolution.* Cambridge: Cambridge UP, 1992.

Goscilo, Helena. "The Gendered Trinity of Russian Cultural Rhetoric Today—or the Glyph of the H[i]eroine." *Soviet Hieroglyphics. Visual Culture in Late Twentieth-Century Russia.* Ed. Nancy Condee. Bloomington: Indiana UP, 1995.

Green, William C., and W. Robert Reeves, eds. *The Soviet Military Encyclopedia.* Vol. 3. Boulder: Westview Press, 1993.

Hemer, June, and Ann Stanyer. *Handbook for Widows.* London: Virago, 1978.

Hoffman, David. "Stalin's 'Seven Sister' 'Wedding Cake' Style 1950s Towers Define Moscow Skyline." *Washington Post.* 29 July 1997.

Holmgren, Beth. *Women's Works in Stalin's Time. On Lidiia Chukovskaia and Nadezhda Mandel'shtam.* Bloomington: Indiana UP, 1993.

Hubbs, Joanna. *Mother Russia. The Feminine Myth in Russian Culture.* Bloomington: Indiana UP, 1988/1993.

Hufton, Olwen. "Women, Work, and Family." *A History of Women in the West,* vol. 3, *Renaissance and Enlightenment Paradoxes.* Ed. Natalie Zemon Davis and Arlette Farge. Cambridge, MA: Belknap Press of Harvard UP, 1993.

Hyman, Herbert H. *Of Time and Widowhood.* Durham: Duke Press Policy Studies, 1983.

Ivanova, Tamara. *Moi sovremenniki, kakimi ia ikh znala.* Moscow: Sovetskii pisatel', 1987.

Ivinskaia, Ol'ga. *A Captive of Time.* Trans. Max Hayward. New York: Doubleday, 1978.

———. *V plenu vremeni; gody s Borisom Pasternakom.* Paris: Fayard, 1978.

Kelly, Catriona. *A History of Russian Women's Writing 1820–1992.* Oxford: Clarendon Press, 1994.

Kenez, Peter. *Cinema and Soviet Society 1917–1953.* Cambridge: Cambridge UP, 1992.

Labarge, Margaret Wade. *A Small Sound of the Trumpet: Women in Medieval Life.* Boston: Beacon Press, 1986.

Lahusen, Thomas. "'Leaving Paradise' and Perestroika: *A Week Like Any Other* and *Memorial Day* by Natal'ia Baranskaia." *Fruits of Her Plume.* Ed. Helena Goscilo. Armonk: M. E. Sharpe, 1993.

Laird, Sally, trans. *Immortal Love* by Ludmilla Petrushevskaya. London: Virago, 1995. English translation of *Po doroge boga Erosa: povesti, rasskazy* by Liudmila Petrushevskaia.

Levin, Eve. *Sex and Society in the World of the Orthodox Slavs, 900–1700*. Ithaca and London: Cornell UP, 1989.

Mandelshtam, Nadezhda. *Hope Abandoned*. Trans. Max Hayward. New York: Atheneum, 1974.

Matthews, Owen. "A Magazine for Pigs, and Proud of It." *The Moscow Times*. 7 June 1995.

Mauss, Marcel. *The Gift. The Form and Reason for Exchange in Archaic Societies*. Trans. W. D. Halls. London: Routledge, 1990.

Michelson, Annette. "The Kinetic Icon and the Work of Mourning: Prolegomena to the Analysis of a Textual System." *In The Red Screen. Politics, Society, Art in Soviet Cinema*. Ed. Anna Lawton. London: Routledge, 1992.

Mirrer, Louise, ed. *Upon My Husband's Death*. Ann Arbor: Michigan UP, 1992.

Modleski, Tania. *Loving with a Vengeance*. New York/London: Methuen, 1982.

"Monument to Sakharov unveiled in St. Petersburg." Interfax-Northwest. 5 May 2003.

Nagibin, Iurii. *Dnevnik*. Moscow: "Knizhnyi sad," 1995.

Nayman, Anatoly. *Remembering Akhmatova*. Trans. Wendy Rosslyn. London: Peter Halban, 1991.

Olga's Gallery. 5 May 2003. <http://www.abcgallery.com/list/2003may05.html>

OMRI Daily Digest. Daily news summary of the Open Media Research Institute published between 2 Jan. 1995 and 28 Mar. 1997.

Paret, Peter, Beth Irwin Lewis, and Paul Paret. *Persuasive Images: Posters of War and Revolution*. Princeton: Princeton UP, 1992.

Petrushevskaia, Liudmila. *Po doroge boga Erosa: povesti, rasskazy*. Moscow: Olimp-PPP, 1993.

Pirozhkova, A. N. *At His Side. The Last Years of Isaac Babel*. Trans. Anna Frydman and Robert L. Busch. South Royalton, VT: Steerforth Press, 1996.

Polevoi, Boris. *A Story about a Real Man*. Moscow: Foreign Languages Publishing House, n.d.

Proffer, Carl R. *Widows of Russia*. Ann Arbor: Ardis, 1987.

Proffer, Ellendea. *Bulgakov*. Ann Arbor: Ardis, 1984.

Proffer, E., ed. *Neizdannyi Bulgakov*. Ann Arbor: Ardis, 1977.

Pushkareva, Natalia. *Women in Russian History*. Armonk: M. E. Sharpe, 1997.

Sachs, Susan. "Tobacco Wars. Smoking under Siege. Cigarette Glut Fouls Russia." *Newsday*. 5 June 1997.

Sandler, Stephanie. "Pushkin's Last Love—Natal'ya Nikolaevna in Russian Culture." *Gender Restructuring in Russian Studies*. Ed. M. Liljeström, E. Mäntysaari, and A. Rosenholm. Tampere: University of Tampere, 1993.

Schiff, Stacy. "The Genius and Mrs. Genius." *The New Yorker*. 10 Feb. 1997: 41–47.

Shamgar-Handelman, Lea. *Israeli War Widows*. South Hadley, MA: Bergin & Garvey, 1986.

Sokolov, Y. M. *Russian Folklore*. Hatboro: Folklore Associates, 1966.

Taves, Isabella. *The Widow's Guide*. New York: Schocken Books, 1981.

Thompson, Suzanne. "Russians Take on Joe Camel in Tobacco War." *Saint Petersburg Times*. 9–15 June 1997.

Trofimov, A. *Sviatye zheny Rusi*. Moscow: Khram Rozhdestva Presviatoi Bogoroditsy v sele Poiarkovo, 1993.

Tynianov, Iurii. *Arkhaisty i novatory*. Priboi, 1929; Rpt. Ann Arbor: Ardis, 1985.

Vasilieva, Larissa. *Kremlin Wives*. Trans. Cathy Porter. New York: Arcade Pub., 1994.

Vladi, Marina. *Vladimir, ili Prervannyi polet*. Moscow: Progress, 1989.

Volkov, Solomon. *St. Petersburg: A Cultural History*. Trans. Antonina W. Bouis. New York: Free Press Paperbacks/Simon and Schuster, 1995.

Vysotskii, Vladimir. *"Ia, konechno, vernus'."* Moscow: "Kniga," 1988.

———. *Pesni i stikhi.* New York: Izd. "Literaturnoe zarubezh'e," 1981.

V. Vysotskii: Vse ne talk. Memorial'nyi al'manakh-antologiia. Moscow: Bakhazar, 1991.

Walton, David. Review of *An Appointment with Somerset Maugham and Other Literary Encounters* by Richard Hauer Costa. *New York Times Book Review.* 23 Apr. 1995: 20.

Waxman, Sharon, and Andrew Decker. "Picasso, Inc. Pain and Profit." *Art News.* Sept. 1995.

Weir, Fred. "Chechen women join terror's ranks." *Christian Science Monitor.* 12 June 2003.

———. "Sakharov's ideals: lost in the new Russia?" *Christian Science Monitor.* 6 May 2003.

Yampolsky, Mikhail. "In the Shadow of Monuments: Notes on Iconoclasm and Time." *Soviet Hieroglyphics. Visual Culture in Late Twentieth-Century Russia.* Ed. Nancy Condee. Bloomington: Indiana UP, 1995.

Zholkovsky, Alexander. "The Obverse of Stalinism: Akhmatova's Self-Serving Charisma of Selflessness." *Self and Story in Russian History.* Eds. Laura Engelstein and Stephanie Sandler. Ithaca and London: Cornell UP. 46–68.

Zorkaya, Neya. *The Illustrated History of Soviet Cinema.* New York: Hippocrene Books, 1989.

THREE | Mothers of Communists

Women Revolutionaries and the
Construction of a Soviet Identity

ELIZABETH JONES HEMENWAY

Aroseva, Mariia Avgustovna (Vertynskaia). Led by the Whites from the Spasska prison on the 18th of September 1918 and shot eight versts from the city. Mariia Avgustovna was fifty years old. Her crime lay in the fact that she conducted cultural-enlightenment work among the peasants, and also in the fact that she was the mother of a communist.

—Aleksandr Arosev (*Pamiatnik* 27)[1]

     The first lines of Mariia Aroseva's memorial, included in a 1923 Communist Party publication, demonstrate the ambiguities inherent in defining the new Soviet state, while at the same time suggesting a number of important details about Aroseva's activity as both a revolutionary and a model for other Soviet citizens. First, as a populist, she was committed to improving the lives of peasants in the "dark [ignorant] village" by teaching them to read and conducting reading circles. For Aroseva this work was not simply a job, but a moral duty. Second, she not only gave birth to a son who later became a communist, but also served as the caretaker and metaphorical mother for the peasants she taught, shaping their internal revolution, which, she believed, would ensure their future.[2] Third, her death at the hands of the enemy elevated Aroseva to the status of a martyr to the cause, a "devoted friend of the people" who selflessly "poured her entire soul" into her work for the masses and the revolution. As described in this account, however, her crime consisted not of her activism in support of the Bolshevik Revolution, but of her role as teacher and mother; she was guilty of helping "to give birth" to the Bolshevik Revolution of 1917. Aroseva's case, in other words, illustrated how under certain circumstances Family could mean Fatality despite an official rhetoric of positive kinship.

Juxtaposed to the discourse producing the mother-martyr are the words of Emelian Iaroslavskii, who wrote about "Lenin's family" shortly after the Bolshevik leader's death in 1924: "I speak here not only of those people close to Lenin—those related by blood—with whom he lived his life, who surrounded him in childhood and youth, raised him, and worried about him during his illness. Lenin's family is much broader. Lenin created a communist family of many millions. We all consider ourselves Lenin's brothers, sisters, and children" (Iaroslavskii 1–3). Both these accounts draw direct connections between the nuclear or "small family" (*malaia sem'ia*) and the "big family" (*bol'shaia sem'ia*) of the Soviet nation, institutionalized by Stalin in the 1930s. As described by Katerina Clark, the *bol'shaia sem'ia* had roots in Russian peasant culture, where one's family could extend horizontally to include any number of blood or non-blood relations. The critical aspect, however, of both the small and the big family was their vertical power structure, in which authority derived from the patriarch (Clark 114–35). One can thus imagine the Bolshevik "family tree" consisting not only of metaphorical brothers and sisters, but also of parents and children, with Lenin as the main patriarchal figure. As early as 1918, Soviet publications carried the image of Lenin as the idealized leader of the Party/family. Using imagery drawn from religious literature, folklore, and heroic tales, Soviet writers began to elaborate the image of Lenin that would be unified only after his death in 1924, under Stalin's self-promoting guidance. Bolshevik activists simultaneously used kindred language to describe the lives of their fallen comrades who perished during the Civil War (Tumarkin 74–111).[3]

The two passages quoted above exemplify the ways in which early Soviet narratives used the family motif, though at times in ways that broke from the traditional concept of the patriarchal family. In particular, themes of equality among revolutionaries and the importance of women's activity enjoyed a prominence unknown in earlier Russian public discourse. During the late nineteenth and early twentieth centuries women entered the political realm and became visible actors in the revolutionary process, pressing not only for revolution but also for suffrage and equal rights. Indeed, some, such as Aleksandra Kollontai, believed that the desacralization of tsarist autocracy that culminated in the Revolutions of 1917 would lead to the establishment of a new kind of state, based on the equality of all people irrespective of class, gender, or ethnicity.[4] Women's increased visibility and the socialist commitment to address the "woman question" notwithstanding, by the mid-1920s the image of revolutionary women had become limited to two rather restrictive models, subordinate to that of the benevolent, fatherly leader.[5]

The tensions among the various representations of "family" members—such as the concept of women as sisters and equals in the revolutionary struggle, declarations of the equal rights of women, the concept of women as mothers of revolution, and the persistence of the patriarchal state with Lenin at its head—reveal gaps in the process of constructing a Soviet identity during the early 1920s. If the Soviet Union was to be a new kind of nation, one that stood for the liberation of all humankind, then theoretically it had to reject the old patriarchal models and metaphors of national identity and create new ones. But the persistence of these models—especially the idea of a patriarchal state—suggests an inconsistency in the discourse of Soviet national identity. Was the Soviet Union composed of a collective of equals, and in that case a radical departure from the previous political order in Russia, or was it imagined as an enormous family, created by Lenin, the kindly, all-knowing father (Tumarkin; Borenstein; Fitzpatrick, et al.)?[6] Scholars have argued that both of these conceptions of Soviet identity existed during the 1920s, when Soviet leaders and citizens worked to construct a Soviet "imagined community." As models for a nation of equals, however, these concepts of community had self-evident limits, for they rhetorically restricted or eliminated the role of women.

How were women's identities as revolutionaries and Soviet citizens constructed in a way that acknowledged their diminished role within the "revolutionary brotherhood" and subservient role within the communist family, while at the same time depicting themselves as integral, if not essential, members of the Soviet national community? The roles and experiences of women revolutionaries as they and their comrades described them provide insights into this question and expose the difficulties inherent in the project of forging a Soviet identity. The writing of "memorial literature," or narratives about deceased comrades published in newspapers, journals, and special volumes devoted to the fallen, constitutes a critical element in the narrative of revolution elaborated during the early period of Soviet rule. These testimonials, written by the colleagues of fallen revolutionaries, recited the dedication and achievements of the individuals, and emphasized the qualities that made them part of a larger revolutionary collective or "Lenin's family."[7] The memorials to women revolutionaries in particular illustrate the tensions among three competing discourses: the proclamation of sexual equality; the conception of a Soviet national family; and the role of women revolutionaries as mothers and sisters in the revolutionary family.

While seeming to be straightforward hagiography, the memorial literature of the early 1920s demonstrates the power of narrative in shaping both historical experience and individual and collective identity—what Joan Scott calls a "contested terrain" (Scott 22–40). Scott argues that an individual's experience is not a transparent, self-evident entity, but rather a discursively constituted entity (or text) that contains several possible meanings or interpretations—an idea related to Hayden White's notion of historical accounts as coherent structuring narratives. By insisting on the essential role of language in creating historical experience, Scott urges historians to examine the "multiple and conflicting claims" of identity. Thus the writers of memorial accounts faced a contested terrain in writing about their friends, comrades, and spouses that compelled them simultaneously to affirm and to deny their subjects' individual identities, identities that the authors composed not from direct experience, but from memory and perhaps the few written texts the deceased had left behind.[8] As described in these accounts, to join the revolutionary movement and live underground, in prison or in exile, women revolutionaries had to reject their femininity and join the "band of revolutionary brothers," while at the same time they were expected to uphold certain ideals of feminine virtue. This phenomenon paralleled a similar tension between the roles of revolutionary "sister" and "mother." Similarly, the assertion of an individual revolutionary identity was problematic within a mass movement that emphasized the collective, and a particular tension arose between women's identities and new standards of sexual behavior. As the authors of memorial literature attest, women struggled with their assertion of an individual identity, on the one hand, and the need to blend with a collective concept of revolution that rendered them invisible, on the other. Their narratives of the 1917 Revolutions reveal how these authors portrayed female revolutionary participants as navigators in the contested terrain of individual and collective identities.[9]

Building a Soviet Identity between 1917 and 1927

According to Benedict Anderson, the nation is imagined as "a deep, horizontal comradeship" or fraternity (7). This notion certainly held true for the Soviet Union, for in the immediate aftermath of the Revolution the Soviet nation conceived of itself as a revolutionary fraternity or "band of brothers" who had thrown off the oppressive shackles of the old patriarchal order and united in a collective attempt to establish a community of equals. The core member of the Soviet "imagined community" was the revolutionary activist or hero, a figure that had emerged and developed long before 1917. The revolutionary hero appeared as early as the 1870s in folk tales and stories describing the injustices of tsarist rule and dreams of revolutionary change.[10] Always a male figure, the revolutionary hero not only represented the shared experiences and desires of his social group (workers and peasants), but also belonged to a massive unit of brothers who fought against the Russian tsarist order for fundamental social, economic, and political change. While the band of brothers did not explicitly exclude their revolutionary sisters, women typically appeared on the margins of these stories, as well as of other accounts of revolutionary activity published in newspapers, leaflets, pamphlets, and books during and after 1917.[11] Tales of revolution sharply contrasted this egalitarian fraternity with the archaic, unjust, patriarchal state led by the tsar-*batiushka,* or little father.

The egalitarian model of the new revolutionary national family or *bol'shaia sem'ia* that became central to Soviet identity had two major advantages for the members of the revolutionary collective. First, it was not dependent on biological relationships, thereby enabling members to sever relationships with parents, siblings, spouses, or children that may have interfered with the new way of life and to establish a nascent "great family."[12] Second, the concept of the Soviet family could be expanded or contracted to include or exclude "others." Thus, once they had undergone the appropriate conversion, former members of the bourgeoisie, women, non-Russians, old Mensheviks, or Socialist Revolutionaries could join the Soviet family.

After Lenin's death in 1924, and, arguably, during the years preceding his death, the Soviet family acquired a new element: the heroic Lenin as father or grandfather (Tumarkin 59–62). Lenin's death marked the final phase of a shift from the egalitarian "band of brothers" to a patriarchal family with, as Iaroslavskii notes, the leader as its head and creator. The memorial literature of the early 1920s, including the obituaries of Lenin, served as a transition between the egalitarian and patriarchal models of the Soviet nation and as a link between individual experiences of revolution and the construction of a collective narrative of revolution that was to cement the entire Soviet family. As the revolutionary brotherhood evolved into a Soviet nation with a more traditional imagined family structure, however, the ambiguity of women's place within the symbolic family became more pronounced. The women who had participated in the revolutionary movement and in the founding of the Soviet state, paradoxically, came to be seen as somehow outside this collective. The memorial literature of the early to mid-1920s, then, served the function of asserting the importance of women's revolutionary activity while simultaneously situating that activity within a more traditional gender structure, in which the women appeared as faithful mothers and sisters, "friends of the working class," and assistants in the birthing process of revolution.

The Attributes of a Woman Revolutionary

Part of the larger project of documenting the history of the revolutionary movement and the 1917 Revolutions, and of constructing a collective Soviet national identity, involved telling thousands of individual life stories through a variety of texts. The official history of the Bolshevik Revolution was handled largely by the Section for Study of the History of the October Revolution and Bolshevik Party (known by its acronym, *Istpart*), which founded a revolutionary archive on the basis of autobiographical questionnaires and "evenings of reminiscences."[13] Another practice instituted by the Communist Party during the 1920s was the compilation of volumes such as *The Brothers' Tomb* [*Bratskaia mogila*] and *Memorial to the Fighters for the Proletarian Revolution* [*Pamiatnik bortsam proletarskoi revoliutsii*], which contained testimonials to comrades who had perished during the October Revolution and Civil War.[14] A number of journals, including *The Past* [*Byloe*], *Penal Servitude and Exile* [*Katorga i ssylka*], and *The Woman Communist* [*Kommunistka*], also published obituaries and extended essays commemorating the lives of deceased revolutionaries.[15] In addition, certain individuals merited entire volumes of their own, such as the collections of essays dedicated to Inessa Armand (1876–1920) and Konkordiia Samoilova (1876–1921).[16] While these accounts adhere to a common framework of revolutionary narrative in its broad outline of awakening, activism, and revolution, they also include elements that feminize women's identity as revolutionaries.

These narratives follow a general pattern that reappears in later accounts of Russian women's revolutionary activism and combines three forms of traditional Russian Orthodox saints' lives—biographies (*vitae*) of revolutionary saints, stories of martyrs, and catalogs of virtues (*encomia*).[17] Just as Orthodox hagiography conformed to certain conventions and paradigms, so Soviet memorial literature comprised set structures and phrases that would be familiar to readers and listeners. According to Jostein Børtnes, the subject of the hagiographical text embodies a religious—or revolutionary—ideal and thereby joins the pantheon of saints. Børtnes further explains that the texts describing lives of saints emphasize the contrast between earthly and "upper-worldly" existence, so that "the earthly lives of the saints are seen as negative parallels of their eternal glory" (33). In a similar manner, although the lives of Bolshevik heroes and heroines may have resembled those of other humans, their enshrinement in memorial literature after 1917 ascribed to them special experiences and qualities elevating them above ordinary Soviet citizens and established them as models for emulation.[18]

In this way, we can view memorial literature and the volumes that contained it (*Pamiatnik* and *Bratskaia mogila*) as revolutionary versions of "The Lives of the Saints." For a woman the "plots" usually describe her expanding consciousness and conversion to the cause, which typically occurs during her youth and results in her complete dedication to the revolutionary cause and "family." This process often includes her and others' education in the fundamentals of revolutionary doctrine. A common feature of the memorial account is a recitation of the individual's many virtues, justifying her status within the pantheon of revolutionary hero(in)es. Unwavering commitment to the cause usually required that a woman sever ties with her biological family and deny herself a private life separate from the cause. Moreover, part of her role within the revolutionary movement often entailed caring for her fellow revolutionaries as a mother or sister. Memorial accounts invariably conclude by summarizing the circumstances of the heroine's often premature and tragic death, frequently resulting from her exclusive devotion to the cause and thus providing the impetus for the memorial. While this veneer of heroic sainthood helped to establish women revolutionaries as admirable models of activism and Soviet citizenship, it also reveals an underlying contradiction in the role of the woman citizen and, more broadly, of the implicit concept of nation.

The topos of female revolutionaries' expanding consciousness constituted an important initial phase in the biographical literature, marking the birth of the individual's "awakening" and life in the revolutionary cause, which subsequently became her new family. Modes of reaching such an awakening varied, however, depending on women's social position and

3-1 Inessa Armand. (From *Frauen der Revolution: Porträts hervorragender Bolschewikinnen* [Berlin, 1960])

level of education. Women raised in the middle and upper classes generally experienced a kind of intellectual, moral, or spiritual awakening to the injustices of the world and committed themselves to correcting those inequities through Party activism. For example, the numerous biographies documenting the life of Inessa Armand, the first head of the Women's Section (*Zhenotdel*) of the Bolshevik Party, contain a description of her upbringing in a conventional bourgeois household, where as a teenager she began to read forbidden books and to develop her socialist (and eventually Bolshevik) sympathies.[19] Her "enlightenment" prompted her to assist peasants in a nearby village, including the mothers of illegitimate babies, and culminated in a "spiritual crisis" after the birth of her first child in 1895 (Krupskaia 5–33). For Armand, as for other revolutionary women, conversion necessitated rejecting her biological family and the class privilege associated with it.

Converts from privileged backgrounds typically went on to bring enlightenment to others by opening village schools. Such activism was especially prevalent during the 1890s and the early 1900s. Lidiia Antonovna Basova, for instance, organized Party study circles and a school in Tula, where "children from poor families found things their families could not provide—warmth, light, joy," and knowledge (*Pamiatnik* 51–52). Using educational techniques learned abroad, Basova combined games with studies to teach children in the most appealing manner possible. As noted above,

3-2   Klavdiia Mikhailovna Smirnova. (From Tsetsiliia Samoilovna Zelikson-Bobrovskaia, *Zapiski riadovogo podpol'shchika*, vol. 1, 1894–1914 [Moscow, 1922])

Aroseva taught peasants to read and sought to improve everyday life in the countryside. Similarly, Armand opened a school in 1894 for the peasants near her family's estate. Other women, such as Klavdiia Mikhailovna Smirnova and Nadezhda Stepanovna Baturina, obtained jobs in tsarist schools while conducting underground propaganda and hiding party comrades in their state-provided apartments.[20]

Teaching their comrades in Party circles and schools was another key role fulfilled by highly educated Bolshevik women. Armand worked tirelessly to teach her comrades, especially during times of exile or imprisonment. While living in France and Switzerland, she established circles and worked in the Party schools (where the best workers from Russia were sent), making a strong impression on the other activists who studied with her. Konkordiia Nikolaevna Samoilova, also considered a critical figure in the "enlightenment" of female workers and peasants, exerted every effort to attract both categories "to the communist banner and raise them in the spirit of [. . . the] Party, to make of them warriors for the general good" (Kollontai 8–11). Women from bourgeois backgrounds thus tended to be represented as maternal figures, at times echoing the image of *Rodina-mat'* (see the chapter by Zaitseva in this volume).[21]

Working-class women, by contrast, usually followed another path to Bolshevism and activism, often taking on more "sisterly" roles within the revolutionary collective. Evdokiia Pavlovna Chamova, a blacksmith's daughter, directly felt the pain of loss, oppression, and injustice when her father's

3-3 Konkordiia Nikolaevna Samoilova. (From *Frauen der Revolution: Porträts hervorragender Bolschewikinnen* [Berlin, 1960])

death forced her, at the age of eleven, to seek employment to support herself and her family. Joining a tailor's workshop, she "worked tirelessly, almost like a martyr" eighteen or more hours a day. "Living such a nightmarish existence, she naturally dreamed of better circumstances, of a better life.` She searched and searched, but only the same thing was found over and over. The search only aroused class hatred and class consciousness within her" (*Bratskaia mogila* 2: 248–50). The revolutionary movement offered Chamova an escape from the nightmare of her childhood, an escape fueled by hatred and despair.

The account of Mil'da Turin's life portrays a similarly arduous childhood. Her mother died when Mil'da was a young child. Sent to live with a family of farm workers, she later moved to the city, found a job in a factory, and was entirely swept up by the wave of the workers' movement. From that moment her conscious fight for the working class began. Despite arrests, exile, and near-starvation, she remained "motivated by a deep faith in a better future" (*Bratskaia mogila* 2: 241–42). In short, women of the working classes, with personal knowledge of deprivation and oppression, became passionate fighters for revolution and members of the revolutionary collective, while upper-class women tended to assume the roles of teachers and inspirational speakers.

As in hagiographies, so in memorial literature about women revolutionaries, a litany of the subject's many admirable qualities figured prominently:

dedication to the cause, a heroic attitude toward work, moral uprightness, and nurturing concern for colleagues. Comrade Platova, like other women activists, we learn, was strong, energetic, and a tireless worker, who devoted her entire life to the liberation of the working class ("Odna iz mnogikh" 21). A young woman of only twenty, Mariia Iakovlevna Bogdanova never wavered in her commitment to the Party, listening to all appeals and giving everything she could to the workers' cause (*Pamiatnik* 72).[22] Party leaders, such as Armand and Samoilova, embodied the essential virtues of a Bolshevik Party member. According to one source, Armand steadfastly believed in the revolutionary cause, remaining at her post even under the most trying circumstances during the war, and inspired similar dedication in others. Like other female revolutionaries, Armand showed herself to be a "true friend to the working class" through ceaseless work (*Pamiatnik* 24–26). Samoilova, who reportedly shared her virtues, was deemed the "embodiment of the best hopes of our [i.e., the Bolshevik] party" (Kollontai 8–9). A talented orator, she demonstrated unusual initiative in her efforts to protect the interests of women workers and peasants, convinced that "women would play a decisive role in the struggle for Soviet power" in 1917.

While emphasizing revolutionary women's aptitude for energetic, tireless work, the memorial literature makes clear that their activities were nearly invisible, owing to their embraced ideal of modesty. L. K. Ammosova's modesty, for example, reportedly enhanced her colleagues' respect for her and for those women who evaded arrest by operating "quietly, calmly, and unnoticed" among people of the city and the countryside ("Tov. L. K. Ammosova" 27; *Pamiatnik* 27). At the same time, this quality led to women's erasure as individuals within the collective. Chamova, for instance, emerges as a worker-revolutionary who was "simple, modest, considerate, not even noticeable at first glance, but irreplaceable in the work process" (*Bratskaia mogila* 2: 248–50).[23] These revolutionary sisters blended into the collective so well that they were hardly noticed.

Memorials repeatedly note that for many women, commitment to the cause entailed sacrificing a comfortable existence and a private life. Armand, for example, "refused a life of wealth and pleasure in the bourgeois milieu into which she had fallen as a result of her marriage, in order to exchange it for the life of the underground revolutionary, eternally persecuted and pursued." Political dedication demanded that middle-class Party members forego the material comforts of their class and sever familial bonds, especially during the period of underground activity when revolutionaries regularly risked imprisonment or exile. Consequently, women revolutionaries were either childless or dependent on others to care for their offspring. A case in point was Mariia Baryshnikova, who, after her husband's death during the Civil War, "left her only child with a working-class family and volunteered for the Polish front as a nurse (*v kachestve sestry*)"

(*Bratskaia mogila* 1: 36). In fulfilling the role of revolutionary, then, some revolutionary women had to abandon a traditional maternal role.

The case of Armand illustrates the degree to which a woman's complicated private family life could be almost entirely expunged from her official representation. In their drive to build a specific image of Armand, the narratives omitted mention of her sporadic presence in her children's lives and, perhaps more importantly, of her unconventional relationship with her first husband and her subsequent relationship with her husband's brother, with whom she had a child in 1903.[24] In a scenario reminiscent of Nikolai Chernyshevskii's proto-revolutionary novel, *What Is To Be Done?* [*Chto delat'?* 1863], her husband, instead of divorcing her, stepped aside and allowed Armand and her lover to continue their relationship unhindered. While a potential model for the kind of free relationship later advocated by Kollontai, this nontraditional arrangement (along with Armand's close friendship with Lenin) was never mentioned in the accounts of Armand's life published during the 1920s.[25]

In the memorial literature the denial of private life constituted not simply a separation between the women's biological and revolutionary families but an acknowledgment that the private had no place within the new Soviet national family. As Armand wrote near the end of her life, "There is no personal life because all [of one's] time and strength are given to the general cause" (Clements, *Bolshevik Women* 221; quoting Volkogonov 311). As revolutionary activists, politicized women set aside everything else for the cause, thereby opening all aspects of their lives to public scrutiny and sharing aspects of revolutionary life (such as child-rearing) with other members of the community. In some cases, however, their private lives could raise troubling questions and require "correction" or effacement. A public discussion of Armand's private history, for example, would bring into question her sexual past, moral uprightness, and suitability as a model for the revolutionary woman.

While memorial literature represents Bolshevik women as marginal in the lives of their biological children, it also represents them as caregivers in a more public and metaphorical mode, as mothers to fellow revolutionaries and the Russian masses. This was especially true of those women from the more elite families. Once again, Armand's example dramatizes the problems of motherhood for many female revolutionaries. Married in 1893 at nineteen, she soon became a mother—a fact mentioned in virtually every account and cited as a central aspect of her identity as a revolutionary. She fulfilled her role as mother, however, with ambivalence. Nadezhda Krupskaia's obituary of Armand, published in *Kommunistka*, explains, "Family life did not serve as a refuge for her. She reacted to everything with her own peculiar passion. When her oldest son was born, she experienced a profound spiritual crisis" (17–20). Her full conversion to socialism followed, and Armand soon landed in prison and exile, all the while working actively with Bolsheviks in Russia and Western Europe.

Whatever the dimensions of the alleged crisis after her son's birth, Armand's mothering of her fellow revolutionaries became a central aspect of her revolutionary identity as it was constructed after her death in 1920. In the underground, in prison, and in exile Armand transferred her maternal skills to caring for other revolutionaries who needed nurture. As Comrade Zubrovich describes his time with her in Arkhagel'sk, "[Armand] was like a mother to us. . . . I especially felt this at the time, almost as if I were her little boy [*mal'chuganom*]" (Zubrovich 14–15). He further relates an incident in 1907, when he was beaten by an inspector; Armand, seeing his injuries, "rushed to [. . . him], scooped [. . . him] up in her arms, and took [. . . him] back to her apartment, where she nursed [. . . him] back to health" (14–15). This relationship continued later when both were exiled in Paris, and Zubrovich briefly lived with her and her three younger children. As depicted in memorial accounts, Armand's reputation in the underground was that of a revolutionary/loving caretaker, who drew those with physical or emotional needs into her family circle and taught them the ways of the Party.

Saintliness in memorial accounts combines limitless moral strength with physical frailty. Repeated references to female revolutionaries' "weak organisms," which could not sustain the intensive demands of revolutionary activist work, become a leitmotif. The modest Ammosova, for instance, suffered from a vulnerable constitution, and her tireless work eventually precipitated an illness that resulted in her death ("Tov. L. K. Ammosova" 27). Overwork and self-neglect also undermined the health of others, such as Chamova, whose organism otherwise might have flourished (*Bratskaia mogila* 2: 248–50).[26] In all such cases, bodily weakness stemming from indifference to their own well-being made these politically engaged women susceptible to tuberculosis, typhus, and cholera, which often proved fatal. As in Victorian England, with its cult of female invalidism, these women's fragility, as spotlighted in the memorials, was identified specifically with femininity. It was valued as an exemplary characteristic of a good Soviet revolutionary and citizen.[27]

Poor health or not, the paradigm of the revolutionary woman depicts her as struggling for the cause to the very last. The twenty-year-old Bogdanova, disregarding both her illness and her comrades' pleas that she rest, volunteered for an expedition to obtain bread in the Saratov region and perished in the process (*Pamiatnik* 72). Others endured terrible living conditions, often without adequate food, clothing, or heat. At least one author cited these poor conditions as a major contributing factor in revolutionary women's early deaths. Armand, who during the Revolution and Civil War had invested her energies on behalf of both women and the Revolution, acquired more demanding duties as the Party rose to power in 1917, and she sought to eliminate anything that could interfere with her fulfillment of them. She stepped up her already impressive political contribution, traveling throughout the countryside and helping to establish the *Zhenotdel* in 1919, of which she became the first director. This constant activity and stress wore her down to the point of endangering her health. By 1920 Armand's neglect of her health and diet (not to mention appearance, for she wore faded skirts with holes, while surviving on tea and bread) caused her to become seriously ill, and perhaps clinically depressed (*Bratskaia mogila* 1: 20; Clements, *Bolshevik Women* 220–22; Elwood 262–66).

These aspects of Armand's mode of life during her last years consolidated her image as a Bolshevik martyr—an image enabled by the self-abnegating decisions she made when confronted with emergencies. Though unwilling to leave her post for even a brief period, she agreed to travel to the Caucasus for a rest only when her youngest son's illness necessitated his removal from Moscow. During their stay at the Party sanatorium in Kislovodsk, the White army pressed close to the city, forcing Armand to evacuate. On the journey back north she contracted cholera and died, thereby cementing her image as a self-sacrificing revolutionary martyr, a quality that was evident even as she lay on her deathbed. According to one account, her dying words to the doctor in attendance showed concern not for herself, but for him: "Leave me. You have a family and you might get infected" (*Bratskaia mogila* 1: 20–21).

In the contested terrain of Soviet narratives of revolution, then, the idealization of the female revolutionary constituted part of the revolutionary hagiography that flowered during the 1920s and valorized the words and deeds of the heroines who had perished serving the Revolution. As a model for the good Soviet citizen, the idealized female of the violent transition to the Soviet regime had totally dedicated herself to the cause to fulfill the nation's revolutionary goals. After 1920 and especially after Lenin's death in 1924, however, woman's proclaimed "political" role metamorphosed into that of caretaker and nurturer to members of the Soviet "great" family, or of a loyal helper or "sister." These changes relegated her to traditional niches for women and inscribed her in a space where her service to the nation was privileged above all else. With Lenin as father and the entire population as his brothers, sisters, or children, female revolutionaries assumed (or were assigned) subordinate identities that acquired an inflexibility and vulnerability preventing subsequent recognition of them as empirical entities. The autobiographies of two prominent female revolutionaries in a 1927 collection suggest that these qualities had been adopted by other women, as well. Aleksandra Kollontai wrote of the "patriarchal values" of her family that prevented her from attending high school. Kollontai rebelled against these restrictions and became a revolutionary, later turning to work in the *Zhenotdel* on motherhood and infancy. Nadezhda Krupskaia described how she spent most of her career teaching and working with young people. "All [my] life, beginning in 1894, [I] assisted, as much as possible, Vladimir Il'ich Lenin in his work" (*Deiateli* 194–201, 236–37). In the symbolic family as conceived by Iaroslavskii, living and breathing women had little role. In political and popular rhetoric, the nation became figured as *Rodina-mat'*, a mythologically feminized entity to be defended by real men. Meanwhile, women Bolsheviks continued to function as surrogate mothers and sisters, their work conceived as both distinct from, and morally superior to, that performed by men. Women revolutionaries' collective role of symbolizing the spiritual and moral side of the Revolution corresponded to traditional Russian conceptions of femininity. Such a moral elevation not only restricted the range of female representations, but also overlooked or erased significant aspects of these women's lived experience, as amply attested by Armand's case.

In addition to idealizing and circumscribing women's roles, memorial literature desexualized women. The Soviet system of representation acknowledged no sexual identity in the female revolutionary, enabling her to appear strong without being perceived as a threat to the new, developing social order. Certainly, the counterexample of Kollontai, the perceived advocate of free love, dispatched on a series of diplomatic missions beginning in the mid-1920s, suggests that powerful, sexually liberated women bred anxiety in the Communist Party.

Memorial literature of the 1920s, then, constituted a means of honoring those women who perished in service to the Revolution, while constructing their saintly profiles to fit within the emerging portrait of the period's rhetorically proclaimed Soviet national family. In that context, these brief obituaries and memorials are not merely transparent summaries of individual experience; rather, they are documents that contributed to the building of an ideology of a new social order, an ideology that concealed as much as it revealed. Lenin's acclaimed primacy as that order's father-creator relegated women revolutionaries to a subordinate, and ultimately allegorical, role that would fit within the familiar patriarchal family structure. Official accounts of female revolutionaries' lives ignored all aspects of their lived experience that failed to correspond to the topos of a nurturing, self-sacrificing martyr to the male-conceived cause. Such sanitized narratives modeled on hagiography left radical women's idealized lives uncorrupted and the balance of the Soviet national family undisturbed.

Notes

A National Endowment for the Humanities Summer Stipend and grant from the Xavier University Center for Intercultural and International Programs supported the research for this essay. The views expressed here are the author's own.

1. From *Pamiatnik bortsam proletarskoi revoliutsii pogibshim v 1917–1921 gg.,* hereafter referred to as *Pamiatnik*. This account was originally published in the first edition of *Pamiatnik* in 1922 (the second edition came out in 1923). *Pamiatnik* was an encyclopedic collection of memorial literature about activists who had died during the period of Revolution and Civil War. *Pamiatnik* possesses two distinct characteristics. First, it includes a broad spectrum of revolutionary activists as regards age, occupation, and geography. Second, many of the entries first appeared in other periodical publications, such as local newspapers or Party journals, at the time of the individual's death. Thus, it is safe to say that large portions of *Pamiatnik* were read out-

side of the presumably limited readership of the encyclopedia itself. I sampled every tenth entry in this source and included every entry for a woman, arriving at a database of 323 entries (94 women and 229 men).

2. Aleksandr Arosev (1890–1938) was a prominent Bolshevik Party activist and writer who occupied several important posts during the Revolution and Civil War. A member of the Soviet diplomatic corps during the late 1920s and early 1930s, he was arrested in 1938 and died in prison.

3. According to Tumarkin, the idealized representation of Lenin as father figure and great leader of the Revolution became widespread in the fall of 1918 after Fania Kaplan's assassination attempt. Tumarkin argues that this early manifestation of heroic Lenin images was not entirely consistent and became more consolidated after his death in January 1924, with the rise of the "Lenin cult." I see the family motif emerging during the Civil War and early 1920s.

4. For a discussion of the narratives and rituals of tsarist authority, see Wortman. Their disintegration is discussed in my article "Nicholas in Hell: Rewriting the Tsarist Narrative in the Revolutionary *Skazki* of 1917." For Kollontai's views, see Clements, *Bolshevik Feminist* and *Bolshevik Women* 213–14, 226–27.

5. See Tumarkin; Petrone; Stites, *Revolutionary Dreams* 246–53 and *Women's Liberation* 233–77, 317–45.

6. For a comparative perspective, see Hunt, *The Family Romance of the French Revolution,* especially the chapter "The Band of Brothers" 53–88.

7. I employ memorial accounts because of their prevalence during this period and the particular nature of the genre, which attempts to fix a specific image of an individual at the time of—or shortly after—his or her death. Other modes of writing, such as published first-person accounts, are less common during the early 1920s and do not appear regularly until the later 1920s and the 1930s. See, for instance, *Deiateli,* which contains numerous autobiographical accounts of revolutionary activity. For another discussion of revolutionary women's autobiography, see Liljestrom.

8. Although the authorship of memorial literature is not always clear, signed articles were usually written by close comrades and friends in the Party.

9. I am indebted to Scott's essay and to the significant recent work on women and revolution in Russia, including Clements, *Bolshevik Women;* Wood; Goldman; and Engel, *Mothers and Daughters* and *Women in Russia.*

10. For examples of this model, see Basov-Verkhoiantsev and Bednyi. For an analysis of this model in the late nineteenth century, see Pearl.

11. Certainly, there were exceptions to this phenomenon, especially among women who were active during the late nineteenth century, such as Sofiia Perovskaia, Vera Figner, Vera Zasulich, Ekaterina Breshko-Breshkovskaia, and others. For a sampling of these women's stories, see *Five Sisters,* ed. Engel and Rosenthal.

12. Indeed, one part of the ideal of the new Soviet society involved the dissolution of the "bourgeois" family, and the promotion of collective child-rearing and communal living. See Stites, *Women's Liberation* 346–91.

13. The most detailed account of this process of history-making is Corney, *Telling October.*

14. Together the *Bratskaia mogila* volumes included biographies of more than three hundred fallen comrades of the Moscow party organization, among them twenty-seven women, which is slightly less representative of the total number of women Bolsheviks, who comprised ten percent of Party members in 1917. A third volume, containing fifty-three names (none of them women) was announced in the second volume. For

a thorough history of Bolshevik women, see Clements, *Bolshevik Women*.

15. These were the most prominent accounts of individual revolutionaries during the Civil War period and early 1920s. Autobiographical writings almost never appeared until the publication of the Granat encyclopedia in 1927 (*Deiateli*).

16. See Krupskaia; Breslav; *Revoliutsionaia deiatel'nost'*.

17. See Liljestrom; Børtnes.

18. Tumarkin explains that shortly after the October Revolution agitational organizations began to use religious language in describing revolutionary events and concepts. Hagiographical accounts of Lenin began to appear after the attempt on his life in August 1918. Tumarkin 64–74, 80–91.

19. Not surprisingly, many accounts (Armand's included) effaced the route that many women—and men—took to Bolshevism, which often passed through the Socialist Revolutionary or the Menshevik Party. Those women revolutionaries who had strayed from the path of Bolshevism were shown as traitors to the cause, even though formerly they may have been portrayed as positive figures. One account about Vera Zasulich, for example, states, "Now we see that all of the old leaders of the revolution have abandoned the proletariat just at the moment when it began the implementation of its tasks and aspirations. Such was Zasulich [who sided with the Mensheviks against Lenin in 1903]." *Pamiatnik* 236–37; originally published in *Pravda,* 10 May 1919.

20. *Bratskaia mogila* 1: 36–37; 2: 234–36; originally published in *Kommunisticheskii trud,* 25 July 1920.

21. For an extended discussion of the relationship between the images of motherhood and the Russian nation, see Hubbs; Waters; Kirschenbaum.

22. Authors of accounts often commented on the youthfulness of their subjects, who might have joined the Party at the age of sixteen or seventeen and often evinced extraordinary enthusiasm for the cause. Two-thirds of the thirty-three women included in *Pamiatnik* for whom an age is listed were younger than twenty-five years old when they died, suggesting that the authors considered their subjects' youth a notable fact. Bogdanova was pregnant at the time of her death.

23. It is also important to note that many revolutionaries received only a few lines in *Pamiatnik* or *Bratskaia mogila*. Aside from the most prominent figures' memorials, the ordinary Party workers' comprised between one and three paragraphs.

24. Needless to say, her involvement in the revolutionary underground (not to mention repeated prison terms) meant that she could not care for her children continuously on her own. Indeed, her estranged husband and mother-in-law raised the children, whom Armand saw only at irregular intervals. Elwood 33–35.

25. For discussions of the relationship between Armand and Lenin, see Elwood 173–89, and Clements, *Bolshevik Women* 220–22.

26. See also "Deriabina, Serafima Ivanovna," *Pamiatnik* 177–78; originally published in *Pravda,* 25 Apr. 1920.

27. Although a number of the male revolutionaries in *Pamiatnik* and *Bratskaia mogila* also succumbed to illness, they were not described as having weak constitutions.

References

Anderson, Benedict. *Imagined Communities: Reflections on the Origins and Spread of Nationalism.* Rev. ed. New York: Verso, 1991.

Basov-Verkhoiantsev, S. A. *Konek-Skakunok. Russkaia skazka.* Petrograd: Narodnaia Volia, 1917.

Bednyi, Dem'ian. *Pro zemliu, pro voliu, pro rabochuiu doliu. Povest' v piati chastiakh.* Moscow: Gosudarstvennoe izdatel'stvo, 1920.

Borenstein, Eliot. *Men Without Women: Masculinity and Revolution in Russian Fiction, 1917–1929.* Durham: Duke UP, 2000.

Børtnes, Jostein. *Visions of Glory: Studies in Early Russian Hagiography.* Trans. Jostein Børtnes and Paul L. Nielsen. Atlantic Highlands, NJ: Humanities Press International, 1988.

Bratskaia mogila. Biograficheskii slovar' umershikh i pogibshikh chlenov moskovskoi organizatsii R.K.P.(b). Issues 1 and 2. Moscow: Moskovskii rabochii, 1922, 1923.

Breslav, B. *Konkordiia Nikolaevna Samoilova.* Moscow: Gosudarstvennoe izdatel'stvo, 1926.

Clark, Katerina. *The Soviet Novel: History as Ritual.* 3rd ed. Bloomington: Indiana UP, 2000.

Clements, Barbara Evans. *Bolshevik Feminist: The Life of Aleksandra Kollontai.* Bloomington: Indiana UP, 1979.

———. *Bolshevik Women.* Cambridge: Cambridge UP, 1997.

Corney, Frederick C. *Telling October: Memory and the Making of the Bolshevik Revolution.* Ithaca: Cornell UP, 2004.

Deiateli Soiuza Sovetskikh Sotsialisticheskikh Respublik i Oktiabr'skoi revoliutsii. 1927. 2nd ed. Vol. 41. Moscow: "Kniga," 1989.

Elwood, R. C. *Inessa Armand: Revolutionary and Feminist.* Cambridge: Cambridge UP, 1992.

Engel, Barbara Alpern. *Mothers and Daughters: Women of the Intelligentsia in Nineteenth-Century Russia.* Cambridge: Cambridge UP, 1983.

———. *Women in Russia, 1700–2000.* Cambridge: Cambridge UP, 2004.

Engel, Barbara Alpern, and Clifford Rosenthal, eds. *Five Sisters: Women Against the Tsar.* New York: Schocken Books, 1975.

Fitzpatrick, Sheila, Alexander Rabinowitch, and Richard Stites, eds. *Russia in the Era of NEP: Explorations in Soviet Society and Culture.* Bloomington: Indiana UP, 1991.

Goldman, Wendy. *Women, the State, and Revolution: Soviet Family Policy and Social Life, 1917–1936.* Cambridge: Cambridge UP, 1993.

Hemenway, Elizabeth. "Nicholas in Hell: Rewriting the Tsarist Narrative in the Revolutionary *Skazki* of 1917." *Russian Review* 60 (Apr. 2001): 185–204.

Hubbs, Joanna. *Mother Russia: The Feminine Myth in Russian Culture.* Bloomington: Indiana UP, 1988.

Hunt, Lynn. *The Family Romance of the French Revolution.* Berkeley: U California P, 1992.

Iaroslavskii, E. "Sem'ia Lenina." *Kommunistka* 4 (Apr. 1924): 1–3.

Kirschenbaum, Lisa A. "'Our City, Our Hearths, Our Families': Local Loyalties and Private Life in Soviet World War II Propaganda." *Slavic Review* 59.4 (Winter 2000): 825–47.

Kollontai, Alexandra. "Tvorcheskoe v rabote K. N. Samoilovoi." *Kommunistka* 3–5 (May 1922): 8–11.

Krupskaia, N. K., ed. *Pamiati Inessy Armand.* Moscow: Gosudartsvennoe izdatel'stvo, 1926.

Liljestrom, Marianne. "The Remarkable Revolutionary Woman: Rituality and Performativity in Soviet Women's Autobiographical Texts from the 1970s." *Models of Self: Russian Women's Autobiographical Texts.* Ed. Marianne Liljestrom, Arja Rosenholm, and Irina Savkina. Helsinki: Aleksanteri Institute, 2000. 81–100.

"Odna iz mnogikh (Pamiati tov. Platovoi)." *Kommunistka* 5 (Oct. 1920): 21.

Pamiatnik bortsam proletarskoi revoliutsii pogibshim v 1917–1921 gg. Comp. L. Lezhava and G. Rusakov. 3rd ed. Moscow-Leningrad: Gosudarstvennoe izdatel'stvo, 1925.

Pearl, Deborah. *Tales of Revolution: Workers and Propaganda* Skazki *in the Late Nineteenth Century.* Carl Beck Papers. Pittsburgh: Center for Russian and East European Studies, U Pittsburgh, 1998.

Petrone, Karen. "Masculinity and Heroism in Imperial and Soviet Military-Patriotic Cultures." *Russian Masculinities in History and Culture.* Ed. Barbara Evans Clements, Rebecca Friedman, and Dan Healey. New York: Palgrave, 2002. 172–93.

Revoliutsionnaia deiatel'nost' Konkordii Nikolaevny Samoilovoi. Sbornik vospominanii. Moscow: Gosudarstvennoe izdatel'stvo, 1922.

Scott, Joan. "'Experience.'" *Feminists Theorize the Political.* Ed. Judith Butler and Joan Scott. New York: Routledge, 1992. 22–40.

Stites, Richard. *Revolutionary Dreams: Utopian Vision and Experimental Life in the Russian Revolution.* New York: Oxford UP, 1989.

———. *The Women's Liberation Movement in Russia: Feminism, Nihilism, and Bolshevism, 1860–1930.* Princeton: Princeton UP, 1978.

"Tov. L. K. Ammosova." *Kommunistka* 10 (Oct. 1923): 27.

Tumarkin, Nina. *Lenin Lives! The Lenin Cult in Soviet Russia.* Enlarged ed. Cambridge, Mass.: Harvard UP, 1997.

Volkogonov, Dmitrii. *Lenin. Politicheskii portret.* Vol. 2. Moscow: Novosti, 1994.

Waters, Elizabeth. "The Female Form in Soviet Political Iconography, 1917–32." *Russia's Women: Accommodation, Resistance, Transformation.* Ed. Barbara Evans Clements, Barbara Alpern Engel, and Christine D. Worobec. Berkeley: U California P, 1991. 225–42.

Wood, Elizabeth. *The Baba and the Comrade: Gender and Politics in Revolutionary Russia.* Bloomington: Indiana UP, 1997.

Wortman, Richard S. *Scenarios of Power: Myth and Ceremony in Russian Monarchy.* 2 vols. Princeton: Princeton UP, 1995, 2000.

Zubrovich, Tov. "Armand Inessa Fedorovna (dobavlenie k vyp. No. 1 'Br. mogily,' str. 5)." *Bratskaia mogila* 2: 14–15.

FOUR | Forging Soviet Masculinity in Nikolai Ekk's *The Road to Life*

LILYA KAGANOVSKY

The pleasure that comes from exercising a power that questions, monitors, watches, spies, searches out, palpates, brings to light; and on the other hand, the pleasure that kindles at having to evade this power, flee from it, fool it, or travesty with it. The power that lets itself be invaded by the pleasure it is pursuing; and opposite it, power asserting itself in the pleasure of showing off, scandalizing, or resisting. Capture and seduction, confrontation and mutual reinforcement. . . . These attractions, these evasions, these circular incitements have traced around bodies and sexes, not boundaries not to be crossed, but *perpetual spirals of power and pleasure.*

—Michel Foucault, *The History of Sexuality,* Vol. I

Nikolai Ekk's 1931 film *Putevka v zhizn'* [*The Road to Life*][1] is the story of a group of "wild boys" who find themselves subjects of "an unprecedented experiment" (*nevidannyi opyt*). Captured by the Soviet authorities, the boys are offered a chance to leave behind their lives of crime to form a labor commune at the site of a former monastery. Here they will be converted from dangerous criminals who exist on the margins of society and beyond the rule of the state into productive citizens of the fledgling Soviet nation. A recognizable narrative of conversion or *perekovka, Putevka v zhizn'* is loosely based on the educational experiments of Anton Makarenko, whose youth colonies tried to solve the problem of *bezprizorshchina*—children left orphaned and homeless by the Revolution and Civil War—through discipline, isolation, and hard labor.[2]

Putevka v zhizn' tells the story of the forging of Soviet masculinity—and Soviet national identity—through voluntary submission to the experiments of the new Soviet state. Beyond the narrative of conversion of boys into men and homeless youth into Soviet citizens, *Putevka v zhizn'* also tells the story of Soviet cinema's conversion to sound and the anxiety attendant upon creating the new national cinema. The first conversion narrative centers on the deployment of disciplinary power—not jail but labor will help to reform "wild boys" into Soviet men. The second conversion narrative centers on the deployment of pleasure—with *Putevka,* Soviet cinema "learns to talk," to laugh, and to sing. Yet, as Foucault suggests in *The History of Sexuality,* power and pleasure are always caught up in a mutual game of "capture and seduction, confrontation and mutual reinforcement," which means that in *Putevka,* the site of disciplinary power is also the site of pleasure, of engagement and resistance, while the site of pleasure is always already penetrated by structures of power (45).

Cinema for the Millions

The 1927 release of *The Jazz Singer* (dir. Crosland, USA) coincided with an ongoing crisis in Soviet cinema that was financial, aesthetic, and technological. The Party Conference on Cinema held in March 1928 focused attention on the problem of the Soviet film industry and its preparation for the period of cultural revolution that was to accompany the First Five Year Plan (Taylor and Christie 191). For cinema, the notion of cultural revolution involved, first of all, the creation of what Boris Shumiatskii later referred to as "cinema for the millions"—cinema that was simultaneously intelligible to the masses, entertaining, ideologically sound, and lucrative.[3] As Anatoli Lunarcharskii put it in his speech to film workers, "Our film production must stimulate the public appetite . . . if the public is not interested in a picture we produce, it will become boring agitation and we shall become boring agitators." "Boring agitation," he concluded, "is counter-agitation" (cited in Taylor and Christie 197).

By 1929 the advent of sound was the focus of a major debate in cinema circles. The suggestion of incorporating speech into Soviet cinema had met with opposition from its best-known filmmakers, who argued that speech would undermine the "international nature of cinema" and "destroy the culture of montage" (Eisenstein, Pudovkin, and Alexandrov; cited in Taylor and Christie 234–35). Their pronouncement, though consistent with worldwide debates about sound in cinema, only helped to underscore the need for a different kind of Soviet cinema from a different set of filmmakers, ones who would employ sound for the purposes of intelligibility, not of "formalist" contrapuntal aesthetics.

With the "silent" establishment of Soiuzkino in February 1930, all aspects of the film industry—technical, financial, artistic, and ideological—

were gathered under the leadership and administration of Boris Shumiatskii, and the first sound films went into production.[4] Yet, even though Abram Room's *Plan velikikh rabot* [*The Plan for Great Works*] was released in March 1930 and many of the leading directors of both documentary and fiction cinema in the Soviet Union were now working with sound, nonetheless, the editors of *Kino i zhizn'* were able to pose the "fateful question": "Is There a Soviet Sound Cinema?" (Taylor and Christie, doc. 122, 310–11). One of the principal problems, as Richard Taylor and Ian Christie have pointed out, was that the first Five Year Plan had been drawn up in 1927/8, before the impending arrival of sound had been widely discerned and fully comprehended (Taylor and Christie 285). Moreover, the technological breakthrough coincided with Stalin's decision to sever economic ties with the West and make the Soviet Union "self-sufficient" by means of aggressive industrialization. For cinema, this meant that the new sound equipment necessary for moving Soviet cinema forward into the bright future could not be bought from the U.S. but had to be "invented." Thus, it was not until the year 1931 that the first films relying on sound appeared: Dziga Vertov's *Entuziasm: Simfoniia Donbassa* [*Enthusiasm: The Donbass Symphony*], Grigorii Kozintsev and Leonid Trauberg's *Odna* [*Alone*], Sergei Iutkevich's *Zlatye gory* [*The Golden Mountains*], and Nikolai Ekk's *Putevka v zhizn'*, which came to be widely known as the "first Soviet sound film."

The 1971 volume of *20 Rezhisserskikh biografii* [*20 Directors' Biographies*] lists twenty "talented and unusual directors who stood at the cradle of the Soviet cinema (*u kolybeli sovetskogo kino*) and through their efforts helped to formulate the principles of the new art, which became the method of socialist realism" (5–6). Nikolai Ekk occupies a privileged place among the twenty as the first-time filmmaker responsible for solving the problem of synchronized sound, which "had stumped world-renowned directors" (Vladimirtseva et al. 5–6). Unlike Vertov's *Entuziasm,* which had a soundtrack but no dialog, or Kozintsev and Trauberg's *Odna,* which added sound to a film originally conceived as a silent, Ekk's *Putevka v zhizn'* from the beginning was conceived as a "talkie," despite the presence of a significant number of inter-titles.

Billed by the Amkino Corporation, which distributed the film in the United States in 1932, as a "startling drama of Russia's 'Wild Children,'" *Putevka v zhizn'* was heralded as "the first Soviet sound film" and called a major success (*The Road to Life,* Pacific Film Archive). Completed and released before the other films (opening in theaters on June 1, 1931), *Putevka v zhizn'* was "the first film in which the quality of sound registration met the highest acoustic requirements" and was greeted with the "warmest response" from the general audience: "In one Moscow theater, *Koloss, Putevka v zhizn'* played non-stop for over a year. . . . For the first time, the viewer saw protagonists who had gained the right to speak" (Kalashnikova et al. 280).

Soviet advertisements and reviews from 1931 note that *Putevka v zhizn'* was the first film to utilize new sound technology "created by director Ekk, cameraman Pronin, and sound-operator Nesterov," and shot with "the Soviet [sound] camera, Tagafon."[5] Filmed with Soviet equipment by Soviet cameramen, and directed by a brand new filmmaker using brand new technology, *Putevka v zhizn'* signified not simply a technological breakthrough but the dawning of a new era for Russia's national cinema. As Maia Turovskaia has suggested, in *Putevka,* the combination of synchronized sound and mass appeal made possible a new paradigm: "ideology plus profitability plus sound" (45).

Highly entertaining, a box office success both in the Soviet Union and abroad, *Putevka v zhizn'* gave Soviet cinema its first speaking protagonist. The fact that the protagonist, Mustafa *"Fert"* ("fop" or "dandy," played by Iyvan Kyrla[6]), spoke broken Russian and sang in Tatar should have answered the anxiety of Eisenstein, Pudovkin, and Aleksandrov about the "international status" of sound cinema.[7] Yet the effect—achieved in part through Mustafa's tragic end—was quite the opposite. Mustafa's inability to speak proper Russian and his foreign song (played without subtitles as pure, incomprehensible exuberance), suggested that Soviet citizenship was limited to those capable of expressing themselves in standard Russian—the new language of Soviet cinema.[8] Mustafa's carnivalesque body and his inability to hold his (foreign) tongue marked him for death and suggested that Soviet national identity—which the new sound cinema would bring to the screen—would be forged through bodily discipline and linguistic control.

From Boys to Men

Putevka v zhizn' is set in the year 1923, a period during which the problem of *besprizorshchina* reaches its political apex, and its narrative describes the means by which that problem is resolved. After a raid on their hideout by a group of social workers from the *detkommissiia,* the *besprizorniki* are given a chance to participate in an "unprecedented experiment": instead of jail or orphanages, Sergeev (Nikolai Batalov) offers to take the boys to a monastery and put them to work making boots and furniture. Discipline through hard labor, he argues, will ensure the transformation of young criminals into useful members of society. His experiment succeeds when Kol'ka (Mikhail Dzhagofarov) gathers together the remaining "wild boys" and leads them to the steps of Juvenile Hall under the banner, "We want to go to the commune! We want to make boots!" (*Khotim ekhat' v kommunu! Khotim sami shit' sapogi!*).

The ideological message of *Putevka v zhizn'* is articulated via the interjection (through inter-titles) of Lenin's decree about *besprizorniki:* "In the Soviet Republic there must be no deprived or homeless children. Let there be young, happy citizens."[9] Indeed, by the third "decisive" year of the first Five Year Plan (1930), and the year before *Putevka's* release, "socialist construction" had gathered enough force that numerous officials, resolutions, and individual authors began to voice confidence that enlightenment would soon expunge homelessness. A slogan appearing in the journal of the People's Commissariat of Enlightenment read: "In 1931, not a single *bezprizornyi* in the Soviet Union!" (cited in Ball 194). In other words, *Putevka v zhizn'* took up the problem of homeless children precisely when that problem became obsolete, or at least discursively eliminated.

Part of the *agitprop* message of the film, Lenin's directive points to the way Soviet subjects are addressed and constituted by structures of power. Homeless children are called upon to become citizens via a performative discourse ("There must be no ... Let there be ...") that erases their old identity and makes their new identity possible. In this way, *Putevka v zhizn'* resembles Kozintsev and Trauberg's *Odna*—a film that also straddles the silent/sound divide—in which the heroine hears the "voice of power" addressing her directly from a loudspeaker in the town square. In *Putevka,* Lenin's words produce a similar effect. Though the attribution connects the speech to a body, that body remains completely outside the diegesis, leaving instead the voice of power that "hails" the individual as a Soviet subject (Althusser 174).

Another set of titles makes explicit the means by which the boys' conversion is to take place: they will be born again through "the awl, the chisel, and the saw" (*shilo, rezets i pila zanovo razhdali liudei*). Work at a monastery-turned-labor-colony will ensure the boys' transformation into men through physical discipline. What remains implicit—but mandated by Lenin's decree mentioned above—is the psychic discipline that accompanies physical labor. The boys will be reborn/remade into citizens only when they begin to perceive themselves subject to a power that addresses them directly. The early actions of the *besprizorniki*—their petty criminal offenses, their homeless and vagabond existence—initially enable them to function outside the system of power that seeks to control them, and hard labor alone is not enough to bring the *besprizorniki* under Soviet rule. Rather, they require "super-vision": discipline by means of observation.

By juxtaposing homelessness with citizenship, Lenin's decree, and by extension, *Putevka v zhizn',* shows that the children are homeless not only as members of a gang, but even as members of a family: both Mustafa (a street urchin) and Kol'ka (a model son) have to be removed from their harmful environments before they can become citizens of the new order. Thus, the very word, "*besprizornye,*" points to a necessary connection between super-vision and citizenship. The children are not only without homes, but also *bez prizora*—unwatched.[10] In order to be constituted as citizens, they must forgo the pleasures of evading the power that seeks to control them and, instead, embrace the pleasures of being subject to its observation.

It is easy to see the ways Soviet power founded its authority on spectacles of force. Yet, as *Putevka v zhizn'* suggests, alongside what Foucault has called "traditional" power, the Soviet state also exercised "disciplinary" power. In *Putevka,* after the initial gathering of the boys by the police, for example, power's operations appear, as D. A. Miller has put it, both petty and diffuse, while its policing actions are "under cover of other, nobler or simply blander intentionalities (to educate, to cure, to produce, to defend)" (18). Sergeev's insistence that the boys not be locked up, the very nature of the commune as an untraditional site of reeducation, and the "invisibility" (*nevidannyi opyt*) of the "unprecedented experiment"—all point to the way in which, in this film, overtly coercive Soviet power translates into silent disciplinary power. Soviet "subjection"—that is to say, "(people's) constitution as subjects in both senses of the word"—requires the apparent elimination of visible force and its replacement by invisible operations of disciplinary power (Foucault 60).[11]

Men without Women

In *Putevka v zhizn'*, the formation of the Soviet subject is constrained by a number of factors: by "national" identity, as Mustafa's narrative shows, by age, and by gender. Adults such as Zhigan, and even Kol'ka's father, cannot be reeducated and must remain on the sidelines of Soviet subjectivity, while gender turns out to be the defining characteristic for membership in the new Soviet society. Although the film initially seems to privilege women by foregrounding their presence on screen and introducing Lel'ka Mazikha (Mariia Gonta) as Zhigan's main operative, it also underscores the impossibility of their conversion by (silently) excluding them from the commune.

The absence of women in the film is partly explained by the directive, *Protokol No. 45*, from the Secretariat of the Arts, written on March 16, 1930.[12] Here the Secretariat offers two main editorial suggestions regarding Ekk's film: the first asks Ekk to shorten the montage sequence of "debauchery" (*razgul*); the second requests that he severely reduce the number of scenes starring "that famous Soviet prostitute," Mariia Gonta, whose on-screen presence might introduce into the picture a "boulevard style (*bul'varnyi stil'*) otherwise foreign to it." The link between debauchery and Mariia Gonta is not incidental. Except for the two mother figures—Kol'ka's mother, who dies early in the film, and the social worker Skriabina, who plays a marginal role—*Putevka v zhizn'* suggests that, like vodka, association with girls is one of the main sources of the boys' corruption. Answering questions before the committee in Juvenile Hall, one of the "wild" girls describes herself as a streetwalker ("*guliashchaia, ia*"), while a close-up of her record clearly shows the word "syphilis." As a contaminant, she is immediately packed off to a hospital, without being given the chance to hear about the "unprecedented experiment."

Similarly, *Protokol No. 45* indicates that the delinquency of the girls is not limited to the film's diegesis, but has the power to contaminate its audience. In *Putevka*, girls appear only in order to tempt boys away from their labor and the goals of the State. Unlike male subjectivity, which can be forged by awls, chisels, and saws, female subjectivity remains un-forgeable, serving only to distract the boys on their road to becoming new Soviet men.[13] This principle seems to apply even to Kol'ka's mother, whose death makes possible Kol'ka's conversion to Soviet citizenship. In the beginning, Kol'ka appears in soft focus, under the spell of his love for his mother and her love for him. Viewers are given to understand that, however reassuring, that love would continue to seduce Kol'ka into classless impassivity, preventing his true maturation into adult Soviet masculinity.[14] His father's later refrain, "*Ushla, Kol'ka, mat'-to*" (literally: "[She] left, Kol'ka, mother") collapses "Kol'ka-mother" into a single unit. And as Kol'ka wanders the streets of Moscow, he is haunted by memories of his mother that he must forget before his transformation into the new Soviet man can begin.

The mother's death suggests that her presence posed a threat to male collectivity. As Eliot Borenstein has pointed out, domesticity and traditional femininity have no place in the world of factories and battlefields, and Kol'ka's mother certainly appears as a backward force standing in the way of the socialist struggle (3). Moreover, in a film concerned with the corrupting influence of women, the mother's domesticity represents temptation. Her death is eroticized, first by the posture of her dying body, both when she is carried back to the apartment and in her final death throes, and after, by Kol'ka's act of watching, by her final moan, "Kol'ka!" addressed to him, and by her haunting presence as Kol'ka roams the city streets. The mother's death also underscores the failure of the old type of masculinity, personified by Kol'ka's father. Her death leads the father to drink, and his manifest self-indulgence and lack of bodily control (he staggers, stammers, and hits Kol'ka for no reason) are evidence of his paternal impotence. Ekk himself comments that Sergeev is "like father and mother" to the boys (*kak rodnoi otets i mat' vmeste vziatye*), demonstrating the way in which *Putevka* successfully replaces the entire traditional family with the State.[15]

Whether following on the heels of the '20s' utopianism (which visualized a world of "men without women") or trying to reflect the composition of Makarenko's colonies (which were primarily, though not exclusively, male), *Putevka v zhizn'* envisions Soviet collectivity as first and foremost a masculine collectivity achieved through the expulsion of women. *Putevka's* labor colony certainly privileges traditional masculine activities: it trains the boys to become cobblers, machine operators, and railroad engineers in the traditionally masculine setting of a monastery. The "hallmarks of traditionally masculine ethos: production rather than reproduction, participation in the historic process rather than domestic ahistoricity, heavy industry, construction, and, of course, 'the struggle'"—all these, together with the notions of danger and corruption, ensure the exclusion of women from the collective (Borenstein 3).

Unsurprisingly, this exclusion produces a homoerotic tension that underlies the formation of the "new Soviet man." By disrupting the possibility of heterosexual eroticism, *Putevka v zhizn'* retranslates the boys' seduction

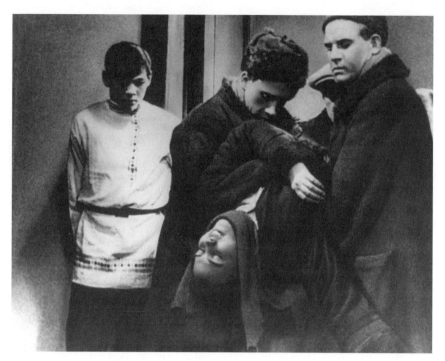

4-1   The Mother's Death. (British Film Institute)

in terms of their relation to Soviet power. National (Soviet) identity is formed through the boys' voluntary submission to the experiments of the new Soviet state, whose "power" tools include cigarettes, money, guns, and knives. In *Putevka,* the dual mechanism of pleasure and power produces the desire for establishing bonds between men and ensures that the structures of disciplinary power function by means not of coercion but of seduction. Moreover, as part of the mechanism of power, pleasure itself becomes, in Foucault's formulation, a "police matter"—not so much repressed as regulated, structured, and rigidly controlled. Mustafa's role appears here most clearly: more than Kol'ka's, Mustafa's negotiations with the state take the form of flirtation, submission, and resistance. His death is partly an escape from the mechanisms of power and pleasure that operate in *Putevka v zhizn'* and to which his foreign body provides the only possible site of resistance.

Between Men

Mustafa's privileged position vis-à-vis the state is made clear by his first interaction with the social workers at Juvenile Hall. Sneaking into the room uninvited, Mustafa performs a series of carnivalesque bodily acts that draw adult attention and help to disrupt established hierarchies. Unlike the other

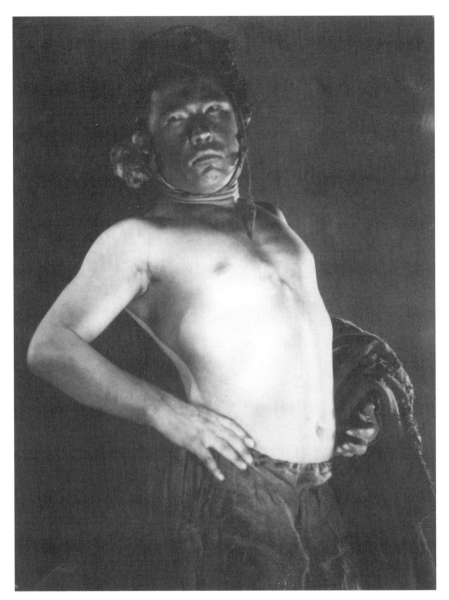

4-2 Mustafa-the-Dandy. (British Film Institute)

children, he greets each adult by name, forcing them to answer him. "Where hasn't he been? Who doesn't know him?" murmur the adults, answering: "Everyone knows him. He's the head of an entire gang!" They name the orphanages from which Mustafa has run away, and it is precisely here that Mustafa's incorrect use of language for the first time manifests his incorrigible individuality: in answer to every inquiry, "Did you run away from . . . ?" (*Iz . . . ubezhal?*), Mustafa affirmatively echoes, "Run away!" (*Bi-azhal!*), causing greater and greater laughter. And, as an exasperated social worker threatens to put him in prison and behind bars, Mustafa taunts, "Run away, anyway!" (*Vse ravno, ubiagu!*).

It is clear from this exchange that prison bars and orphanages represent the structures of coercive Soviet power by which Mustafa cannot be contained. The special committee's interrogation, on the other hand, is meant to produce an account of the boys, a knowledge of who they are and where they come from, which will make it easier to fit them back into a system that so far they have eluded. To constitute the boys as objects of knowledge is also to constitute them as subjects of power—and Mustafa, by remaining outside the boundaries of the interrogation, also remains outside subjecthood.

The fact that even his language produces the effect of a disruption—not only is he not speaking "proper" Russian, but his every word generates uncontrollable laughter in others—suggests that this simple exercise in knowing will not suffice to bring Mustafa under control. E. Margolit and V. Filimonov argue that Mustafa's incorrect speech points to his uniqueness and individuality: he is capable of transforming language and altering its meaning through the simple act of speaking it. "*Ubezhal*" is a deed punishable by law, they write, whereas "*ubiazhal*" is a simple and ordinary feat (95). Not only do Mustafa's words change a criminal action into something simple and natural, but they also take him outside the law, beyond its rules. And by generating laughter in the audience, they also threaten the special committee with lawlessness. The site of resistance—Mustafa's language and the laughter it produces—defies the disciplinary forces trying to forge Mustafa's new identity. Sergeev clearly understands this message, since his "unprecedented experiment" is to give Mustafa and the boys the impression of self-control and voluntary participation.

Sergeev's proposal is structured as a game of pleasure/power, an erotic initiation of the boys into Soviet subjectivity. The sequence opens with a shot of an empty room, and as the camera tracks back, it reveals a window, a bench, and a single source of light, evoking a large prison cell or interrogation room. The boys enter what appears at first to be a perfectly empty space, which Mustafa unexpectedly greets with the words, "Hello, comrade cop!" His greeting seems to summon Sergeev, who emerges out of the darkness as a kind of apparition (and from a visually impossible place in the room, located behind the camera), to stand silently before them.[16]

Mustafa immediately approaches this new figure, and his encounter with Sergeev makes clear that this is a scene of seduction. To begin with, Mustafa assures the others that Sergeev is a doctor and immediately begins to undress. Arguably, the difference between openly coercive and secretly disciplinary power is located precisely between Sergeev's two mis-appellations of "cop" and "doctor." As a cop Sergeev would openly police the boys; as a doctor he is interested in power through knowledge, a knowledge that

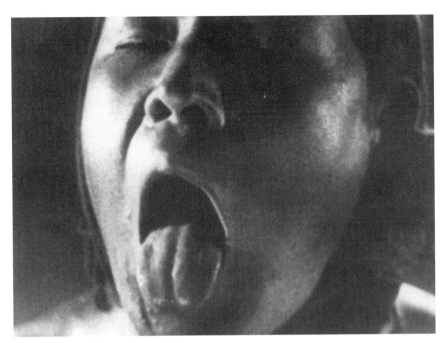

4-3   The Medical Exam. (British Film Institute)

would, as Foucault suggests, "contact the body." While Sergeev looms silently over the boys huddled together in the corner, Mustafa throws down his hat, pulls off his jacket and shirt, and asks the now smiling Sergeev, "Do you want us to take off our pants?" (*Shtany snimat'?*). Without waiting for an answer, he removes his. A reverse shot shows Sergeev looking down, on a right-to-left top/down diagonal, at the naked Mustafa. "You *are* a doctor?" (*Ty zhe doktor?*), Mustafa asks again and, bringing his face very close up to Sergeev's, sticks out his tongue and says "Aaaa."

Sergeev's towering presence and the boys' submission to his (implied) authority under the mistaken identity of "doctor" create an aura of erotic tension. Describing the scene in his notes, Ekk writes, "Having thrown off his clothes, Mustafa stands before Sergeev in all his glory—filthy, provocative, wearing a woman's leather hat."[17] Sergeev and Mustafa are "playing doctor." With a small laugh and pat on the head, Sergeev orders the boys to get dressed. He then describes the "unprecedented experiment," a proposal the boys greet with a string of obscenities. In response, Sergeev "shows them his": suddenly becoming serious, he reaches into his pants' pocket to pull out, not the gun that the suddenly hushed boys probably expect, but a box of cigarettes.

As a key moment of erotic male bonding, this scene merits closer attention. Sergeev's initial laughter at the boys' vulgar shouts disappears when he reaches into his pocket. Though cigarettes do not necessarily signify masculine power, in *Putevka* they are linked in a chain of signifiers that includes knives and guns (and further on, money and sausages). The opening shot of the movie is a close-up of the gang leader Zhigan's face, cigarette in mouth, and the caption, "His reputation cannot be questioned." The reputation, and with it, the meaning of the cigarette, is secured when the camera pans down to the knife suspended on his belt, linking the cigarette and the knife in a chain of phallic signification and establishing Zhigan as a source of power and authority.

Sergeev's offer of the cigarettes is an offer of both power and pleasure. On the one hand, these are "state" cigarettes, and the boys' willingness to take the state's handout brings them a step closer to accepting state-issued subjectivity. The close-up of the many hands together reaching into the box proffered by Sergeev shows us the first instance of the boys' "communal" spirit. The symbolic promise of their new social role carries with it the conferral of a particular kind of power that derives exclusively from the master signifier. The cigarettes represent nothing less than Soviet power that Sergeev is willing to share with the boys.

At the same time, cigarettes are what the boys desire. The initial tension, the hungry grabbing, and the subsequent moment of relaxation in which the boys lean back, smoking their cigarettes, suggest that Sergeev is offering pleasure as well. As Sergeev lights up, two eager faces, each with cigarette in mouth, move toward him to light theirs on his. And as he turns his head back and forth in a half-hearted effort to avoid the two boys, Mustafa enters the frame from the bottom left corner, bringing his cigarette to meet Sergeev's in a prolonged nicotine kiss.

Both Sergeev's role of redeemer[18]—saving the lost souls and bodies of the boys from the horrors of orphanages, the streets, and jail—and his proposal, which underscores voluntary choice, are permeated by ambiguity. While ostensibly offering liberty, Sergeev actually offers the boys hard labor on a secluded island; the boys buy freedom from jail at the price of self-imprisonment.[19] As the film goes on to suggest, by accepting the pact the boys will become what they most hate. In remaking homeless youth into Soviet citizens, Soviet power will also transform criminals into policemen, and regular people into informants. In other words, the boys become not just those who are regulated and policed, but who themselves regulate and police, internalizing the mechanisms of disciplinary power that earlier they had been able to elude.

An important feature of this discipline, generally overlooked in the literature on *Putevka v zhizn'*, is the film's time-specific (1930–1931) ideological presentation of this particular kind of labor as *voluntary*.[20] When trying to sell the idea of the commune to the boys, Sergeev emphasizes that the boys will be "fully trusted and free" and that they will "always have time to leave." Moreover, when they are reluctant to follow him out of Juvenile Hall because there seems to be no police supervision, Sergeev announces smugly, "There's no convoy, you've come voluntarily" (*konvoia ne budet, vy dobrovol'no*). Arguably, their transformation begins at this point. The boys must police themselves, as they will later learn to police others. As the boys walk from Juvenile Hall to the train station, they are frequently separated from their new leader, Sergeev. At one point, there is an agonizing pause while Sergeev (as well as the camera) waits on one side of the tracks, while streetcar after streetcar blocks his and our view of the boys. The sequence is punctuated by inter-titles repeatedly asking, "Will they run away?" Of course, they do not, and the dramatic tension underscores the boys' willingness to "come voluntarily." Again, this sequence traces precisely the movement from coercion (police escort) to discipline (voluntary submission). Sergeev's project is fully redeemed when—later, after the success of the commune reaches the other *besprizorniki*—a large group of orphans led by Kol'ka storms Juvenile Hall, requesting to be taken to the commune to make boots, in a moment of "voluntary collectivization."

Before the Law

The anxious inter-titles ("Will they run away?") that punctuate the initial trip to the train station, however, point to the possibility of failure, which the next scene makes explicit. The test of the boys' commitment culminates in partial disaster when Mustafa is given money to buy provisions for the train ride to the monastery. This scene also shows that Mustafa's enjoyment—the particular pleasure he takes in defying Sergeev's authority—is one of the main obstacles to his conversion. As the time for departure approaches, the tension on the train grows: will Mustafa-the-thief make good or will he take the government's money and disappear? Finally, as the train begins to move and Sergeev gives up all hope, Mustafa reenters the compartment, carrying not only the bread and canned food sanctioned and bought with the government's money, but also, unexpectedly, with what Ekk himself describes as an enormous sausage (*priogromneishaia kolbasa*), hidden inside his jacket.[21] Laughing heartily, he slowly withdraws the sausage, to Sergeev's astonishment and everyone's amusement.

The film leaves little doubt as to the meaning of the sausage, whose length is emphasized by its slow extraction from the interior of Mustafa's coat. Most importantly, however, the sausage allows the film to articulate Mustafa's relationship to pleasure and power. As in the earlier scenes in Juvenile Hall, wild laughter is Mustafa's persistent answer to the state's imposition of the mechanisms of control. By literally laughing at power, Mustafa remains beyond its reach, and his bodily pleasure, for which the sausage stands as a marker, effectively removes him from the field of power's operations. Sergeev's look of disapproval and his warning that this is "the last time" that Mustafa will get away with such stunts suggest that he is aware of the true stakes of this power play. As with the cigarettes, Sergeev has offered Mustafa a share in the patriarchal order by giving him government money and real purchasing power in the new economy. Instead of unproblematically assimilating into this new economy, however, Mustafa has returned with "something extra"—something, in fact, that the government could not afford—thereby revealing the government's poverty and his own fundamental inability to work within the rules of the system.[22] Mustafa's "last" criminal act demonstrates that the policing of bodily pleasures is one of the goals of the boys' reeducation.

Indeed, the overall process of reeducation is structured in terms of the imposition of structures of bodily control. The disciplining of the body takes place slowly, as the boys learn to exercise self-restraint. When first brought to the monastery, they are abandoned to the full enjoyment of the bathhouse, where again the visual parade of naked bodies is overlaid by the sound of Mustafa's laughter. This scene of pure, idiotic "enjoyment" (Lacanian *jouissance*) is intercut with a similar scene taking place back at Juvenile Hall. Skriabina had just received a telegram from Sergeev that all the boys made it to the commune and none ran away. The happy news causes the head of the *detkommissiia*, Volkov, to literally jump for joy as he tries to grab Skriabina and give her a kiss. Again, the prohibition against heterosexual eroticism at work in this movie prevents Volkov from actually touching Skriabina, but the matching juxtaposed shots of the boys' activities in the bathhouse and the social workers in Moscow reveals the way pleasures in *Putevka* are contagious.

The next moment of enjoyment, however, is already surreptitious. As the cobbler shows the boys how to cut out shoe soles from pieces of leather, we see in flashback Mustafa's memory of his days on the street: some quick knife work lets him cut out a large swath of fabric from the back of a lady's fur coat, revealing her underpants, much to the amusement of a male passerby. Armed with this memory, Mustafa can easily do his new job of making boots, yet the job has been compromised by the pleasurable memory of the street, for the flashback allows us to see once again Mustafa's ability to produce pleasure at the site of discipline.

The reverse is also true, and the co-optation of pleasure for purposes of discipline marks the first step in the process of conversion. The boys must become their own opposites: they must abandon their positions as individuals outside the law to become not only subjects of the law but also subjects who carry out the law. In *Putevka v zhizn'* this reformation is encoded in the binary opposition, "*besprizornyi*" and "*legavyi*" / "*ment*" (police informant/cop). The binary is first introduced during the social workers' raid on the boys' hideout, when the boys yell, "*Bei mentov, bei legavykh!*" (Beat the cops! Beat the stool pigeons!) As the boys voluntarily subject themselves to the process of reeducation, however, and as the work at the monastery progresses, the assumption of Soviet national identity is marked by the transformation of *besprizorniki* into stool pigeons and cops.

Evidence of this transformation occurs the first time the boys are left alone without Sergeev's supervision and with nothing to do. As the hot, lazy days go by, the boys' increasing restlessness finally tips over into wild abandon. In the ensuing brief spell of anarchy, the boys run around smashing the monastery's windows and breaking the equipment. This activity is squelched by a two-pronged controlling force, one led by Mustafa, the other by Kol'ka (the latter under the banner, "Save the machines!"). But before the rebellion is completely put down and the offending boys properly tied up, Ryzhii, the instigator of the rebellion, hurls an eloquent insult at Mustafa, calling him *"legavaia svoloch'"* (police swine).

The next episode occurs during the construction of the new railroad. Mourning the loss of Mustafa and Kol'ka, the gang leader Zhigan explicates the nature of the boys' conversion. "The Soviets have thought of a clever trick," he says, strumming on his guitar, "They've transformed criminals into cops." The context for this pronouncement is in itself telling. Zhigan is drinking with his girls, surrounded by multiple signs of debauchery: vodka, cards, the guitar, lacy lingerie, and the girls themselves. Moreover, as will be made clear with Mustafa's final song, Zhigan's mournful ballad, though apparently quite popular with the audiences, is yet another sign of his dissipation. In *Putevka*, singing is just one more form of bodily pleasure (like vodka and girls) that must be brought under control.

To test the limits of the boys' conversion Zhigan opens up a small "house of entertainment" on the edge of the collective, and every night more and more boys disappear there, only to return the next day drunk, exhausted, and unwilling to work. When the first group of revelers makes its way back to the construction site, Kol'ka gives instructions for their punishment: fifteen days of isolation. Here the binary opposition between the *besprizorniki* and the police, as well as between the commune and the jail, collapses. Zhigan's house of entertainment is also a kind of commune, as his prior Moscow operations had a "coherence of delinquency as a structured milieu" (Miller 4, emphasis omitted). As in the monastery-commune, Zhigan's gang established rules of the workhouse, with apprenticeship, membership, and hierarchies that mimic those of the "outside" world, and the main difference between the two systems is the deployment of pleasure. Importantly, not Sergeev or Mustafa, but Kol'ka gives the order for the boys' arrest. Kol'ka is the model Soviet subject: unlike Mustafa, who never has the chance to become the commune's "first engineer," Kol'ka becomes its first conductor—and, by implication, future leader. As in the earlier scene of anarchy in the monastery, his role as the state's policeman is secured.

Finally, to get rid of Zhigan and his gang once and for all, Mustafa and Kol'ka organize a raid, reminiscent of the original *detkommissiia* raid on the boys in their "underground den." Pretending to have succumbed to the pleasures being offered within, they visit the house of entertainment, whose entrance is marked by a big heart-shaped sign with the words, "Here you can drink, smoke, dance, and kiss the girls." Instead of drinking, dancing, and kissing the girls, however, Mustafa and Kol'ka surreptitiously pour their vodka on the floor, so that when the time comes to pull out their guns and destroy the establishment, they are perfectly sober, leading Zhigan to observe, "So Mustafa's become a spy!" (*Tak, tak, Mustafa legavyj stal!*).

4-4 Kol'ka—the New Soviet Man. (British Film Institute)

Thus, for the third time, the boys are identified with the disciplinary forces at work in the film.

This repeated conflation of criminal and cop, of *besprizornik* and informer, describes precisely the nature of the boys' conversion. At the same time, the raid on the house of entertainment also makes explicit the co-opting of enjoyment/pleasure by disciplinary self-restraint. Indeed, the moment of pleasure's interruption is made visually explicit. A point-of-view shot from the perspective of a very drunk Zhigan shows a spinning room and a wildly dancing Mustafa. As the camera spins faster and faster, we lose all sense of orientation, until suddenly we are shown a close-up of a gun. A similar pattern occurs in the original *detkommissiia* raid on the boys: the incoherent struggle between the boys and the social workers is suddenly interrupted by a close-up of a knife, with which one of the boys kills a policeman. Clearly, each of the raids is about the exercise of power—traditional, coercive—but only the second is also about the destruction of pleasure. The presence of girls in this scene both underscores their absence in the rest of the movie and reveals them for what they "are." Tied up, with smudged make-up and messy clothing, the girls, too, have undergone a certain conversion: they have been permanently removed as pleasurable objects of desire.

The Uses of Pleasure

The raid on Zhigan's pleasure den initiates the climax and finale of the film, in which Kol'ka, rather than Mustafa, emerges as the proper Soviet subject and new Soviet man. Chosen as the commune's representative to meet the delegation from Moscow, Mustafa sets out alone at night in a handcart to meet the train at the Moscow station. Riding along the tracks, Mustafa bursts into loud and incomprehensible song: after speaking proper Russian throughout the second half of the film, he suddenly reverts to his Chuvash/Tatar origins. It is clear that in this, as in earlier scenes, Mustafa's accent, while adding the necessary "international" element to the story, also singles him out as the outsider who does not quite belong in the Soviet collective. His incorrect use of the Russian language, like his outrageous hat and his skill in jumping out of barrels, signals an irrepressible individuality, one that—even when smilingly tolerated by figures of authority—potentially endangers that authority. From the moment he enters the monastery Mustafa seems to blend in: neither his language nor his clothes mark him as the irrepressible individual he is at the beginning of the narrative. His loud, incomprehensible song as he rides along the railroad, however, suddenly reminds the viewer that despite everything, Mustafa is not like the others. Tellingly perhaps, the only lyrics in the song that can be easily deciphered are *"bespartiinyi molodets"* (a young man, not a Party member), which underscore Mustafa's nonmembership—in the Party, in the commune, and ultimately, in Soviet subjectivity.

Mustafa's "regression" into foreignness prepares us for the ensuing disaster: his handcart suddenly goes off the rails, tripped by a missing length of track. As a final act of vengeance, Zhigan had aimed to derail the train and sabotage the commune's construction project. He stabs Mustafa and leaves him to die on the tracks. The following day when the train with Kol'ka at the helm reaches the spot of the struggle, Mustafa's body lies stretched across the tracks, marking the missing length of track.

Zhigan's knife, found nearby, has a monogram that presumably will enable the commune to avenge Mustafa's death. The close-up of the knife and all the different hands holding it together recall the eager hands that earlier reached out for Sergeev's cigarettes. A master signifier from a different system, the knife is now appropriated into the right chain of signification and substitution (cigarettes, money, guns, knives), co-opted and proffered by communal Soviet power. Too much of an individual while alive, with his death Mustafa effects that necessary "socialist realist" transition from individual to collective: his death saves the construction project and, with it, the commune. His body symbolically and literally fills in the missing piece, allowing the boys to come together as a totality. And yet despite this last, successful transformation, Mustafa's death does not allow the film to end on a note of happiness, looking forward to a bright future. With Mustafa stretched on the cowcatcher, the train pulls into the commune. The slow movement of the train interrupts the music and cheers that Sergeev and the boys prepared for this moment. Mustafa's funeral now replaces the planned collective celebration.

Catherine De la Roche and others have commented on the final scenes of *Putevka* as early examples of the possibilities of sound effects: "the metallic noise of wheels and Mustafa's carefree song, as he rides alone in a rail hand-cart; further along the line, the stillness of the night, broken only by croaking frogs and the light clinking of tools while the murderer loosens a rail; then Mustafa's distant song becoming louder and louder as he approaches danger" (Dickinson and De la Roche 41). The Pacific Film Archive similarly notes the "memorable instance," in which the sound of steam from a locomotive "expresses the grief of hundreds of onlookers."[23] The role of sound in the film simultaneously marks Mustafa as an outsider, and silences the last of bit of pleasure in favor of grief and self-restraint. Ekk reserves much of the sound track of *Putevka* for sounds of exuberance and joy—laughter, singing, jokes—most of which belong to Mustafa. By the time the train carrying Mustafa's body pulls into the station, the only sound effect left is the hiss of steam from the locomotive that slowly dies in the distance as the hundreds of onlookers bare their heads in silence.

The gloomy ending of *Putevka v zhizn'* is unrelieved (unlike those of the Vasilii Brothers' 1934 *Chapaev* and other early '30s films) by speeches about progress, a symbolism of rebirth, or shots of troops wreaking vengeance on the enemy. Even the actor Kochalov, whose two poetic monologs frame the film, does not bring a more uplifting closure to the narrative when he dedicates the film to Feliks Edmundovich Dzerzhinskii, the first director of the children's commission of the VtsIK (the All-Russian Central Executive Committee) and head of the Cheka.

Thus the film appears to end with the final destruction of pleasure. Not only does Mustafa's death bring the commune's celebration to a halt, but it also prevents the film's audience from feeling the proper joy at the fulfillment of the socialist task and the creation of new Soviet men. Participation in the new Soviet order and the creation of a new national identity requires the co-optation of pleasure by the operations of power. Mustafa's continuous negotiations of the power/pleasure dynamic result in his death at the moment of formation of the new commune, signifying that Soviet power, after all, has the means to coerce those it fails to discipline.

And yet the enthusiastic reception of *Putevka v zhizn'* proved that the different pleasures that the film introduced and then tried to erase created pockets of resistance inside a narrative about the successful imposition of disciplinary structures. Despite Ekk's reedit following the directives of *Protokol No. 45*, which removed many of the scenes of delinquency and privileged the themes of labor, the audiences remembered the film mostly for its criminal songs (*blatnye pesni*), Mustafa's bizarre appearance ("*Kyrlia tak odelsia, nadel takuiu neveroiatnuiu shapku i nachal tak dvigat'sia . . .*" Shklovskii 157), and girls. When speaking to workers of a Khar'kov factory after the film's screening, Ekk was appalled to learn that many of the audience members applauded during the songs. "No one applauded the criminal songs," he insists, "No one laughed. And if they did laugh, that was the way it was, that's not how it is today. Today, in the Soviet Union, with our industrial progress, we have no prostitution as such."[24] Laughter, as *Putevka* has shown, is both disruptive and contagious, and Ekk's traumatically repeated negatives only work to show that consistent denial always produces that which it tries to repress. Moreover, Ekk's own odd semantic link between applause and prostitution suggests that though not itself a "body genre," *Putevka* nevertheless succeeded in generating bodily effects[25]: audience members clapped, sang, laughed (even possibly cried), and thought about girls.

Notes

I am indebted to Andrea Lanoux and Helena Goscilo for their attentive and provocative readings of this chapter, and to Eric Naiman, whose question about laughter in *Putevka v zhizn'* led to this analysis.

1. Archival materials on the film—interviews, production notes, letters, advertisements, decrees, photographs, newspaper articles, and reviews—are located in the Russian Federal Archive for Literature and the Arts (RGALI), fond 2794, op. 1, ed. khran. 49 (N. Ekk); fond 2794, op. 1, ed. khran 228 (materialy k podgotovke *Putevki v zhizn'*); fond 2639, op. 1, ed. khran. 60 (Regina Ianushevskaia). Materials on the American reception of the film, including John Dewey's introduction of the American release, are located at the Pacific Film Archive, Berkeley, Calif. File: *The Road to Life.*

2. From 1920 to 1935, Anton Makarenko was in charge of two of the most famous colonies for homeless youth. Ekk had visited Makarenko's colonies; however, he indicated in his notes that when it came time to make the film "no written material was available" (RGALI, f. 2794 (Ekk), op. 1, ed, khran. 49, l. 174). Part One of Makarenko's best-known novel, *Pedagogicheskaia poema* [*Pedagogical Poem;* translated as *The Road to Life,* 1936], was first published in 1933, while the novel in its entirety was published in 1936.

3. The resolution of the December 1928 Conference of Soiuzkino workers deemed that an essential part of any experimental work was to be "artistic expression that is intelligible to the millions." It was Shumiatskii's 1935 *Kinematografiia millionov* [*A Cinema for the Millions*], however, that used the phrase "cinema for the millions" to describe the main goal of Soviet cinematography.

4. In 1930, Sovkino was silently renamed Soiuzkino (the change was not mentioned in the press) and given greater authority over the studios of the national republics. Kenez 95.

5. RGALI, f. 2794 (Ekk), op. 1, ed. khran. 261.

6. Iyvan Kyrla seems to have come from the Republic of Mari (Mari El), which borders Kirov, Nizhnii Novgorod, the Chuvash Republic, and the Tatar Republic.

7. The opposite is true, for example, in *Oliver Twist.* As D. A. Miller points out, Oliver's story, like his Standard English, will entitle him to full integration into middle-class respectability. Miller 9. Conversely, in *Putevka*, Mustafa's nonstandard Russian will ensure his exclusion from Soviet subjectivity.

8. Viktor Shklovskii relates the following story about a "nameless homeless orphan who distinguished himself" from the other extras during the shooting of *Putevka v zhizn'*: "The boy, Kyrla . . . came to the shoot. There was no role for him. . . . But when

they spread out the old disinfected trash and asked the boys to pick out the costumes themselves, Kyrla dressed himself in such a way, put on such an impossible hat, and started to move in such a manner, that he became the main star of the picture" (157). Margolit and Filimonov, however, argue that Shklovskii's Iyvan Kyrla was actually named Kirill Ivanov and a student of GTK (the State Cinema Polytechnic) (74–98).

9. "V sovetskoi respublike ne dolzhno byt' obezdolennykh i besprizornykh de-tei. Pust' budut iunye, molodye i schastlivye grazhdane." Also cited in Ball 127.

10. Ball maintains that "the singular *besprizornyi* means 'unattended' or 'neg-lected', though 'homeless' or 'waif' would be closer to the meaning intended by most Russians" (xii). He also cites usage by journalists in the 1920s, who "began to refer caustically to inanimate objects, left to deteriorate through abandonment or neglect, as *besprizornye*" (201, n. 5). Translated "literally," however, *besprizornyi* means "un-watched" or "un-(super)-vised," as, for example, *zorkii*, -aia, -oe. 1. Someone who sees well both small and large objects. 2. *fig.* Penetrating, vigilant. Ozhegov, "*zorkii.*"

11. On the debate of Foucault's applicability to Russian and/or Soviet studies, see Engelstein; Paperno et al.; Kotkin; and Kharkhordin. The Foucauldian model at-tempts to understand the place of the subject in relation to power. As Stephen Kotkin notes, Foucault "focused on what he called the problem of subjectivity, or the process by which individuals are made, and also make themselves, into subjects under the aegis of the state" (22).

12. RGALI, f. 2794, op.1, ed. khran. 228 (materialy k podgotovke *Putevki v zhizn'*).

13. In response to questions from a film screening in Khar'kov, Ekk states that it was not possible to include girls in the film because they were mainly prostitutes, but that he is devoting another large project to them. RGALI, f. 2794 (Ekk), op. 1, ed. khran. 49, l. 68.

14. Ekk states that Kol'ka comes from a family of workers and that is why the mother must have long hair. The family's class, however, is not clearly articulated in the film. Their one-room apartment seems to be filled with all manner of bourgeois items, such as a samovar and lace curtains. B. Alpers, writing for *Sovetskoe iskusstvo* (May 1931), suggests that a formulation of the family's class status is absent alto-gether and that Kol'ka ends up on the street because of "private circumstances" and not as a result of the imperialist war or the intervention. RGALI, f. 2639 (Regina Ianushkevich), op. 1, ed. khran. 60, l. 43.

15. RGALI, f. 2794 (Ekk), op. 1, ed. khran. 49, l. 184.

16. Indeed, although the special committee interviews two other *besprizorniki*, as well as Kol'ka's father, before Mustafa, Sergeev appears for the first time only once Mustafa enters the room, establishing a strong visual connection between the two characters.

17. RGALI, f. 2794 (Ekk), op. 1, ed. khran. 49, l. 185.

18. Among others, Dmitry Shlapentokh and Vladimir Shlapentokh call Sergeev "Plato's enlightened philosopher-king," and Jay Leyda refers to him as the "good angel." Shlapentokh and Shlapentokh 88; Leyda 284.

19. The site of their voluntary incarceration is not incidental, as monasteries were the first structures to be converted by Soviet authorities into labor camps.

20. In his "Golovokruzhenie ot uspekhov" ["Dizzy from Success"], pub-lished in *Pravda* on March 2, 1930, Stalin writes, "The success of the collective-farm policy, by the way, is explained by the fact that it leans on the *voluntary na-ture* of our collective farm movement. . . . We must not seed the collective farms by force. That would be foolish and reactionary" 193 (emphasis in the original).

Just as Dmitry and Vladimir Shlapentokh argue that Ekk's film "glorified collectivism and its ally, new technology," I take the emphasis on the boys' *voluntary* participation as indicative of Ekk's incorporation of current Party rhetoric. Shlapentokh and Shlapentokh 87.

    21. RGALI, f. 2794 (Ekk), op. 1, ed. khran. 49, l. 187.

    22. Ekk notes that the very large sausage (*kolbasishchia*) cost more than all the money that Mustafa had, so even if he had wanted to, he would not have been able to pay for it with Sergeev's money. (RGALI, f. 2794 (Ekk), op. 1, ed. khran. 49, l. 187).

    23. Pacific Film Archive, *The Road to Life*, screening 26 Nov. 1986.

    24. RGALI, f. 2794 (Ekk), op. 1, ed. khran. 49, l. 68.

    25. For "the spectacle of a body caught in the grip of intense emotion," see Carol J. Clover, "Her Body, Himself: Gender in the Slasher Film"; see also Linda Williams, "Film Bodies: Gender, Genre, and Excess."

References

Althusser, Louis. *Lenin and Philosophy, and Other Essays*. New York: Monthly Review Press, 1971.

Ball, Alan M. *And Now My Soul Is Hardened*. Berkeley: U California P, 1994.

Borenstein, Eliot. *Men Without Women: Masculinity and Revolution in Russian Fiction, 1917–1929*. Durham: Duke UP, 2000.

Clover, Carol J. "Her Body, Himself: Gender in the Slasher Film." *Representations* 20 (Fall 1987): 187–228.

Dickinson, Thorold, and Catherine De la Roche. *Soviet Cinema*. London: Falcon Press, 1948.

Doane, Mary Ann. "The Voice in Cinema: The Articulation of Body and Space." *Yale French Studies* 60 (1980): 33–50.

Eisenstein, Sergei, Vsevolod Pudovkin, and Grigorii Aleksandrov. "Zaiavka." *Zhizn' iskusstva*. August 5, 1928.

"Ekk, N." RGALI. fond 2794, op. 1, ed. khran. 49.

Engelstein, Laura. *The Keys to Happiness*. Ithaca: Cornell UP, 1992.

Entuziasm: Simfonia Donbassa. Dir. Dziga Vertov. Ukrainfilm, 1931.

Foucault, Michel. *The History of Sexuality. Volume I: An Introduction*. New York: Random House, 1978.

"Ianushevkaia, Regina." RGALI. fond 2639, op. 1, ed. khran. 60.

The Jazz Singer. Dir. Alan Crosland. Warner Bros., 1927.

Kalashnikova, Iu. S., et al., ed. *Ocherki istorii sovetskogo kino v trekh tomakh*. Moscow: Iskusstvo, 1956.

Kenez, Peter. *Cinema & Soviet Society, 1917–1953*. Cambridge: Cambridge UP, 1992.

Kharkhordin, Oleg. *The Collective and the Individual in Russia*. Berkeley: U California P, 1999.

Kotkin, Stephen. *Magnetic Mountain*. Berkeley: U California P, 1995.

Leyda, Jay. *Kino: A History of the Russian and Soviet Film*. Princeton: Princeton UP. 1983.

Makarenko, Anton. *Pedagogicheskaia poema*. 3 vols. Moscow: Gos. izd-vo khudozhestvennoi literatury, 1934–1936; volume 1 translated by Stephen Garry as *The Road to Life*. London: Stanley Nott, 1936.

Margolit, E. Ia., and V. P. Filimonov. "Proiskhozhdenie geroia (*Putevka v zhiz'* i iazyk narodnoi kul'tury)." *Kinovedcheskie zapiski* 12 (1991): 74–98.

Miller, D. A. *The Novel and the Police*. Berkeley: U California P, 1988.

Odna. Dir. Grigorii Kozintsev and Leonid Trauberg. Sovkino, 1931.

Ozhegov, S. I. *Slovar' russkogo iazyka*. Moscow: Russkii iazyk, 1987.

Paperno, Irina et al. "Symposium." *Slavic Review* 53.1 (Spring 1994), 193–224.

Plan velikikh rabot. Dir. Abram Room. Soiuzkino, 1930.

Putevka v zhizn'. Dir. Nikolai Ekk. Mezhrabpomfil'm, 1931.

"Putevka v zhizn', materialy k podgotovke." RGALI. fond 2794, op. 1, ed. khran 228.

The Road to Life. Pacific Film Archive. Berkeley, California.

Shklovskii, V. *Za 60 let raboty o kino*. Moscow: Iskusstvo, 1985.

Shlapentokh, Dmitry, and Vladimir Shlapentokh. *Soviet Cinematography, 1918–1991: Ideological Conflict and Social Reality*. New York: A. de Gruyte, 1993.

Shumiatskii, B. *Kinematografiia millionov*. Moscow: Kinofotoizdat, 1935.

Stalin, Iosif. *Sochineniia*. Vol. 12. Moscow: Gosudarstvennoe izdatel'stvo politicheskoi literatury, 1949.

Taylor, Richard, and Ian Christie, ed. *The Film Factory: Russian and Soviet Cinema in Documents 1896–1939*. New York: Routledge, 1988.

Turovskaia, Maia. "The 1930s and 1940s: cinema in context." *Stalinism and Soviet Cinema*. Ed. Richard Taylor and Derek Spring. New York: Routledge, 1993.

Vladimirtseva, I. N., et al., ed. *20 rezhisserskikh biografii*. Moscow: Iskusstvo, 1971.

Williams, Linda. "Film Bodies: Gender, Genre, and Excess." *Film Quarterly* 44.4 (Summer 1991): 2–13.

Zlatye gory. Dir. Sergei Iutkevich. Soiuzkino, 1931.

| Reflecting Individual and Collective Identities

Songs of World War II

S U Z A N N E   A M E N T

The second World War signaled a break in the Stalinist era, as national and gender identities shifted from an official Soviet rhetoric of collectivity and gender equality to constructs grounded in community and traditional notions of gender. World War II songs composed by state arts institutions and the general population were performed throughout the war, and played a significant role in stabilizing identities in a time of crisis. Concepts of national identity became increasingly individualistic and territorial, and songs encouraged men and women to make a difference through their personal contributions to the war effort. Despite the unprecedented participation of women serving in the armed forces (estimated at one million) and the fact that diversity in gender roles aided in the ultimate goal of victory, World War II songs tended to highlight and celebrate unexamined age-old gender roles (Stites 2). As expressions of nostalgia, desire, hope, and lived experience, today these songs offer valuable insights into the perception and expression of gender and national identity during this period of Soviet history.

The dramatic reformulation of collective identity during the war reshaped the song genre. Songs extolling the ideology of communism, communist leaders, and relevant institutions thrived during the outbreak of the war, but quickly faded into the background in favor of songs with apolitical or less political themes. As Robert Rothstein aptly notes, "'Songs of collective emotion' became secondary to 'songs of individual emotion'" (77). This shift necessarily rebalanced perceptions of nation and self, collective and individual patriotism, and the understanding of male and female roles in the resultant paradigms. Stereotypical images of loyal, passive, and gentle women resurfaced, notwithstanding women's active participation in all spheres of military activity, including front-line combat. Paradoxically, these very images became a driving force in the war effort. Adhering to the scheme of conventional gender oppositions recently deconstructed by Hélène Cixous, Toril Moi, and others, which equates the feminine with nature, pathos, emotion, and the Imaginary (the mother), and the masculine with culture, logos, reason, and the Symbolic (the father), during the war both the state and the population at large emphasized the feminine spheres of emotion, nature, and family (Cixous 63–64; Moi 104).

In this regard, collective identity took on an individual-national, rather than collective-state, character. As mobilized by and depicted through song, the war effort concentrated on a national identity with the common goal of defeating the enemy and protecting the homeland, much like the stand against Napoleon in 1812. The "new" emphasis on Russian national identity rather than Soviet state identity, in fact, harked back to older, Russian, even universal human reactions to the threat of war. Many war survivors noted that this was a special time when people helped one another and were united in an unprecedented way. This sense of unity was powerful precisely because each member of the national collective was entrusted and credited with fulfilling a particular role in the unfolding events. The songs written and performed during this period fostered the feeling that each individual played a unique part in the eventual achievement of victory. The emphasis was on the people (*narod*), who, though peace-loving, would rise up in unity to defend their homeland.[1]

"The Sacred War" ["*Sviashchennaia voina*"], a popular anthem of the war years, expressed these sentiments most directly to somber yet uplifting music:

> Arise, huge country! Arise to the fatal battle/with the fascist dark forces,/with the accursed horde./Let noble rage build like a wave./The people's war, a sacred war, is being waged./ . . . We fight for light and peace,/and they for the kingdom of darkness . . . ./Let us go and break them with all our strength,/our hearts and our souls,/for our dear land, for our great union.[2]

This song presented a model for Russian national identity and a summation of national objectives: all members of the population, no matter what their status, would invest their energy in the noble cause of defending the honor of a just people and the territory they called home. Simply because they were just and the enemy was evil and corrupt, victory was presumed inevitable; but indignation and rage were also required to ensure the desired result.[3] This song is nonspecific as regards gender: "country" (*strana*) and "people" (*narod*) include everyone, the feminine and masculine gender of these respective words notwithstanding. Not the fatherland or the Soviet Union, but the country and people are highlighted in lyrics that evoke the physical and geographic rather than political aspects of Russo-Soviet identity.

The popularity of certain songs suggests that the population found solace in those texts that downplayed or ignored political factors and underscored a more basic connection with Russia. The "motherland," not the Party, was associated with nation, and images of the people (*narod*), the family, and familial roles replaced political terms. Since songs were discussed and promoted at officially sponsored plenums and conferences throughout the war, the Communist Party was fully aware of this preference. It relinquished its control over this aspect of cultural production and took into account the opinions of soldiers, composers, journalists, and performers who argued for songs they deemed helpful to the war effort. The composer Anatolii Novikov recalled, "Everyone was drawn to action and felt that he should either go to the front to fight or participate by creating art as a weapon. Patriotic feelings united us. We met and showed each other songs" (Krasil'shchik 124). In other words, song composition was considered a contribution no less essential than participation in military combat, and through arts and media organizations the state actively solicited troops' opinions in the creative process. The newspaper *Soviet Fighter* [*Sovetskii boets*] requested soldiers to send in the titles of songs they wanted to see printed in its pages or in special brochures. Nearly a thousand letters came back with titles and composers' and poets' names, as well as fragments of text that reflected individual preferences. In this manner, the troops themselves helped to produce forty-nine song brochures (*Krasnaia zvezda,* 22 May 1945: 3).

As the war moved westward and away from Soviet territory, attempts to give the soldiers a connection to their homeland acquired a stronger political component. Yet the Party and its artistic organizations redoubled their efforts to promote a national identity grounded primarily in heritage and ties to the motherland rather than in state ideology or politics. The government vigorously encouraged the composition and dissemination of songs, recognizing their psychological role in the war. Calls went out for new songs specifically based on Russian themes, musical style, and content. The minutes of a 1943 plenum on song, which issued a direct appeal for more folk songs, noted that directors of ensembles and choirs did not adequately understand the importance of this music. G. Polianovskii, an administrator with the board of musical activities, insisted that domestic tradition was crucial to these compositions, whether it originated in Russian peasant or urban music or in old soldiers' songs (Ibid; *Pravda,* 16 June 1943: 3). Some supported this nationalistic stance in order to avoid types of music that might smack of "the decadent West," "pernicious jazz," or "frivolousness." Others realized that composers, artists, and audiences yearned for lyrical music and lighter fare, whatever its roots.

This debate remained open throughout the war years, and as a result a wide array of song styles enriched the general repertory. While soldiers, composers, and poets collaborated in determining both music and dominant themes, political organizations followed their lead and promoted a given motif or message through newspaper promotions, contracts, and contests. This flexibility and the willingness to consider the Russian masses' views and individual opinion as key elements in shaping official policy represented a significant change in propaganda during the war.

Women—including brigade directors, administrators, singers, dancers, and musicians—also shaped the process of song production and distribution. Participants in these arts groups included such famous singers as Lidiia Ruslanova and Klavdiia Shul'zhenko, whose recordings gained popularity at the beginning of the war.[4] A member of the first official brigade to visit the front on a two-week trip, Lidiia Ruslanova received an honorary membership in the fifty-seventh tank brigade, complete with full uniform, for her efforts (Filippov 27–64; Sakharova 26–29; *Krasnaia zvezda,* 5 Sept. 1941: 3). Lesser-known artists from theaters, philharmonic orchestras, and choirs also joined these brigades, as did amateur singers and musicians and students from conservatories and institutes.

Despite their broad participation, however, women sometimes perceived gender or ethnic discrimination as a factor limiting their access to certain spheres in the war effort. E. Arskaia, for instance, wrote a letter of complaint, claiming that gender accounted for her not having been appointed a brigade director, and she countered the argument that the assignment was too close to the front by pointing out that she also had been denied permission to tour in the Urals region (Arskaia). Another brigade performer noted that she was forbidden to travel near the front or the borders, purportedly because of her maternal status: as the mother of two small children at home with their grandmother, she should not be put at risk. Since her husband was also prohibited from traveling, however, she believed that their being Jewish sooner explained the restrictions imposed on their mobility (Elizaveta).

Although fully integrated into the artistic distribution system as performers, directors, radio announcers, and recording artists, women were all but absent from the professional process of song composition. Out of the hundreds of war songs reviewed and approved, only a few female names appear among those of lyricists or composers. In fact, Nina Makarova is the sole woman among approximately sixty-five professional composers of this repertory. Trained at the Moscow Conservatory, by the 1940s she was over thirty and not a fledgling composer, though her contribution to war songs was small. Similarly, though various sources mention a few female lyricists, the famous children's writer, Agniia Barto, stood out as the only woman among approximately fifty professional poets writing songs during the war. Indeed, one of her songs entered the frequent contests held for compositions on specific themes or occasions (Lempert; Khrennikov).

Though a thorough exploration of the reasons for this pronounced gender imbalance in writers' and composers' unions lies beyond the scope of my essay, it is important to note that when women did make contributions to the corpus of wartime songs, it was as amateur poets and composers. Consequently, much of their work was not publicized or preserved. Nevertheless, women submitted verses to local and front newspapers, and readers set some of these poems to music. In some cases, singers or administrators pointed composers in the direction of lyrics from newspapers or journals, as in the case of Irma Iaunzem. The singer read a verse in a paper just before the war and commissioned Leonid Bakalov to compose music for it.

The result was a version of "Sailor's wife" ["*Moriachka*"] (Lukovnikov 57–58). In short, even if women did not usually compose songs, they occasionally participated in the process of song composition, and as performers they influenced the success of given selections.[5]

However circumscribed women's roles in song production, their symbolic function within songs reached new heights, and feminized images of homeland, rivers, and the natural world constituted the driving themes of many songs. As in "The Sacred War," feminine traits and concepts—especially in the image of the *rodina* (homeland or motherland)—were exalted. Some songs impassionedly summoned Russians to defend the nation; others conveyed a longing to return home. Despite occasional references to Soviet national identity, more often Russia is evoked, though many of the places and peoples implied in the songs' lyrics were not ethnically Russian. Thus, "Russia" summed up all that needed to be defended, and songs emphasizing Russia's natural landscape—birch trees, forests, and the steppe—reinforced the idea of a native homeland/motherland.

The indivisibility of the native locus and its inhabitants figured prominently in the theme of dislocation. Songs from the beginning of the war period emotionally emphasize people's profound attachment to their immediate environment through heartfelt farewells, such as those expressing sadness at parting with "the rocky cliffs" of the northern peninsula, the Dniepr River, the cities of Kiev and Leningrad, "cities and homes," and "native villages." Songs narrating the wrenching departure of soldiers leaving for the front or of citizens evacuating and fleeing the Germans likewise underscore a profound identification with native soil. The composer Vasilii Solov'ev-Sedoi composed the song "Evening on the Quay" ["*Vecher na reide*"] after watching a naval ship readying to sail the following day.[6] This simple description of a crew and its captain preparing for war is known for its most famous line, "Farewell, beloved city"—that is, Leningrad.[7] Attachment to homeland likewise finds poignant expression in "The Cherished Stone" ["*Zavetnyi kamen'*"], which depicts the harrowing experience of troops in the Crimea and Sevastopol subjected to defeat and evacuation. It is based on the popular legend of a sailor who upon departure carried a piece of granite from the shore and when dying entrusted it to another comrade, who in turn passed it along to others, to ensure that after victory the rock would be returned "home." The message is clear: soldiers identify with the land and nation in concrete, physical terms.

As the war progressed, the theme of physical proximity as a marker of national identity developed, and usually included comparisons with other locales. By the time the war neared its end, songs portrayed Russia as a place superior to and more desirable than all other countries visited by the troops. "Russia" ["*Rossiia*"] and "Under the Balkan Stars" ["*Pod zvezdami balkanskimi*"] extol Russian rivers, cities, and landscapes over those in the rest of Europe. "Under the Balkan Stars" clearly associates Russia with love and feminized natural landscapes: "Where are you, dark eyes? Where is my

homeland? Bulgaria is in front of me and the Danube is behind. We have
traveled many *versts* in campaigns on land and on water, but we have never
forgotten our Soviet motherland. . . . The country of Bulgaria is good, but
Russia is better then all of them" (Lukovnikov 210–11). "Dear native country" ["*Storonka rodnaia*"] compares European cities and concludes that none
holds a candle to Russia. It vows, "Somehow I will find my way home to
my Soviet native country."

As in earlier songs, "Russia" dwells on the physical features of the Russian land:

> Russia, beloved land, native birches and fields, how dear you are to the soldier.
> . . . The sons and fighters have sworn to stand up for that which the fathers
> and grandfathers have created. . . . Many lives have been ruined. Many *versts*
> have been traversed, and many souls have been laid to rest for you, Mother
> Russia. We are carrying on a sacred war . . . for your beauty and your treasures.
> The bloody battles will end. We will come home with glory and once again
> the nightingales will return to the dense forests. (Biriukov, *POV* 231)

This song expressively condenses elements of a kenotic national identity in
currency during the war: Soldiers must sacrifice their lives in order to preserve the beloved, now threatened, world built by their ancestors. Accordingly, men defend the honor, the glory, and the survival of the land that is
their nourishment and existence—indeed, their spiritual foundation. Religion, history, and aesthetics merge in the optimistic prophecy of natural
harmony to be reinstated by the sacrifice of the fighting men. These later
songs reconfirm identification with homeland and territory, village and
family, and with a stable life (here cast as an idyll) disrupted by war and the
vast transitions it effects.

During the first part of the war, gender roles in songs adhered to age-
old traditions: men were courageous, marched off to the front, and at
some future date would return home victorious. Women, by contrast,
were depicted as safekeepers of hearth and home, sending off their men
and waiting for their return. Patient waiting became a symbol of feminine loyalty to one's husband, boyfriend, or son, but it also stood more
broadly for women's fulfillment of their patriotic duty. One of the earliest and clearest models of traditional attitudes towards gender informs
the prewar song "Katiusha," which premiered in February 1939 and became extremely popular during the war (Biriukov, *PVD* 107–9). In the
original text, a girl, Katiusha, comes to the riverbank and asks the song
she is singing to fly after the bright sun and carry her love to a soldier at
the border. The final verse exhorts: "Let him remember the simple girl,
let him hear her sing, let him guard the native homeland while Katiusha
guards their love." Written in the tempo of a march, the song is stirring
and uplifting in mood, which suggests why it was co-opted by many
amateur poets and songwriters for their own lyrical variations. Literally

hundreds of versions appeared during the war,[8] in one of which the border guard answers the girl by vowing faithfulness to her and to the defense of country. Traditional gender roles, in short, are shown to inspire better fighting.

Variants of this and similar songs reflect changes in gender roles during the war and alternative ways of promoting the objective of victory. Some variants break with long-standing stereotypes, as when Katiusha herself opts for more active service in the war. She leaves her "high riverbank" to become a nurse, a soldier, or a partisan—functions that women actually fulfilled. Since these versions were written by amateur songwriters and people serving in the war, this shift reflected lived reality rather than officials' attempts to recruit women into more active engagement. Amateur lyricists captured the feelings of real Katiushas and Mashas: women contributed not only by staying home and waiting; for even if not recruited, they recognized the importance of their active part in fending off the enemy. Women's commitment to the war effort allowed for not only traditional (domestic, feminine) but also newly created military service roles, both categories richly represented in songs of the era.[9]

As the theme of faithful waiting continued to thrive, it gradually acquired increasing importance as a matter of life and death. Wives' and girlfriends' devotion at home became a reason for men in combat to fight harder, to believe in the future, and to survive. An exemplary text in this regard is "Wait for Me" ["*Zhdi menia*"] by Konstantin Simonov (see Goscilo's chapter in this collection). Much later the poet noted that the text originally was rejected as too intimate for publication, but by January 1942 the official line had changed. Numerous composers set Simonov's verses to music,[10] stimulating responses in the form of songs often titled "I'm Waiting for You" ["*Zhdu tebia*"]. These affirmed the patient loyalty of the woman at home, whose love would protect the soldier's life and vouchsafe his victorious homecoming. Other songs on this theme included "In the Dugout" ["*V zemlianke*"], in which a soldier is kept warm by the knowledge of his beloved's awaiting his return. "The Dark Night" ["*Temnaia noch'*"] reiterates this theme, adding a historical element by envisioning the solder's wife keeping watch over their child. Maternal care for existent children or the promise of future children upon the soldier's return are common themes that extol women's immemorial, primary social role—particularly revered during wartime as a guarantor of life.

Some songs cast the topic of remaining true to the absent male from the woman's perspective. "Sailor's Wife" ["*Moriachka*"] inspired many melodies after its first composition, but the text remained unchanged. The song tells of a girl's encounter with a sailor who "gives her his heart," but she jokes that she does not know where to keep such a gift. Once the sailor leaves, she waits for news of him, thinking,

He was probably offended and said farewell at the gate. Somehow he didn't understand a girl's joke—a slow-witted sailor—and I waited in vain for the mailman. The sailor doesn't write a single word, not even his address. I'm sad and depressed. Grief overwhelms me. I didn't say the right thing, I wasn't tender, and it's even sadder because around town everyone calls me a sailor's wife (*Moriachka*) and it's not clear why. (Biriukov, *POV* 217–18; Lukovnikov 57–58)

The regret and uncertainty spotlighted here imply that frivolity has no place in the serious matter of war, with its constant threat of extinction. Another song, "Little Flame" ["*Ogonek*"], translates fidelity into quasi-religious terms as a girl burns a candle for her soldier to demonstrate her loyalty, whereas a more down-to-earth version geared to lived reality rather than an ideal chastises a girl for giving up on her soldier boyfriend when he is wounded (Rothstein 84). Whatever the variations, the thematic core of countless songs comprised women's stalwart patience and faithfulness.

Other songs treat not so much stoic fidelity as the specific functions carried out by women both before and during the war, and absorb standard traits and symbols associated with femininity. For instance, the combination of courage and tenderness deemed characteristic of nurses serving at the front colors such songs as Iu. Slonov's "Nurse Aniuta" ["*Medsestra Aniuta*"] and Dolmatovskii's "Sister" ["*Sestra*"]. While the latter shows the nurse's medical role in tending the wounded as crucial, it also focuses on the womanly qualities of nurturing and devotion requisite for sustaining the wounded.[11] In other words, the authors of these songs transposed stereotypical feminine images into a new wartime context.

Women workers on the home front provided another version of feminine loyalty during the war, but, unfortunately, only a tiny percentage of songs glorifying them have survived. One example is the popular "Girl from the Urals" ["*Uralochka*"], which, in addition to elaborating the standard themes of family and waiting, also praises the effort and work carried out by women in the factories on behalf of the national objective:

My Urals girl's so far away, but I can't forget her. . . . It's hard for my letter to reach you; but, my bride, work and don't be sad, and if you get sad, then cry just a bit, not a lot, because our cause is true . . . and because we will live together, free, for a hundred years. No one's seen a metal worker like you; so, work, and then I'll return and we'll think of a name for our son. (Biriukov, *POV* 216; *PVD* 246–48; Lebedev 361)

Lauding women's extraordinary toil on the home front, these songs acknowledged the burden placed upon them by the exigencies of war and provided hope for a brighter future. In the song cited above, the promise of motherhood illuminates a projected future reality and is intended to serve as both solace and inspiration for the female metal worker serving her nation.

As the war neared its conclusion, songs gradually incorporated the new theme of soldiers' return to their loved ones. Like earlier compositions, these narratives of reunion downplay the collective body of the nation in their focus on individuals and their intimate relationships. Songs about returnees present the decisive moment from the viewpoint of those at home and those rejoining them. Surprisingly, one such song was written days before war actually broke out and was resurrected in the middle of it. "I Walk Along the Familiar Road" ["*Idu po znakomoi dorozhke*"], also known as "Return" ["*Vosvrashchenie*"], lists the range of likely reactions to the soldier's return home as envisioned by him: "Maybe you will meet me smiling, or maybe you will sternly knit your brows. Maybe you will hardly remember me, or maybe your heart will ignite with tender love" (Lukovnikov 108–10; Biriukov, *POV* 214).[12] Perhaps even more surprisingly, some of these songs considered the possible negative outcomes of reunion: indifference as a result of protracted waiting, or undesirable changes in the relationship.

Many of the songs noted above demonstrate a tendency to characterize women in terms not of their physical attributes, but of abstract qualities, such as loyalty, tenderness, warmth, courage, and maternity (see, for example, "In the Dugout," "Wait for Me," and "The Dark Night"). Rarely presented as objects of visual desire, women more typically appear as sources of emotional reassurance. Exceptions to this rule are signaled by the famous phrases "blue kerchief" and "dark eyes," which appeared as metaphorical metonyms for femininity or the beloved in some of the most famous hits from the war period. The song "The Blue Kerchief" ["*Sinii platochek*"], popularized between 1939 and 1941, initially relayed a light-hearted story of a man's flirtation with the owner of a blue kerchief. In the middle of the war, however, a new, more serious version of the song appeared, reflecting the conditions of a soldier's life:

> [A]nd often your memory guides me into battle. I feel that you, with your loving gaze, are beside me. You are always with me. How many beloved kerchiefs we keep with us; we remember tender talks and girls' shoulders as we remain in the battle ranks. For those dear ones, those desired and beloved ones, the gunner fires for the sake of the blue kerchiefs that covered our beloveds' shoulders. (Biriukov, *POV* 213–14; *PVD* 237–40; Lukovnikov 61–63; Lebedev 24)

Many versions of this song circulated during the war, including one printed on cereal packaging. Moreover, the symbol of the kerchief was adopted in a number of other songs, such as "A Mother Saw Her Son Off" ["*Provozhala mat' synochka*"] and "Evening on the Quay." In the latter, a sailor sees a familiar blue kerchief fluttering as his ship sails out of the harbor. The kerchief repeatedly symbolizes not only the women in a man's life, whether it be mother or lover, but also the comforting sign that someone is waiting for him.

The physical specification "dark-eyed" (*cherno-glazaia*) in "The Dark Moldavian Girl" and other songs symbolizes the beauty of women unavoidably left behind by their men and harks back to images of women in gypsy songs from the nineteenth and early twentieth centuries. Toward the end of the war, several such songs acquired a flirtatious and sexual tone. "In the Sunny Meadow" ["*Na solnechnoi polianochke*"] contains the line: "Play, little accordion, tell about how my dark-eyed one drove me crazy"; the soldier in "The Dark Moldavian Girl" "blushed and got flustered" when he met the dark-eyed girl (Lukovnikov 224–26). Such songs, however, are few, for the repertory primarily sought to stimulate loyalty, kinship, and personalized patriotism—hardly emotions grounded in sexuality. Even rarer were songs in which women coquette with men, one of the infrequent such compositions being "The Cossacks are in Berlin" ["*Kazaki v Berline*"], portraying a signal girl initiating a flirtation with a mounted Cossack who is taking the horses to drink. She stops traffic for them to cross, and innuendo leads the listener to believe that later the two will meet again back in the "wide steppes of Ukraine."

Gendered images in songs, of course, are not limited to women. Masculine images tend to focus on physical characteristics, the need for brotherly companionship, and the reliance on such vital equipment as weapons and other necessities. Many songs document soldiers' daily lives, friendships, and male bonds, as well as their military gear, which is cast in gendered images.[13] Some prewar songs, such as "A Little Smoke" ["*Makhorochka*"] and "Three Tankists" ["*Tri tankista*"], address the themes of camaraderie, friendship, and military life based on experiences from the Russian and Spanish civil wars. Various units adapted "Cavalry Song" ["*Konarmeiskaia*"], about Semen Budennyi's cavalry unit, and reworked it to reflect their own particular experiences and exploits in battle. Echoing the focal motif of "A Little Smoke," in "Let's Have a Smoke" ["*Davai zakurim*"] smoking together is depicted as a bonding experience when a friend or fellow soldier shares a highly prized commodity. The song "Where Are You Now, My War Buddies" ["*Gde zhe Vy teper' druz'ia odnopolchane*"] adopts an optimistically prophetic stance, depicting a soldier who after victory misses his close wartime friendships and the men with whom he served.

Like smoking, drinking was not simply a physical activity, but a symbol of solidarity and friendship. "Our Toast" ["*Nash tost*"] presents the raising of glasses as a celebration of community and common aims; images of war interweave with images of the dinner table, and the tradition of hospitality is associated with hearth and home. Written in 1942, "Our Toast" lists individuals, institutions, and things that deserve a toast: Stalin and the motherland, brave people, the powerful army, the honored navy, the wise glorious Party, victory banners, children, happiness, good fortune, and a reunion with an unspecified "you."

Although less common, songs about meetings of men and women at the front also circulated during the war. One such song, "The Chance Waltz" ["*Sluchainyi val's*"], recounts a brief encounter between a man and a woman, both far from home, who share a brief dance on an unusually quiet evening. Official circles attacked this lyrical song for its "frivolity," "sentimentality," and "lightheartedness," but popular opinion outweighed this critique.[14] The song's original title, "Officer's Waltz," was changed in order to suggest that everyone—soldiers of all ranks, as well as civilians—could identify with such an experience.[15] The connection to home is made explicit in the line "It's as if I'm home again." While the romantic dance causes sparks to fly between the two, the song's emphasis falls on remembering home.

Lyrics personified weapons, clothing, and other daily tools, comparing them to nurturing women and girlfriends to underscore soldiers' reliance on their equipment. One example, "Song about the Flask" ["*Pesnia o fliazhe*"], states, "You campaign flask of mine, my noble girlfriend (*blagorodnaia podruga*) . . . , you and I together will fight honorably and never let anyone down." The verses describe the restorative uses of water: drinking, washing wounds, and helping needy comrades (Lebedev 298–99). Other songs honored parts of uniforms and clothing, including the pea coat (*bushlat*), navy cap (*beskozirka*), and greatcoat (*shinel'*), which became objects of intimacy and attachment. The song "Gray Greatcoat" ["*Seraia shinel'*"], evoking Gogol's famous story, notes that, even after returning home, the soldier will care tenderly for the coat that kept him warm and dry and protected him from harm.[16] Songs also expressed reverence, affection, and respect for the weapons used in the war. "Two Maxims" ["*Dva maksima*"], for instance, played on the English name for the machine gun (Maxim gun) and the common Russian first name. A machine gunner and his Maxim gun are in such harmony with each other that they even speak alike: "Just so, just so (*tak tak tak*), said the gunner, rat tat tat (*tak tak tak*) said the gun." Some found the humor in this song distasteful, and early on in the war the selection was criticized for its light tone; yet its popularity among soldiers reflected their intimate bond with their weapons.

Additional variations on the song "Katiusha" introduced the theme of weaponry in lyrics set to the familiar melody (Biriukov, *PVD* 107–9). New texts depicted the prowess of the powerful Soviet mortar rocket, known as the Katiusha rocket. Variations described both the power of the gun against the enemy and the love soldiers felt for this invaluable weapon.[17] The connection in multiple versions of the text is clear: the rocket, like the girl back home, did its part to protect the soldier from harm and ultimately to bring peace and love back into life. Other songs similarly mixed unlikely themes with weaponry: "Tula Rifle" ["*Tulskaia vintovka*"] and "Firing Samovars" ["*Samovary samopali*"] play humorously on the Tula factories, famous for their samovars, which began producing weapons during the war (Lukovnikov 43–45; Biriukov, *POV* 203). Blending ferocity with fabled Russian hospitality, they produce a deadly blend of tea: "Tula tea is not sweet for uninvited guests. The Tula brand of tea comes with fire and lead." The unlikely combination of such images as rifle barrels functioning as tea spigots enabled the mixing of traditional gender roles to emphasize the individual makeup of the collective effort exerted to win victory: feminine hospitality joins with masculine bravery and physical strength to repel the enemy and restore peace.

Just as motherhood is a prominent image of feminine patriotism, paternal images are also evoked, sometimes in the figure of the archetypal father, Joseph Stalin. As the leader of both the Party and the nation, Stalin appears in songs or in titles of song collections as a father figure whose very presence vouchsafes victory. Songs underplayed his role of Party leader, or *vozhd'*, which appeared in other, more formal musical genres toward the end of the war. One songbook titled *For the Motherland, for Stalin* [*Za rodinu za Stalina*] merges familial national symbols by presenting the nation's leader as father and the land itself as mother. Although not explicitly articulated in any one song, the juxtaposition of motherland and Stalin as its leader adverts to the Big Family—part of Stalin's psychologically astute domestic rhetoric of national consolidation. The people follow the father's example as they defend and are nurtured by the mother—the physical homeland. These early songs sometimes directly link success with the leadership of the country, as in the song, "For the Motherland, Forward" [*"Za rodinu vpered"*]: "March more confidently, / Keep the ranks straighter, / Stalin is with us, / the people are with us . . . / Forward against the enemy for the sake of the motherland" (*Pesni* n.p.).

The theme of Stalin as linchpin in the war effort undergoes endless variations. In the song "Beat the Enemy" [*"Bei po vragam"*] his pronouncement of Soviet triumph makes it a *fait accompli:* "Stalin says victory will be ours, the Bolshevik country is unconquerable." Elsewhere, as in "Song of Courage" [*"Pesnia muzhestva"*], Stalin is elevated to the status of inspirational source infusing those in combat: "Stalin is the will of a soldier, Stalin is the heart of a soldier, Stalin is the banner and the glory of a soldier" (*Pesni* n.p.; *Krasnoflotskie pesni* n.p.). His expertise is not limited to one branch of the service. Evoking a nautical image of Stalin steering the country to victory in a 1933 poster disseminated throughout the country, "Stalin's Sea Song" [*"Morskaia stalinskaia"*] glorifies the Leader as "the wise flagman of the country of Bolsheviks," the sailors' father and friend. Data indicate that these songs—and others extolling political commissars, generals (such as Voroshilov, Budennyi, and Timoshenko in the song "Three of Stalin's Friends" [*"Tri stalinskikh druga"*]), and Lenin—were published and broadcast intermittently, but few, if any, seem to have lasted throughout the war, and they rarely appear in lists of performance pieces.

Part of the drive to encourage and reward patriotism by recognizing heroes and heroic acts entailed the creation of songs in praise of heroism, not only of individuals, but also of units, divisions, entire cities, or those involved in particular battles or events. Poets and composers were sent out to the front to write songs commending units that had achieved honors and were granted the title of "Guard" (*gvardeiskii*). Receiving a professionally composed song to commemorate the unit's achievements was an honor similar to receiving a medal or scroll. The honorees ranged from entire fronts or entire military branches, such as the artillery or the cavalry, to ships, regiments, and specialists such as drivers, members of a tank crew, or scouts. A few such songs were widely distributed and enjoyed currency long after the war, such as "Song of the Moscow Defenders" ["*Pesnia zashchitnikov Moskvy*"], "The Sea Guards" ["*Morskaia gvardeiskaia*"], and "Song about the Soviet Army" ["*Pesnia o sovetskoi armii*"]. Yet most did not last beyond the war or were only known in the limited circles of those whom they directly concerned.

Songs from the World War II era left a legacy for the nation as well as for individuals; they helped people to survive hardship, express emotions, visualize the future, and cope with rapid change. They achieved all these goals by providing a balance between projected ideals and the daily realities of life. The image of women waiting loyally at home was only valid for a portion of the population, just as songs about the bravery of soldiers charging the enemy did not apply to all men. Yet gendered images of stoic waiting, loyal and unconditional love, motherhood, and tenderness infused both soldiers and housewives with hope not only for national victory, but also for the intimate reunion with loved ones. Thus, something in these songs was close enough either to lived experience or to an imagined ideal to make listeners request them over and over again.

In many ways, the war challenged individual and national identities by inflicting grief, hardship, and loss, and the songs written and performed during this period helped to define and stabilize those identities. Songs that balanced optimistic images of a bright future with the demanding reality—that the achievement of such a future required enormous effort—proved the most popular within a huge repertory. Thus, an accommodation between ideal and real was what rendered a song effective and powerful. One final example, of a song written by an amateur composer and lyricist, Ivan Zuev, is illustrative. In "*Koptika*" (an improvised lamp made of bullet casings, a wick, and oil), the author mournfully recalls the bright past, which he contrasts with the gloomy present: "Once a person could walk all night under the light of street lamps, but when the Germans attacked, things grew dark and people parted. Now all that remains is the light from the little *Koptika*, my girlfriend in these difficult days" (Zuev). The bright lights represent peace, normalcy, and family; reduced in size, the little light nonetheless is as dear as a beloved girlfriend. The romantic feminine image of this "beloved" (*liubimaia*) bears no resemblance to the official communist ideal of the "bright future" (*svetloe budushchee*), a gender-neutral image (and neuter noun) that stands in stark contrast to the tentative flickering flame of the *koptika*. Such songs lent a human face to the war experience and acknowledged the complexity of emotions and relationships that existed for each citizen. They helped to shape national and gender identities on both the individual and the collective level.

Notes

1. Early examples of such songs include "For the Honor and Glory of the Soviet People" ["*Za chest' i slavu sovetskogo naroda*"] and "For the Komsomol, for the Motherland, Forward!" ["*Za Komsomol za rodinu vpered!*"].

2. A. E. Lukovnikov, *Druz'ia odnopolchane* 9–14; Iu. E. Biriukov, *Pesni, opalenye voinoi* 195, hereafter referred to as *POV*; Iu. E. Biriukov, *Po voennoi doroge* 136–38, hereafter referred to as *PVD*.

3. Other, lesser-known songs took up these themes as well, such as "Rise up, People" ["*Podnimaisia, narod*"] and "To Battle, Sons of the People" ["*V boi, syny naroda*"], which stressed the need for a unified response. Songs such as "We Will Destroy the Fascists" ["*My fashistov razab'em*"], "Obliterate the Enemy" ["*Bei vraga v pukh i prakh*"], and "The Enemies Will Be Sunk" ["*Poidut vragi na dno*"] continue the theme of the just nature of the war and the vision of ultimate victory.

4. For more information on these and other performers and arts workers, see Richard Stites, "Frontline Entertainment," in *Culture and Entertainment in Wartime Russia,* 126–40, and Suzanne Ament, *Sing to Victory.*

5. Another indication that women were active poets more often than the sources indicate is the tradition of *chastushki* (musical limerick). Although men did participate in their composition, often village women would sing improvisational lyrics set to specific dance tunes. This practice is still widespread in Russia today. Both men and women would actively participate in this entertaining practice on holidays and more recently in televised national contests.

6. The song had personal meaning for him as well, for soon after, the Arts Committee evacuated him to Siberia because of his prominence as a composer.

7. "Song about the Dniepr" ["*Pesnia o Dnepre*"] was written after the fall of Kiev in 1941: "The enemy is drinking your water . . . but the glorious hour will come when we will go forward and see you again." This song had such an emotional impact that its first performance left all the choir members in tears.

8. After the war, the original version of the text was again the most popular, while the other variations faded into obscurity or were collected in compilations of wartime folklore.

9. A number of songs also pursue this theme. In "The Dark Moldavian Girl" ["*Smuglianka moldovanka*"], a girl tells her admirer that she will love him only if he joins the partisans. When he does, he finds that she is already a member of the partisan unit.

10. Only the text is well known today, as no song version was ever extremely popular. One melody, however, by M. Blanter was exported and published more widely than the others. Two songs that stress the general theme of waiting are "In the Dugout" ["*V zemlianke*"] and "The Dark Night" ["*Temnaia noch'*"]. "The Dark Night" was composed for the 1943 film *Two Fighters* [*Dva boitsa*].

11. There were some songs portraying nurses that actually played down such feminine symbols as the blue kerchief, stating that these women traded in their kerchiefs for white coats or helmets. Lebedev 309; Rothstein 85.

12. "Quiet in the Hut" ["*Tikho v izbushke*"] tells of the soldier's return from a mother's point of view: "Your son will return to you, and early one morning an unexpected guest, the warrior, will appear. He will embrace you tightly, take off his felt boots, and sit down with you at the table. You will watch him, not taking your eyes away for a moment. You will shake your head over and over and sometimes you will cry quietly as you listen to his stories." Biriukov, *POV* 223.

13. Men's appearance is likewise discussed in concrete, physical terms. In "Beard at the Front" ["*Frontovaia boroda*"], a soldier notes that long beards and an unkempt look have become the norm at the front. Biriukov, *POV* 221. "Partisan Beard" ["*Partizanskaia boroda*"] elaborates, "Now scouting, now hiding, there is no time to shave. A beard is unavoidable trouble for a partisan. . . . Once they said I had a brush for a beard, now they call it a broom. . . . I'm not worried, though; let it grow to my waist and as soon as we finish fighting, then I will take to the razor and get dressed up and dance with our girls. . . . [T]he only problem with this beard is that it covers up my partisan medals." Biriukov, *POV* 209.

14. The story may be based on a true account, an experience a pilot recounted to the poet. Lukovnikov 179–81; Biriukov, *PVD* 242–44; *POV* 214–15.

15. The song was composed and first played on a weeklong train trip. In describing its nearly instant popularity, the authors said it was as if the song preceded the train at every stop; as they sang it along the way, people would learn it and sing it to one another. Interview with Evgenii Dolmatovskii.

16. The melody was written by the amateur composer and singer Anna Venchikova, who read the verse and wrote her own melody while at the second Baltic front as a mechanic. Lebedev 304–7.

17. It is not clear how the song and the rocket came to be associated, despite Robert Rothstein's claim that the rocket was in fact named after the song. Rothstein 78.

References

Ament, Suzanne. *Sing to Victory: The Role of Popular Song in the Soviet Union during World War II*. Ph.D Dissertation, Indiana U, 1996.

Arskaia [no first name given]. Letter to Solodovnikov. 15 Sept. 1941. TsGALI, fond 962, opis 3, doc. 950.

Biriukov, Iu. E. *Pesni, opalenye voinoi*. Moscow: Voenizdat, 1984.

———. *Po voennoi doroge*. Moscow: Voennoe izdatel'stvo, 1988.

Cixous, Hélène, and Catherine Clément. *The Newly Born Woman*. Minneapolis: U Minnesota P, 1986.

Dolmatovskii, Evgenii Aronovich. Personal interview. 7 May 1991, Moscow.

Elizaveta [surname omitted by request]. Personal interview. 13 Aug. 1989.

Filippov, B. M. *Muzy na fronte: Ocherki, dnevniki, pis'ma*. Moscow: Sovetskaia Rossiia, 1975.

Khrennikov, Tikhon. Personal interview. Feb. 1991.

Krasil'shchik, S., comp. *Muzy veli v boi*. Moscow: Agenstvo pechati i novostei, 1985.

Krasnaia zvezda. 5 Sept. 1941; 22 May 1945.

Krasnoflotskie pesni. N.p.: Muzgiz, 1942.

Lebedev, P. F., comp. *V boiakh i pokhodakh*. Moscow: Sovetskii kompozitor, 1975.

Lempert, [No first name given]. Report on Moscow composers in Sverdlovsk. Meeting of the presidium of the Orgkom of the Union of Soviet Composers. Protocol 4, 25 May 1942. TsGALI fond 2077, opis 1, doc. 52.

Lukovnikov, A. E. *Druz'ia-odnopolchane*. Moscow: Voenizdat Ministerstva Oborony SSSR, 1975.

Moi, Toril. *Sexual/Textual Politics: Feminist Literary Theory*. London and New York: Routledge, 1985.

Pesni Otechestvennoi voiny. N.p.: Central House of the Railway Workers, 1942.

Pravda. 16 June 1943.

Rothstein, Robert. "Homeland, Home Town, and Battlefield: The Popular Song." *Culture and Entertainment in Wartime Russia.* Ed. Richard Stites. Bloomington: Indiana UP, 1995. 77–94.

Sakharova, I. N., comp. *Iskusstvo v boevom stroiu: vospominaniia, dnevniki.* Moscow: Iskusstvo, 1985.

Stites, Richard, ed. *Culture and Entertainment in Wartime Russia.* Bloomington: Indiana UP, 1995.

Zuev, Ivan. Personal interview. 25 Apr. 1994.

SIX | The Post-Utopian Body Politic

Masculinity and the Crisis of National Identity in Brezhnev-Era TV Miniseries

[The Hero] is recognized by a mark, a brand (a wound, a star marking) or by a thing given to him. . . . The hero is also recognized by his accomplishment of a difficult task (this is almost always preceded by an unrecognized arrival). Finally, the hero may be recognized immediately after a long period of separation.

—Vladimir Propp, *Morphology of the Folktale*

The Fate of Men: Soviet Masculinity after the Father

Volumes have been written about the plight of contemporary Russian women who are burdened by traditional male chauvinism and the devastation wrought by twentieth-century history. Yet, precisely because of these hardships, Russian women were marginal subjects in the sweeping modernization that defined the past century. Aside from the brief moment of early postrevolutionary equality discourse, women had a stable identity, which fully coincided with Russia's traditional self-image as a kenotic entity.[1]

Russian men never had it that "easy" with their self-image. This statement seems less paradoxical if we consider the pressure of carrying on one's shoulders the entire edifice of Soviet mythology. The Soviet story of origins was largely a male story. In Stalinist mythology, national identity rested on the myth of the "unalloyed masculinity" of the Father of All Peoples and his children, represented in film and art as embodying the national ideal. While in theory the constructed "Soviet person" (*sovetskii chelovek*) represented both genders, the process of nation-building was primarily associated with masculinity.[2] Whether through an individualized hero such as

Chapaev, or through revolutionary masses of sailors, workers, and soldiers in Eisenstein's films, the labor pains of Soviet power were invariably attributed to men, both as agents of change and as sacrificial figures.

Among the most important reasons for this masculinization of culture was the destruction of the traditional, nuclear family in the 1920s–1930s. The new ideology declared class origin and political worldview to have a monopoly on the process of socialization and identity formation. Hence the complexity of family relations, emotions, and the entire sphere of the erotic was replaced by a vertically constructed love for the Big Family, with the Soviet Union imagined as a state-wide orphanage, looking up to and modeling itself on the Father figure. Within this system, Soviet male identity was unequivocally one-sided: although male heroes (metro builders, aviators, polar explorers, etc.) were the state's currency in demonstrating the success of the nation's modernization, men's status as fathers and household patriarchs was undermined by the state's ideological claim of providing primary control over and care for individuals and the family. Thus, as Sarah Ashwin notes, "Men were encouraged to realize themselves in their work—that is, their self-realization was to have a public character, which coincided with the purposes of the regime" (12).[3]

In the 1950s, the Soviet "imagined community"—an ideological phantom rather than a nation-state—and its primary subject, the heroic Soviet male, received their first blow. With Stalin's death and the ensuing criticism of the worst aspects of the totalitarian state policies, utopian ideals of political and cultural modernization and reeducation were shaken and the natural family stepped in to fill the gap left by the compromised Father. For a short time Thaw celluloid men seemed to regain wholeness: while not giving up on their heroic public image, they acquired a positive private side. They were allowed to cry and to show personal weakness; they adopted children and were generally softer than women. Indeed, the major figure of Thaw cinema is the man-orphan, who metaphorically represented the nation recovering after the loss of its founding myths and finding the strength to reconfigure the family/community.[4] But whether portrayed as victors or survivors of the turmoil of history, men felt secure, bolstered as they were by state mythology.

The major cultural outcome of the failed reforms of the Thaw was, to use Boris Groys's expression, an acute sense of "living outside of history" (75). Devaluation of national symbols, fragmentation of national mythology, arrested economic development, and impotent gerontocratic leadership marked the crisis of national identity in the 1970s. Unlike the more traditional image of femininity, Soviet masculinity as cultural construct was built primarily on the foundation of the political utopia, and once the latter started showing signs of decay, masculinity as the icon of Soviet modernity underwent a crisis. Similarly to soldiers who cannot adjust to peacetime life, men found themselves lost and displaced once the constraints of the state loosened and self-realization in the public sphere lost its heroic overtones. Decimated by the purges and the war, the Soviet man was plagued by alcoholism, domestic violence, an astronomical divorce rate, and the shared feeling that society made it very hard to do "man's work." As Lynne Attwood remarks, "The notion of the country's dire social problems being largely or partly traceable to a 'feminization' of men and 'masculinization' of women was held by very large numbers of people" (354). These parallel crises of male identity and Soviet identity were perhaps best captured by posters of the decade: androgynous figures on nondescript backgrounds of generic factories, framed by empty slogans.

In other words, the loss of historical momentum led to the loss of heroics both on the level of Big Narratives (typical of Stalinist culture) and on the level of individual identity (typical of the Thaw's reformulation of Stalinism). This gap between official discourse and people's daily experience resulted in the Brezhnev period's obsession with memory and the past, which underwent intensive "narrativization" (Groys 94) as the era of true heroes, clear goals, and resolved (and resolvable) conflicts. The search for "heroism in our contemporary life" became a recurrent cliché in 1970s newspaper articles, radio, and television programs. Among major narratives that formed the foundation of 1970s ideology were the story of revolution—the Soviet story of origins—and of the Great Patriotic War (WWII). The Revolution and the Civil War (the Soviet version of the Wild West) were sufficiently removed in time to have their romanticized aura restored.[5] The cultural centrality of WWII in the 1970s rested on the fact that despite its devastating effect on the country's population and economy the war remained the only uncompromised collective experience.[6]

War mythology in particular proved to be an efficient basis for national identity in the post-Stalin era. By returning to "simple" times, when black and white, weak and strong, female and male were unambiguously defined, this mythology gave a boost to ideology and responded to public and private sensibilities. It fed into rituals (for instance, public spectacles of grief for war victims) and provided material for visual and verbal culture. Moreover, the return to more heroic times allowed the Soviet male a ready-made and sanctified space for fantasizing about a regained sense of mission, resolution, and action—in short, the standard masculinity set.[7] The interrelationship between model manhood and model nationhood was evoked, for instance, through the rhetoric of war sacrifice. Since the majority of veterans were men, evocations of the heroic period of national greatness were invariably gender-coded.

As Catriona Kelly argues, "war mythology also carried the seeds of its own destruction as a consolidating force. Though official commemorations could, and often did, adequately express private feelings, the clichés of official propaganda were so melodramatically overstated, and so often repeated, as to invite ridicule" (265). Kelly provides a striking example of such ironic reversal: Aleksandr Galich's song "How Klim Petrovich Spoke at a Meeting in Defense of Peace," in which the hero, a master workman, is handed a ready-made speech. As he mechanically starts reading the prefabricated lines, he realizes that it has been written to be said by "a mother, a woman, and a widow" (265–66).

Galich's parody, as well as a score of Vladimir Vysotskii's songs in which he assumes a female identity,[8] signals more than a ridicule of empty patriotic slogans. The simultaneous fragmentation of Soviet ideological discourse and the idealized vision of Soviet masculinity suggest a deep link between the two. Indeed, in Galich's song, despite the hero's horror, the audience does not notice the "gender fraud," blindfolded as it is by the ritualistic nature of the speech. The weakened mythology only underscores the diluted sense of male identity, with all of its Brezhnev-era blights: lack of initiative; collective responsibility; cultural conservatism; and social paralysis.

The visual culture of the Brezhnev era, and especially television as the most popular of all official cultural forums of the time, faced the double task of fostering Soviet mythology and reestablishing masculinity as the "avatar of a potent nationhood" (Shapiro 140). Television, and in particular the young but booming industry of serial productions, was charged with the task of portraying strong heroes, capable of expressing Soviet culture's concerns. The domestic setting was a healing space where people could find refuge after long days at unsatisfying jobs, hours of standing in line, public insults and humiliation, and the general senselessness of existence. At the same time, this enormous television audience constituted the avid consumer of virtually anything different from the idealized cardboard heroes represented in Soviet newscasts.

The task of creating shows for such an audience was not an easy one, however, primarily because Western-style action films, with their individualistic heroes, violence, and sexualized "hard bodies,"[9] were not a welcome genre in the Soviet Union. Moreover, the Soviet national mythology insisted upon women's liberation and equality as one of its political foundations. Hence, the restoration of male status and the national identity could not be achieved through commodification and marginalization of women by rampaging men reasserting a shaken mythology. Even more problematic was the necessity of creating popular productions while preserving ideological *dominantas,* especially the untouchable authority of the Soviet state in the process of both nation-building and male identity formation.

Television's marginal status as a "nonartistic" form of cultural production simplified the process of incorporating popular genres into regular programming. The dual crisis of Soviet national mythology and of the conventional image of the "real man" brought about gendered TV scheduling: on the one hand, the television schedule was flooded with genres traditionally considered attractive to male spectators: spy thrillers, detectives, police procedurals; on the other hand, serialized melodramatic narratives became staples of 1970s Soviet television. For the most part, serial productions and made-for-TV films offered narratives about the already canonized past, which gave directors more freedom in treating conflicts while addressing political and cultural anxieties of the present. Genre productions were ideally suited for the project of recuperating the obsolete masculinity of Soviet patriarchy's golden days.

Brezhnev-era television offered two models for linking nation and gender: the hyperrational, urban, intellectual narrative model (spy thriller, police procedural, and the *"detektiv"* [murder mystery])[10] and a traditional, peasant, grassroot model (historical melodrama). The two differ in their respective strategies of constructing and linking the "national imaginary" with the "masculine imaginary." In the first, neo-*Stalinist* model, the nation is replaced by the state (or, more precisely, the empire) as the mechanism of power and control, with masculinity represented as an extension of this power. In the second, traditional *Russian* model, in contrast, the state is only an implied frame, whereas the topoi of the "natural" nation are central to the formation of idealized maleness. The remaining part of this chapter focuses on two genres of Stagnation television series: the spy thriller and the historical melodrama. While the two could not differ more in their strategies of representing national and gender identity, both are engaged in the process of rearticulating Soviet national mythology by linking it to complementary aspects of representations of masculinity.

Imperial Fantasies: Men in (Virginal) Black

Seventeen Moments of Spring [*Semnadtsat' mgnovenii vesny,* 1973] emerged as an unmatched leader among Brezhnev-era TV spy thrillers. This twelve-episode blockbuster, based on a Iulian Semenov novel, exemplifies the paradox of "official popular culture": while the production was closely supervised, and even inspired, by the KGB and the Party,[11] it succeeded in achieving cult status by touching on the sensibilities of the 1970s. The Soviet superagent protagonist, Isaev-Shtirlits, is composed, terse, dressed in the "virginal black" of the Nazi uniform and, above all, hyperrational. Forced to live undercover for twenty years, he infiltrates the perfect machines of the SS, SA, and Gestapo and deceives his experienced Nazi "colleagues" not through action (of which there is next to none in the series) but through his extraordinary intellectual abilities—and, of course, his love for the Motherland. The latter, truth be told, rarely appears in the series. As a spy, Shtirlits acts as a perfect member of the German bureaucratic elite: he sits in his office, drinks cognac, drives a Mercedes, and lives a comfortable life in his villa. But beneath his façade of reserve and military gentility throbs not the heart—but the mind of a "real Soviet man."[12]

6-1 Isaev-Shtirlits in *Seventeen Moments of Spring* (Dir. Tat'iana Lioznova, 1973).

In each episode the hero has "moments of reflection," in which various cinematic documentary sequences go through his mind. These include footage depicting the rise to power of various Nazi leaders, their fictionalized dossiers, compilation sequences of major WWII battles, and Stalin's fictional conversations with Soviet intelligence authorities. All this overwhelming information has been absorbed by the protagonist, who now has to process it in order to determine which of the four major Nazi players—Goering, Goebbels, Himmler, or Bormann—is behind the separatist negotiations with the treacherous American diplomats. The fate of the Soviet Union and of the world thus depends on this one man's analytical powers.

As if this stunning regression to the Stalinist representation of male rationality were not enough, *Seventeen Moments of Spring* features a voice-over. Dispassionate and detached, the narrator relates past and future events, fills in pieces of official dossiers and of private conversations, and even interprets the psychophysiological conditions of characters. For example, when Shtirlits naps in his car before continuing his struggle with Evil, the voice-over informs the viewer, "In exactly fifteen minutes he will wake up. The mechanism perfected over many years will work again." In Lioznova's production, past and future, the public and the private, history and myth are collapsed into the voice-over as the only accessible authority. Omniscient, ubiquitous, and omnipotent, the voice-over controls the development of the plot, the meaning of History itself, and the actions of the male protagonist. After all, focused on his mission, Shtirlits does not know that the Motherland has just awarded him the title of Hero of the Soviet Union and thus elevated him to the pantheon of her ideal "sons."

Shtirlits's dual identity, as both a Nazi and a Soviet intelligence officer, functioned as a dreamscape for the disempowered Soviet viewer, but especially for the male spectator, and in no way undermined Shtirlits's status as the ideal Soviet man. On the contrary, this double identity raised his symbolic value, as attested by his official dossier, which features the standard menu of model male characteristics: "Nordic character, ruthless toward enemies of the Reich, friendly and open with colleagues, good family man, did not have any compromising liaisons." The universal nature of these catalogued qualities and the image of the strong, supranational empire they evoked, in fact, conveniently eschewed the feeble rhetoric of Soviet ideology, merging it with the culturally vibrant icon of the ideological "Other." As a double agent, Isaev-Shtirlits could claim a "double dose" of ideal patriotic virility.

The iconography of a spy, with its links to both Stalinist culture and Western popular forms, plays a major role in constructing Shtirlits's status as the ideal hero. John Cawelti names clandestineness as one of the major components of the spy plot, the basic elements of which hold certain psychological attractions that provide a narrative impulse and constitute a powerful mechanism for stimulating audiences' fantasies. Among such fantasies, Cawelti mentions invisibility and the resultant pleasures of voyeurism and license; the fascination with disguises either as a temporary escape from one's own identity or as a means of creating one; the secret exercise of power; a strong image of belonging to some organization or community; and, finally, shifts from profound loyalty to extraordinary forms of betrayal (9). Shtirlits, then, embodies a perfect escape into another identity, removed from the effeminizing daily grind, into a world of political intrigue and familiar—but no less invigorating—tropes of heroism, sacrifice, and license.

The transparency of these tropes of model manhood and nationhood is ensured by the tight control over space and time in the series. The twelve-episode series is set over a few weeks in the spring of 1945, foregrounding the urgency of the mission. The naming of places and timing of events in *Seventeen Moments* has no meaning outside of the structure of patriarchal discourse. All twelve episodes are set in the limited, contained, and controlled space of office walls and long corridors punctuated by identical, statue-like guards. An ingredient important to the picture of an ideal nationhood is surveillance, which reinforces the tight boundary controls of nationalism and controls sexuality, as well (see Chapter 4 by Kaganovsky in this volume). While the community of middle-aged males in *Seventeen Moments of Spring* evokes homoerotic associations, at no point does the series suggest a transgression of strictly heterosexual behavioral boundaries. More precisely, it is the absence of *any* romantic or erotic liaisons that both illustrates the series' anachronistic, Stalinist ideal of masculinity and betrays its late Soviet male angst.

6-2   Reich Central Security Office
in *Seventeen Moments of Spring*
(Dir. Tat'iana Lioznova, 1973).

Comparing *Seventeen Moments of Spring* with James Bond movies, Marina Adamovich argues that they are strikingly similar in their use of strategies to link supermasculinity with concerns over troubled national identity. Indeed, while for a Western viewer the ideal male figure is constituted by action, initiative, and hypersexuality, the ideal spy for post-Stalin Soviet audiences combines superior intellect with sexual sterility. As Adamovich notes, "In the ideological Soviet state of the 1970s, nobody was interested in the kind of stud you were. Whether castrated or impotent—it's no big deal; it was much more terrifying to turn out to be a fool, an intellectual impotent" (80).

The calm resolve and intellectual superiority of "our" man was unchallenged and focused entirely on the task at hand. More importantly, this superiority was not threatened by female influence. Shtirlits's wife appears in one five-minute-long flashback and does not say a word. His only female acquaintances are an old German lady and his Russian radio operator, who gets pregnant and thus is not only useless in her professional capacity, but also has to be rescued as a woman and a mother. The only "active" and threatening female is a German sergeant, who flirts with Shtirlits and argues that a sexual encounter between the two healthy and politically sound adults will benefit the Aryan nation. Unlike the symbolic "copulation" of the Nazi national myth with the Soviet one, such a liaison involves a bodily contact, which would threaten the purity of the Soviet male. The ideological seductress is immediately shot. *Seventeen Moments,* thus, outlines the boundaries of the "national imaginary" and, at the same time, the boundaries of ideal masculinity in its imperial, Stalinist version. The genre of spy thriller functions as a dreamscape, where national and gender borders are secured by the patriarchal structures of representation. This narrative of control revolves around male intellect deciding the fate of the world.

Melodramatic History: Male Angst and the Soviet Story of Origins

The other feature of exemplary masculinity, male sexual potency—
which for many decades had been excised from Soviet culture—became a
primary metaphor for national strength in 1970s historical melodramas.
The latter proved an efficient tool for fostering official state mythology
through visual and narrative codes of popular culture. Unlike the spy
thriller, which had "ancestors" in Stalinist defense films and films about Soviet scouts,[13] 1970s TV dramas had no immediate Soviet models. In her
book *Fol'klor. Lubok. Ekran,* Neia Zorkaia argues that such TV series as *Shadows
Disappear at Noon* [*Teni ischezaiut v polden',* 1971] and *Eternal Call* [*Vechnyi zov,*
1974–1977] hark back to the dime novels at the turn of the century. Specifically, their simple plots, flat and predictable characters, and melodramatic
conflicts are reminiscent of *lubok* dramas, a popular genre of fairgrounds entertainment. Indeed, in covering Russo-Soviet history of the twentieth century, *Eternal Call* and, to a somewhat lesser degree, *Shadows* follow the logic of
carefully selected images that by the 1970s had acquired the status of legend
in the popular consciousness and offer a "folklorized" version of the Soviet
story of origins.[14] What was even more important for 1970s culture, however,
was melodrama's propensity to break taboos and its focus on intimate relations as a way of reestablishing the nation's vitality.[15]

While some productions of the seventies and eighties deal with history
in the broad sense, the majority of miniseries address specifically twentieth-
century history and evoke the genre of historical-revolutionary films,[16]
which is adjusted to the narrative conventions and visual codes of melodrama. Both *Shadows Disappear at Noon* and *Eternal Call* were based on historical novels by Anatolii Ivanov and made by the two young TV directors
Valerii Uskov and Vladimir Krasnopol'skii. The two productions trace the
life of several generations in Siberian villages over many decades of prerevolutionary and Soviet history. Designed as national epics, both conceive
family as the site of class conflict and ethical dilemmas. The series' melodramatic plots revolve around the conflict between the private self (the
realm of love, emotion, and family) and the self's realization in the public
sphere, offering a glimpse of private dramas underlying political and social
change. In other words, the narrative as a whole may follow the model of a
historical-revolutionary genre, but history in its canonical Soviet instantiation happens in the gaps between episodes, while individual episodes focus
on the traumatizing impact of the Revolution, the Civil War, dekulakiza-
tion, etc., on people's daily lives.

Given the epic design of both productions, the political dimension is
important to the interpretation of the twentieth-century history that the
series offer. The landmark events that define that history, however, happen
elsewhere (in Saint Petersburg and Moscow, neither of which appears in the
series), whereas life "in the sticks" follows different laws and a different
rhythm. By linking national identity to the peasant milieu, the productions

set out to reclaim traditional Russian identity to complement and strengthen the weakened Soviet mythology.[17] The other, equally compelling reason to use the vast Siberian expanses as the setting was the opportunity to incorporate images of strong patriarchs. A peasant father was a traditionally powerful figure, whose authority was unchallenged both at work and at home. In fact, these two spheres were far less separated in village communities than in the urban environment. Hence the beleaguered "real Soviet man" was to be transformed into a real *muzhik*, whose tribulations were informed by, but not reduced to, political paradigms.[18]

As Jesús Martín-Barbero remarks in connection with soap opera in Latin America, the genre's popularity may be ascribed primarily to the link between melodramatic plots and national cultures: "The melodrama speaks of a *primordial sociality*," at the center of which there is "a plot of the tightly woven fabric of family relationships" (277). While political binaries are important for the ideology of both Soviet series, they find expression through moral polarization, redefining innocence and villainy along gender/sexual lines. The two series tell retrospective stories of Russia's modernization and class struggle, conveyed in traditional melodramatic codes. Love, adultery, rape, and even incest are intertwined with the political history of the Soviet Union and with the personal maturation of individual characters. Both series privilege gesture, visual excess, and musical cues over narrative continuity. At the center of the narrative is the troubled Russian male, whose cultural lineage extends from Stepan Razin through Chapaev to Vasilii Shukshin's Egor Prokudin.[19] This version of Russian masculinity, unlike *Seventeen Moments,* marginalizes reason and political consciousness in favor of more traditional values—communal life, spontaneity, "genuine" emotions—with the attendant vaunted "Russian" features: behavioral extremes and irrational swings from good to evil.

Shadows Disappear at Noon: Revolution as Male Hysteria

Shadows Disappear at Noon portrays the new socialist world-in-the-making as a product of an ambiguous combination of class and gender struggle. The narrative moves briskly through the prerevolutionary and early revolutionary periods. All of the opening sequences focus on women and help to construct female sexuality as dangerous and playing into the hands of class enemies. While the two female leads, Mariia and Serafima, are political opponents, their class essence and behavior are linked to, and articulated through, their bodies. What is striking, however, is the departure from the traditional representation of women as mothers. While both women have children, neither of them is shown as child-rearing or domestic, their energy directed outward, into the political sphere. In contrast, men's behavior in the series is determined by loss—of wealth, status, or a loved one. Violence is the domain of men, particularly men of the "revolutionary generation," and it frequently assumes the form of hysterical, irrational behavior.

The series begins with a scene in which a crowd of kulaks incites a drunken man, Anisim, to show his power over Mariia, his lover and the mother of his daughter. Anisim orders Mariia to bring back a bear's pelt from the taiga. Mariia's survival against all odds and her arrival with the pelt of an enormous bear mark not only her triumph as an individual, but also a challenge to the patriarchal order in terms of gender relations and political struggle. Predictably, her transformation occurs simultaneously on the personal (she abandons Anisim) and on the public level (she joins a revolutionary cell in the nearby town and eventually becomes the first head of the kolkhoz in her village).

Both visually and narratively, however, the episode constructs Mariia as first and foremost a sexual being. She emerges out of the woods half-naked, her body barely covered by clothes torn after her struggle with the beast. This new Amazon's "raised consciousness" does not stop Anisim, and another man, Frol, from stalking her. Mariia rejects them both, choosing instead the ascetic life of a revolutionary. This rejection precipitates Anisim's "sobering up" and personal maturation, but also results in a sexually barren life. Symbolically castrated, he becomes an ideal father to Mariia's daughter after Mariia is killed.

In contrast, Frol becomes an involuntary accomplice in Mariia's death. His desire for Mariia and his jealousy of Anisim are used by two kulak brothers, who convince him to kidnap Mariia. Once she opens the door, the brothers knock down the intoxicated Frol, drag Mariia to a cliff, and smash in her head with a stone. In a gender reversal of the Soviet narrative of sacrifice,[20] Mariia's violent death begins her symbolic life. For the village community, her memory is that of the revolutionary spirit. Just as both men's desire for Mariia's body is intertwined with her revolutionary struggle, so does the cliff combine all of the meanings of Mariia's death. The purely cinematic, extreme long shot of "Mariia's cliff" and the crane shot of the village as seen from the cliff recur in every episode, marking moments in the intersection of both the epic (Mariia of the legend, overseeing the progress in her native village) and the personal meaning (Anisim's and Frol's painful memories).

The urgency of eliminating Mariia as the physical body, so as to elevate her memory, slots neatly into the framework of the Soviet sacrificial narrative. Significantly, however, her death opens a vacancy for her male comrade, Zakhar, to become the kolkhoz leader. By equating the turbulent revolutionary period with female influence, *Shadows* establishes the paradigm of a normalizing representation of masculinity. Hereafter, the building of the Soviet commune in the village proceeds under normative male guidance.

Frol's "original sin" of weakness and betrayal—attributed to lust and alcohol—is later reenacted when the enemy blackmails and forces him to marry a woman he does not love, but whom he steals from her wedding with Zakhar, the new kolkhoz leader and Mariia's successor. Frol is able to come to terms with life and find happiness only decades later, after he returns from WWII and starts an affair with a widow. Although villagers frown at his adultery (he is still married to the woman he stole from Zakhar), Frol is able to consummate his desire for the first time. Predictably, he also becomes a productive member of the kolkhoz. His male strength and maturation, then, are closely related to the Soviet nation's history as it metonymically grows from an unstable, female-guided, and past-haunted village to a tightly organized and victorious patriarchal community.

The subplot of class enemies involves similar structures of meaning, but in the negative. Serafima, the daughter of a rich merchant who inherited his gold mines, first appears at a party, where the father places her chair on the dinner table and orders his guests to kiss her shoes. This initial humiliation of, and triumph over, men anticipates her sadomasochistic relationship with Konstantin, her future husband and comrade-in-arms in her fight against the Bolsheviks. Konstantin is the only one who refuses to kiss her shoes. After both of them lose their wealth, status, and parents to the revolution, the two accidentally meet and end up living in a monastery. Under the names Pistimeia and Ustin—the peasants they had murdered—they move to Mariia's village, Green Vale, to continue fighting against the new regime by using people's weaknesses, anxieties, and secrets to manipulate them. Though Ustin executes these vile plots, the design and the hatred fueling them come from Pistimeia-Serafima, whose black garb and "unwomanly" power suggest her identification with a witch, who "sets out to unsettle boundaries between the rational and the irrational, the symbolic and imaginary" (Creed 76).

Her transformation from the spoiled heiress Serafima into the religious fanatic Pistimeia is neither motivated nor shown—quite in the tradition of the Stalinist representation of enemies—and adds a disturbing dimension to the political/sexual knot of meanings. She initially taunts Konstantin for his weakness in the face of adversity and rejects his sexual advances, reminding him of his refusal to kiss her shoes. When she is praying half-naked, Konstantin forces himself on her, after which Serafima declares him her husband and master "first after God." As a payoff for her taunting and to demonstrate his absolute power over Serafima, Konstantin orders her to walk through the village in her underwear. This perverse exercise of power, however, is nothing more than hysteria and a sign of abnormal relations. The narrative repeatedly emphasizes the unnaturalness of their family, ruled as it is by a strong female figure. Gender relations outside the "normal" patriarchal order have a destructive effect on the family. Their son Fedor grows up a stranger to his parents and frees himself from the oppressive domestic atmosphere by following the path of a good Soviet youth. Captured by the Nazis during the war, he meets his father, who, in keeping with his "perverse" conduct, offered his services to the invaders. Afraid that Fedor might denounce him as a traitor, Ustin kills his son in a fit of panic.

The juxtaposition of the healthy and unhealthy communities culminates and resolves in organic, rather than political, terms: the "good" family of the village poses for a group photograph, while the "bad" family destroys itself (Ustin's madness and suicide, Pistimeia's flight). Ustin's insanity is signaled by nightmares in the form of flashbacks: a haunting vision of Fedor as repentance for filicide, and a vision of Pistimeia on the day he raped her in the monastery. Ustin whispers "Witch!" before, consumed by his dark origins and dark desires, he shoots himself in the cellar.

By drawing on age-old cultural and gender stereotypes, *Shadows Disappear at Noon* achieves a double objective. First, it revitalizes the waning revolutionary mythology by encoding it through power relations between genders. Second, it directly links the progress of building socialism in Siberia with the establishment of a "normal," i.e., patriarchal, family and community structure.

Eternal Call: Soviet History à la Karamazov

Compared to the somewhat idiosyncratic vision of the revolution in *Shadows,* the signally titled *Eternal Call* offers a more conventional view of the Soviet story of origins. The series engages more directly in trafficking Soviet national icons of masculinity in their ideologically approved, heroic/sacrificial version. The nineteen episodes of *Eternal Call* allow for a bigger cast, repeated mass scenes, detailed representation of underground Party cells, the Civil War, etc., and consequently for the adherence of the selected moments of Soviet history to the canon mastered by students in Soviet secondary schools.

At the same time and in striking contrast to *Shadows Disappear at Noon, Eternal Call* dwells extensively on prerevolutionary history—the legitimate environment for family dramas and illicit passions. While historical teleology brings the story closer to the "radiant present" of the Brezhnev era, family and love conflicts nevertheless remain the same throughout the narrative. More specifically, heroes' actions in the first three episodes, and all the conflicts, family secrets, and passions that emerge, define characters' fates. Narrative fragmentation and lack or delay of closure create ambiguity, which prevents the knot of complications from being resolved. As Jeremy Butler points out in connection with soap operas, their "audial and visual style . . . [is] uniquely adapted to the preservation of enigmas, rather than their resolution" (67).

Like *Shadows,* the series chronicles more than six decades in the life of a Siberian village and focuses on three Savel'ev brothers—a hybrid of a fairy-tale formula and a Dostoesvky motif. Anton, the oldest brother, leaves the village while still an adolescent, joins a Bolshevik group, is repeatedly jailed, and returns home only for brief moments. This absence from the life of the community is meaningful, for Anton's exemplary life of a reeducated youth and a dedicated communist—a positive version of Ivan Karamazov stripped of his complexity—makes him a rather superfluous figure. Equally insipid and predictable are other figures of Soviet party bosses,

6-3   Fedor Savel'ev in *Eternal Call*
(Dir. Valerii Uskov and Vladimir
Krasnopol'skii, 1974–1977).

largely recycled from *Shadows Disappear at Noon*. Designed to recast Soviet national mythology in "human" terms, these characters nevertheless conform to the worn-out iconography of the positive hero.

It is the two younger brothers who are central to the narrative. Fedor, the middle son, is an extremely contradictory figure. With his gypsy appearance, glaring and passionate eyes, lust and yearning for power, Fedor is a poorly disguised replica of Mitia Karamazov. The blond, slightly built Ivan—the youngest son—is Fedor's competitor for the love of Anna, the daughter of the local kulak Kaftanov. The representation of Ivan, especially his unwillingness to fight evil with evil, is not far removed from Alesha Karamazov's kenotic ideals—adjusted, of course, to the Soviet context.

The Dostoevskian lineage—and the logic of visual titillation—demands "Father Karamazov" as well. Since the series' class approach disallows such a figure in the Savel'evs' father, a poor peasant, Kaftanov becomes a dark force ruthlessly ruling over villagers' lives. More importantly, he is Dostoevskii's depraved sensualist, whose hut in the forest is the locus of constant debauchery and violence, and a source of temptation for Fedor and Ivan. The association of the "dark forces" of history with lust, debauchery, and promiscuity both satisfies ideological orthodoxy and offers a legitimate source of titillation for the viewer.

The most terrifying figure, however, is not Kaftanov. His cruelty, sexual hyperactivity, and absolute power render him an almost mythological being, an epic villain akin to the multi-headed dragon so vividly captured by Evgenii Shvarts's 1943 play. The true horror resides with Dem'ian Iniutin, Kaftanov's second-in-command and Smerdiakov's replica. A poor peasant, he returns from the Russo-Japanese War one-legged and disgruntled, and offers Kaftanov his services as a watchdog. Unable to do "man's work" because of his disability (and thus his symbolic castration), he compensates for his inadequacy by spying on and viciously prosecuting other men.

By following textbook logic, the series is consistent in showing that people's lives, from childhood to old age, are predetermined by their class origins. But once characters are lined up along these political lines, the immediate motivation for their behavior is invariably painted in melodramatic terms. Ivan joins Kaftanov's White regiment out of despair, after Anna chooses Fedor, and his entire life pays for this choice: he spends years in a camp and forever becomes an outsider in the community he rejoins. Fedor, who marries Anna, cannot forgive her short affair with Ivan and suspects that his oldest son is, in fact, Ivan's. But the dark secret is much darker than he suspects. In the novel, the child results from incest—Kaftanov's rape of his own daughter as a punishment for her joining the Red guerillas. For the TV script, Ivanov produced a "softer" version of the story: Kaftanov ordered one of his henchmen to rape her. The scene, however, is ambiguous. As Ivan rushes into the barn to rescue Anna, it is Kaftanov who towers over Anna's ravaged body and declares his absolute power over her. Ivan shoots Kaftanov and carries Anna to the Reds, but the literal and figurative "evil seed" defines many of the future events. In the final analysis, then, it is not the logic of class struggle but melodramatic coincidence that rules history.

In contrast to the narrative restraint and visual discipline of *Seventeen Moments*, *Eternal Call* plunges the viewer into the midst of politically and sexually coded passions. Imperial sterility gives way to a generous exchange of bodily fluids; bodies are undisciplined and on display—a paradigm especially evident in Fedor's violent relationship with the women in his life. His individualism, ruthlessness, moral ambiguity, and desire for domination over his own fate and those of other people (Ivan, Anna, Kir'ian, and Kir'ian's wife) make for a problematic socialist realist hero. Yet he is an ideal figure to represent the troubled masculinity of the twentieth century, as troubled, in fact, as Russia itself. While the extremes of Fedor's character pay homage to Dostoevsky's self-lacerating men, who never stop searching for self, the road traveled by the Savel'ev brothers in the series is more reminiscent of an epic journey.

The two series are neither purely cinematic texts, which in the Soviet tradition came to be associated with the masculine sphere of action and violence, nor purely televisual soaps, which, at least in an American context, are considered a woman's form. The narratives oscillate between socialist realist and melodramatic aesthetics. But it is the latter's heterogeneity that, in Christine Gledhill's words, "facilitates conflict and negotiation between cultural identities" (37).

Politically, Soviet miniseries of the 1970s were designed to resuscitate state mythology, reconfiguring it through popular genres. In a related project, however, and perhaps more importantly, these texts attempted to rearticulate Soviet masculinity as the pillar of a rediscovered national mythology. By the 1970s, both the "neo-Stalinist" and the "*lubok* Russian" models for linking masculinity with national mythology were marginal to the post-utopian Soviet cultural landscape. The national ideal was temporally displaced into the past and spatially fragmented and decentered, i.e., located in the West (Berlin) or in the East (Siberia), but not in Moscow. It was precisely this anachronistic iconicity and the shameless recycling of the familiar and tested tropes, however, that gave a boost to the ailing ideology.

Ivanov's widow recounts an anecdote about casting for the early 1990s TV series *Ermak* (based on another of Ivanov's epic novels) about the sixteenth-century Russian Cossack-explorer, whose name is synonymous with Russia's conquest of Siberia. According to her, America offered to pay Russia $50 million if Arnold Schwarzenegger could be cast in the role of Ermak. This offer reportedly enraged Ivanov: "Never! How can an American play a legendary Russian hero!"[21] Indeed, he could not and most certainly did not aspire to such a role. And yet, both the timing of this anecdote—the crisis of Russia's self-image after the collapse of the empire—and the choice of candidate for such national fantasy are quite revealing. While Schwarzenegger's gender identity is beyond doubt, inscribed upon his body and enacted through violence in every action film, his national identity is questionable, making him a marginal cultural figure. With Russian culture "gone global" and the pool of available male heroes expanded, who would be a better candidate for the impossible task of bridging Russia's past and present than the Austrian-American "hard body," speaking in ironic one-liners?[22]

Notes

1. For a detailed discussion of Russia's feminine self-image, see Hubbs. In Stalinist culture, the newly liberated Soviet woman featured predominantly as a symbol of transformation under the influence of the male idea, as in Vsevolod Pudovkin's *Mother* (*Mat'*, 1926), or of the male guiding hand, as in 1930s musicals.

2. In Sergei Livnev's provocative film *Hammer and Sickle* [*Serp i molot,* 1994], the heroine Evdokiia is forced to undergo a sex-change operation, to become a living illustration of the Party's slogan: "Some of our heroic women are not satisfied with being just women: they want to become men." The new Soviet "man" functions well as a model worker and a model family patriarch, until s/he stumbles onto the man who used to be the lover of "Evdokiia." This triggers a total emotional breakdown, which results in the hero's attempt to free himself from the system and to kill the Father—Stalin.

3. On the construction of Soviet masculinity in the Stalin era, see Haynes.

4. Thaw men-orphans are protagonists in such films as Marlen Khutsiev's *Two Fedors* [*Dva Fedora,* 1958] and Sergei Bondarchuk's *Man's Fate* [*Sud'ba cheloveka,* 1959].

5. In the late 1960s and early 1970s the Civil War emerged as a perfect setting for adventure films. For instance, Edmond Keosaian's *The Elusive Avengers* [*Neulovimye mstiteli,* 1966] tells the story of a group of teenage boys fighting the White Army. This successful remake of Ivan Perestiani's film *The Red Imps* [*Krasnye d'iavoliata,* 1923] was attended by 54 million people in 1967, while its two sequels (1968 and 1971) gathered 66 and 61 million viewers respectively. Zemlianukhin and Segida 283.

6. For a discussion of the place of WWII mythology in the 1970s, see Kelly, 263–66.

7. In such films as Andrei Smirnov's *Belorussia Station* [*Belorusskii vokzal,* 1970] or Vladimir Rogovoi's *Officers* [*Ofitsery,* 1971], the narrative starts in the present, with protagonists, who went through the Revolution and the war, having a reunion or reminiscing about the past. Contemporary life and the younger generation are portrayed as lacking values. The rest of the narrative unfolds as a trip to the past, to heroic times and historical optimism. This trip typically ends with a lesson to posterity, best exemplified by a scene from *Officers*. Addressing his preschool grandson, the general says: "There is such a profession, Ivan—defending your Motherland."

8. For instance, Vysotskii's "Dialogue by the TV Set" ("Dialog u televizora") alternates between voices of spouses. The foolish wife compares what she sees on TV with her husband and his male friends—the comparison not in their favor. The husband's only defense is alcohol and a threat of violence. The perception of men as henpecked by women and unable to live up to cultural expectations is also a central theme in *bytovoi* (slice-of-life) film, which often focused on male midlife crisis but indirectly commented on society. Such films as *Autumn Marathon* (*Osennii marafon,* dir. Georgii Daneliia, 1979) were metaphorical but poignant expressions of the "double identity crisis."

9. For a discussion of the politics of linking forms of masculinity with nationhood see, for instance, Jeffords; Mosse; and Shapiro, especially 139–57.

10. The two most famous 1970s police procedurals are *The Investigation Is Conducted by Experts* [*Sledstvie vedut znatoki,* 1971–1986] and *The Meeting Place Cannot Be Changed* [*Mesto vstrechi izmenit' nel'zia,* dir. Stanislav Govorukhin, 1979]. The former follows a more intellectual model; the latter, featuring Vysotskii as a Stalin-era policeman, combines mild critique of vigilantism with populist ideology. In the miniseries *Born in the Revolution* [*Rozhdennaia revoliutsiei,* dir. Grigorii Kokhan, 1974–1977], which traces the sixty-year history of the Soviet police forces, the protagonist outlives his wife by thirty years. This longevity—a reversal of the actual male/female life expectancy—both provides him with a subjectivity outside of his job (the last two episodes are punctuated by the hero's painful flashbacks) and gives him a reason to demonstrate his male qualities even in senility (he eventually tracks and arrests the murderer of his wife).

11. The story of both the novel and its television adaptation is quite remarkable. The idea of the novel was suggested to Iulian Semenov by Iurii Andropov, then head of the KGB. The novel came out in 1968 and enjoyed some popularity, although the notorious Soviet "book deficit" made Semenov's works virtually unavailable to the general public. In 1969 Andropov offered Semenov the chance to start working on the script for a television production based on the novel. The official reason for the project was the approaching thirtieth anniversary of the Soviet victory in WWII. Andropov ordered General Semen Tsvigun, his deputy and Leonid Brezhnev's close friend, to supervise the production. The second line of support for the miniseries came from the Central Committee of the Communist Party. G. Ezhov, a "consultant on historical issues" of the CC, published in the *Literary Gazette* a positive review of Semenov's novel, and, together with the "consultants" from the KGB, was listed in the miniseries credits. The documentary, released in 1998 to celebrate the twenty-fifth anniversary of the release of *Seventeen Moments,* claims that the production was nothing short of a "brilliant PR move by the KGB": the miniseries suggested that during the war Soviet secret agents helped "to decide the fates of the world, and, presumably, continue to do so in the present." *Seventeen Moments* thus was made under

the auspices of the two most powerful agencies in the country, something that no other popular television production could ever dream of.

12. It is no accident that chess, which had always enjoyed high status in the Soviet Union, became a pawn in political games in the 1970s. After Anatolii Karpov's victory over Viktor Korchnoi, who defected to Holland two years earlier, at the 1978 World Championship, Leonid Brezhnev sent a congratulatory telegram to Karpov and personally decorated him with the Labor Red Banner medal.

13. "Defense literature" and "defense films" (*oboronnaia literatura* and *oboronnye fil'my*) appeared in the 1930s in an attempt to boost vigilance. A typical plot involved imperialism's attempts to penetrate a Soviet border and sabotage or undermine socialist construction. Boris Barnet's 1947 film *The Scout's Exploit* [*Podvig razvedchika*] introduced "films about Soviet scouts," which conformed to the "defense" model ideologically but generically were adventure war films, portraying Soviet agents crossing enemy (usually Nazi) lines.

14. For a discussion of *The Eternal Call* and *Shadows Disappear at Noon,* see Zorkaia, *Fol'klor. Lubok. Ekran,* 95–107.

15. On the uses of the melodramatic mode in Russian culture, see *Imitations of Life: Two Centuries of Melodrama in Russia,* ed. Louise McReynolds and Joan Neuberger. See also Kate Baldwin's, "Montezuma's Revenge," a discussion of the Russian reception of the Mexican soap opera *The Rich Also Cry.*

16. The "historical-revolutionary film" appeared in the 1920s, displacing the historical film in the genre system. This new genre answered the state's need to articulate an agreed-upon mythology of origins. The two major settings for these films were the October Revolution and the Civil War. The classic historical-revolutionary film is also the canonized exemplar of the socialist realist method in cinema—*Chapaev.* Eisenstein's *October* and, to a lesser degree, *Battleship Potemkin* [*Bronenosets Potemkin*] also belong to this genre.

17. Soviet cinema of the 1940s–1950s produced several films about multigenerational workers' family—a mini-model of the modernizing society. See, for example, *A Great Life* [*Bol'shaia zhizn',* dir. Leonid Lukov, part one—1939; part two—1946/1958] and *The Big Family* [*Bol'shaia sem'ia,* dir. Iosif Kheifits, 1954]. The shift from representation of the working class to the traditional peasant milieu marks a crisis in the Soviet utopia.

18. Village prose, which emerged in the 1950s and flourished through the 1970s, assumed the task of representing the Russian countryside and voicing concerns about the encroachment of modernization. The works of Valentin Rasputin, Vasilii Belov, and Viktor Astaf'ev portrayed the traditional Russian way of life in the process of becoming extinct, owing to the thoughtless use of technology, neglect, ignorance, and greed. The conflict between the old and the new, which in Stalinist literature and film is always resolved in favor of the latter, in village prose is reversed: from universal modernist projects to a rediscovery of traditional Russian values, invariably located in the past.

19. Stepan (Stenka) Razin, the legendary hero of many songs and the first Russian film made in 1908, was the commander of a band of Don Cossacks, who in 1670–1671 roamed the countryside, massacring the rich and helping the poor. For some time he successfully challenged Moscow troops, before being captured and publicly executed. The myth of the "people's avenger" is complemented by Razin's notorious cruelty. He fell in love with the captured Persian Princess, causing a stir among his men. To stop accusations of weakness and betrayal, Razin cast the Princess overboard.

Vasilii Chapaev is the Russian Civil War hero and the protagonist of the 1934 film *Chapaev.* His popularity both with his men and with the generations of Soviet viewers rested as much on his bravery and military prowess, as on his archetypally Russian "spontaneity"—swings from calmness to rage and violence.

Egor Prokudin is an ex-convict from Vasilii Shukshin's novella *Snowball Berry Red* [*Kalina krasnaia*] and the 1973 eponymous film. His attempt to sever his connections with the criminal past and find new life with a devoted woman is thwarted by his prison habits and his former gang, who eventually kill him. These figures embody the contradictory "male imaginary" of the Russian identity: toughness and even cruelty, on the one side, and unbound generosity, camaraderie, and unreflexive patriotism, on the other.

20. Despite its antireligious rhetoric, Soviet ideology embraced many Christian paradigms and tropes. For instance, scores of verbal and visual texts produced from the 1920s through the 1970s follow a hagiographic mode and narrate the exemplary lives and deaths of "martyrs for Soviet power." Cf., for instance, the canonical story of Pavlik Morozov. The vast majority of these narratives had male heroes. Among the best-known Soviet female martyrs are members of the anti-Nazi resistance in Krasnodon, described in Aleksandr Fadeev's 1945 novel *The Young Guard* [*Molodaia gvardiia*], and Zoia Kosmodem'ianskaia, who was hanged by the Nazis. As Helena Goscilo argues in her article in this collection, widowhood was the only position that allowed women to produce alternative narratives of self-abnegation.

21. "On vospel izmenu, no byl veren zhene." Interview with Galina Ivanova, *Komsomol'skaia Pravda*, <http://www.kp.ru/daily/23024.5/3455/>

22. Aleksandr Rogozhkin's series of films of various "particularities" of national culture sets out to transcend the divide between Russian and Soviet identities through bonding male bodies, united in drunken bliss that is accompanied by one-liner dialogue. Ironically, the only carrier of the memory of the beautiful Tolstoian Russia is a Finn—a former marginal subject of the Russo-Soviet empire.

References

Adamovich, Marina. "Ne dumai o 'Mgnoven'iakh' svysoka...." *Iskusstvo kino* 3 (2002): 74–85.

Ashwin, Sarah, ed. *Gender, State, and Society in Soviet and Post-Soviet Russia*. New York: Routledge, 2000.

Attwood, Lynne. "Gender Angst in Russian Society and Cinema in the Post-Stalin Era." *Russian Cultural Studies: An Introduction*. Ed. Catriona Kelly and David Shepherd. New York: Oxford UP, 1998. 352–67.

Baldwin, Kate. "Montezuma's Revenge: Reading *Los Ricos También Lloran* in Russia." *To Be Continued...: Soap Operas around the World*. Ed. Robert C. Allen. New York: Routledge, 1995. 285–300.

Butler, Jeremy. "Notes on the Soap Opera Apparatus: Televisual Style and *As the World Turns*." *Cinema Journal* 25.3 (Spring 1986): 53–70.

Cawelti, John. *Adventure, Mystery, and Romance: Formula Stories as Art and Popular Culture*. Chicago: U Chicago P, 1976.

Creed, Barbara. *The Monstrous-Feminine: Film, Feminism, and Psychoanalysis*. New York: Routledge, 1993.

Ellis, Frank. "The Media as Social Engineer." *Russian Cultural Studies: An Introduction*. New York: Oxford UP, 1998. 192–222.

Flitterman-Lewis, Sandy. "All's Well That Doesn't End—Soap Opera and the Marriage Motif." *Private Screenings: Television and the Female Consumer*. Ed. Lynn Spiegel and Denise Mann. Minneapolis: U Minnesota P, 1992. 217–26.

Gledhill, Christine. "The Melodramatic Field: An Investigation." *Home Is Where the Heart Is*. Ed. Christine Gledhill. London: BFI Publishing, 1987. 5–39.

Groys, Boris. *The Total Art of Stalinism: Avant-garde, Aesthetic Dictatorship, and Beyond*. Trans. Charles Rougle. Princeton: Princeton UP, 1992.

Haynes, John. *New Soviet Man: Gender and Masculinity in Stalinist Soviet Cinema*. Manchester: Manchester UP, 2003.

Hubbs, Joanna. *Mother Russia: The Feminine Myth in Russian Culture*. Bloomington: Indiana UP, 1993.

Jeffords, Susan. *Hard Bodies: Hollywood Masculinity in the Reagan Years*. New Brunswick, NJ: Rutgers UP, 1994.

Kelly, Catriona. "The Retreat from Dogmatism: Populism under Khrushchev and Brezhnev." *Russian Cultural Studies: An Introduction*. Ed. Catriona Kelly and David Shepherd. New York: Oxford UP, 1998. 249–73.

Lipsitz, George. "The Meaning of Memory: Family, Class, and Ethnicity in Early Network Television." *Private Screenings: Television and the Female Consumer*. Ed. Lynn Spigel and Denise Mann. Minneapolis: U Minnesota P, 1992. 71–110.

Martín-Barbero, Jesús. "Memory and Form in the Latin American Soap Opera." *To Be Continued...: Soap Operas around the World*. Ed. Robert C. Allen. New York: Routledge, 1995. 276–84.

McReynolds, Louise, and Joan Neuberger, eds. *Imitations of Life: Two Centuries of Melodrama in Russia*. Durham: Duke UP, 2002.

Mosse, George. *The Creation of Modern Masculinity*. New York: Oxford UP, 1996.

Neuberger, Joan. "Between Public and Private: Revolution and Melodrama in Nikita Mikhalkov's *Slave of Love*." *Imitations of Life: Two Centuries of Melodrama in Russia*. Ed. Louise McReynolds and Joan Neuberger. Durham: Duke UP, 2002.

Propp, Vladimir. *Morphology of the Folktale*. Trans. Laurence Scott. Austin: U of Texas P, 2000.

Rofel, Lisa. "The melodrama of national identity in post-Tiananmen China." *To Be Continued...: Soap Operas around the World*. Ed. Robert C. Allen. New York: Routledge, 1995. 301–20.

Semnadtsat' mgnovenii vesny [*Seventeen Moments of Spring*]. Dir. Tat'iana Lioznova. Screenplay by Iulian Semennov. Perf. Viacheslav Tikhonov, Leonid Bronevoi, Oleg Tabakov, Ekaterina Gradova, Rostislav Pliatt. Gorky Film Studios; commissioned by Gosteleradio, 1973. 12 episodes.

Semnadtsati mgnovenii vesny. 25 let spustia [*Seventeen Moments of Spring. 25 Years Later*]. Dir. Sergei Kozhevnikov and Aleksandr Lebine. NTV/Dixi, 1998.

Shapiro, Michael J. *Cinematic Political Thought: Narrating Race, Nation, and Gender*. New York: New York UP, 1999.

Teni ischezaiut v polden' [*Shadows Disappear at Noon*]. Dir. Valerii Uskov and Vladimir Krasnopol'skii. Screenplay by Anatolii Ivanov. Perf. Petr Vel'iaminov, Nina Ruslanova, Lev Poliakov, Vladimir Samoilov, Aleksandra Zav'ialova. Mosfilm, 1971. 7 episodes.

Vechnyi zov [*Eternal Call*]. Dir. Valerii Uskov and Vladimir Krasnopol'skii. Screenplay by Anatolii Ivanov and Konstantin Isaev. Perf. Valerii Khlevinskii, Vadim Spiridonov, Petr Vel'iaminov, Ivan Lapikov, Ada Rogovtseva. Mosfilm, 1974–1977. 19 episodes.

Zemlianukhin, Sergei and Miroslava Segida. *Domashniaia sinemateka: otechestvennoe kino, 1918–1996*. Moscow: Dubl'-D, 1996.

Zorkaia, Neia. *Fol'klor. Lubok. Ekran*. Moscow: Iskusstvo, 1994.

SEVEN | From "Demographic Crisis" to "Dying Nation" The Politics of Language and Reproduction in Russia

MICHELE RIVKIN-FISH

In Natal'ia Baranskaia's 1969 novella, *A Week Like Any Other* [*Nedelia kak nedelia*], the women researchers of a polymer lab are required to complete a questionnaire explaining their reproductive behavior and measuring their ability to fulfill both work and domestic responsibilities. "If you have no children, then for what reason: medical reasons, living conditions, family situation, personal considerations, etc. (Underline your reason)," the survey demands. "Days excused from work on account of illness: yours, your children's (the number of work days for the past year; we ask you to give the information based on the time sheet)." The office of human resources calculates the workdays each has lost owing to her children's illnesses and makes the grand totals public. For most of the coworkers, these numbers express in condensed terms a complex set of dilemmas that all female worker-mothers endure under conditions of socialist shortages, and they inspire sympathy for the personal dimensions of a socially based double burden. Yet for a minority of the women, the questionnaire makes visible an authentic collective concern about fertility decline that has led their country to a "serious and even dangerous" demographic crisis (Baranskaia).

Through the researchers' immediate reaction to the questionnaire and the ensuing events in the novella Baranskaia exposes in stark terms the frantic, frustrating rhythms of Soviet women's daily grind, their dire lack not only of choice in reproductive matters but also of control over their personal and professional destinies. Yet few Soviet officials recognized or appreciated these dilemmas. From the late 1960s to the early 1990s obligatory demographic surveys such as the one motivating Baranskaia's plot were a standard mode of establishing why women failed to bear sufficient numbers of children for "society's sake." Official publications continuously informed the Soviet and post-Soviet public that the country's demographic situation must be studied and made a matter of everyone's concern, while experts proposed policies to raise the birthrate in European regions of the Soviet Union and Russia for just as long. Russian women largely have responded to such efforts as does Baranskaia's fictional character Olga: with cynicism, frustration, and a determined insistence on keeping reproductive decisions personal.

This chapter examines the ways reproductive politics in Russia have shifted from the late 1960s, when the government announced a "demographic crisis" in the European regions of the Soviet Union, until the year 2003. The concerns over low fertility that Baranskaia used to depict her society during the Brezhnev era persist amidst post-Soviet reforms and have acquired even greater cultural and political salience. Indeed, the monitoring of fertility rates and attempts to manipulate them constitute a primary vehicle for nationalist revival in contemporary Russia. Similar processes have occurred since the 1990s throughout Eastern Europe. At the same time, pronatalism and opposition to abortion manifest a degree of cultural specificity in Russia, and it is instructive to analyze the particular arguments and coalitions that have—and have not—emerged in Russian reproductive politics. Throughout, I underscore the centrality of discourse in reproductive politics, for the negotiation and manipulation of language is what reinscribes and imbricates population and nation, women and Russia in the Soviet and post-Soviet public spheres.

Debates surrounding demography and reproduction illuminate both the politics of gender and the broader political transformations currently underway in Russia. Alarm over the size and quality of "the Russian nation" increasingly pervaded public discourse during the 1990s.[1] Long-standing concerns with falling fertility rates transformed into a social panic and yielded imagery of an impending national catastrophe. In an extraordinary move, Communist opponents sought to impeach Boris Yeltsin on grounds that included his role in advancing the "genocide of the Russian people" through population decline. Vladimir Putin, in his first address to the public upon taking office, warned that the country's decreasing population posed a serious threat to "Russia's survival as a nation, as a people. . . . We are really threatened with the prospect of wasting away as a nation" (Putin; Feshbach, "Russia's Population Meltdown" 15–22). Communist and nationalist supporters tended to be the most apocalyptic in their descriptions, often comparing Russia's population losses with the ravages of war, bombings, and plague; one demographer and communist supporter characterized the falling population as a "demographic Chernobyl" (Khorev 1–45). With discussions of fertility rates closely linked to issues of women's sexual, reproductive, and professional practices on the one hand, and national survival on the other, reproductive politics represents an arena of central importance for analyzing the mutually constitutive entities of gender and nation in contemporary Russia.

In examining the centrality of gender to post-socialist transitions throughout Eastern Europe, Susan Gal and Gail Kligman note that control over reproduction became a key arena for reconstituting political agency and renewing legitimacy for political elites (Gal 256–86; Gal and Kligman). When state systems undergo radical transformation, elites may politicize reproductive issues for several goals: facilitating the reconfiguration of relations between citizens and the state, establishing new criteria for asserting political and moral legitimacy, and constructing women as certain kinds of citizens whose roles and responsibilities may be defined through politically useful categories (such as biology/nature, social norms, or liberal ideologies of the rational subject). Additionally, reproductive politics enables those vying for power to pursue campaigns for nationalist supremacy against ethnic others defined as outsiders and threats (Gal). Reproductive issues are thus important for post-socialist political contenders in part because, as elsewhere in the world, the nation is defined as a biological entity, with the national essence (blood, genes, etc.) transferred and preserved—or lost—through the physical process of procreation (Borneman; Brubaker; Herzfeld; Ginsburg and Rapp). In this paradigm, the nation's continuity cannot be achieved through cultural or social processes alone. Childbearing is deemed necessary, resulting in the constant monitoring of fertility—that of one's own nation and of others'.[2]

While Russian discourses on demographic crises and reproductive politics bear the traces of a Soviet legacy in which gender and nation have long been mutually implicated (Massell), current versions also reveal one of the ways the country is reconfiguring national identity following the dissolution of the Soviet Union. Since Soviet ideology rejected discrimination on the basis of ethnic or national identity,[3] demographic discourses before 1991 muted overtly nationalist rhetoric. By contrast, contemporary discourses on population dynamics and reproduction increasingly emphasize putative biological properties of the Russian nation, glossed as the Russian "gene pool" (see the chapter by Borenstein in this volume). They often construct the presence of other ethnic groups in Russia as competition, if not outright threats, to the nation's security and prosperity. This intensification of ethnic-based discourses has occurred in the context of unprecedented population trends triggered by the breakup of the Soviet Union in 1991. Although Russia experienced a declining birthrate since the late 1960s, it fell further after the collapse of the Soviet Union, while the mortality rate rose.

In 1992, the Russian Federation registered negative population growth. The Russian media seized on this demographic event as an ominous sign of physical loss and linked it conceptually with a range of other signs of Russia's diminishing vitality: territorial losses following the dissolution of the Soviet Union, population losses resulting from Russians' increased emigration to the West, and new patterns of migration from former Soviet republics into Russia. Public discourses spotlighted these substantial changes in population size and composition, which many sociologists and politicians characterized as signs of profound national vulnerability (DaVanzo; Demko, Ioffe, and Zayonchkovskaya). The representation of these trends has shifted the discursive framing of population processes themselves, as well as the significance attributed to demographic trends for the society and the nation.

Soviet demographic discourses of the 1960s and 1970s cited the state's needs to rationally plan and ensure adequate supplies of labor, pension resources, and military personnel as the chief reasons for concern over population trends and low fertility (Perevedentsev 12–13; Borisov). Other reasons included the Soviet Union's stature in the geopolitical realm and, what was a more sensitive and thus less openly discussed matter, the perceived need to maintain numerical balances between non-Slavic and Slavic ethnicities in the multiethnic state (Desfosses, "Population Policy"; Kvasha). The threat of depopulation loomed in the background—as a worrisome but distant possibility that might begin in a hundred years or so (Borisov). When fertility declined dramatically and negative population growth began, politicians, journalists, and demographers seized upon chilling demographic and public health statistics to establish the parlous state of the Russian population. Professional observers of Russia throughout the world contributed to this perception, repeating the notion of a severe demographic "crisis" (Feshbach, "A Country on the Verge"; Field; Eberstadt; Tayler). While some continued to discuss the implications of falling population size for questions of labor supplies and pension funding, Russian nationalists took this discourse to another level of panic, hyperbolically, as evidence that the nation was literally "dying out." Demographic indicators became a staple ingredient of broader public laments that fashioned Russia as undergoing massive societal disintegration and disarray; demographic analyses themselves frequently became framed as litany, a culturally resonant genre in Russia that, as Nancy Ries has persuasively shown, links individual and collective moments of suffering with the eternal saga and destiny of the Russian people (Ries). By appropriating such genres, analysts of fertility, mortality, and public health data tapped into key sources of cultural power and extended the scope of their authority from bureaucratic matters of state planning and politics to the very production of Russianness, the Russian experience, and the future of the Russian nation.

In seeking to reverse demographic decline, Russian nationalists took longer than their counterparts in neighboring Eastern Europe to limit abortion access. Whereas conservatives in Poland, Hungary, and Germany openly attacked abortion at the legislative level immediately after independence in the early 1990s, Russian activists initially eschewed the outright pursuit of criminalization, to which there has been widespread public opposition. Instead, their tactics employed indirect strategies for limiting women's reproductive options by working symbolically to delegitimize abortion and empirically to cripple the work of newly established family planning organizations and sex educators. Nationalists, for example, portrayed contraceptive services as a danger for the survival of the Russian people, and as strategic tactics by Western organizations intended to accelerate Russia's depopulation through the introduction of family planning programs. In draft laws proposing to restrict women's access to abortion, they surreptitiously buried the abortion issue within broader legislation concerning "bioethics" or the "protection of mothers and children" (Bateneva, "Nevezhestvo" 1,7; Ballaeva). The discourse on the "death of the nation" thus served as a legitimating framework for promoting policies with little support among the public at large. Tapping into widespread anxieties about Russia's vitality and global position, reproductive political maneuvers enlisted gender and sexuality in the struggle for a nationalist revival. By the summer of 2003, nationalists achieved success: the Russian Ministry of Health instituted the first restrictions on abortion since Stalin.

Soviet Debates over the "Demographic Crisis"

To understand the significant kinds of shifts that have occurred over the last decade, it is first necessary to examine Soviet-era discourses on reproduction and demographic crisis. An aspect of this history that has already been well documented involves the hypocrisy of Soviet reproductive health policies, which strongly discouraged abortion but provided almost no alternative methods of fertility control (Popov and David 223–77, esp. 241–42). Fewer scholars have examined the broader contours of Soviet efforts to boost population growth through reproductive politics (Lapidus 293–95; Desfosses, "Pronatalism"; Rivkin-Fish, "Anthropology"). Yet demographic debates over childbearing have had important implications for women's domestic and public roles; they paved the way for the recent marriage of post-Soviet reproductive politics and vibrant nationalism.

By the late 1960s, Soviet demographers realized that in the two decades since the end of World War II, there had been no significant or sustained rise in fertility. This pattern was worrisome, since demographers and politicians widely viewed a national demographic politics as necessary for planning the socialist state; predicting and organizing labor supplies and pension resources; accumulating military power; and maintaining the Soviet Union's status as an international superpower (Perevedentsev). These experts and politicians also interpreted the fertility rate as a measure of social stability: declines in childbearing, in conjunction with rising divorce rates, appeared as evidence that marriages were unstable and individuals were insufficiently committed to realizing "societal interests" in and through their family life.

Attempts to explain the causes of low fertility throughout the 1970s and 1980s, however, were cause for debate, with no consensus on how best to increase childbearing. Within demographic circles, one group of scholars argued that many women were limiting their births because poor material conditions prevented them from bearing and raising children. They argued that decreased childbearing stemmed from the burdens women faced in trying to manage domestic responsibilities while being employed full-time (Piskunov and Steshenko; Volkov; Kuznetsova 33–35). Low fertility would best be surmounted, in their view, by offering more services to working mothers, socializing child care more completely, and reducing women's work responsibilities by providing part-time options and longer maternity leaves. They emphasized the results of extensive survey data that revealed disparities between women's ideal and expected numbers of children in order to highlight the impact of difficult living conditions on reproductive decisions. These demographers' writings, which reproduced the hegemonic pronatalism of the Soviet era, should be read with caution and placed in the context of the times. Without challenging the notion that the state must work to raise the birthrate—an ideologically inadmissible position during the Soviet era—these experts nonetheless sought to introduce what they termed "the needs of the family" into discussions of reproductive policy. Thus, they also advocated increased availability of contraceptive services and technologies, to enable families' control over conception and to reduce the rates of abortion and secondary infertility that often resulted from the process. One may read their analyses and policy recommendations as oblique criticism of the state dominance over personal life practiced under the Soviet regime (Rivkin-Fish, "Anthropology").

Another group of fertility specialists, by contrast, argued that direct interventions to immediately increase the fertility rate must be the unequivocal priority of demographic politics. These discourses depicted women's refusal to bear more than one or two children as a selfish rejection of both family life and the demographic needs of society. Some experts considered the possibility that women's "emancipation" into the labor force had resulted in the loss of their "maternal instinct" (Kvasha 151). Policy recommendations deriving from this perspective placed minimal emphasis on the value of improving living standards because, as one prominent specialist emphasized, better economic conditions are associated with lower, not higher, fertility (Antonov, *Sotsiologiia rozhdaemosti*). The alleged solution was to mobilize the state's arsenal of propaganda tools in order to promote the status of motherhood, to make the prospect of having multiple children more popular, and to celebrate the importance of home life (Antonov, *Demograficheskoe povedenie;* Sinel'nikov 47–51). These experts portrayed women's concerns and perceived obstacles to childbearing as at best misguided and at worst morally corrupt. At its core, their perspective denied the possibility that women and/or families could have legitimate interests that contradicted the needs of society as a whole. Demographers in this camp argued that all of society had shared interests, that population experts were best suited to discern these demographic and familial interests, and that they should therefore develop a national demographic policy to raise fertility in European regions of the USSR. The desired norm was two to three children per couple, to be achieved by instilling the value of a "midsize family" in the public consciousness. Justifying the need for this policy, demographers argued that the family should see no contradiction in complying with the state's demands to bear more children even in difficult living conditions, because in the long run, higher fertility would lead the nation as a whole to greater wealth and development (Kvasha 116–17).

As attention to fertility increased throughout the 1970s and 1980s and the "values" theory of reproductive motives gained prominence, experts and the media more frequently depicted childbearing as women's "most important biological and social function" and the "family's obligation to society" (Antonov, *Sotsiologiia rozhdaemosti*). In the view of one fertility specialist, Anatolii Antonov, small families (defined as those with one or two children) were a deviant and dangerous phenomenon that had arisen from the combination of two main factors: the loss of children's economic value to family survival, and the rise of a destructive, self-indulgent consumer mentality (*Sotsiologiia rozhdaemosti*). Leading the debates on demographic crisis since the mid-1970s, Antonov continually has urged the government to combat what he identified as the one-child family mentality (*odnodetnaia sem'ia*) rampant among the educated and professional classes and threatening to the moral and demographic base of Soviet/Russian society (*Sotsiologiia rozhdaemosti;* Antonov and Medkov; Antonov, *Sem'ia i deti;* Antonov, "Sem'ia kak institut"). To some extent, policy makers listened: it was certainly cheaper and easier to generate messages about family values than to resolve housing shortages and invest in child care resources.[4] So-called sex-role socialization courses were instituted in high schools to ensure that young women would not be derailed from cultivating their "maternal instinct" and that all young adults would be disciplined to embrace traditional stereotypes about women's and men's characters and societal roles (Attwood). Significantly, while few part-time opportunities or other improved conditions for women's employment materialized, policy makers extended maternity leaves. Writers in the popular press highlighted images of women as mothers and nurturers rather than workers (Posadskaia 79–88). Such representations were not coincidental: They often consciously remarked on the need to replace Bolshevik-era representations of women as the physically and mentally strong equals of men who would participate in all aspects of the building of communism with a renewed feminine image of maternity and domesticity.

The textbook used in high school sex-role socialization courses established during the late 1980s, *The Ethics and Psychology of Family Life,* launched a frontal attack against these perceived distortions in sex roles. Women have become "harsh, rude, and authoritarian," the textbook claims, and have "lost" characteristics once "inherent to feminine nature: spiritual kindness and attention to people, softness in manner and tact, gentleness and caring, and an ability to yield, to be weak": "The issue is that equal rights do not mean identity, sameness. The difference in the sexes has an existence in reality; nature has implanted in each girl and young woman a future mother and, consequently, placed on her a responsibility not only for herself, but for her future child" (Grebennikov et al. 69–70).

The new socialization efforts of the anxious, pronatalist state sought to disabuse adolescents of the notion that socialism had liberated them from biological and social imperatives. Equal rights did not extend to the creation of autonomous personal destinies: all girls were to recognize and accept their responsibility as future mothers. In this new ideology, the needs of nature and society fortuitously coincided.

From "Demographic Crisis" to the "Death of the Nation"

When the Soviet Union dissolved in 1991, Russian society entered a period of rapid and sweeping sociocultural transformation coupled with an acute economic crisis. Public health indicators of morbidity, mortality, and fertility expose the trials these changes inflicted on the lives of ordinary citizens. Morbidity rates in almost all categories of disease rose in the 1990s, not infrequently reaching epidemic proportions (Feshbach, "Russia's Population Meltdown"; Field). Diagnosed cases of active tuberculosis, for example, increased 2.2 times between 1991 and 1998, reaching a rate of 76 cases per 100,000 population (in comparison with U.S. rates of approximately 10 per 100,000); sexually transmitted diseases (STDs) rose astronomically, with syphilis reaching a rate of 277.6 per 100,000 population in 1997 (an increase of 64.5 over statistics for 1989, *Naselenie Rossii 1999*, 86). Children and adolescents experienced significant rises in morbidity as well: cancer in this demographic age group, for example, rose 2.9 times between 1991 and 1998, and diseases related to the endocrine system, digestive system, and immune system rose 3.9 times in the same period (*Naselenie Rossii 1999*, 90). Life expectancy for men fell from 64.87 years in 1987 to 57.49 years in 1994; it rose again in 1998 to 61.30 years but then fell to 58.96 in 2001 (*Naselenie Rossii 2001*, 99). At the same time, the birthrate plunged to new lows. The average number of children a woman would bear in her lifetime (the total fertility rate or TFR) fell from 1.89 in 1990 to 1.17 in 1999 and 1.25 in 2001 (*Naselenie Rossii 2001*, 36).[5] With high male mortality and sharp decreases in fertility, Russia has experienced a net population decline since 1992. As scholars have noted, such a rapid and intensive decline of public health indicators as occurred following the collapse of the Soviet Union is unprecedented in any country in modern history during peacetime (Field).

What has received far less attention than these statistics are the significant political and social effects of Russia's public health dilemmas, effects that transcend their physical and biological dimensions. For example, the specific ways this crisis has been reported in the Russian media and constructed in public debate have changed the significance attributed to population issues and the tenor of debates over fertility. Eclipsing Soviet-era concerns over low fertility as a problem for future labor supplies and state planning issues, current discourses make urgent, if not hysterical, claims that the Russian people have already begun the process of dying out. Headlines in mainstream newspapers announce that "Russia Has 100 Years to Live," or contain ominous announcements such as "Pediatricians Confirm That Russian Children Everywhere Are Physically and Mentally Deficient" (Derzhavina 1–2; Malakhova 1). Terms such as "dying out" (*vymiranie, ubyl'*), "depopulation" (*depopulatsiia*), and "degeneration" (*degredatsiia*) pervade newspapers, transforming demographic analysis into litany. The performative effects of this stylized discourse, a conventional genre in Russian history and culture for the expression and creation of "the people" (*narod*), the nation, and the essence of Russia, are multiple and profound. In its form and content the litany reproduces the cultural salience of Russia as long-suffering, enduring, and tragic. It likewise affirms the shared substance of the Russian people as a single, unified, biogenetic entity. Finally, it establishes conceptual closure, mobilizing a misrecognition of its own culturally productive work by banishing alternative discursive genres from its domain (Ries). My discussion combines the first two of these effects, then addresses the third.

Public health and population discourses explicitly and implicitly encourage readers and viewers to imagine the Russian nation as a single entity unified in common biological substance and suffering. This phenomenon occurs at one level through a constant discussion of physical demise and bodily illness. But it also proceeds from the litanous construction of the health crisis as a quintessentially *national* phenomenon, with the Russian populace *as a whole* depicted as ill, frail, and vulnerable. Some of this panicked and panic-causing reporting emanates from nationalist and communist activists, for whom "the death of the nation" offers a rhetorically sensational means of impugning market reforms and advocating a return to Soviet-style rule or nationalist alternatives. "The demographic situation . . . is called a crisis. That's not accurate. It's not a crisis, it's a national catastrophe. . . . The annihilation (*ubyl'*) of the population has acquired a stable pattern," said one activist from Zhirinovsky's Liberal Democratic Party in an article titled "To Stop the Nation from Dying Out" (*Ostanovit' vymiranie natsii*) in the newspaper *Izvestiia* (Semenov). The Communist Party introduced impeachment proceedings against Boris Yeltsin in part for perpetuating the "genocide of the Russian people" through his economic reforms. One prolific Communist demographer blamed market economics for "sentencing Russia to extinction" in part through "the feminization of poverty." He called for the eradication of the market, a return to price controls, and the reinstitution of a socialist welfare system (Khorev, "V chem ostrota"; Khorev, "Rynok").

Yet it is not only nationalist politicians who make the conceptual leap from acknowledging the public health crisis to litanizing about the "death of the nation." In the summer of 2000 the mainstream business newspaper *Delovoi Peterburg,* for example, invited a range of community leaders and concerned professionals to a roundtable discussion about the demographic crisis and necessary steps for resolving it. "Petersburg knows how to make babies, but can't," mourned the headline of an article covering the event, which was described as a conversation about "the extent of the tragedy and measures for raising fertility" ("Kak delat' detei" 8–9). The two-page spread included a color photograph of four bony, adolescent-sized legs buried in hay, a morbid image of life cut off, extinguished. Notably, while

the newspaper emphasized the negative consequences of population decline for the "market," "economic and social spheres," and the "development of productive ideas," the specialists participating in the discussion focused on the dire national and moral consequences of the below-replacement
birthrate, making explicit links between national continuity, reproduction,
and the need to preserve the Russian "gene pool." The introduction to the
article announced that the survival of the nation itself was at stake, suggesting in its opening paragraphs that "in order to avoid the degeneration
of the nation" Russia should heed the example of prosperous countries,
which "pay mothers substantial entitlements to enable them to raise children without being impoverished" ("Kak delat' detei" 8).

The article included comments by a medical director from the Russian-
based International Center of Reproductive Technologies, which treats infertile couples in part through the use of donor sperm. He lamented that only
a tiny proportion of men who answered the center's inquiry to become donors
were deemed healthy enough to do so. Without providing specifics regarding
the kinds of health problems or criteria for assessing men's health, he stated
that out of 2,000 respondents, only seven became donors. The status of men's
health holds national importance, he claimed: "I agree that it's necessary to
strengthen the health of future mothers, but it is also necessary to attentively
study men's health. Nobody's dealing with the maintenance of the gene pool.
That should be a government program" ("Kak delat' detei" 9).

As this passage reveals, laments about Russia's ill health underscore the
presumed genetic basis of the Russian nation and make it the springboard
for a renewed reproductive politics. Russia's decline and suffering are directly linked with its failure to reproduce, often explained now as the physical inability to do so. Many texts portray Russians as incapable of producing healthy offspring: repeated abortions have left women infertile (Baidan
3), and men likewise suffer diminished fertility levels ("Kak delat' detei" 9).
Similarly, discussions of pregnant women emphasize complications such as
toxemia, extra-genital infections, and other illnesses; babies who are carried
through to term are described as suffering from birth traumas, birth defects,
and health insufficiencies (Baidan; Gorbachova; Kostiuk). Children continue to undergo nutritional inadequacies and other health problems
throughout their childhood, according to these litanies (Baranov). The
country's chief pediatrician, Aleksandr Baranov, has reported appreciable
declines in all main categories of children's physical health, including
weight, height, chest size, and muscle strength. The universalizing portrayal of all Russians as equally vulnerable and diseased is thus qualified
only by age and sex: men's illnesses and low life expectancy owing to accidents, alcoholism, and cardiovascular disease receives attention, though
most often without qualifications as to the contributing role of socioeconomic status on these indicators. Articles on girls' and women's health also
disregard socioeconomic issues but focus the analysis even more narrowly on
reproductive issues, while concerns unrelated to fertility and women's roles as

mothers are generally ignored (the main exception being the media's vast coverage of beauty-related matters, Bassom 233–63). One typical article reads:

> The state of health of our fellow citizens has deteriorated substantially. Women are ailing and therefore give birth to ailing babies. Normal births account for 31.8%, and in some regions only 25%. Infertility occurs among 15% of married couples.
>
> But even those babies who are born are often unhealthy. One in three newborns has defects. . . . Among schoolchildren, only 10% to 12% in the younger grades are healthy, 8% in the middle grades, and 5% in the upper grades are [healthy]. . . . Fifty percent of teenagers aged 15 to 17 suffer from chronic ailments. The frequency of gynecological diseases among girls has tripled, and one in ten abortions is performed before the age of 19. One can imagine the kind of offspring that today's children may produce. An ailing generation is now entering the active working and childbearing years. (Gorbachova)

In this passage, the scope of analysis quickly moves from the nation as a whole, of "our fellow citizens," to the health of women, whose morbidity is exclusively a matter of their reproductive capacities. As the generalized discussion of schoolchildren turns to focus on girls' health, the emphasis again shifts to discuss reproductive potential alone: the text underscores gynecological problems and abortions, with no mention of broader health factors. Nationalists in numerous historical and contemporary contexts have found this limited view of women as mothers or sex partners (in both cases, as determined by their biology) instrumental in facilitating a vision of the nation as ethnically homogeneous. Anxiety over the nation's purity legitimizes efforts to harness women's sexuality and reproductive potential for national needs (Ginsburg and Rapp; Anagnost; Davin; Grossman; Haggis; Korac; Ram and Jolly). Indeed, at the same time that Russian nationalists advocate the implementation of immediate pronatalist measures to save the Russian people from extinction, many reports in the mass media express anxiety over the presence of nonethnic Russian migrants. Newcomers from the Caucasus and former republics of the Soviet Union with largely Islamic populations are seen as posing particular threats to the preeminence of the Russian people on account of their higher fertility rates and supposed tendencies to embrace religious fundamentalism (Shumilin). Many observers advocate policies that will encourage the "return" of ethnic Russians from outside the Russian Federation to combat the demographic and social effects of non-Russian migration into Russia. Nationalists and others (referred to in local parlance as "patriots" and "Russophiles") also openly criticize intermarriage between Russians and non-Russians on this basis (Santana; Goble).

Framed as litanies, such demographic and public health analyses appear particularly persuasive, and not only because they seem to measure, chart, and warn of the nation's precarious state; by deploying a standard (and thus invisible) cultural idiomatic structure, they also disguise the partial and selective character of the data they present. Such "litany analyses" present demographic statistics without comparative data, either from other countries or from Soviet history. Experts and journalists alike rarely cite the sources of their data and virtually never include commentary about their methods of gathering data or the theories used in their analysis: numbers presumably speak for themselves. This undisciplined flood of statistics makes demographers, public health experts, and other observers of population dynamics seem like the nation's modern fortune-tellers, foreseeing its future by means of graphs and charts, and offering statistics-as-facts to create prognoses about whether current political efforts to save the nation from total extinction will succeed.

Almost none of these reports discusses the stratified character of health and disease, the ways poverty, wealth, and different forms of social displacement shape the health of distinct social groups. They assume poverty to be another characteristic of "the Russian nation," and rather uniformly distributed. Notably, few ever report health indicators of ethnic minorities within Russia. Nor does one get a sense of how some children *are* actually born healthy, who they are, and how they acquired their positive start— explanations that could potentially measure the particular effects of socioeconomic status, social capital, and education on people's lives. Nor do we find analyses of the particular factors that caused specific babies who were born healthy to deteriorate and suffer later in childhood. Instead, the imagery deployed creates a picture of Russia suffering as a collective: deprived of decent nutrition and health care, and exposed to myriad environmental dangers from infectious diseases to poor ecology and to the (apparently equally distributed) risks of substance abuse, drug addiction, alcoholism, and sexually transmitted diseases. What substitutes for a differentiated analysis is the sweeping image of the nation in its entirety as a shrinking, deteriorating, biological entity (Baranov).

An important exception to this trend is the work of demographers who since the 1970s have critiqued the discourse on the demographic crisis and continue to oppose pronatalist measures as antidemocratic and ineffective.[6] During the Soviet era these scholars argued against directed pronatalist interventions, maintaining that families should have the right to make their own choices about childbearing. Limited, indirect support of childbearing could be provided, they insisted, by offering better social services, child care, and health care resources such as contraceptives. Since the emergence of negative population growth and the latest pronatalist panic, these scholars have reformulated their argument about low fertility specifically to counteract self-proclaimed patriots' sensationalist laments that the nation is dying out. They emphasize specific causes of morbidity and mortality, including alcohol, cardiovascular disease, and trauma, which affect Russian men in particular (Shkolnikov), and they underscore universalizing trends of fertility decline found throughout the world. Instead of pronatalism, they advise the need for public health policies that target the problems of chronic diseases (Vishnevskii, "Russia"). These scholars call attention to the mythic character of pronatalist and alarmist discourses and strategically work to debunk "demographic myths," which they consider "hullabaloo" and the work of "dilettantes" (Zakharov). While claims to scientific objectivity are common among demographers in other countries, these Russian scholars' emphasis on the need for scientific objectivity is undoubtedly also a response to the Soviet legacy of ideologically motivated science and demography (Vishnevskii, "Ideologizirovannaiia demografiia"). Aligning themselves with the authority of science also serves as a defense against charges they have encountered that their opposition to pronatalism constitutes a betrayal of Russia and promotes "anti-patriotic" aims (see, for example, Khorev, "V chem ostrota"). Accordingly, scholars opposed to pronatalist politics privilege the necessity for retaining scientific objectivity in their analyses far more frequently and vocally than they advocate women's right to make childbearing decisions without state interference. They emphasize the significance of population dynamics for the state's development of social services such as pensions, housing, employment, and health care, ultimately because they speak to Russia's economic vitality and ability to compete successfully in a global market (Zakharov; Zhukov 44–46). Yet these arguments have not overcome the incendiary laments that the Russian nation is in its last gasp—a perspective that consumes the media and shapes public opinion.

Reproductive Politics: Fighting Abortion and an "Undeclared War" Against Russia

The Russian Federation guaranteed the right to abortion in a law passed on 23 June 1993. Article 36 of the law states: "Each woman has the right to make the decision about motherhood independently. The artificial termination of pregnancy is provided on the woman's demand up to 12 weeks of pregnancy, for social reasons up to 22 weeks pregnancy, and in the case of medical indicators and with the woman's agreement, irrespective of the time of gestation" (cited in Ballaeva 37).

In 1996, the list of acceptable "social reasons" was formalized to include pregnancy resulting from rape, the woman's unmarried status, occurrence of a divorce, the husband's death, homelessness, refugee status, incarceration of the woman or her husband, loss of parental rights, having a disabled husband or disabled child to care for, having three or more children already, loss of the woman's or her husband's job, and having a salary lower than the minimum living standard for one's region (Mishle 356). Despite this recognition that economic constraints often lead women to seek abortions, the state's rapid withdrawal of funding for health care in general, and the creation of loopholes that enable local governments to exclude abortion services from the list of insured medical procedures, restricted the actual availability of the procedure throughout the 1990s (Ballaeva 41–47).

Moreover, by the summer of 2003, nationalists succeeded in establishing restrictions on second-trimester abortions for the first time since the Stalin era. The new rules limit abortion to the first twelve weeks of gestation except under conditions of rape, imprisonment, the death or severe disability of one's husband, or the loss of parental rights. These new restrictions effectively cancel out the previously acceptable criteria known as "social reasons" (Pravitel'stvo RF; Timashova; Myers). This significant revision was not the first proposed, for throughout the 1990s nationalists drafted several bills aiming to chip away at abortion access. Deploying manipulative language intended to obscure the actual purpose of the proposed legislation, in 1993 abortion opponents submitted to Parliament a draft legislation bill entitled "For the Defense of the Family." It proposed establishing "the defense of rights of future mothers" by endowing citizenship rights to fetuses. Another legislative effort in 1998 to restrict abortion placed the procedure under the rubric of "bioethics" (Bateneva, "Nevezhestvo"). While neither of these bills passed, the ideas they represent have clearly gained increased legitimacy.

A politics of language sits at the core of these efforts. As pronatalists and nationalists vociferously oppose abortion, openness about sexuality, and the use of family planning, they have deployed the stratagem of reframing health issues and women's interests in terms of nationalist needs. Their attacks have taken place in large part through the manipulation of language and meaning—by denying the relation between contraceptive use and women's health and by redefining family planning programs as tactical weapons in a Western conspiracy to weaken Russia and hasten the nation's impending extinction.

The irony of pronatalists' hostility to family planning efforts cannot escape the observer familiar with organizations and practitioners of Russia's reproductive health establishment, for the content of their sex education and family planning projects reveals how devotedly they work to ensure women's capabilities to successfully bear children, to promote the moral revitalization of traditional families, and to support the nation's future vitality. Many Russian reproductive health clinics receive financial and moral support from Western antiabortion organizations for their work against abortion, including video players and videos such as *The Silent Scream,* a film that purports to show the suffering a fetus endures during an abortion. Donated literature from American antiabortion organizations abounds. During fieldwork in 1994–1995 in Saint Petersburg's women's clinics, for example, I saw on the walls of the area where women were waiting for their abortions graphic posters displaying photographs of aborted fetuses, framed by antiabortion propaganda declaring the procedure "murder." Many practitioners whom I met in Russia, including those working in clinics that provide abortions, asserted that they viewed abortion as "a sin" and "murder." In fact, none of these institutions wants to be identified—either tacitly or explicitly—with its promotion or moral sanction.

Even those Russian organizations with ties to the global reproductive rights movement do not publicly advertise the issue of reproductive rights. When the Russian Family Planning Association was established in 1992 as a branch of the nongovernmental International Federation of Planned Parenthood, it received the blessing of the Yeltsin administration for its contribution to the reduction of abortions and to the solution of the country's demographic crisis. Activists in the early 1990s who first attempted to develop sex education programs for Russian schoolchildren and teenagers conceived their cause as strengthening reproductive health and family life. The doctors and psychologists who initiated such projects were concerned and horrified at the sharply rising rates of pregnancy and sexually transmitted disease among teens. These experts determined to combat both the ignorance created by the Soviet regime's campaign to eradicate sexuality from public life and the vulgar misinformation disseminated in the ubiquitous pornography accompanying post-Soviet market "democracy." Accordingly, their lectures didactically insisted that sexual desire is a natural and necessary part of human life and that sex is most safely and morally experienced when contained within family life and expressed in "cultured" ways (Rivkin-Fish, "Sexuality Education"). These fledgling steps in sex education did not lead to its institutionalization in Russian schools or elsewhere. Clinics offering such programs were often specialized centers in reproductive health staffed by highly educated, liberal members of the intelligentsia unafraid to risk publicly addressing such taboo topics as masturbation, sexual pleasure, and homosexuality. Some clinics forged ties with international organizations that developed sex education programs and received support in the form of supplies, educational resources, and moral encouragement. Many also gladly accepted such assistance from international antiabortion organizations, without necessarily seeing a contradiction between the two. Among Russian activists, extensive cooperation exists between many reproductive health clinics and antiabortion proponents, described in the Web sites of organizations such as Human Life International (*Culture of Life*).

Nevertheless, nationalist activists portrayed sex education and family planning programs as morally outrageous, foreign intrusions designed to warp Russian youth psychologically and to brainwash them into a contempt for family life. Targeting for particularly vociferous protest one pilot program sponsored by UNESCO, nationalist opponents depicted the project as a foreign conspiracy to pervert Russian children and promote the nation's depopulation (Baidan). Their success in derailing the UNESCO project inspired more attacks and has led to the wide delegitimation of sex education. Projects I observed operating in 1994–1995 in Saint Petersburg had disappeared by 2000, their supporters unable to withstand pressure from critics and public protest.

The politics of reproduction thus has recourse to the politics of language: nationalist, pronatalist attacks on family planning reveal the power of rhetoric. One revealing text, for instance, equates sex education and family planning programs with the deliberate tactics of an "undeclared, neo-fascist war against Russia," an imperialist battle whose weapons are cynical deception and conspiracy (Medvedeva and Shishova). It posits historical links between today's family planning movement and eugenics advocates from the turn of the twentieth century. Margaret Sanger, the American birth control crusader and founder of the family planning concept, is portrayed as the architect of a rationalized, effective, and affordable model of genocide that gradually lulls victims into committing mass suicide by controlling and curtailing their fertility (Medvedeva and Shishova). The article impugns current family planning work in Russia for putatively concealing its eugenic purposes in order to perpetuate the fascist goals of eliminating undesirables: in this case, Russians. Educating people to accept sterilization, they explain, is a much more effective way of reducing their vigor than bombing them. The main tactic for realizing these machinations, nationalists assert, involves a method pioneered by Sanger and maintained today: the use of an Orwellian language of euphemism that purposefully camouflages the actual goals and ultimate objective of family planning/sex education programs.

> Our fatherland's [*otechestvennye*] followers of Margaret Sanger use phrases such as "reproductive health," "reproductive rights," "healthy lifestyles," "safe motherhood," "responsible parenthood," and "healthy and wanted children" to deceive Russians into accepting and complying with programs that aim to reduce Russia's vitality and ultimately, further its national extinction. (Medvedeva and Shishova)

Although acknowledging that some (misled if not disloyal) Russians have been drawn into the enemy camp, this discourse pivots on a fundamental dichotomy between Russians and alien, hostile Westerners: Russians love children and family, while Westerners have little interest or time for offspring; Russians are ailing and weak, while Westerners seek to further their demise by emphasizing the need to reduce populations and control births. One article claims that 20 percent of couples in England reject childbearing, while Stockholm is labeled a "post-family city," where two-thirds of the residents have been so permeated with Sanger's idea of "free love" that they never had or plan to have a family (Medvedeva and Shishova 4). Associated with this alleged difference between Russians and Western outsiders is the inherent link between traditional, rigid gender differences and Russian national identity. Another article by a Russian criticizes sex education programs for representing ideas alien to "Russian people's thinking, culture, and way of life," manifested in the programs' "language, style, overall thrust and approach . . . [which are replete with] translations and paraphrases from a foreign language" (Molodtsova). To contrast with such perverse ideas, this writer affirms the masculine virility of the Russian peasant (*muzhik*). In a defensive attack against a sex education program in Vologda, which is accused of trying to "impose behavioral patterns that are characteristic of the opposite sex," the article cites what is supposed to be a typical statement from the project (quoted but not referenced in any way): "In order to be a real human being, a man must not only be strong and brave, but [must] also adopt a number of traditionally 'feminine' qualities." The article goes on to challenge this notion as absurd and dangerous: "Now tell me, what does a future Vologda farmer need with traditionally 'feminine' qualities? Will they help him plant crops, fell timber, harvest grain or embrace women, so that after passionate caresses they'll give birth to robust boys to carry on the family name?" (Molodtsova 5). It is the Russian peasant, with his traditional habits and character, who epitomizes the essence of masculinity, the author insists, as she rhetorically berates audacious foreigners for daring to pollute Russia's cultural, biological, and genetic stock with their subversive program for crossing genders.

Such efforts have directly interfered with the work of the Russian Family Planning Association. In the spring of 1997, representatives of conservative coalitions, who had formed a public committee called "For the Moral Regeneration of the Fatherland," sponsored by the Russian Orthodox Church, working in collaboration with the nationalist activists, submitted to the Duma batches of signed petitions asking the government to rescind funding for family planning. The Duma made the topic the subject of a roundtable discussion on "Family Planning in the Context of Russia's National Security" and subsequently voted to end funding of its presidential family planning program, which had been established in the early 1990s. The funding and moral support of this program has not been reinstituted (Babasyan). On the legislative front, Church organizers promoted a 1997 draft law that would have made abortion illegal in all but medically indicated cases (Bateneva, "Na sobach'em urovne"). While this draft law failed to pass, the growing strength of this coalition between church-based abortion opponents and nationalist activists should not be underestimated. Their strategies for forging a politics of reproduction through the political manipulation of language have succeeded in linking childbearing to the nation's survival and entangling anti-Western sentiment with opposition to family planning in a substantial proportion of public debate. With the necessity to reverse population decline deemed ever more urgent, and invoked by calls for moral revival in the face of corrupting Western ideologies, nationalists' insistence on seizing control over women's fertility appears increasingly acceptable.

Conclusion: The Paradox of Women's Responses

In marked contrast to their equivalents in some parts of the former socialist world, Russia's women's organizations and self-identified feminist groups have not taken an active interest in reproductive politics. To some extent, what accounts for this phenomenon is the reluctance, both among the Russian public at large and among most experts in the reproductive health field, to entirely criminalize abortion (Borisov, Sinelnikov, and Arkhangelsky 24). At least for now, the memory of Stalinist repression remains a sobering reminder of the futility of criminalization, even among many Russians who equate abortion with "murder." Yet the near-absence of an active opposition to pronatalist and antiabortion rhetoric is particularly striking in the context of broader changes in media representations of women's lives. Discussions in the popular press regarding the obstacles facing women who attempt to combine labor inside and outside the home—a staple of public discourse on fertility rates and demographic crisis during the Soviet era—have been eclipsed under the new market conditions: Low fertility is now more often construed as a symptom of economic turbulence for the family as a whole, with women's participation in the labor force no longer seen as inevitable (Bridger, Kay, and Pinnick). Working with strained energies and resources, women's groups have focused much of their energy on women's practical and economic survival, not on public relations campaigns to link women's economic constraints with the issue of reproductive autonomy (Sperling; Hemment). The urgent economic concerns of daily life have taken precedence over what seem to be less immediately threatening and longer-range struggles, such as the defense of reproductive rights and access to abortion and contraception.

By contrast, advocates of the idea that abortion entails "murder" and "sin" have led lively public campaigns and succeeded in thwarting or impeding family planning and sex education programs initiated in the 1990s. Moreover, nationalists, communists, and many demographers persistently formulate political proposals for the immediate implementation of pronatalist measures. As antiabortion politics around the world demonstrates, the legislative path towards prohibition often works in stages, gaining public support gradually and establishing partial restrictions on the way towards complete criminalization. There is no guarantee that Russian opposition to restricting abortion further will remain widespread.

I suggest that Russian women's avoidance of reproductive politics may result from the hegemony achieved by the rhetoric and politics of pronatalism. In a context where citizenship is increasingly coming to be defined on the basis of ethno-national identity, and the biogenetic substance of the ethno-nation is perceived at risk, defending reproductive rights undoubtedly courts the danger of appearing to oppose the very survival of "the Russian nation." Claims that women have the "right to choose," to reject childbearing, could leave women's groups vulnerable to charges of national betrayal, of working in concert with foreign interests against the nation. Accordingly, even family planning services in Russia represent themselves as strengthening women's reproductive health and family life, never as defending the right to abortion. The Russian Family Planning Association, for example, has neither criticized the latest restrictions on second trimester abortion nor called attention to the hardships this policy will bring some women. As nationalists and others engage in reproductive politics to save the Russian "gene pool" from extinction, they place the burden of national survival largely on women's childbearing and maternal obligations. In entangling concepts of women and nation in mutually constituting, naturalizing ways, they make the potential costs of resistance appear dire.

Notes

1. Russians have expressed concern over demographic processes since the 1920s, but arguments that the nation is "dying out" are a post-Soviet phenomenon. For an analysis of the earliest demographic anxieties, see Solomon.

2. Slobodan Milosevic, for example, warned Serbs of the threat posed by Albanians' high birthrate in order to instigate a sense of national vulnerability and to justify pronatalist measures. Similarly, nationalists in Bulgaria view Turks and Roma as ethnic others whose higher rates of reproduction must be combated to save "the Bulgarian nation." Daskalova 351.

3. Of course, Soviet policies on nationalities and subnational groups were neither as simple nor as straightforward as state slogans pretended. See Edgar; Hirsch; Massell; Slezkine; Suny.

4. The pronatalist cause received some economic support, but nothing near the sweeping investments proposed by those demographers who appreciated the impact of women's double burden on their reproductive strategies. In 1974, the Soviet state established a child allowance program and extended maternity leave benefits. It further expanded these entitlements in 1981 for second and higher order births. The latter policy extended partially paid maternity leave to all women for increasingly longer periods, eventually culminating in a three-year maternity leave that exists to this day. See Helen Desfosses, "Pro-Natalism"; Feshbach, *The Soviet Population Policy Debate* 25; Zakharov and Ivanova, "Fertility Decline"; Jones and Grupp 275. The 1981 program called for enterprises to provide options for part-time work, flexible working hours, and work within the home, yet few such opportunities actually materialized. Despite the financial incentives offered for second and higher order births, fertility rates rose only briefly and did not stay high. Demographers examining these fluctuations in birthrates that followed the institution of pronatalist incentives argue that incentives affected the timing of births by motivating women to bear children earlier than they otherwise would, but did not impact the overall number of children women would have. See Zakharov and Ivanova, "Fertility Decline"; Zakharov.

5. For comparative figures, in 1995 Italy had a TFR of 1.17, Japan 1.42, and Denmark 1.80. Zakharov 44.

6. Zakharov and Ivanova, "Fertility Decline" and "Regional Fertility"; Zakharov; Vishnevskii, "Konservativnaia revoliutsiia," "Russkii krest" Parts 1–3, "Russia," and "Serb i rubl'."

References

Anagnost, Ann. "A Surfeit of Bodies: Population and the Rationality of the State in Post-Mao China." *Conceiving the New World Order.* Ed. Faye D. Ginsburg and Rayna Rapp. Berkeley: U California P, 1995. 22–41.

Antonov. A. I. *Demograficheskoe povedenie i vozmozhnosti sotsial'nogo vozdeistviia na nego v usloviakh sotsializma: po materialam mezhdunarodnoi nauchno-prakticheskoi konferentsii v Vilniuse, 1985 g.* Moscow: Akademiia nauk SSSR Intitut sotsiologicheskikh issledovanii, 1986.

———. *Sem'ia i deti.* Moscow: Izdatel'stvo Moskovskogo Universiteta, 1982.

———. "Sem'ia kak institut sredi drugikh sotsial'nykh institutov." *Sem'ia na poroge tret'ego tysiacheletiia.* Ed. A. I. Antonov and V. V. Negodin. Moscow: Institut Sotsiologii Rossiiskoi Akademii Nauk, Tsentr obshchechelovecheskikh tsennostei, 1995. 182–98.

————. *Sotsiologiia rozhdaemosti: Teoreticheskie i metodologicheskie problemy*. Moscow: Statistika, 1980.

Antonov, A. I., and V. M. Medkov. *Vtoroi rebenok*. Moscow: Mysl', 1987.

Attwood, Lynne. *The New Soviet Man and Woman: Sex Role Socialization in the USSR*. London: MacMillan/Centre for Russian and East European Studies, U Birmingham, 1990.

Babasyan, Natalia. "Freedom or 'Life': Secular and Russian Orthodox Organizations Unite in a Struggle against Reproductive Freedom for Women." *Current Digest of the Post-Soviet Press* [*CDPSP*] 51.12: 14. Rpt. and trans. from *Izvestia* 26 Feb. 1999.

Baidan, Natal'ia. "You Have to Save Up to Have a Baby." *CDPSP* 51.36: 16–17. Rpt. and trans. from *Vremya MN* 24 Aug. 1999: 3.

Ballaeva, E. A. *Gendernaia ekspertiza zakonodatel'stva RF: reproduktivnye prava zhenshchin v Rossii*. Moscow: Proekt gendernaia ekspertiza MTSGI [Moscow Center for Gender Studies], 1998.

Baranov, Aleksandr. "A Real Threat to the Nation's Future." *Russian Social Science Review* 39.4 (1998): 4–13.

Baranskaia, Natal'ia. *A Week Like Any Other* [*Nedelia kak nedelia*]. *The Massachusetts Review* (1974): 657–703. The story originally appeared in *Novyi mir* 11 (1969).

Bassom, Ann. "The Russian Press: Coverage of Women's Health." *Medical Issues and Health Care Reform in Russia*. Ed. Vicki L. Hesli and Margaret H. Mills. Lewiston, NY: Edwin Mellen Press, 1999. 233–63.

Bateneva, Tat'iana. "Na sobach'em urovne." *Izvestiia* 1 Apr. 1997: 5.

————. "Nevezhestvo pod vidom bioetiki." *Izvestiia* 13 Oct. 1998: 1, 7.

Borneman, John. *Belonging in the Two Berlins: Kin, State, Nation*. Cambridge Studies in Social and Cultural Anthropology. New York: Cambridge UP, 1992.

Borisov, Vladimir A. *Perspektivy rozhdaemosti*. Moscow: Statistika, 1976.

Borisov, Vladimir, Alexander Sinelnikov, and Vladimir Arkhangelsky. "Expert Opinions on Abortion in Russia." *Choices* 26.2 (1997): 23–26.

Bridger, Sue, Rebecca Kay, and Kathryn Pinnick. *No More Heroines? Russia, Women and the Market*. New York: Routledge, 1996.

Brubaker, Rogers. *Citizenship and Nationhood in France and Germany*. Cambridge: Harvard UP, 1992.

Culture of Life Being Rebuilt in Russia. Human Life International. 25 July 2001. Captured 4 Oct. 2001. <http://www.hli.org/Content/Dynamic/Articles/000/000/000/756biwba.asp>

Daskalova, Krassimira. "Women's Problems, Women's Discourses." *Reproducing Gender: Politics, Publics, and Everyday Life after Socialism*. Ed. Susan Gal and Gail Kligman. Princeton: Princeton UP, 2000. 337–69.

DaVanzo, Julie, ed. *Russia's Demographic 'Crisis'*. Santa Monica: RAND, 1996.

Davin, Anna. "Imperialism and Motherhood." *History Workshop Journal* 5 (1978): 9–65.

Demko, George J., Grigory Ioffe, and Zhanna Zayonchkovskaya, eds. *Population Under Duress: The Geodemography of Post-Soviet Russia*. Boulder, CO: Westview Press, 1999.

Derzhavina, Olga. "Russia has 100 Years to Live: The Country is Experiencing an Unprecedented Crisis." *CDPSP* 50.49: 16. Rpt. and trans. from *Segodnia* 7 Dec. 1998: 1–2.

Desfosses, Helen. "Population Policy in the USSR." *Problems of Communism* 22.4 (1973): 41–55.

————. "Pronatalism in Soviet Law and Propaganda." *Soviet Population Policy: Conflicts and Constraints*. Ed. Helen Desfosses. NY: Pergamon Press, 1981. 95–123.

Eberstadt, Nicholas. "Russia: Too Sick to Matter?" *Policy Review* (June–July 1999). <http://www.policyreview.org/jun99/eberstadt_print.html>

Edgar, Adrienne. "Genealogy, Class, and 'Tribal Policy' in Soviet Turkmenistan, 1924–1934." *Slavic Review* 60.2 (2001): 266–88.

Feshbach, Murray. "A Country on the Verge." *New York Times*. 31 May 2003. Rpt. in Johnson's Russia List. 7203, 31 May 2003.

———. "Russia's Population Meltdown." *Wilson Quarterly* 25.1 (2001): 15–22.

———. *The Soviet Population Policy Debate: Actors and Issues*. Santa Monica: RAND, 1986.

Field, Mark. "The Health Crisis in the Former Soviet Union: A Report from the 'Post-War' Zone." *Social Science and Medicine* 41.11 (1995): 1469–78.

Gal, Susan. "Gender in the Post-Socialist Transition: The Abortion Debate in Hungary." *East European Politics and Societies* 8.2 (1994): 256–86.

Gal, Susan, and Gail Kligman. *The Politics of Gender after Socialism: A Comparative-Historical Essay*. Princeton: Princeton UP, 2000.

Ginsburg, Faye D., and Rayna Rapp. *Conceiving the New World Order: The Global Politics of Reproduction*. Berkeley: U California P, 1995.

Goble, Paul. *Russia: Analysis from Washington—A Demographic Threat To Russian Security*. Radio Free Europe/Radio Liberty. 16 Feb. 2001. Captured 10 Apr. 2001. <http://www.rferl.org/nca/features/2001/02/16022001105257.asp>

Gorbachova, Ada. "Russia's Demographic Twilight." *CDPSP* 52.30: 7–8. Rpt. and trans. from *Nezavisimaya gazeta* 6 July 2000: 9.

Grebennikov, I. V., et al. *Etika i psikhologiia semeinoi zhizni: posobie dlia uchitelia*. Moscow: Prosveshchenie, 1987.

Grossman, Atina. "The New Woman and the Rationalization of Sexuality in Weimar Germany." *Powers of Desire: The Politics of Sexuality*. Ed. Ann Snitow, Christine Stansell, and Sharon Thompson. New York: Monthly Review Press, 1983. 153–75.

Haggis, Jane. "Good Wives and Mothers or Dedicated Workers: Contradictions of Domesticity in the Mission of Sisterhood, Travancore, South India." *Maternities and Modernities: Colonial and Postcolonial Experiences in Asia and the Pacific*. Ed. Kalpana Ram and Margaret Jolly. New York: Cambridge UP, 1998.

Hemment, Julie Dawn. "Gender, NGOs and the Third Sector in Russia: An Ethnography of Post-Socialist Civil Society." Ph.D. Dissertation, Cornell U, 2000.

Herzfeld, Michael. *The Social Production of Indifference: Exploring the Symbolic Roots of Western Bureaucracy*. Chicago: U of Chicago P, 1992.

Hirsch, Francine. "Toward an Empire of Nations: Border-Making and the Formation of Soviet National Identities." *Russian Review* 59 (Apr. 2000): 201–26.

Jones, Ellen, and Fred W. Grupp. *Modernization, Value Change and Fertility in the Soviet Union*. Cambridge: Cambridge UP, 1987.

"Kak delat' detei, Peterburg znaet. No ne mozhet." *Delovoi Peterburg* 22 June 2000: 8–9.

Khorev, Boris. "Rynok: podi pri nem rodi. . . ." *Pravda* 30 Mar 1995: 1–2.

———. "V chem ostrota demografand cheskoi problemy v Rossii?" *Rossiia i Mir (Informatsionnyi ekspress biulleten' dlia deputatov Gosudarstvennoi Dumy). Communist Party of the Russian Federation* (June 1997): 1–45.

Korac, Maja. "Ethnic-Nationalism, Wars and the Patterns of Social, Political and Sexual Violence against Women: The Case of Post-Yugoslav Countries." *Identities-Global Studies in Culture and Power* 5.2 (1998): 153–81.

Kostiuk, Elena. "'Government Contracts' for Babies Might Save the Nation." *CDPSP* 52.40: 17–18. Rpt. and trans. from *Vremya MN* 30 Sept. 2000: 1, 5.

Kuznetsova, Larisa. "Glazami Zhenshchiny." *Novoe Vremia* 10 (1989): 33–35.

Kvasha, Aleksandr I. Akovlevich. *Demograficheskaia politika v SSSR.* Moscow: Finansy i statistika, 1981.

Lapidus, Gail Warshofsky. *Women in Soviet Society: Equality, Development, and Social Change.* Berkeley: U California P, 1978.

Malakhova, Alla. "'Tsvety zhizni' vianyt na glazakh: Pediatry konstatiruiut povse-mestnuiu fizicheskuiu i umstvennuiu degradatsiiu russkikh detei." *CDPSP* 51.9: 7–8. Rpt. from *Novye izvestiia* 21 Jan. 1999: 1, 5.

Massell, Gregory J. *The Surrogate Proletariat: Moslem Women and Revolutionary Strategies in Soviet Central Asia, 1919–1929.* Princeton: Princeton UP, 1974.

Medvedeva and Shishova. "Demograficheskaia voina protiv Rossii." *Nash Sovremennik* 1. Rpt. at <http://nashsovr.aihs.net/main.php>

Mishle, Nadezhda. *Iuridicheskii spravochnik: zhenshchiny i deti: semeinoe pravo, trudovoe pravo, sotsial'nye l'goty.* Moscow: Filin', 1998.

Molodtsova, Viktoriia. "Public Sin Is Getting Thunderous Applause." *CDPSP* 51.45 (1999): 18. Rpt. and trans. from *Rossiiskaia gazeta* 22 Oct. 1999: 25.

Myers, Steven Lee. "After Decades, Russia Narrows Grounds for Abortions." *New York Times.* 24 Aug. 2003: 3.

Naselenie Rossii 1999. Moscow: Institut Narodnokhoziaistvennogo prognozirovaniia RAN Tsentr demografii i ekologii cheloveka, 2000.

Naselenie Rossii 2001. Moscow: Institut Narodnokhoziaistvennogo prognozirovaniia RAN Tsentr demografii i ekologii cheloveka, 2002.

Perevedentsev, V. "Continuation of a Controversy." *Studies in Family Planning, U.S.S.R.: Views on Population/Family Planning Theme.* 1.49 (1970): 12–13.

Piskunov, V. P., and V. C. Steshenko. "O demograficheskoi politike sotsialisticheskogo obshchestva." *Demograficheskaia politika.* Ed. V. C. Steshenko and V. P. Piskunov. Moscow: Statistika, 1974. 15–27.

Popov, Andrej, and Henry David. "Russian Federation and USSR Successor States." *From Abortion to Contraception: A Resource to Public Policies and Reproductive Behavior in Central and Eastern Europe from 1917 to the Present.* Ed. Henry David. Westport, CT: Greenwood Press, 1999. 223–77.

Posadskaia, A. I. "Tendentsii izmeneniia zakonodatel'stva v oblasti sotsial'noi zashchity materinstva." *Zhenshchiny i sotsial'naia politika: gendernyi aspect.* Ed. Z. A. Khotkina, Demografiia i sotsiologiia. Moscow: Institut sotsial'no-ekonomicheskikh problem narodonaseleniia, 1992. 79–88.

Pravitel'stvo RF. Postanovlenie No. 485. 11 Aug. 2003. "O perechne sotsial'nykh pokazanii dlia iskusstvennogo preryvaniia beremonnosti." Rpt. in *Demoscope Weekly* No. 123–24, 25 Aug.–7 Sept. 2003. <www.demoscope.ru/weekly/2003/0123/tema03.php>

Putin, Vladimir V. "The Kind of Russia We Are Building." *CDPSP* 52.28: 4–7. Rpt. and trans. from *Rossiiskaia gazeta* 11 July 2000: 1, 3.

Ram, Kalpana, and Margaret Jolly, eds. *Maternities and Modernities: Colonial and Postcolonial Experiences in Asia and the Pacific.* New York: Cambridge UP, 1998.

Ries, Nancy. *Russian Talk: Culture and Conversation During Perestroika.* Ithaca: Cornell UP, 1997.

Rivkin-Fish, Michele. "Anthropology, Demography, and the Search for a Critical Analysis of Fertility." *American Anthropologist* 105.2 (2003): 289–301.

———. "Sexuality Education in Russia: Defining Pleasure and Danger for a Fledgling Democratic Society." *Social Science and Medicine* 49 (1999): 801–14.

Santana, Rebecca. "Mixed Marriages Make Moscow a Melting Pot, Some Russians Fear Minorities' Growth." *Atlanta Journal and Constitution* 24 Aug. 2003. Rpt. in Johnson's Russia List No. 7198, 25 Aug. 2003.

Semenov, S. S. "Ostanovit' vymiranie natsii." *Izvestiia* 13 Sept. 1996.

Shkolnikov, Vladimir. "Striking Widening of the Educational Mortality Gap in Russia in the 1990s: Components and Impact on Mortality of the Total Populuation." Paper presented to the Harvard University Conference on Health and Demography of the Former Soviet Union, 29 Apr., 2005.

Shumilin, Vadim. "Russians are Leaving the Volga. Change in Ethnic Balance is an Extremely Painful Process." *CDPSP* 52.36: 13. Rpt. and trans. from *Nezavisimaya gazeta* 5 Sept. 2000: 9, 11.

Sinel'nikov, A. B. "Sotsial'nye i emotsional'no-psikhologicheskie aspekty i potrebnosti individa v sem'e i detiakh." *Planirovanie sem'i i natsional'nye traditsii*. Ed. A. I. Antonov, Sh. Kh. Kadyrov, and Giorgi Tsuladze. Moscow: Institut Sotsiologii AN SSSR, 1988. 47–51.

Slezkine, Yuri. "The USSR as a Communal Apartment, or How a Socialist State Promoted Ethnic Particularism." *Slavic Review* 53.2 (1994): 414–52.

Solomon, Susan Gross. "The Demographic Argument in Soviet Debates over the Legalization of Abortion in the 1920s." *Cahiers du monde russe et soviétique* 33.1 (1992): 59–82.

Sperling, Valerie. *Organizing Women in Contemporary Russia: Engendering Transition*. Cambridge: Cambridge UP, 1999.

Suny, Ronald Grigor. *The Revenge of the Past: Nationalism, Revolution, and the Collapse of the Soviet Union*. Stanford: Stanford UP, 1993.

Tayler, Jeffrey. "Russia Is Finished." *The Atlantic Monthly* (May 2001). <http://www.theatlantic.com/issues/2001/05/tayler-pl.htm>

Timashova, Natal'ia. "Mediki vvodiat ogranicheniia na pozdnie aborty v nadezhde povysit' rozhdaemost'." *Novye izvestiia* 19 Aug. 2003. Rpt. in *Weekly* 123–24. 25 Aug.–7 Sept. 2003. www.demoscope.ru/weekly/2003/0123/tema03.php.

Vishnevskii, A. G. "Ideologizirovannaia demografiia." *Vestnik Akademii Nauk SSSR* 10 (1991): 3–18.

———. "Konservativnaia revoliutsiia v SSSR." *Mir Rossii* 5.4 (1996): 3–66.

———. "Russia: The Demographic Situation." *Studies on Russian Economic Development* 6.1 (1995): 35–45.

———. "Russkii krest." Parts 1–3. *Novye izvestiia* 24–26 Feb. 1998.

———. *Serb i rubl': Konservativnaia modernizatsiia v SSSR*. Moscow: OGI, 1999.

Volkov, A. G. *Sem'ia-Ob''ekt Demografii*. Moscow: Mysl', 1986.

Zakharov, Sergei V. "Fertility, Nuptiality, and Family Planning in Russia: Problems and Prospects." *Population Under Duress: The Geodemography of Post-Soviet Russia*. Ed. George J. Demko, Grigory Ioffe, and Zhanna Zayonchkovskaya. Boulder, CO: Westview Press, 1999. 41–58.

Zakharov, Sergei V., and Elena I. Ivanova. "Fertility Decline and Recent Changes in Russia: On the Threshold of the Second Demographic Transition." *Russia's Demographic 'Crisis.'* Ed. Julie DaVanzo. Santa Monica: RAND, 1996. 36–82.

———. "Regional Fertility Differentiation in Russia: 1959–1994." *Studies on Russian Economic Development* 7 (1995): 354–68.

Zhukov, Boris. "Men'she narodu-bol'she kislorodu." *Itogi*. 16 Mar. 1999: 44–46.

EIGHT | **Selling Russia** Prostitution, Masculinity,

and Metaphors of Nationalism after

Perestroika

ELIOT BORENSTEIN

As Western ships approached a port in Sevastopol, Ukraine, in late April of 1997, a group of prostitutes lined up to greet them. Given the long-standing connection between shore leave and sex-for-hire, this was hardly unusual in and of itself, but these women planned a welcome with pickets rather than open arms. The sailors were part of the North Atlantic Treaty Organization's Operation Sea Breeze, a set of practice maneuvers in the Black Sea. NATO could not have picked a worse time or a more troubled spot: the Russian government was outraged over plans for the organization's imminent expansion to include former Warsaw Pact countries, while the Crimea (the largely Russian-speaking region including Sevastopol that was given to Ukraine by Soviet leader Nikita Khrushchev as a "gift" in 1954) has been the focus of a simmering territorial dispute with Ukraine since the collapse of the USSR. On Russia Day, which commemorates the incorporation of the Crimea into the Russian Empire by Catherine the Great, the local Russian-language newspaper, *The Crimean Times* [*Krymskoe vremia*], reported that a group of prostitutes declared a boycott on NATO sailors: "Let them be serviced by the wives of the officers who let NATO ships into the Black Sea," one of the prostitutes-turned-activists was quoted as saying. "We for our part will shower the uninvited guests with tomatoes and rotten eggs" (Lodge [translation adjusted for the sake of idiom]). Her words are almost too good to be true, and one suspects that the reporter might well have fabricated them to spice up his story.[1] Whether real or fabricated, they exemplify the sexualization of boundaries that so often characterizes prostitution as a metaphor for international relations: the prostitute refuses access to NATO sailors, just as the country should have refused them access to its precious and vulnerable warm water port.

For the past decade, the Russian prostitute has been routinely deployed in the symbolic battle for Russia's soul. The collapse of the Russian state, the decline of patriotism, and the absence of a workable national idea share center stage in the Russian media and culture industry with tales and images of sexually uninhibited young women offering their bodies and their services to paying clients. Just as the media and culture industry themselves are often pilloried for the boom in prostitution that began in the last years of perestroika (the assumption is that young girls and women throughout the country wanted to be just like the high-priced Russian prostitutes they saw on the silver screen), so are perestroika and the subsequent attempts at economic "shock therapy" blamed for turning the entire country into a nexus of buying and selling, where everything of value is offered cynically to the highest bidder.

At issue here is prostitution as metaphor rather than social phenomenon. Certainly, prostitution and sexual slavery are very real and serious problems in Russia today; barely a month passes without some Western news outlet reporting on the physical and psychological humiliation suffered by women in the former Soviet Union who have joined the swelling ranks of prostitutes either out of dire economic need or from the mistaken assumption that selling their bodies will give them the "good life." Newspapers are filled with reports of naïve young women in the former Soviet Union lured abroad with promises of high-paying jobs, only to find themselves sold into sexual slavery in brothels throughout Europe and the Middle East. But the real-life trials and tribulations of actual prostitutes are beyond the scope of this chapter, whose subject matter is defined in terms of representation and consumption, not daily life or individual psychology. At issue is the way in which Russia, Russian culture, and Russianness (*russkost'*) are constructed in the country's mass media and culture industry for a domestic audience. In Russia, millions of viewers and readers have a strong sense of the chaos into which their country is falling, not only because of their day-to-day experiences, but also because the media and culture industry create specific narratives for constructing and understanding that chaos, narratives that are calculated to appeal to their audience. The plight of actual post-Soviet prostitutes is horrific, but this is not their story.

Indeed, it is not a woman's story at all.[2] More often than not, the network of artistry and ideology that has created the metaphorical post-Soviet prostitute functions like the prostitute herself: its primary target is men. A brief overview of the prostitute's function in Russia's cultural mythology before perestroika will show that the prostitute has rarely been a subject in her own right; usually, she is a foil for the male hero or an important step in his moral or psychological development. The post-Soviet prostitute is no exception. Burdened with a symbolism that might seem wildly disproportionate to her status, she becomes a sign of Russian national humiliation—of the desperation of a country forced to sell off its natural and spiritual resources to unscrupulous clients from other lands. Sometimes the scenario is more optimistic, the prostitute representing the nation's enduring pride and moral superiority in the face of hostile enemies. This is in keeping with centuries-old traditions of representing Russia as feminine, as a woman who alternates between a stern and forbidding Mother Russia rallying her sons to her defense and a helpless, innocent virgin despoiled by invaders from both East and West. Yet despite this pervasive feminization of the country on the symbolic level, and despite the fact that male prostitution is rarely raised as an issue, the Russian prostitute symbolizes national humiliation as male, rather than female, experience.[3] She represents the anxieties of a post-Soviet masculinity in crisis, where the loss of empire, the onslaught of the market, and competition with a triumphant West are construed as a kind of male sexual humiliation. Even though Russia is embodied by a female prostitute, even though her victimization unfolds within a context of specifically heterosexual violence and commerce, and even though her story fits classical patterns for the heroines of melodrama, in terms of the Russian cultural imaginary, her darkest secret is that, symbolically if not sartorially, she is a cross-dresser. This does not render her story a kind of *Crying Game à la russe*. Quite the contrary: whereas Jaye Davidson's character shocked her would-be lover when she spread her legs to reveal a penis, the post-Soviet prostitute is the perfect expression of Russian male anxiety because, powerless and alluring, she does not have a phallus at all.

The Russian Prostitute and Her Literary Pedigree

> When out of the gloom of error
> With the heated word of conviction
> I drew out your fallen soul,
> And, full of deep torture,
> Wringing your hands, you cursed
> The vice that had corrupted you.
> ....
> Believe me: I listened, not unmoved,
> I greedily caught every sound...
> I understood everything, unhappy child!
> All is forgiven and all is forgotten.
> And come into my house boldly and freely
> As its full mistress!
> —N. A. Nekrasov, "When out of the gloom of error"
> ["Kogda iz mraka zabluzhden'ia"] (Nekrasov 101–2)

All appearances to the contrary, the post-Soviet prostitute of fiction and film has an impeccable pedigree, tracing her ancestry back to classic Russian novels, short stories, and verse.[4] The Russian literary tradition is quite tolerant of the fallen woman, who is often treated less as an individual character than as the embodiment of a moral dilemma. N. A. Nekrasov's "When out of the gloom of error" (1845), cited above, establishes a pattern for the literary prostitute that resonates to this very day: the speaker inevitably hears the prostitute's tale of woe, facilitating her redemption by asking her to marry him: "And come into my house boldly and freely / As its full mistress!" (102). In her article "A Typology of Fallen Women in Nineteenth Century Russian Literature," Olga Matich observes that the fallen woman "brings together two major themes of Russian fiction: those of moral integrity and socio-economic status" (327).

Her words apply equally well to the post-Soviet prostitute, as does her typology itself: examining some of the most important heroines in nineteenth-century Russian fiction, Matich develops a classification system that divides the fallen woman and her "male complement" into four groups: Female victim and Male victimizer, Female victim and Male redeemer, Female victim-redeemer and Male victim, and Female victimizer and Male victim (327). That the fallen women should be defined in terms of suffering and redemption should come as no surprise to readers of Russian fiction, since these themes are central to the entire literary tradition in general (and to the works of Dostoevsky in particular). Matich reminds us of the numerous attempts by Russian heroes to "save" the prostitute or fallen woman, who is usually depicted as a victim of harsh circumstances: Nekhliudov and Katiusha Maslova from Leo Tolstoy's *Resurrection,* the Underground Man and Liza from *Notes from Underground,* and, of course, Kirsanov's transformation of Nastia Kriukova from prostitute to utopian socialist seamstress in Chernyshevsky's *What Is to Be Done?* The impulse to "save" such women may be attributed to a variety of motives, from a combination of vanity and a misguided sense of social duty to a selfish need to dominate. Indeed, one might argue that attempts at redemption work precisely in that they sublimate the initial, sexual arousal provoked by the prostitute into a moral one: it is her plight, and not her body, that is so seductive. In 1899, Tolstoy's Katiusha Maslova, the last in a long line of the century's literary prostitutes, so clearly understands her spiritual and sexual status that one might almost suspect she was familiar with Matich's typology. She resolves not to let off so easily the man who seduced her and ruined her life: "She would not give herself to him, would not allow him to use her spiritually as he had used her bodily" (Tolstoi 10: 259). For the attempt at salvation to be made, the male protagonist must first transform the prostitute in his own mind from a sex object to a moral object.[5]

Yet, as Matich's framework suggests, the prostitute could also be the *instrument* of salvation rather than its object. All but one of Matich's models are predicated on sexual role reversal, in which the man is "socially degraded" (338). Her third model, female victim-redeemer and Male victim, is most fully pronounced in the works of Dostoevsky. Although Dostoevsky did not invent the theme of redemption through suffering, it quickly became associated with both his work and with the moral imperatives of the Russian literary tradition as a whole; his focus on female sacrifice and redemption played a decisive role in the formation of the image of the self-sacrificing Russian heroine. In the aforementioned *Notes from Underground,* the narrator's fantasy that he will "raise up" the prostitute Liza is a parody of the utopian idealism of similar scenes in Chernyshevsky's *What is to Be Done?*; by the end of the story, Liza, aware of his degradation, "assumes the role of redeemer in a redistribution of power and an inversion of the classical redemption model" (339). Sonia from Dostoevsky's *Crime and Punishment* is certainly a victim to the extent that she turns in her passport for the prostitute's yellow ticket in order to save her family from destitution. Yet her primary role in the novel is to facilitate the hero's rejection of the path of sin, hubris, and murder. As Matich and numerous others have noted, "It is Sonja who is the Christlike savior in the novel" (340).[6]

Although the suffering woman as both victim and redeemer would stubbornly persist into the Soviet period (with Solzhenitsyn's Matryona being one of the most famous examples), after the 1920s she was only rarely a prostitute. Certainly, prostitutes would be found throughout the literature documenting the Russian Revolution and Civil War, from Kat'ka in Aleksandr Blok's "The Twelve," the prostitute who had disrupted the comradely harmony of the revolutionary soldiers (a harmony that would be restored only after her death), to the camp followers of Isaak Babel''s *Red Cavalry* stories. During the New Economic Policy, the prostitute resurged as a social and cultural phenomenon: the prevalence of prostitutes both responded to the newly restored market forces and, in literature and film, reflected them.[7] Now prostitution was treated as a social problem to be eradicated through labor and reeducation rather than romantic idealism; if anything, the role of redeemer was now co-opted by the state and by doctors who were acting in the name of "enlightened science."[8] By the 1930s, victory was declared in the war on prostitution, and the phenomenon officially ceased to exist. The prostitute vanished from the horizon, reappearing only after Gorbachev's perestroika was well under way. Of course, women continued to perform sex for hire in train stations, in hard-currency hotels for foreign visitors, and by special arrangement for the Party elite. Yet if there is ample evidence that prostitution actually persisted as a social phenomenon, it vanished as a discursive one: it was no longer a subject fit for literature and art.

Perestroika Prostitutes

> Making that film is tantamount to actually luring women into prostitution. It should be prosecuted under the law.
> —A Moscow policeman, 1989 (Belova 44)

The prostitute's disappearance from Soviet discourse was necessitated by the supposed eradication of prostitution as a social ill; but her loss of currency also points to more fundamental characteristics of Soviet culture before glasnost. In a society where money and market relations were not the dominant means of exchange, the metaphorical power of prostitution was diminished. Even when the country was represented as feminine, Mother

Russia's problem was not that she was selling her services to foreign customers. In World War II, clearly the Soviet Union's greatest international crisis, Mother Russia had to be protected from rape by a violent invader rather than seduction by a rich exploiter. When forbidden by law, prostitution is a classic example of a "victimless crime": no direct harm comes to anyone as a result.[9] The resolution of moral dilemmas under Stalin (and even Brezhnev) did create victims: as a metaphor, prostitution is woefully inadequate when applied to the denunciation of friends and neighbors to the authorities. The dominant metaphor for "selling out" in Soviet times was Faustian rather than whorish: avoiding the mediation of the cash nexus entirely, one sold one's *soul* rather than one's *body*. One of the challenges faced by the art of the Thaw was to address not just the victims of Stalinism, but those who actively colluded to ruin people's lives.[10]

Among the oppositional intelligentsia after Stalin, "selling out" to the authorities or to the crushing dictates of Soviet life was a matter of either submission to blackmail (denial of basic rights or privileges if one fails to go along) or invidious compromise (a series of small concessions that led one down the primrose path to total capitulation). The man who conveyed this dilemma the best, indeed, the undisputed master of the genre, was Brezhnev-era author Iurii Trifonov; his 1976 novel *House on the Embankment* [*Dom na naberezhnoi*] tells of a perfectly normal and likeable young man who betrays his teacher during the Stalin era, while his 1969 novella *The Exchange* [*Obmen*] shows the more mundane deals with the devil made during Brezhnev's "period of stagnation": step by step, a man parts with his principles in order to swap his tiny apartment for a larger one.

With the advent of perestroika, the dominant metaphors changed. Not only did the state rapidly lose much of its ability to force its citizens into ethical compromises with the system, but the system itself quickly became preoccupied with issues of money and market relations. One of Russia's most prominent, and most controversial, fiction writers appeared to have anticipated this shift earlier than most: between 1980 and 1982, Viktor Erofeyev wrote a novel called *Russian Beauty* [*Russkaia krasavitsa*], which would be published in the USSR only in 1990. The novel's obscene language (which was unprintable before the late 1980s) and graphic descriptions of sexual violence did not exactly endear it to the Russian intellectual readership, while its stream-of-consciousness narration was a bit too daunting for those who were simply looking for titillation. *Russian Beauty* tells the tale of Irina Tarakanova (her last name means "cockroach"), a beautiful, high-class slut who, although not strictly speaking a prostitute, services the communist *nomenklatura*, artists, and various hangers-on. As the female embodiment of a debased and mercantile Russia on the cusp of perestroika, Tarakanova is perfect: at a time when connections and favoritism can make or break someone's life, Tarakanov implicitly sells her services without taking cash. She is not a prostitute, but she is a whore. As in so much of Erofeyev's work, underneath the modernist narrative techniques and scandalous four-letter words of *Russian Beauty* are themes resurrected from the literary classics: in this case, the suffering, beautiful female "fallen woman" as a symbol of Russia's salvation. Erofeyev is one of Russia's most self-conscious postmodernists, and his approach to the theme is easily identifiable as parody: as Helena Goscilo has noted, Irina clearly represents the new Russia ("two fates were to be decided: Russia's and mine" [227], Goscilo 43). She is convinced that she will be Russia's spiritual savior, because "beauty will save the world" (Prince Myshkin said as much in Dostoevsky's *The Idiot,* so it must be true).

Ultimately, it would not be "high art" like *Russian Beauty* that would establish the image of the perestroika prostitute; that honor would fall to a novel and movie called *Intergirl* [*Interdevochka*]. Viktor Kunin's 1988 novel and Petr Torodorvskii's movie of the following year tell the melodramatic story of Tania, a nurse's aid by day and foreign-currency prostitute by night. Although Tania uses her ill-gotten income for luxuries and fine clothes, her main concern is the welfare of her friends and her mother, a middle-aged woman of poor health. After many trials and tribulations, Tania marries one of her clients, a Swedish businessman who takes her away from both mother and Motherland to install her in a house with all the modern conveniences of Western suburbia and all the warmth of a Scandinavian winter. Tania's relationship with her husband rapidly deteriorates as she is overcome by boredom and homesickness; her only solace is her friendship with the Soviet truck driver who is her one link to her past life. By the story's end, the truck driver has lost his job for consorting with Tania, her mother has discovered her secret life and committed suicide, and a distraught Tania dies in a car accident.

This wildly successful potboiler simply begs for a political reading. In her discussion of Todorovskii's film, Lynne Attwood argues convincingly that the prostitute is a symbol of Soviet society as a whole: "everybody is forced, metaphorically, into prostitution" (Attwood 72).[11] Katerina Clark offers a more provocative interpretation of the *perestroika* prostitute: such works as *Intergirl* highlight the intelligentsia's anxiety over the fate of culture in the era of the international marketplace (Clark). As Goscilo observes, "the dominant lexicon of *Intergirl* is that of economics (not sex)" (144). The novel itself, which was published along with a brief foreword by the prominent Russian sexologist Igor' Kon praising Kunin's work for its social utility, is remarkably chaste in its language, containing neither obscene words nor explicit descriptions of sexual acts (the American Motion Picture Association would be hard pressed to give it an "R" rating). In *Intergirl,* Goscilo discovers a prurience of a different sort: a "preoccupation with various brands and names of commodities, which relentlessly repeat themselves whenever clothes, cars, makeup, perfumes, etc., are mentioned. Needless to say, these are all Western imports, weapons with which the corrupt materialist West invades innocent Russia to tempt and degrade it" (Goscilo 144). Of course, crucial to all these readings of *Intergirl* is the fact that Tania is a *foreign-currency* prostitute, one who disdains mere rubles in her quest for dollars and

Deutschmarks. Indeed, Tania meets her death in a foreign car whose name seems to point back to the body parts with which she earned her keep: a Volvo. When we recall the frequent recourse to female symbols to represent Russia, Tania's melodramatic story becomes a transparent allegory of Russia's relationship with the West: rich in natural beauty, Russia sells herself to foreign suitors only to be overcome by nostalgia and regret.[12]

Although *Intergirl* was just a novel and movie, the work represents a turning point for the social construction of the Russian prostitute. Contemporary reviewers of the movie feared that its depiction of its star, Elena Iakovleva, decked out in foreign clothes and enjoying imported luxuries, would prompt millions of young Soviet girls to follow in her spike-heeled footsteps.[13] And although the media are too easy a target to blame for all contemporary social ills, it is true that the number of prostitutes in the former Soviet Union began to skyrocket in the years following the movie's release. Unquestionably, there are clear socioeconomic reasons for this phenomenon that have nothing to do with the corrupting power of film and fiction, but the movie did provide an easily digested narrative for becoming a prostitute that could have exacerbated it.[14] Over a decade later, *Intergirl* is still routinely blamed for Russia's prostitution problem. The May 1999 issue of *Kino-Park,* a popular movie magazine, featured an article called "How *Intergirl* Was Accused of Prostitution," in which professors, policemen, and even prostitutes themselves make the case that, despite its tragic ending, Todorovskii's film is to blame for luring girls from the path of righteousness. Curiously, the metaphor of prostitution is used to explain how a film about prostitution led real girls and women to turn tricks for a living: the movie's producers are essentially accused of pimping the Russian public.

After 1991: On the Market

> There are nations and cultures that simply *know how* to sell and buy women. . . . In theory, Russian *high* culture (*kul'tura*) couldn't stand that. Buying and selling gave it [culture] convulsions. It was uniquely un-mercenary. Without investigating the matter thoroughly, it declared woman priceless. That's why Russian culture's attitude toward prostitution was so strained.
> —Viktor Erofeev, "The Price of the Prostitute" ["*Tsena prostitutki*"] (Erofeev, *Muzhchiny* 108)

Intergirl appeared only two years after the paradigmatic moment when sexuality reemerged as an important part of Russian discourse, when a member of the Russian studio audience for a 1987 Soviet-American "space bridge" hosted by Phil Donahue and Vladimir Pozner declared that, in the Soviet Union, "We have no sex!" Her words were only semi-serious, and certainly their meaning was misunderstood (she was referring to sex as subject matter in the media and entertainment, not physical sexual activity), but they functioned as a call to arms: for the past fourteen years, Russia has been doing its best to prove her wrong. Talk shows, films, novels, and how-to manuals are now impossible for the Russian consumer to ignore, while those who live in the capitals can now visit one of many sex shops and bring home a variety of plastic objects and battery-operated devices that never quite made it as categories for production targets under the old Soviet five-year plans. And despite legislators' frequent attempts to restrict or ban pornography altogether, sexually explicit magazines and videos are almost as easy to acquire as a loaf of black bread, if not as cheap. Since Russian culture can be said to have undergone both a market revolution and a sexual revolution simultaneously (although both claims are problematic), the discourse of sex has become inextricably linked with the discourse of economics.[15]

The result has been a commodification of women's bodies and female sexuality that is unprecedented in Russian history. For almost a decade now, want ads casually announce secretarial vacancies for attractive young women who are "*bez kompleksov*" or "uninhibited," a none-too-subtle code for explaining the secretary's horizontal duties to her boss. And just as American and European commercials use beautiful women to sell cars and beer, Russian ads routinely feature half-naked, sexually available beauties to promote the most unlikely of products: a recent billboard for a copy machine has a sexy woman lying on top of it, with the slogan "*ona ne otkazhet*" (a play on words suggesting that the copy machine will not break down and the woman will not say no). Equally evocative is a 1999 billboard for "West" cigarettes: in it, a beautiful stewardess sits next to a handsome male passenger, smiling broadly as her breasts, barely covered in a black-lace bra, spill out of her unbuttoned uniform. Although the man is looking her in the eye, the cigarette's logo points straight to her cleavage, while the slogan above their heads proclaims: "Everything is possible."

This last ad is particularly significant, since it brings together female sexual commodification and the tortured relations between Russia and the West. The man's clothing and the women's face strongly suggest that both are Russian, but the artifact responsible for their unlimited possibilities is packaged as foreign: the color scheme is a rip-off of Marlboro's, which had been the undisputed favorite among Russia's smokers with the money to pay for them, while the product's name speaks for itself. West presents a relatively uncomplicated connection between sexuality, Russian male sexual success, and Western consumer culture. But as the 1990s drew to a close, this utopian idyll was more the exception than the rule. Here again, the figure of the prostitute plays a central role: repeatedly standing in for Russia as a whole, she sells her services, herself, and often her pride.

Post-Soviet Russia's drama of international prostitution is thus always played out on a number of levels simultaneously: on the empirical level, there is the unchecked growth of highly paid call girls serving "New Russians" and foreign businessmen, the boom in Russian "mail-order brides," and the notorious trafficking in women from the former Soviet Union throughout the world; allegorically, the "export" of Russian women is inevitably compared with the shortsighted marketing of the country's oil reserves for Western consumption. The Russian woman has become part of a constellation of symbols for Russian anxieties over commodification. In the Russian imaginary, the prostitute who caters to Western clients serves much the same function as the baby adopted by American and European childless couples, or the victims of kidnapping in popular urban legends whose organs are harvested for the underground transplant market. In each case, something that might normally be considered intimate or even sacred is thrown to the tender mercies of the postcommunist international market, turning Russia into a depot for human spare parts. Rita Prozorova, the heroine of Sergei Pugachev's 1999 novel *You're Just a Slut, My Dear* [*Ty prosto shliukha, dorogaia!*], escapes from sexual slavery in the provinces only to be lured into a black-market organ-harvesting scheme in the capital. She escapes solely because she has heard enough news stories on TV to recognize the imminent danger: "The heart valve of some millionaire in Chicago fails him, and a man in Moscow or Petersburg disappears. She'll disappear the same way, so that her kidney can process American urine somewhere in San Francisco. To die, just to piss in San Francisco? Screw that!" (296). Rita's escape from the organ harvesters parallels her escape from prostitution: refusing to be a victim, she does not hesitate to commit murder herself.

Rita's story is unusual, however, in that she is not only the action hero but also an irredeemably unattractive character (the novel begins with her murdering her mother, a neighbor, and a policeman, all in thirty pages). Nor is she a professional prostitute. The professional prostitutes in Russian popular narrative are usually far more appealing, and their story is calculated to arouse numerous conflicting feelings in the male audience. On the sexual level, the Russian prostitute's story contributes to a growing complex of inferiority and insecurity among Russian men, one that is amply demonstrated by the numerous publications and broadcasts aimed primarily at male consumers. Indeed, the very existence of "men's magazines" and softcore pornography in Russia inevitably points back to the threat of foreign competition: no matter how hard they may try to be unique, male heterosexual erotica and pornography in Russia betray their foreign origins. The *Playboy* clone *Andrei,* the first slick "men's magazine" in the former USSR, makes such anxieties crystal clear in a cartoon in its very first issue: two prostitutes display their wares on a Moscow street: the first, a Russian woman standing under the "M" of the metro sign, looks on in horror at a black woman leaning against the "M" of a McDonald's sign (*Andrei* 27).[16] Such publications trumpet the virtues of Russian women, repeating the male mantra that women in Russia are the most beautiful in the world; but they also reinforce the threat that these women will attract the attention of rich foreign men (through associated projects such as *Andrei*'s own Web site). Ironically, these publications, which shamelessly borrowed from Western models such as *Playboy* and *Penthouse,* eventually found themselves retreating behind national chauvinism when *Playboy* and *Penthouse* began publishing their own Russian editions. Magazines such as *Andrei* experienced the same anxieties as their Russian male readers when faced with foreign competition.

If the media, pornography, fiction, and film are any indication, Russian masculinity is often represented as embattled by potential threats from all sides, both on the home front and in relation to the West. The 1990s have witnessed a burgeoning literature on the supposedly pathetic state of post-Soviet manhood: Lina Tarakhova's 1992 *Raising a Man* [*Vospitat' muzhchinu*], V. Z. Vladislavskii's 1991 *If You're a Man* [*Esli ty muzhchina*], and A. Nikulin's 1990 *Men's Talk* [*Muzhskoi razgovor*] all share the argument that Russian men are an endangered species. These books are largely pedagogical, focused on returning traditional male values to the younger generation; these are books for boys and for the teachers of boys. They appear to respond to a complaint more often voiced by Russian women than Russian men, the charge that the Soviet system rendered its men "infantile" and "dependent." Perhaps the most prominent exponent of this view is none other than Viktor Erofeev, the author of *Russian Beauty,* whose 1997 book of essays *Men* [*Muzhchiny*] is a collection of occasional pieces published in such magazines as *Andrei* and the Russian edition of *Playboy*. The *Andrei* articles were originally printed in a monthly rubric called "The Rights of Men" [*"Prava muzhchin"*], and the sixth issue (1995) contained an essay penned by Erofeev titled "The Flight of the 'Cloud in Trousers'" [*"Polet 'oblaka v shtanakh'"*]. After a self-satisfied diatribe on the dangers of feminism and the controversy over sexual harassment in the West, "The Flight of the 'Cloud in Trousers'" informs us that "Man's fate in Russia looks different, but is no less dramatic," since the Russian man is not merely embattled but has ceased to exist altogether. Thanks to Soviet power (which Erofeev himself admits was instituted by male Russians), the Russian man has lost the honor and freedom that are the hallmarks of true manhood. Though the Russian man is still a "human being" (*chelovek*), still a "guy" (*muzhik*), and still a "husband" (*muzh*), all of these terms represent circumscribed, ultimately unfulfilling roles for the potential "real" man.

Erofeev's essay hints at the spectre that haunts Russian masculinity: the spectre of Western culture and Western men. If the Russian man is a thing of the past, the Russian woman is entirely real: "Woman consists of necessity. In Russia we have necessity by the ton (*neobkhodimosti khot' valiai*). That is why Russia is feminine. And the Russian woman has no illusions: she knows there are no men in Russia. She wants out of Russia."[17] Once again, this sexual threat is inextricably caught up with an economic one: the Russian man posited by *Andrei* laments the competition with Western men, while *Andrei* itself is haunted both by Russia's competition with American pop culture and by the magazine's own attempts to maintain its market share against the threat of "men's magazines" imported from the United States, particularly the Russian-language edition of *Playboy,* whose contents only slightly differ from the American version. "The Flight of the 'Cloud in Trousers'" brings together a popular argument about Russian male inadequacy with the perceived problem of Russian women "exporting themselves" to the West. In a few short paragraphs, the author of *Russian Beauty* links a crisis of Russian masculinity, prostitution, Russia's relations with the West, and international commerce into an overriding discourse of wounded national and male pride.

How, then, does Russian popular culture attempt to exorcise itself of the sense of humiliation and betrayal as symbolized by the prostitute, who shamelessly crosses borders and exchanges bodily fluids? By appealing to a tired cliché of prostitute narratives and adding a nationalist twist: the desirability and value of the prostitute is proven by the fact that the West is willing to pay, but her spirituality, and the ultimate superiority of Russian men, is demonstrated when she performs her services for love, rather than for money. By and large, the prostitute is mercantile only with her foreign johns, bestowing her gifts on the Russian hero for free.

Indeed, the moment when the prostitute stops taking money can be tantamount to the validation of the hero's Russian credentials. In 1993, director Ivan Shchegolev and screenwriter Lev Korsunskii produced a rather ham-handed comedy called *Amerikanskii dedushka* [*American Grandfather*], the last film starring the beloved actor Evgenii Leonov. Leonov plays an émigré who returns from Brooklyn to his native Russia in order to buy a cemetery plot, plan his funeral, and die at home surrounded by loved ones. These same loved ones, however, have far more mercantile ideas. Through the inexplicable logic of film comedy, Leonov has gotten rich in America (after all, that is what America is for), and so he is soon the target of various hangers-on who hope to squeeze as much money out of him as possible before he takes to his grave. Along the way, Leonov goes to a hotel restaurant and meets a Russian woman whom the viewer has little difficulty identifying as a prostitute (she wears the "uniform" of high heels, fishnets, miniskirt, and garish make-up). Incredibly, Leonov fails to realize she is a professional: after all, he has been away from Russia so long, he does not know that the country is now swarming with call girls. Apparently, his experience in America does not give him the street smarts to recognize a hooker; instead, prostitution is implicitly identified as a post-Soviet Russian phenomenon. This being a comedy, and one with the word "American" in its title, it has to have a happy end; and so the tragic finale of the funeral is replaced by the celebration of Leonov's wedding to the prostitute, who is now pregnant. Leonov has come home to live, not to die.

There is much to unpack here: at the very least since the Russian Revolution, emigration and exile have been symbolically linked to images of death, with the foreign countries standing in for the land of the dead.[18] Indeed, *Intergirl* itself makes use of this tradition, turning Tania's new home into a land that virtually buries her alive and ultimately kills her. Leonov's happy end is the mirror image of *Intergirl*'s tragedy: the prostitute finds happiness by marrying a foreign john who turns out to be a Russian; she helps reconcile him with his greedy relatives, and the newlyweds remain in their native land to raise children rather than move abroad to die. Here the prostitute facilitates reintegration with Russia and a reassertion of "family values" rather than exile and the soul-crushing dominance of market relations.

The foreign-currency prostitute plays a similar function as the guide back "home" in the 1997 action film *Everything We Dreamed About for So Long* [*Vse to, o chem my tak dolgo mechtali*], although its end is tragic nonetheless. A young man is tricked by his old army buddy into running drugs from Western Europe into Russia, not realizing that he is being set up to be caught and killed. Although he is told to drive nonstop, he is lured by the bright lights of a German city and makes his way to a strip club, where he is immediately attracted to a platinum blonde exotic dancer who he is convinced is a "real German." Naturally, when he arranges to pay for her services, she turns out to be a Russian (named Natasha, no less—Russian prostitutes throughout Europe and the Middle East are routinely referred to as "Natashas"), and mayhem ensues. He finds himself in jail, and Natasha, who at first disdained him as just another raggedy Russian, soon finds herself in an all-too-familiar role for women from the ex-USSR: she brings him packages in prison. Eventually, she meets up with him after he breaks free, following a kickboxing struggle to the death with a fellow prisoner while clad in nothing but a loincloth and silver body paint. Natasha turns out to be a foreign-language graduate who was lured abroad with promises of work as a translator, only to have her passport seized and her body sold into sexual slavery. Thanks to her, the hero turns his life around. She brings him to a Russian Orthodox Church, where, overwhelmed by the power of the icons, he faints. He returns and is baptized into the faith of his fathers, as a more modestly dressed Natasha looks on, smiling beatifically. Soon she gets pregnant, and the couple starts to make plans for the future. Before she and the hero can start a new life together, however, she is shot by gangsters.

Everything We Dreamed About for So Long is a prostitute melodrama in the Dostoevskian mold, where the heroine facilitates her lover's salvation. But here these hackneyed themes are transposed to the realm of international commerce and national disenchantment. When the hero was still in the army, he and his friend dreamed of the good life, the kind available only in the West; but when he arrives in Germany, the West for him is nothing but a prison. His status in life is both typical for so many young Russian men who leave the army aimless and disillusioned, and symbolic of Russian manhood in general; where once he belonged to something, to an organization of comrades that gave some sense of purpose, now he must try to find a place for himself in a harsh and unfamiliar world. As for Natasha, she charges foreign men for her sexual favors, but gives herself to the hero for free, facilitating his reintegration into traditional Russian spiritual values.

A prostitute named Natasha is also crucial for the redemption of the hero of Viktor Dotsenko's best-selling series of action novels, Savelii Govorkov, nicknamed "Mad Dog" ("Beshenyi"). The fifth novel, *Mad Dog's Revenge* [*Mest' Beshenogo*, 1998], begins at the funeral of Savelii's latest dead girlfriend, Natasha. Virtually all of Savelii's lovers quickly turn into beautiful corpses to be avenged by Mad Dog, with the exception of the underage Rozochka, whom Savelii eventually marries. Right after the ceremony, he meets a beautiful young prostitute who shares his beloved's name, and marvels at this rather unremarkable coincidence. This is Natasha's day off, but when she looks into his eyes, she realizes what he needs. She is no stranger to loss, since her small daughter was killed by a drunk driver three years before, and the sight of the other Natasha's funeral brings back memories of her own daughter's death: "In a purely womanly way, she felt that he needed help, that something tragic had happened to him" (25). She takes him home, where they have numerous shots of cognac, including a toast to the fallen Afghan veterans. Soon enough, they fall into bed together, and the experience is redemptive for both of them: the all-too-experienced Natasha is nervous and excited as though she were with a man for the first time, while Savelii reaches an epiphany that is unparalleled in modern literature: crying out her name, he enters her rectally and communes with the spirit of his departed lover, while the living Natasha experiences the first orgasm of her life (30–32, 39). Now Savelii is able to return to his mission, saving Russia from its enemies, while anal sex with Savelii has transformed Natasha entirely: "Her soul was joyous and calm: for the first time in many long years, she felt pure and immaculate" (34).

By the late 1990s, the prostitute with a heart of gold was once again such a ubiquitous feature in popular culture that she easily lent herself to satire. Viktor Pelevin's 1997 novel *Life of Insects* [*Zhizn' nasekomykh*], a postmodern animal fable in which nearly all the main characters are insects navigating the absurdities of contemporary Russian life, uses the trope of the prostitute to lampoon one of the author's favorite targets: the ultranationalist and pseudo-mystical discourse of Russia's fate. One of the novel's main characters, a visiting American businessman, Sam Sucker, is actually a mosquito who has come to Moscow to sample the local cuisine (i.e., Russian blood).[19] Soon after his arrival, he meets a young fly named Natasha, whom Sam's Russian companions immediately recognize as a prostitute. Here Pelevin manages to send up both *Intergirl* and Kornei Chukovsky's classic children's poem, *Mukha-Tsokotukha* (in which a female fly is rescued by a male mosquito). Like Tania from *Intergirl*, Natasha is a disappointment to her sick mother (in this case, a house-bound widow who consumed the remains of Natasha's father as nourishment while waiting for her eggs to hatch), choosing to sell her body in exchange for a better life. After she and Sam have sex in the pristine countryside, Natasha whispers a naive question to her foreign lover: "Sam . . . is it true that America has lots of shit?" (223). Sam nods indulgently, reassuring her that he really is from the land of plenty. But, as with so many of her predecessors', Natasha's story ends in tragedy. She had been so certain of Sam's love that she was even practicing her English in preparation for their eventual departure ("Please cheese and pepperoni"), but Sam intends to leave her behind. Grief-stricken, Natasha commits suicide, hanging herself on a strip of flypaper (348–49).

Nymphomaniac: The Prostitute as "Spiritual Barometer"

> "I had a country I was proud of. My country was betrayed, ruined, and raped, like the cheapest of sluts. They just let it be desecrated. What's now called the Russian state can't make you proud, only ashamed. The country is a prostitute who lies down under any scum who happens by! And she even eats her young, like a pig! . . . All right, enough. Let's go on. I had ideals. They weren't subtle ideals, but, still, they were respected by any normal person. Now these ideals are mocked, slandered, smeared in shit, any cowardly bastard can publicly spit on them, where before he wouldn't even have dared make a sound! When I see this sort of thing, I want to kill! But I'd have to kill too many people. . . ."
> —Sever Belov, Dmitrii Shcherbakov, *Nimfomanka: besposhchadnaia strast'* (8–9)

So laments the hero of Dmitrii Shcherbakov's lurid potboiler *Nymphomaniac: Merciless Passion* [*Nimfomanka: besposhchadnaia strast'*], the second book in a trilogy describing the adventures of a sex-crazed but highly moral woman and her superpowered husband as they fight Russian and Chechen organized crime. Sever certainly knows whereof he speaks: not only has he spent the best years of his life trying to save a country that doesn't want to be saved, but his wife Mila is a career prostitute whose "disease" (her physiological need to be gang-raped and humiliated) continually drives her back to the brothel after each rescue from the clutches of the latest in a long line of pimps. He is telling his story to his best friend, the surgeon Pavel Kuzovlev, whose dedication to the Belovs led him to retrain himself as a psychoanalyst in order to try to cure Mila of her nymphomania and Sever of a "reactive psychosis" that has led him to attempt suicide. The good doctor's response to Sever's tirade? "You've been watching too much television!" (9).

All three parts of Dmitrii Shcherbakov's "Nymphomaniac" trilogy (*Nymphomaniac, Nymphomaniac: Merciless Passion,* and *Nymphomaniac: A Hooker's Love* [*Liubov' putany*]) date from the late '90s, and, while there is no evidence that they will ever attain the popularity of *Intergirl*, taken together they form the post-Soviet prostitute text par excellence. All of the themes discussed above are present: border crossings, a feminized Russia and the West, the prostitute as symbol of Russia's natural resources, the focus on the male hero, and, most notably, the prostitute as Christ-like redeemer. The first novel is the story of Sever Belov and Mila, both of whom have lost their memory after a car accident. When they meet again, they do not even know that they were lovers before, but they are immediately united by passion. And by something more: each of them has phenomenal powers. They can project an aura that prevents people from remembering what they look like; they possess super strength and an iron will; Belov can kill dozens of people with his bare hands, and he soon teaches Mila to do the same. But Mila has one additional ability: through her erotic dancing, she can drive men and women into a sexual frenzy.

After their accident, Sever finds work as a mechanic, and eventually is employed by the local mafia. Mila becomes the most coveted prostitute in an elite brothel, and as much as she despises herself for her work, she cannot give up prostitution. For reasons that do not become clear until the end of the first novel, she has an insatiable need to be gang-raped and abused, both verbally and physically. Belov's doctor friend even describes her nymphomania as physiological: if her brain does not receive the essential impulses it gets when she is gang-raped, it will literally self-destruct. When Sever and Mila fall in love (for what turns out to be the second time), their relationship is seriously undermined by the fact that, even though Sever's superhuman abilities extend to the bedroom (he usually has sex with Mila throughout the night), he is never enough for her.

All of this unfolds in a context of virulent racism and offhand disdain for democratic reform. Sever's enemies in the first novel consist largely of Chechens and Georgians, whom he routinely dismisses as *"chernozhopaia mraz"'* ("black-assed scum") and *"chernomazy,"* the closest Russian equivalent to "niggers." His solution to the Chechen problem is simple: exile all Chechens from Russian territory and close Chechnia's borders forever. His judgment of Yeltsin's government is equally uncompromising, if a bit less heated: the narrator casually refers to the year 1991 as the time when "American agents of influence" took over the Kremlin. Sever's nationalist credentials, which are established early on, are further strengthened when the reader discovers that, in his past life, Sever was a border guard who devoted all his efforts to preventing the theft of Russia's mineral resources. This detail is particularly important in light of Sever's problems with Mila: even after he rescues her from the brothel, she still has a physiological need to be abused, and by more than one person. His only solution is to form a brothel of his own, in which Mila plays the starring role, and Sever provides the protection. Of course, it is a kinder, gentler brothel, a whorehouse with a human face: Sever and Mila greatly improve the lives of the prostitutes who end up working for him.[20] But Sever, the strong Russian action hero, ends up in the position of pimping for the woman he loves.

By the end of the first novel, Sever's friend Pavel, the surgeon-turned-psychoanalyst, discovers the root cause of Mila's nymphomania. Before the accident, her love for Sever was so strong that it was like a drug; she could not do without him. While she is in the hospital following the accident, an unscrupulous doctor who was in the habit of pushing her female patients into prostitution injects her with an aphrodisiac to determine her erotic potential. Unfortunately for Mila, a group of young criminals is being treated in the hospital for minor wounds at the same time, and they gang-rape

Mila while she is under the influence of the aphrodisiac. Against her will, she is aroused by the experience, but meanwhile she hates herself, knowing that somewhere out there lives her beloved, whose name she cannot recall, and she is betraying him. Subconsciously, she decides she is not worthy of him, and that the world is a terrible place filled with evil people who do evil things. Her only possible value in life could be to let herself be raped and abused, thereby sparing other women her fate. As the doctor puts it, "Mila's system has become a kind of barometer, reacting to the spiritual atmosphere of society. If there is too much evil surrounding her, she tries to reduce its quantity . . . in the only way she can" (Shcherbakov, *Nimfomanka* 493).

Moreover, Mila is uniquely attuned to her native country. Before she and Sever meet again after the accident, Mila is taken to France to dance in a Parisian nightclub. But she has to be flown home immediately, because she nearly dies of a literal form of homesickness. She cannot leave Russia because "Russia is the land of sincerity, and evil here is also sincere, open, with no pretensions to false morality. In the West it's different. The West is hypocritical to the marrow. Evil is everywhere there, but it clothes itself in respectability. . . . The West is soulless in both good and evil. It lives only for a sense of advantage, which . . . usurps any other moral values. And Mila is too sensitive an instrument" (494). Nor can she go to the East, since people are animals there, lacking any sense of good and evil.

Mila is the lowbrow apotheosis of the prostitute as redeemer: her libido is the cross she has to bear. In these novels, it is not beauty, but nymphomania that will save the world. Her status is a source of inverted pride: she is far more moral than almost anyone around her, and her beauty is unsurpassed. Even her humiliation has a higher purpose. But her humiliation is ultimately shared by her man. Sever is in a bind, both as lover and patriot: the object of his affections is as beautiful as ever, but wallows in filth and seems unlikely to recover.

Where, then, does that leave the post-Soviet prostitute? Why should so many artists, writers, pundits, and filmmakers choose her as a vehicle for conveying their thoughts about Russia, masculinity, and the West? To a large extent, the symbolic prostitute recapitulates the allure and the functionality of the "real-life" prostitute: The customer purchases her services for pleasure but has no guarantee that he might not be getting something highly unpleasant in the bargain. The Russian audience consumes stories of fictional prostitutes for their prurient entertainment value, often unaware that they are a vehicle for conveying a specific, and not necessarily welcome, ideological message. Hence, the metaphorical prostitute disseminates ideology as a kind of "textually transmitted disease." Whether she is a source of national pride or solely a cause for humiliation, she is inordinately efficient at bringing in both ideological and financial capital. Where advertisers use the sexually available woman to sell their none-too-sexy wares, the producers of the culture industry peddle the post-Soviet prostitute in order to market their own approach to the "Russian idea" to consumers who buy it as part of the entertainment package.

Notes

1. Indeed, the term "uninvited guests" evokes an ethnic group that is never mentioned in the article but whose spectre must haunt any consideration of Crimea's status: the Tatars. Due to the Mongol Invasion and subsequent "Tatar Yoke," the Tatars serve as Russia's archetypal foreign invader and have entered the everyday linguistic consciousness with the extremely common saying, "Nezvannyi gost'—khuzhe Tatarina" ("An uninvited guest is worse than a Tatar"). The Tatars of Crimea were deported to Uzbekistan during World War II and only had their right to return to their land approved definitively in 1988. Thus, the proximity of NATO warships to Crimea could hardly have been more resonant: a Western alliance was seen to be demonstrating its strength off the coast of a region claimed by both Russia and Ukraine, home to a displaced people who are culturally identified with raping and pillaging "Holy Rus'," the birthplace of both nations.

2. Nor is it the story of male prostitutes; when prostitutes are deployed as metaphors or symbols, they are almost exclusively female. Isaak Babel''s "My First Fee" ["*Moi pervyi gonorar*," 1922–1928] is a rare exception: in this story, an aspiring young writer tells a prostitute that he used to be a "boy for the Armenians," which prompts the young woman to call him "sister" and pay him for his services (Babel', vol. 2: 253). For information about male prostitution as a social phenomenon in Russia before and after the Revolution, see Healey.

3. In her 1993 article "Sex and the Cinema," Lynne Attwood argues that "films about prostitution have one notable feature that sets them apart from the majority of recent films from the former USSR; their protagonists are, inevitably, female. To find women as the centre of attention in films which tackle other themes is increasingly uncommon" (73). While Attwood's assertion is technically correct, focus on the prostitute is neither a guarantee that a film or novel has any investment in a female point of view or in women's experience, nor does it raise the chances that a woman might actually be involved in creating the film. Only superficially do such works deal with the lives of women; their broader themes and concerns tend to concern the fate of the nation itself.

4. For a thorough historical study of prostitution before the Soviet period, see Laura Bernstein, *Sonia's Daughters*. See also Lebina and Shkvarovsii; Engel, "St. Petersburg Prostitutes" and *Between the Field and the City* 166–97; and Stites, "Prostitute and Society" and *Women's Liberation Movement* 178–90.

5. This brief overview of the nineteenth-century fictional prostitute should by no means be considered exhaustive; a more complete discussion would have to include Aleksandr Kuprin's *Iama* [*The Pit*] (1908–1915), a novel about a brothel whose inhabitants and clients bring together every cliché and motif connected with the representation of the Russian prostitute. For more on Kuprin, see Matich; Zholkovskii.

6. For more on the attempts to "save" the literary prostitute, see Borenstein, *Men Without Women* 47–57; Matich; Siegel 81–107; and Zholkovskii.

7. Indeed, the prostitute in NEP Russia functioned as a kind of shorthand for the moral and physical diseases brought on by the partial return to a market economy. Mikhail Bulgakov's infamous stage play *Zoia's Apartment* [*Zoikina kvartira*] is only the most famous example. In their article on the evolution of the Russian procuress, Julie Cassiday and Leyla Rouhi also discuss a 1926 film by O. Frelikh called *A Prostitute/Crushed by Life* [*Prostitutka/Ubitaia zhizn'iu*], which associates prostitution with the evils of the past and provides a happy ending, thanks to the enlightened

policies of the state (413). In her study of Russian public health posters in the 1920s, Frances L. Bernstein observes that the prostitute's image serves to personify the threat of syphilis and other sexually transmitted diseases: she is both temptress and disease vector ("Envisioning Health" 205–7). For more on the Soviet fight against prostitution in the 1920s, see Elizabeth Waters, "Victim or Villain," and Wood.

8. As part of the public health campaign known as "sanitary enlightenment," Soviet doctors under NEP attempted to redeem prostitutes through labor, establishing special clinics to cure their ailments and teach them a trade (F. Bernstein, "Prostitutes and Proletarians").

9. The use of the term "victimless crime" is not meant to imply that prostitutes never suffer as a result of their work, but rather that they do not cause harm to third parties. Where prostitutes themselves are considered victims, the crime in question is pimping rather than prostitution (see Cassiday and Rouhi). Prostitutes in Russia and elsewhere have faced legal prosecution for offenses related to their profession, such as spreading venereal disease to their customers (F. Bernstein, "Envisioning Health" 205–7).

10. For example, Pavel Rusanov, the Party hack in Solzhenitsyn's *Cancer Ward* (1967–1968), is appalled at the prospect that the people he sent to the camps might return and demand their jobs and apartments back, not to mention justice and reparations. Iulii Daniel's haunting novella "Atonement" (1963) presents the Kafkaesque dilemma of a man who finds himself shunned by his circle of friends after one of them returns from the gulag; the narrator discovers that this man holds him responsible for the years spent in the prison camps, even though in actuality the returnee had been denounced by someone else entirely. By the story's end, the narrator nonetheless accepts his guilt, if not for this particular crime, then for his failure to speak out when his friend was caught up in the machinery of the Terror.

11. When Tania's mother expresses her horror at the thought that her daughter is "selling herself," Tania replies: "Correct. But how many of us do *not* sell ourselves?" Attwood 73.

12. The fact that Tania meets her demise in Sweden of all places is also worthy of note. On the level of plot, Sweden is clearly meant to embody the West at its coldest: an efficient land where any act of spontaneity is greeted with suspicion and any expenditure of money must be counted to the last decimal. Symbolically, Sweden still functions as one of Russia's oldest and weakest European enemies, the country whose army was defeated by Alexander Nevsky in 1240, by Peter the Great (most notably at Poltava in 1709), and by Alexander I in 1809.

13. Igor' Kon cites a 1989 survey of high school senior girls in Riga and Leningrad claiming that foreign-currency prostitution "had become one of the top ten most prestigious professions," as well as a survey in which prostitutes ranked higher than journalists, diplomats, and academics among prestigious and lucrative professions admired by Moscow schoolchildren (223). Survey results in the former Soviet Union are notoriously unreliable and should be viewed with a healthy dose of skepticism; nevertheless, the appearance of such survey results in the Russian mass media has been important in defining the role of the prostitute in contemporary Russian sexual discourse. At the very least, the surveys have created the *impression* that prostitution is considered a desirable profession.

14. For information about the rise in prostitution during the perestroika era, see Sanjian; Waters, "Prostitution."

15. For more on the connection between sexual and economic discourses in contemporary Russia, see Borenstein, "'About That.'"

16. The constellation of Russian and black prostitutes with Russian and foreign johns recurs throughout the popular discourse on prostitution in post-Soviet Russia. Edvard Maksimovich's 1997 *Prostitutki Moskvy,* a "handbook" on the lives of prostitutes in the capital, is largely a compendium of horror stories about the miserable lives of young women who make their living performing sex for hire. The cover shows a brazen Russian woman clad in scanty black leather fetish garb with a cigarette hanging out of her mouth, set against the backdrop of a well-known Moscow hotel for foreigners and enlarged reproductions of hundred-dollar bills. But the stories within the book concern lower-class hookers whose customers tend to be Russian, and the photo spread in the middle prominently features African women who have been picked up for soliciting and put in holding cells. In the racist hierarchy of prostitution for export, the presence of African women serving Russian men only heightens the humiliation entailed by exporting Russian women to serve European and American men: Russia exports its riches and imports lower-class commodities. The very composition of the book reflects the prostitute's symbolic importance in terms of her domestic and international role: if the cover's hard-currency hooker, whose clients are presumably foreign, has at least a modicum of glamour, the women in the interior photos (decidedly not for export) are made as repulsive as possible.

17. These last two sentences are present in the *Andrei* text but were left out of the *Muzhchiny* collection.

18. Mikhail Bulgakov's 1928 play *Flight* [*Beg*] and Iurii Olesha's 1931 melodrama *A List of Assets* [*Spisok blagodeianii*] present emigration and death as either virtually equivalent (the émigrés are the living dead) or a matter of cause and effect (even considering emigration leads to the hero's death). See Avins 79–90, 101–16. An American documentary about Soviet émigrés in Brooklyn entitled *The Russians Are Here* was broadcast in the Soviet Union in 1986 under the evocative title *Ex-* [*Byvshie*], suggesting that the émigrés are simply enduring an unpleasant afterlife.

19. Sam's encounters with ordinary Russians inevitably revert to a parody of Russian chauvinism. After getting drunk on a Russian man's vodka-infused blood, Sam attacks his Russian mosquito hosts: "Admit it, *bliad'* [whore]. . . . Don't you suck Russian blood?" (167). Later on, a driver launches into a tirade about the enemies of Russia while Sam quietly sucks the man's blood from behind: "We've been sold . . . . And all our rockets and our navy. They've drained us of our life's blood. . ." (217).

20. Sever's brothel resembles a parody of Vera Pavlovna's sewing cooperative in Nikolai Chernyshevsky's *What Is To Be Done?* Where Vera Pavlovna rescued young prostitutes from a life of shame and redeemed them through labor, Sever gives them a better life without actually changing their profession.

References

Amerikanskii dedushka. Dir. Ivan Shchegolev. Moscow: Iupiter, 1993.

Andrei: Russkii zhurnal dlia muzhchin 1 (1991).

Attwood, Lynn. "Sex and the Cinema." *Sex and Russian Society.* Ed. Igor Kon and James Riordan. Bloomington: Indiana UP, 1993. 64–85.

Avins, Carol. *Border Crossings: The West and Russian Identity in Soviet Literature, 1917–1934.* Berkeley: U California P, 1983.

Babel', Isaak. *Sochineniia.* 2 vols. Moscow: Khudozhestvennaia literatura, 1990.

Belova, Valeriia. "Kak Interdovichku obviniali v prostitutsii." *Kino-park.* May 1999.

Bernstein, Frances L. "Envisioning Health in Revolutionary Russia: The Politics of

Gender in Sexual Enlightenment Posters of the 1920s." *Russian Review* 57.2 (Apr. 1998): 191–217.

———. "Prostitutes and Proletarians: The Labor Clinic as Revolutionary Laboratory in the 1920s." *The Human Tradition in Modern Russia.* Ed. William Husband. Wilmington: Scholarly Resources, 2000. 113–28.

Bernstein, Laura. *Sonia's Daughters: Prostitutes and Their Regulation in Imperial Russia.* Berkeley: U California P, 1995.

Borenstein, Eliot. "'About That': Deploying and Deploring Sex in Post-Soviet Russia." *Studies in Twentieth Century Literature* 24 (Winter 2000): 51–83. Guest ed. Helena Goscilo. Special Issue on Russian Culture of the 1990s.

———. *Men Without Women: Masculinity and Revolution in Russian Fiction, 1917–1929.* Durham: Duke UP, 2000.

Cassiday, Julie A., and Leyla Rouhi. "From Nevskii Prospekt to Zoia's Apartment: Trials of the Russian Procuress." *Russian Review* 58.3 (July 1999): 413–31.

Clark, Katerina. "Not for Sale: The Russian/Soviet Intelligentsia, Prostitution, and the Paradox of Internal Colonization." *Russian Culture in Transition.* Stanford: Stanford Slavic Studies 7: 189–205.

Dotsenko, Viktor. *Mest' Beshenogo.* Moscow: Vagrius, 1998.

Engel, Barbara Alpern. *Between the Fields and the City: Women, Work, and Family in Russia, 1861–1914.* Cambridge, Eng.: Cambridge UP. 1994.

———. "St. Petersburg Prostitutes in the Late Nineteenth Century: A Personal and Social Profile." *Russian Review* 48.1 (Jan. 1989): 21–44.

Erofeev, Viktor. *Muzhchiny.* Moscow: Podkova, 1997.

———. "Polet 'oblaka v shtanakh'." *Andrei* 6 (1995): 44–46.

———. *Russkaia krasavitsa.* Moscow: Vsia Moskva, 1990.

Goscilo, Helena. *Dehexing Sex: Russian Womanhood During and After Glasnost.* Ann Arbor: U Michigan P, 1996.

Healey, Dan. "Masculine Purity and 'Gentlemen's Mischief': Sexual Exchange and Prostitution between Russian Men, 1861–1941." *Slavic Review* 60.2 (Summer 2001): 233–65.

Kon, Igor. *The Sexual Revolution in Russia: From the Age of the Czars to Today.* Trans. James Riordan. New York: The Free Press, 1995.

Lebina, N. B., and M. V. Shkarovskii. *Prostitutisiia v Peterburge.* Moscow: Progress-Akademiia, 1994.

Lodge, Robin. "Crimean Prostitutes to Retreat from NATO." *The Times* (UK). Apr. 24, 1997. Rpt. in *Johnson's List* 24 Apr. 1997.

Maksimovich, Edvard. *Prostitutki Moskvy.* Moscow: Iustitsiia-M, 1997.

Matich, Olga. "A Typology of Fallen Women in Nineteenth Century Russian Literature." *American Contributions to the Ninth International Congress of Slavists. Vol. II: Literature, Politics, History.* Ed. Paul Debreczeny. Columbus: Slavica, 1983. 325–43.

Nekrasov, N. A. *Polnoe sobranie stikhotvorenii v trekh tomakh.* Vol. 1. Leningrad: Sovetskii pisatel', 1967.

Pelevin, Victor. *Zhizn' nasekomykh. Romany.* Moscow: Vagrius, 1997.

Pugachev, Sergei. *Ty prosto shliukha, dorogaia!* Moscow: EKSMO-Press, 1999.

Sanjian, Andrea Stevenson. "Prostitution, the Press, and Agenda-Building in the Soviet Policy Process." Anthony Jones, Walter D. Connor, and David E. Powell (eds.) *Soviet Social Problems.* Boulder: Westview Press, 1991. 270–95.

Shcherbakov, Dmitrii. *Nimfomanka.* Moscow: EKSMO-Press, 1998.

———. *Nimfomanka: Besposhchadnaia strast'.* Moscow: EKSMO-Press, 1998.

Siegel, George. "The Fallen Woman in Nineteenth Century Literature." *Harvard Slavic Studies* 5 (1970): 81–107.

Stites, Richard. "Prostitute and Society in Pre-Revolutionary Russia." *Jahrbücher für Geschichte Osteuropas* 31.3 (1983): 348–64.

———. *The Women's Liberation Movement in Russia: Feminism, Nihilism and Bolshevism (1860–1930)*. Princeton: Princeton UP, 1988.

Tolstoi, L. N. *Sobranie sochinenii v dvenadtsati tomakh*. Moscow: Pravda, 1987.

Vse to, o chem my tak dolgo mechtali. Dir. Rudol'f Fruntov. Moscow: Kvorum, 1997.

Waters, Elizabeth. "Prostitution." *Soviet Social Reality in the Mirror of Glasnost*. Ed. Jim Riordan. New York: St. Martin's Press, 1992. 133–54.

———. "Victim or Villain: Prostitution in Post-Revolutionary Russia." *Women and Society in Russia and the Soviet Union*. Ed. Linda Edmonton. Cambridge: Cambridge UP, 1992.

Wood, Elizabeth. "Prostitution Unbound: Representations of Sexual and Political Anxieties in Post-Revolutionary Russia." *Sexuality and the Body in Russian Culture*, 1993.

Zholkovskii, Aleksandr. "Topos prostitutsii." *Babel'/Babel*. Ed. A. K. Zholkovskii and M. B. Iampol'skii. Moscow: Carte Blanche, 1994. 317–68.

NINE | Castrated Patriarchy, Violence, and Gender Hierarchies in Post-Soviet Film

YANA HASHAMOVA

After the collapse of the Soviet state, Russian cinema explicitly revealed the nation's inherited social and psychological problems and began to reflect emergent changes in Russian society. During the first half of the 1990s, Russian filmmakers disregarded those ideological constraints that previously had prevailed and presented an unremittingly bleak picture of Russian reality. Pavel Lungin's *Taxi-Blues* (1990) and *Luna Park* (1992), Vladimir Khotinenko's *Makarov* (1993) and *The Muslim* (1995), Georgii Daneliya's *Passport* (1990), and Aleksandr Sokurov's *The Second Circle* (1990) portray nationalist obsessions, psychological problems, violence, chaos, poverty, and crime.[1] While films such as these suggest a social structure in disarray, the cinematic production of the late 1990s exhibits tendencies that imply a new Russian social order: specifically, a greater variety of female roles and a traumatic adjustment of men to the most recent social changes.

Although Russian cinema in post-Soviet culture may have lost the popularity it enjoyed in the 1970s and early 1980s, through its archetypes and images of everyday life it still influences the public more than any other artistic media with the exception of television.[2] In today's new political, social, and economic conditions, Russian cinema continues to explore new avenues, take risks, and seek original formulas to attract more viewers. In this regard, contemporary Russian film offers abundant material for cultural analysis by reflecting as well as constructing social paradigms.

This chapter focuses on gender dynamics in post-Soviet cinema in an attempt to draw conclusions on the basis of representative examples, however tentative, about gender developments within the broader picture of change in Russian society and culture. Two key arguments should be outlined here. First, gender roles as represented in post-Soviet Russian films are directly rooted in Soviet experience, inasmuch as the latter provides a social foundation for the male and female screen characters Russian viewers watch today: aggressive, disoriented, and inept Russian men and victimized young women, strong (even when negative) mothers, and successful female professionals. Though some of these male and female images basically represent gender roles very similar to those of their socialist predecessors, there is more diversity in today's celluloid gender representations. This suggests, if not the emergence of new roles, then at least new dynamics in gender paradigms.

Second, the new gender dynamics on the post-Soviet screen are also influenced by contemporary Western "gender hesitations," which stem from the West's discovery of an absence of authority, the Father, or the Other in the Lacanian sense.[3] Russian screen images of men and women reflect the consequences of these hesitations.[4]

The two groups of films discussed below explore the causes of alterations in gender paradigms. The first includes *Mama* (1999), *Death and a Little Love* [*Smert' i nemnogo liubvi*, 2000], and *The Land of the Deaf* [*Strana glukhikh*, 1998], which show a decisive female presence, powerful mothers, and successful female professionals.[5] The second group includes *Taxi-Blues* (1990), *Luna Park* (1992), *Brother* [*Brat*, 1997], and *The Voroshilov Marksman* [*Voroshilovskii strelok*, 1999]. These films depict desperate, angry, and confused men, violent young Russian males occupying a transitory niche in the new symbolic order, and victimized young women.[6] All images, male and female, suggest a new dynamic that, however timidly, pushes against the traditional patriarchal structure.[7] This statement may appear to be at odds with Helena Goscilo's argument that the "treatment of gender in Russian culture today suggests that in one respect, at least, post-Soviet culture is more Soviet than post-" (Goscilo, "Gendered Trinity" 68). While the patriarchal structure is certainly still intact in Russia, the Soviet experience and Western distrust of the function of the Father are destabilizing factors that have challenged its rigidity and thus, perhaps, made it even more brutal.[8]

Soviet Womanhood

In her study of identity and social institutions, Renata Salecl pinpoints the hesitations and problems with identity of individual subjects in post-communist Russia and Eastern Europe (Salecl, *[Per]versions* 80–85). Her work centers on people's nostalgia for the past and poses a variety of theoretical questions, such as: "How is the identity of the subject related to the symbolic order and which memory of the past does the subject invoke?" (80). She argues that in a restrictive society the subject's identity develops in close relation to the symbolic order, the Other, as well as reacting to the positions of other members of society. Salecl analyzes the movie *The Shawshank Redemption* (Frank Darabont, 1994) to illustrate her point:

> Certain prisoners serving life sentences display an impossible desire: they dream endlessly about "freedom", but when they are eventually released, they nostalgically remember the "non-freedom" of their prison life. . . . In the film, the prisoner Red, serving a life sentence, narrates a story about another lifer, Andy, a young banker, convicted of murdering his wife and her lover. Andy is

a special person: he radiates a certain calm, as if the horror of prison does not touch him in his inner being. In contrast, other prisoners are, as Red says, "institutionalized men": their identity depends on the place they have in the prison hierarchy. When released from prison, they become broken individuals who either commit another crime in order to be reincarcerated or decide to end their lives. (81)

What is important for Salecl is how, in the strict order and oppressiveness of the prison, the prisoners organize their identities. They follow rules, often invented by them, form hierarchies, humiliate one another, and pit one inmate against another. The prison institution provides a structure for prisoners' identity: there are those who know how to follow the rules and identify with them, and others who are endlessly at odds with the internal organization of the prison.

Salecl's observations are relevant to the present study, not only for understanding the subject's identity, but also for approaching developments in gender identity during the Soviet period and after the fall of communism, particularly the construction and deconstruction of gender roles in relation to the symbolic order. In examining how men and women form their gender identities vis-à-vis the demands of Soviet and post-Soviet ideology, I acknowledge the significant impact on gender studies of Judith Butler's gender theory and performativity (see Butler), while focusing specifically on the Russian historical and social context. Given that context, Salecl's discussion of institutionalized identities and Paul Verhaeghe's ideas about the collapse of the Father, discussed below, provide a useful lens through which to view Russian gender paradigms in post-Soviet reality.

The Soviet system firmly structured Russians' lives and designated their social roles according to its ideology. To achieve women's emancipation and the abolishment of class differences, legislation guaranteed women's equal rights and access to the means of production, which, according to Engels, would liquidate their dependence on men. On paper, Soviet ideologists vouchsafed all workers' equality in the symbolic order. Men and women were agricultural, industrial, intellectual, and Party workers, and thus, theoretically, at least, occupied the same position in relation to the Other, the Law. However, the restructuring of society and the creation of new roles after 1917 was fraught with contradictions and served state ideology rather than individual women. Stalinist socialism emphasized women's reproductive functions in order to secure new generations of believers and builders of the "bright future" of Russian society, making women "workers, wives, and mothers." The Soviet woman (*sovetskaia zhenshchina*) had to achieve a healthy balance among the three roles assigned to her by society and to strive for perfection in all three.[9]

Women's emancipation under socialism differed from the emancipation of Western women in several important ways. First, the Soviet system rapidly enforced emancipation before preparing society for it. Second, socialism imposed an obligatory triple role on women. Daniel Rancour-Laferriere in his book *The Slave Soul of Russia* mentions another important difference: "The imbalance between hours spent by men and hours spent by women on household tasks was very roughly similar across developed countries. . . . What was different about Soviet women is that they endured the imbalance *and* typically worked full-time" (161).[10] The author explains this endurance as a feature of Russian women's masochistic nature.[11] He concedes, however, that economic and ideological factors contributed to women's double burden and their masochistic behavior (167).

It could be argued, alternatively, that ideological demands structured women's desire, which is the desire of the Other and not their own. Women felt the pressure of Soviet ideology, which required that they be perfect "mothers, wives, and workers." This desire, however, encountered the (Lacanian) real and proved an unattainable goal. As Andrew Horton and Michael Brashinsky have argued, "The development of Marxism-Leninism . . . while vaguely espousing gender, actually supported the patriarchal family structure and puritanical sexual values, and thus never delivered true economic, social, personal, or psychological freedom for women in the Soviet Union" (101). Perhaps women were not forced by men to do what they did, as Rancour-Laferriere argues, but they certainly received little support or help within the family. In "Effects of Perestroika and Glasnost' on Women," Kerry McCuaig reports that a Soviet mother with young children had an average of seven hours and thirty-six minutes a day for sleeping, eating, and personal time (11–14). This clash of the symbolic order of women's roles with the real in Soviet Russia suggests that to a certain extent women's identity escaped complete "institutionalization" (in Salecl's understanding of the term).

As Horton and Brashinsky point out, though women in the Soviet Union made up more than half the population and held 51 percent of the jobs, comprising "75 percent of all teachers, 69 percent of all physicians, and a surprising 87 percent of all economists," they accounted for only 30 percent of the members of the Communist Party, and only one woman ever joined the highest governing structure, the thirteen-member Politburo (Horton and Brashinsky 102). Whatever freedom and economic independence Soviet women may have enjoyed, they were drastically underrepresented in the political sphere, despite the peculiar position in which WWII placed them: With so many men killed either in the war or in prison camps, women frequently had to support their children alone, while also maintaining the local farms or factories. Though promulgated on paper, gender equality failed in the real; it was fallaciously claimed in the symbolic order but actually never left the level of the (male) imaginary.

Already accustomed to contradictions between the symbolic order and the social realities of the Soviet period (or being less institutionalized—which grants them more power and flexibility), women currently exhibit various identity patterns. Whereas formerly ideology mandated that they perform the role of the perfect Soviet woman, today one sees a quite broad range of women's attitudes originating in economic necessity, disillusion-ment with Soviet "emancipation," and long-delayed, repressed reactions to Soviet demands. These reactions manifest themselves, for example, as an-tifeminism and a return to the domestic space, or as an active, decisive so-cial presence and pursuit of professional development.[12] This broadened spectrum of choices available to women in post-Soviet Russia marks a dras-tic departure from previously assigned roles. Today's cultural production in general, and film specifically, reflects the consequences for women of both the imaginary equality and the escape from complete institutionalization.

Western culture's most recent invasion of (post-Soviet) Russia inevitably has affected representations of gender dynamics in Russian cinema. The to-tal collapse of the old political and economic structure, which provided se-curity and order, as well as repression and restraints, reinforces Russia's cur-rent, typically Western, distrust of authority—a distrust that produces effects on gender dynamics similar to those in the West but intensified in the Russian case. As Verhaeghe has argued, the successful feminist move-ment of the last quarter of the twentieth century weakened the function of the Father and, precisely because of its success, simultaneously prompted a longing for the old authority. He writes, "Nowadays popular opinion is ask-ing, sometimes even begging, for a return of law and order, that is a re-turn of the authoritarian father, again both at the individual and at the sociological level" (132). He believes that this striking reversal is due to the widespread distrust of Freud's myth of the primal father and, by ex-tension, of the symbolic function of the father and of any authority. Such a situation affects the way gender roles, and especially the concepts of the Father and femininity, are enacted or viewed. Verhaeghe argues that to al-leviate the prevailing feeling of loss and insecurity the sons install an ab-solute Other, of which there are "abundant contemporary examples, from the return of fundamentalism on a mass scale to the success of smaller sects" (138).

The current distrust of authority amid the prevailing postmodern cyni-cism leads, from a Freudian point of view, to the reversal of this primal fa-ther myth, as deftly summarized by Slavoj Žižek (*Metastases* 205–6).[13] In the reversed version the symbolic function (the paternal metaphor as organiza-tional principle) is destroyed, which results in the creation of what Žižek calls the primal anal father, who seeks only his own *jouissance*. As a result, his sons experience insecurity and lack of protection, which (according to Freud) increases their anxiety, aggression, and violence. This course of events influences the feminine side of the gender paradigm in two dis-tinct ways: aggressive and violent sons abuse and victimize women; at the same time, however, with the disappearance of masculine superior-ity, feminine inferiority also disappears, resulting in an increased and more decisive social presence of professional women.[14] Furthermore,

Verhaeghe claims that mothers, as a category, are marginalized and "while their sons trouble them the most, there is a new coalition in the making with their daughters" (139). These tendencies are certainly reflected in contemporary Russian film.

During the transitional period to a post-totalitarian society, Russian films entered marginal spaces previously proscribed by Soviet ideology. The term *"chernukha"* (from the Russian word "black"), which commentators regularly apply to visual and verbal texts of the 1990s, describes works drawing a bleak picture of reality, featuring criminals, prostitutes, hit men, and New Russians. New words entered the Russian language—"thriller," "killer," and *"uzhastik"* (horror film). In these new social and cultural circumstances, as the film critic Zara Abdullaeva argues, one cannot apply the old artistic criteria of "good" and "bad" to new cinematic Russian productions, but, rather, tends to evaluate them with the modifiers "important" and "unimportant" (Abdullaeva n.p.). To characterize a film as important, one should consider its aesthetic radicalism, social correctness, and viewers' interest. For example, Abdullaeva labels Aleksei Balabanov's *Of Freaks and Men* unimportant, for while the film may be aesthetically challenging, it does not reflect present social concerns and did not strike a chord with the general public. All of the films I shall discuss here belong to popular mainstream cinema and, according to Abdullaeva's criteria, may be considered important. Some of them are artistically and intellectually challenging, and others are trivial; they are stylistically diverse, committed to a portrayal of social reality, and have enjoyed considerable success with Russian audiences.

Screening Female Gender

Denis Evstigneev's *Mama* (1999) belongs to a group of films appearing at the close of the twentieth century that allow women to propel the cinematic narrative and become its agents rather than its victims.[15] It falls within the tradition of maternal images in Russian literature and cinema (one of the most significant being Gorky's—and Pudovkin's—*Mother* [*Mat'*, 1926]). After the death of her husband, Polina decides to organize and manage a family folk band. Called *Happy Family,* the group successfully tours the country, but soon thereafter the mother begins to imagine a better future for her five sons—an aspiration that raises pointed questions about just how happy the *Happy Family* is. Polina engages in the risky, desperate enterprise of hijacking a plane, and fails. After serving fifteen years in prison, she searches for her sons, now scattered all over the country. The oldest, Lenchik, has been in a mental institution all these years, feigning madness to avoid a prison sentence for his part in the hijacking. Polina asks her four other sons to visit her, and within a few days they gather at their old apartment.

After fifteen years of separation the grown men meet their mother with respect and fear. The scene reveals the unusual influence and power Mama wields over her sons: after just a few moments in her company they transform into infantile boys—jumping, laughing, and fighting. The family frees Lenchik from the madhouse and heads for its native village. On the train heading home, Lenchik demonstrates that he, at least, has jettisoned his dependence on Mama; he confronts his mother with her arrogance in trying to mold their lives by attempting to start their collective "happy new life." His last words are, "I need nothing from you, Mama, nothing."[16] Evstigneev softens the conflict between Mama and her sons by creating a second ending: As they all get off the train at a small provincial station in their home village, Mama begins crying and asks forgiveness of her sons. She covers her face with her hands, and when she removes them her sons start laughing, for she accidentally has smeared her face with some black paint stuck to one of her palms. This "happy" ending, however, does not change the overall gloomy impression of the film or of the mother's image. Her blackened face can also be read in a less than "happy" way: her individuality (her human face) disappears at the expense of her omnipotent control. Polina is not a mother (*mat'*) to the young men, but a mama—who has manipulated and ruined her sons' lives, and perhaps will continue to do so. Appropriately enough, within the Russian prison system, Mama is jargon for the seasoned older female criminal who oversees and tyrannizes groups of less experienced male inmates. While Vlasova in Gorky's novel changes her convictions and beliefs under her son's influence and is ready to sacrifice her life for him, the overpowering control of Mama in this film has destroyed her sons' lives. While the gender dynamics in this film feature Mama as a strong female figure, she is demonized as the Negative Mother, who hesitates at nothing to achieve her goals.

Contemporary Russian fiction contains a kindred example of controlling and destructive maternity in Petrushevkaia's *The Time Night* [*Vremia noch'*, 1992]. In her compelling analysis of the text ("Mother as Mothra"), Goscilo writes:

> Indeed, a closer inspection of the text's double-voicing unmasks Anna Andrianovna's vaunted Christian self-abnegation as a mode of unappeasable sadistic control and vampirism—all in the name of love, which she trumpets as the most important thing in life . . . . Beneath her rhetoric we uncover the pre-Oedipal mother, an all-powerful, engulfing figure who theatricalizes the Freudian scenario of the mother-child relationship. (108)

This observation is also applicable to Polina's character and behavior. In addition to the marginalized mother figure as described by Verhaeghe (present also in Balabanov's *Brother,* discussed below), the weak function of the paternal metaphor and the subsequent crisis in the symbolic order create conditions for the resurfacing of the pre-Oedipal mother. Lacan stresses the

9-1   Elena Iakovleva as Major Kamenskaia in *Death and a Little Love* (Dir. Iuri Moroz, 2000).

9-2 Nonna Morkiukova as Mama in *Mama* (Dir. D. Evstigneev, 1999).

function of the paternal metaphor as an organizational principle, which enables a passage from duality to triangularity. The main function of the father figure is to separate the child from the mother in order to ensure the child's healthy maturity. When the paternal metaphor is dysfunctional, as occurs in *Mama* and *The Time Night,* the scenario results in destructive mothers and alienated, disoriented children. Mama in the eponymous film occupies the symbolic positions of both the mother and the father, and this fusion grants her an overwhelming control over her sons; she deprives them of the possibility to identify with the symbolic function of the Father itself. This deprivation, as noted above, condemns her sons to remain perpetually at the level of immature boys, in unresolved fear of the threatening female figure. The film features only a mother-sons relationship—an unsurprising fact considering the structure of the Oedipus complex. The absence of daughters in the film, however, raises the question of the female side of generational gender paradigms. Verhaeghe maintains that the disappearance of the old-style masculine Father figure, or authority, eliminates feminine inferiority, but we can only speculate how Evstigneev might have portrayed Mama-daughter relations.

In their depiction of gender roles Aleksandra Marinina's novels and the films based on them constitute precisely this shift: the disappearance of female inferiority. Marinina's novels about Major Kamenskaia have become a phenomenon in Russian popular culture. While some intellectuals regard them with skepticism, many readers are infatuated by the female protagonist, Anastasiia Kamenskaia.[17] A detective who both analyzes crimes and hunts down criminals, Kamenskaia does not exhibit the typical male traits traditionally inhering in this position. She relies not on muscles but on brains and intuition to investigate and solve crimes. Comfortable and confident within the symbolic order—that is, amid the male assistants, associates, and boss who surround her—she nonetheless has marked her space with thoughtfulness and sensitivity. In her insightful analysis of Marinina's novels, Catherine Theimer Nepomnyashchy points out that "although it would be problematic to identify Marinina as a 'feminist' writer in any recognizably Western sense of that word, viewing her works in the light of some Western scholarship on feminist detective fiction may help to explain her popularity with contemporary Russian readers" (171). Nepomnyashchy draws a detailed portrait of Kamenskaia as a woman surrounded by male protectors: her stepfather, half-brother, and husband in her personal life and her colleagues on the job. Yet Kamenskaia overturns conventional female gender roles insofar as she never uses makeup or feminine clothing to please men, never cooks or worries about housework. When, in *Smert' i nemnogo liubvi*, Marinina decides to bestow some "family happiness" on her female protagonist, Kamenskaia's marriage functions differently from traditional legal unions. She has known her fiancé for years and is comfortable living with him but does not depend on him financially. Moreover, she clearly is active in public spaces, whereas her husband is "domestic." He purchases the groceries, prepares dinner, and even buys her wedding dress when she cannot find the time to complete this task. Nepomnyashchy also points out that Kamenskaia "insists on wearing black to her wedding, the color putatively gendered male," and, moreover, highly inappropriate for the occasion, given its associations with funerals (179).

The popular success of the novels and films about Kamenskaia implies readers' receptivity to feminist ideas that do not reject men but posit gender parity in professional, social, and domestic spheres. Bearing in mind Kamenskaia's relationship with her husband and her behavior at home, this equality certainly differs from the ill-achieved emancipation during the Soviet period. Kamenskaia's position within her family "unit," unlike that, for example, of Baranskaia's heroine Ol'ga in the Thaw novella *A Week Like Any Other*—one of the first texts to raise the issue of women's workloads (see endnote 9)—is not burdened by household chores; on the contrary, she is relieved of most domestic duties by her husband and exhibits few feelings of guilt about this situation. Kamenskaia often gives priority to her professional responsibilities over her domestic ones. Though her profession defines her as woman-the-hunter, in her relationship with her husband, true to long-standing paradigms, she is still desired rather than desiring. And she scorns the stereotypical profile of a loving wife—that is, a housewife.[18] Marinina takes care not to construct her heroine as entirely woman-the-hunter, or entirely the doting wife, for either extreme likely would have reduced her popularity. In this cautious construction of the character's gender position one can uncover the complexities and the contradictions of sexual difference. According to Salecl and others, "Sexual difference is understood . . . as the result of the castration complex which 'makes' a girl (as a sexual role) out of a girl, and a boy out of a boy, although it is not always the case that sexual roles have to correspond to biological sex" (Salecl, *The Spoils of Freedom* 128). Salecl insists that the status of men and women is not naturally determined but ascribed in the symbolic order; they are symbolically mediated. Kamenskaia's female body does not limit her search for equality and even superiority in the workplace. In her social position and in her appearance the heroine refuses to follow any "naturally" determined expectations of her sex, despite her occasional guilt at not fulfilling certain obligations traditionally tagged female. Yet Kamenskaia is desired, not desiring; in her emotional/sexual relationship with men she enacts the passive side.

One can observe here a significant modification in the standard binary opposition: despite the equality in the male-female social positions and the near-disappearance of the fundamental polarization of gender, the opposition of *active* versus *passive* still obtains in the sexual relationship. The popularity of Kamenskaia and her gender construction testifies that for the Russian collective mind sexual difference may be symbolically mediated in the social sphere, but sexual desire is implicated in such traditional oppositions as active/passive.

Anyone seeking more radically feminist ideas in Russian cinema will find them in incipient and contradictory form in Valerii Todorovskii's *The Land of the Deaf*. Based on Renata Litvinova's novella *To Have and to Belong* [*Obladat' i prinadlezhat'*], the film centers on the relationship between a deaf dancer, Iaia, and Rita, the girlfriend of a compulsive gambler, Alesha. Iaia's name is her own invention, consisting of the double personal pronoun "*ia-*

ia" [I-I].[19] This affirmation of her personality and independence reflects her attitude towards men. Working as a dancer in a strip bar, Iaia breaks with her lover when he asks her to sleep with the manager. Tellingly, upon first encountering Rita in the bar, Iaia asks, "Are you in danger? Danger from men?" following up immediately with the statement, "I hate all men." Since Rita needs money to save Alesha from his gambling debts, Iaia proposes that they earn money through prostitution. The ensuing scene between them and the local pimps reveals their dignity and independence as Iaia daringly refuses to accept the pimps' conditions and they leave. Rita finds employment with a deaf, criminal owner of a restaurant to whom Iaia introduces her, who decides to hire her as his "ears": She accompanies him to "business" meetings and warns him of any danger. Iaia teaches Rita sign language, and the two develop a sufficiently strong emotional and physical attachment for Iaia to draw Rita into her fantasy of a land of the deaf—a paradise where people are happy and lack nothing, for money is disbursed to all who are deaf. This fantasy sooner belongs to the imaginary, based on sense evidence, than to the symbolic, mediated by language and controlled and enjoyed by men. Alesha's sudden appearance disturbs the women's relationship when Rita's desire to maintain a relationship with him and help him arouses Iaia's jealous aggression until Alesha leaves Rita after again spending all the money she has earned. At the film's conclusion men from various gangs kill off one another, deafening Rita in the shootout. Only the two women stay alive. Of the men in the film, only the police chalk lines remain.

Despite the unfolding of events that at least partially would seem to indicate otherwise, the overall context of the film remains patriarchal and phallocentric. One could argue, in fact, that the two women are completely dependent on men, even to a degrading extent: Iaia is a stripper and her first idea for making money is to become a prostitute. She seems utterly at the mercy of male-dominated society, unable to see beyond it except in fantasy. Also, since in her relations with Rita Iaia behaves like a capricious and jealous husband, the bond duplicates a standard heterosexual model. Indeed, Nina Tsyrkun reads the gendered fantasy of a land of the deaf as the patriarchal mark on women who wish to take advantage of the capitalistic lavishness awakened in Russia (Tsyrkun 57–66).

I see this fantasy, however, and the pair's caring union as an attempt to break with the strip bar and the compulsive gambler—hackneyed features of masculinist entitlement. Certainly, the utopian land of the deaf is a fantasy, but a fantasy for a different, female economy. Iaia never clarifies whether only women reside in this land of the deaf, but she invites only Rita to join her and share her fantasy as the two women attempt to create a union founded not only on emotional attachment but also on shared lives and finances. What makes this film radical is its readiness to entertain the notion of an economy that, if not lesbian, clearly differs from the failed heterosexual and phallocentric economy presented in the beginning of the film. The film's attempt at a feminist utopian society recalls Charlotte

Perkins Gilman's novel *Herland*, written in 1915 (but published as a complete work only in 1979), which promotes a similar all-female society founded on nurturing and cooperation.

Even though the sexual relationship between Iaia and Rita remains imaginary, the way they execute their sexual identities is significant. Their strong and compassionate sensual union suggests sexual desire in flux—sexual desire not tied to any essential body, as in the case of Kamenskaia's image (see also Brennan). In other words, sexual difference and sexual desire are not prediscursive but are born in signification, in the symbolic or, more precisely, in its failure; hence Iaia and Rita remain trapped in the symbolic and entertain only the fantasy of the imaginary land of deaf. Indeed, the construction of sexual difference as a failure of signification and the attempt to escape the symbolic linger, vague and unanswered in the film, yet as an undeniable conceptual presence.

Soviet Manhood

Focusing on the male side of the gender paradigm, one notes that men's roles changed little after the Revolution of 1917. In addition to maintaining their traditional roles as husbands and fathers, men were guaranteed workers' positions for which in the past they would have had to compete. In his study *Men without Women*, Eliot Borenstein convincingly demonstrates that in the early 1920s, there was a "triumph of affiliation over filial ties, by extension, of masculinity and the social over femininity and the domestic" (17–18). This supposed triumph, however, was "a process enacted [to a large extent] in the realm of the imaginary" (37), similar to the purported gender equality discussed above. When, a decade later, Russian iconography, art, and fiction departed from the masculinization of the 1920s by deploying female images, it did so for specific purposes of propaganda. As Borenstein argues, on the basis of a famous example—Vera Mukhina's statue of the worker and the collective-farm woman (1937):

> On the one hand, it would appear to be a representation of equality, each extending one arm to display a symbol of Soviet power. On the other hand, the traditional gendered hierarchy remains. . . . Agriculture, always the lesser partner in Soviet economic planning, is relegated to a female standard-bearer, while industrialization, the sine qua non of Stalinism, is championed by the man. Moreover, though both the worker and the collective-farm woman are stepping forward, the man is stepping a bit farther ahead. (273–74)

This inclusion of women in strong yet subordinate roles, Borenstein contends, suggests a restoration of male dominance and "of classical patriarchy in Soviet discourse" (274). Such strategies enabled men to avoid the drastic changes experienced by women and to identify more easily with their function as workers, thereby seemingly acceding to the new requirements of the

Soviet system. One could also argue, however, that men had identity problems as workers. The worker's position gave men stability and cemented their patriarchal status, but simultaneously limited their initiative and competitive development. To clarify, one has to mention here that the Stakhanovite movement in the 1930s encouraged competition but did not bring the anticipated results, namely, higher standards of life, and this failure discouraged and frustrated both men and women. As Mikhail Epstein aptly describes the fruitless labor, "How we labored from the twenties to the fifties before becoming lazy in the sixties! Day and night, to bloody blisters and an early grave, we burned to work, as they used to say about zealous laborers. But this didn't make us wealthy, even so" (164). Some men were frustrated by financial and ideological restrictions; others had trouble adjusting to women's economic independence, as reflected in films of the seventies: *Office Affair* [*Sluzhebnyi roman*, 1977], *Moscow Does Not Believe in Tears* [*Moskva slezam ne verit*, 1979]. Yet, it was easier for men than women to identify with their respectively assigned roles: men had to perform the parts of husband, father, and worker, which had been traditionally theirs, and thus, it was not so difficult for them to concede to the gender demands of Soviet ideology, whereas women were cast by ideological directives in unmanageable roles.[20]

In the context of Salecl's argument about the formation of the subject's identity according to his or her position in the symbolic order, one can say that men became more "institutionalized" in their gender manifestations than women because they did not undergo drastic changes in their gender roles. In this regard men surrendered more easily to the gendered terms of ideology, which reinforced their (latent or not) interest in maintaining male dominance. Women became "institutionalized" to a lesser degree, experiencing more directly the inadequacy of the symbolic order and of Soviet ideology, which imposed impossible demands on them. Frustrated and overworked, they performed their assigned roles with difficulty, and could not completely identify with the positions assigned to them. In short, though the population as a whole felt oppressed through subjection to extreme political and social control, the impositions on women were more intolerable.

After the disintegration of the Soviet system and its social organization—that is, after the collapse of the Law in Lacanian terms—both men and women experienced difficulties identifying their places and roles in the new society.[21] In many ways men seemed to confront a harder adjustment than women. They found themselves threatened by the instability of the new symbolic order, which, unlike the Soviet system, left them to locate their niche within society instead of vouchsafing them a secure place within a stable hierarchy. Consequently, they had to find new ways of empowering their positions and restoring their machismo, which some, paradoxically, perceived as having been damaged during the Soviet period by women's emancipation. Viktor Erofeev, a contemporary Russian writer, claims that the Soviet system ruined Russian men because it liberated women socially and sexually, and women's demands threatened and weakened Russian men (51–56, 112–17). Feminist scholars of Soviet society, such as Lynne Attwood, also elaborate on this paradox, observing that men seemingly became weaker and less resourceful since they perceived that women no longer needed their "protection" (see Attwood, *The New Soviet Man and Woman,* also "Sex and the Cinema" 65–88). It must be noted here, however, that just as the equality of male and female workers was achieved only on the level of the imaginary (but claimed in the symbolic), the new male identity crisis and castration complex have occurred on the order of the imaginary. In other words, these are imaginary processes that do not accurately reflect real gender positions.

Screening Male Gender

Pavel Lungin's *Taxi-Blues* (1990) *and Luna Park* (1992) and Aleksei Balabanov's *Brother* (1997) all portray the violent and desperate worlds of disoriented men suddenly deprived of stability and certainty in their identities immediately before and after the collapse of the Soviet system. In *Taxi-Blues* and *Luna Park,* Lungin examines Russian xenophobia. His protagonists, men with a fanatical understanding of Russian identity and what it means to be a decent Russian, find themselves challenged by Otherness. The protagonists experience personal trauma through their intimate interaction with an "Other" and as a result begin to see the world as less black and white than they had previously imagined it.

Lungin presents Lesha in *Taxi-Blues* as a middle-aged man who approaches the new world through his old socialist understanding of society and his own position in it: Russian men should have regular decent jobs and should earn a living through honest hard work. When he meets a musician who follows his passion for music (and for this reason is everything that the taxi-driver despises), hidden desires for spontaneity and personal freedom are awakened in him, but he is unable to face them. Lesha's behavior and identity problems are similar to those of the prisoners in Salecl's example. It is difficult for him, as an "institutionalized" man, to change, to adjust to a new reality, and the film's conclusion emphasizes his confused frustration.

By contrast, Andrei, the protagonist of *Luna Park,* is a young orphan who has found a place in a skinhead gang led and manipulated by a woman, Alena—an evil, destructive force that controls young men's lives by toying with their most vulnerable and sensitive side: their national and social identity. Young, disenfranchised Russians find family, stability, and identity in a nationalist gang, which fuels their extreme intolerance and their propensity for violence. Alena tells Andrei that she knows his father, who is a Jewish composer, and thus, quite contrary to her intentions, she causes Andrei to look for alternatives. After meeting his newfound father, Andrei reevaluates his life and realizes the limitations of the ideals embraced by the skinheads. At the film's end, viewers understand that Alena's depiction

of Andrei's father in derogatory terms was dishonest: Andrei's purported father is not his biological father, but an artist who had rejected Alena's "tal-
ent" when she was young, and she sought to avenge herself by directing
Andrei's anger against him. But events subvert her plans. Andrei befriends
the man and discovers in him the father he never had. The problem of the
absent father figure and of the concomitant lack of security, protection, and an
absolute authority resurfaces in this film. It is unsurprising that Andrei initially
finds his place in a nationalist gang that claims to offer the truth regarding the
Other while in fact offering a lie. His surrogate father provides the truth Andrei
did not find in the gang and inspires Andrei's loving trust. As Verhaeghe insists,
an overwhelming feeling of loss and insecurity drives young people to aggression and violence, urging them to seek certainty, authority, and the truth, but
often they merely find a pseudo-truth, as do the young Russians in *Luna Park*.

Brother likewise focuses on a young man, Danila, who has just finished
his military service in southern Russia. His mother sends him to Saint Petersburg to his older brother, Viktor, who proves to be a hit man. Without
any hesitations or scruples, Viktor involves Danila in the business of killing
and causes him to risk his life. Danila, however, as someone trained for and
in war, successfully deals with his assassins. In an ironic reversal of roles,
Danila, after discovering that Viktor set him up, spares his brother's life,
gives him money, and sends him to live with their mother. At film's end
Danila leaves for Moscow, having established his persona as someone who
abides by his own code, lives for the moment, and kills people of whom he
disapproves rather than contract-killing for money.[22] While Viktor's role as
a hit man reveals a new opportunity for Russian men with no scruples in
the post-Soviet transitional period, Danila's character presents a kind of
Russian Robin Hood who fights and kills for justice as he perceives it. The
two brothers expose conflicting social desires: whereas Viktor embodies the
desire for easy money and an adventurous life, Danila is motivated by a
need for justice in the violent present.

Like *Luna Park,* this film suggests a problematic paternal function and
the nonexistence of the Other, at both individual and societal levels.
Danila's mother complains about his father's meaningless life, and viewers
learn that Danila's father is in prison—the only information given about
him. At the end of the film, when Danila realizes that his older brother
has betrayed him, he does not punish Viktor, for, as he says, his older
brother "was like a father to him." This relationship, however, does not
prevent Danila from taking over the criminal business and sending his
brother home to take care of their mother. The role reversal and change
of power here indicate that no authority figure exists for Danila. This
lack also manifests itself in Danila's behavior, which ignores traditional
morals inasmuch as he kills people callously even while protecting those
he likes. One can argue that *Brother* reveals both the consequences of the
Soviet legacy—Danila's father, a drunk and a criminal—and the recent
distrust in authority.

Women in this aggressive male world function as victims and appendages. Danila's enemies beat up and rape his lover, Sveta, who, moreover, stays in an abusive relationship with her husband, accepting it as fate. The film presents Kat, Danila's young female acquaintance in the city, hooked on drugs with no future or dreams, as a product of Western influence, frequenting McDonald's and parties hosted by foreigners. Danila and Viktor's mother is an exhausted elderly woman with neither a genuine knowledge of, nor a true relationship with, her sons. She corresponds well to today's marginalized mothers as defined by Verhaeghe. The various female images in the film reflect the desperate position of post-Soviet women, who bear no resemblance to the ideal of Soviet womanhood.

This group of films consistently spotlights blood, violence, disoriented men, and killers, on the one hand, and victimized women, on the other. Three of these four films (the exception being *Luna Park*) clearly present a society in which men possess power and dominate women. Stanislav Govorukhin's film *The Voroshilov Marksman* (1999), however, focuses on young males (finally) deprived of their abusive dominance. Though Govorukhin also presents a male-dominant world, he incapacitates his young male characters through the unusual device of literal castration.

The film opens with elderly Russian men playing chess in a courtyard surrounded by apartment buildings. The next, contrasting scene introduces young Russians drinking beer on the balcony of one of the buildings. They are New Russians whose affluence evidently comes from criminal activity, since viewers never see them working or earning this money. The opening scenes establish the location for the unfolding story, the neighborhood, and also mark one of the film's major themes—clashing generational values. Situating the conflict in the neighborhood where people know one another intensifies the mutual pain they inflict. Fedorovich, who appears to be the heart of the elderly company, and his granddaughter, Katia, live alone. He is portrayed as a tender and caring grandfather, who is both surrogate mother and surrogate father to Katia. The young men invite Katia to their apartment under the pretext of celebrating their friend's birthday and proceed to gang-rape her. In its voyeuristic and painstaking representation of the rape the camera objectifies Katia's body and at the same time exposes the young Russians' lack of morals, sensitivity, and regard for others' dignity and life. In her article "Sex and the Cinema," Lynne Attwood argues that behind the scenes of rape and violence against women in Russian cinema on a subconscious level lies the threat to patriarchal gender relations discussed above in connection with the perceived masculine crisis caused by women's emancipation (85). Outraged at the brutality of the young hoodlums, her grandfather files a report with the local policeman, who quickly releases the young men after the colonel-father of one of them intercedes on their behalf. Furious and desperate at this blatant corruption of justice, Fedorovich takes matters into his own hands: He methodically shoots two of the young men, taking care not to kill, but to castrate, them. When the colonel tries to save his son by letting him into his apartment, the son, mistaking him for someone else, shoots his father through the door, and is taken by the police. He thereby escapes castration but loses his sanity.

The director, Govorukhin, who is a member of the Russian parliament, and as such might be expected to advocate lawfulness, here endorses taking justice into one's own hands.[23] The film intriguingly combines the killing of the primal father with the workings of the castration metaphor. The destabilizing role of the primal father, represented by the colonel, produces uncertainty and violence among the sons, who in turn are castrated and thus completely disempowered. The director employs the literal castration of the sons as a method of retribution and punishment, but the symbolic castration metaphor inevitably unveils problems in the phallocentric structure.

Fedorovich's character powerfully conveys the desperation of a generation whose beliefs and goals have been crushed by the new era of corruption and chaos. With no other recourse, he feels forced to use his past skills as an excellent marksman, most likely acquired during WWII, in order to deliver justice. The older generation of Russians may have escaped literal and metaphorical castration, but they have become almost impotent or deprived of the clear-cut gender markings promulgated throughout the Soviet era. Viewers see Fedorovich shopping for groceries and cooking dumplings (*pel'meni*) for Katia. He is visibly confined to the domestic sphere, which extends only to the yard and his chess playing—understandably so, given his function as surrogate for both parents to Katia. The young men's activities are confined to driving expensive cars, drinking, and violating young women. Their lives have no meaning or substance, and their literal castration ultimately results from their spiritual emptiness—a consequence, the film proposes, of their upbringing. The colonel, who misunderstands the paternal function, has not taught his son to accept responsibility or to face the consequences of his actions. Instead, he infantilizes him by regularly protecting him and supplying him with material goods, which the father himself identifies with comfort and enjoyment, both of which he likes to indulge. In other words, the figure of the colonel suggests the reversal of Freud's primal father myth and comes close to Žižek's understanding of the primal anal father who seeks his own *jouissance*. Symbolically castrated by their own lack of responsibility, morals, and order long before Fedorovich takes to the task, and growing up under the full protection of their parents in a corrupt society with unstable values, the young men have become violent and disoriented, afloat in an easy but questionable mode of life.

All of the films discussed so far reveal a violent and chaotic phallocentric society, with *The Voroshilov Marksman* most clearly reflecting the breakdown of a rigid patriarchal system. The film's last scene suggests hope, but only for Katia, not for the male characters. For the first time since the rape she takes up her guitar and sings—an image often used in Soviet film to signal nostalgia for the past, projected by the director onto one of his screen personae. The film ends on a note of serenity: Katia has recovered from her traumatic experience. She has the unmistakable strength and inner spiritual force to move on. In its depiction of the younger generation, the film contrasts a strong woman who endures humiliation and finds the courage to go on living with inept Russian males who fail as products both of their parents' overly indulgent upbringing and of the new, volatile social order.

A significant change in the (re)presentation of gender is evident in the series of comedies *Peculiarities of the National Hunt in Fall* (1995), *Peculiarities of National Fishing* (1998), and *Peculiarities of the National Hunt in Winter* (2000), written and directed by Aleksandr Rogozhkin.[24] Conceived as a "people's comedy," the first film became an instant success.[25] It features a group of friends from various social strata (including a general with the Dostoevskian surname of Ivolgin) united by their unusual enthusiasm for hunting: they value the sport not for the result, but for its chronotope—the opportunity to enjoy friendship at a specific time in a specific place. The film lacks a traditional story line; the only development is an increase in the quantity of vodka consumed. The image and role of vodka in these films achieves hyperbolic dimensions reminiscent of Rabelais's *Gargantua and Pantagruel* and Venedikt Erofeev's novel *Moskva-Petushki* [*From Moscow to the End of the Line*, 1968]. If, however, *Moskva-Petushki* is a tragic poem, these films are slapstick comedies. The characters do nothing but drink and get in and out of ridiculous situations. They constitute a typical male minisociety, though the vodka they consume makes them dense and inept, rendering them impotent, in a sense, as they lose the vaunted male capacity to dominate. In her analysis of *Peculiarities of the National Hunt in Fall,* Susan Larsen notes that the film deflates violence and disaster: the hunters are in pursuit, rather, of beauty, friendship, and brotherhood ("In Search of an Audience").

Even more significant is the change in the characters' gender profile in the most recent film in the series, *Peculiarities of the National Hunt in Winter,* which features a strong, "iron woman" (*zheleznaia zhenshchina*), Masliuk. She is an ecologist (a "nurturer of nature") who visits the hunters to check the legality of their activities. Her character is parodically exaggerated: Fastidiously refusing to drink vodka (Russian males' favorite occupation), she is so large and strong that she knocks down a bear with one blow. At the end of the film, however, influenced by the men's example, she drinks like the rest of them. Verhaeghe points out that today's woman, when invested with the ancient masculine fear of her strength, becomes woman-the-hunter, a paradigm into which Masliuk fits most comfortably. Despite this ironic touch of masculinization, she remains a female presence in this male company of hunters, who, presumably through contact with her, become more thoughtful and intellectual. The host, Kuzmich, grows interested in Eastern philosophy and stops drinking. The twist in gender roles introduced by the director—Kuzmich giving up drinking and Masliuk taking up the habit—reflects a blurring of gender roles, while also perhaps suggesting men's fear of strong women and simultaneously a possible change in male

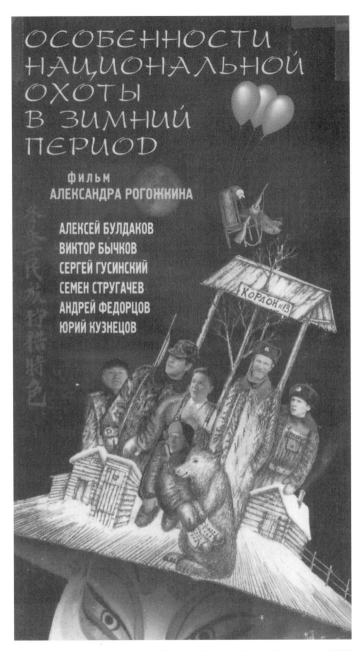

9-3   *Peculiarities of the National Hunt in Winter* (Dir. Al. Rogozhkin, 2000).

attitudes towards feminine sensitivity and thoughtfulness. Such a gender shift comes as no surprise in the context of the increasingly weak function of the paternal metaphor within Russian cinema. Of course, images of strong women are not unusual in Russian culture, as I argue in my discussion of *Mama*. Most often such women appear as mothers, sustaining the metaphor of woman as a symbol of the Motherland. Masliuk, while not a mother, is connected to the Russian land as an ecologist: her profession and her conscience demand that she protect and preserve the Mother*land*.

Seeking innovative formulas, the more recent post-Soviet cinema has changed its genre profile since the early 1990s. Such genres as melodrama, lyrical comedy, and fairy tales, neglected in the first years following desovietization, have been resurrected, recalling films from the Soviet cinema of late stagnation, especially the 1970s.[26] Bleak films (*chernukha*) seem to be disappearing, as audiences increasingly enjoy revamped versions of Soviet-style cinema in the form of thrillers, action films, comedies, and melodramas that propagate "faith, hope, and honest and pure love without sex" (Urizchenko). In *Offending Women Is not Recommended* [*Zhenshchin obizhat' ne rekomenduetsia*, 2001], for example, the screenwriter, Valentin Chernykh, revives the style and some of the themes of his *Moscow Does Not Believe in Tears*. Valerii Akhadov, the film's director, readily admits that he is a Soviet director and has no problem resuscitating some of the sentiments and ideas of that era while placing them in a new context (Urizchenko). The film's protagonist, Vera Kirillova, is an independent, intelligent, and charming high school teacher who succeeds in securing investments and future contracts for the company she inherited from her father; nevertheless, her personal life suffers. After a successful trip abroad, Vera and Sasha, the vice president of the company, return to Russia, where Vera triumphantly announces that she is going back to her school and leaves the company in Sasha's hands. The film ends here and implies that Vera and Sasha will live "happily ever after." The creators of the film offer a Soviet-style ending, updated according to the circumstances of post-Soviet life. The ending looks like a modern repetition of the Mukhina statue. Alternatively, one can argue that the world of caring and nurture is morally superior to that of business success, and woman has become the ethically more moral and spiritually nobler sex. The film, however, suggests nothing to support this claim. Returning the woman to her former profession of schoolteacher, a more traditional and accepted profession for a woman than entrepreneurship, and showing her sacrificing professional success for personal happiness is an ending that falls outside a standard Western feminist approach.

In this respect the Kamenskaia films and *The Land of the Deaf* appear to share more similarities with contemporary Western sensibilities regarding gender. And yet *Offending Women...* presents a woman different from those in Russian cinema of the early nineties: Vera accepts the challenge of heading a big company and copes admirably with the task. *Offending Women...*, along with *Come Look at Me* (2000) and *The Envy of Gods* (2000), visibly increases the presence of intelligent, decisive women on screen—women capable of succeeding in the male world—thereby attesting to shifts in both genre and gender within contemporary Russian cinema.

Discussing sexual representations in films from the period of perestroika and the early 1990s, Attwood writes, "To find women as the centre of attention in films which tackle other [than prostitution] themes is increasingly uncommon. This is partly because, in the latest batch of domestic film releases, detective and adventure films have emerged as the most popular genres" ("Sex and the Cinema" 73). Many of the films analyzed above, however, reveal a shift in such a gender representation that invests female characters with more leading power in the cinematic narratives. In an article about the new types of hero offered on the Russian screen, Mariia Arbatova, writer, media personality, and outspoken feminist, registers this shift. Arguing that Russian cinema today represents violent or impotent Russian men, notably in the images of Danila and the characters in *Peculiarities of the National Hunt,* on the one hand, and surprisingly more positive female characters (Kamenskaia, Iaia, Rita), on the other, Arbatova concludes: "Here's a paradox. How can you place the Russian female 'Robin Hood,' Kamenskaia, next to the Russian male 'Robin Hood,' Danila Bagrov? There's no way. The only possible physical contact between them could be the handcuffing of Bagrov's rough hands by Kamenskaia's tender hands" (40).

In conclusion, male characters from post-Soviet cinema such as Lesha, Andrei, Danila, and the young men from *The Voroshilov Marksman* experience more problems and painful adjustments to the new post-Soviet reality than female characters such as Kamenskaia, Iaia, Rita, and Vera. Female identity patterns represented by these protagonists are certainly diverse, but the heroines do not suffer the kind of trauma in their new roles that blights the post-Soviet male. As argued above, this difference between men's and women's adaptation to new social conditions depends on the degree of their "institutionalization" (to use Salecl's term) during the Soviet era. While discourse of the phallus, masculinity, power, and aggression unambiguously dominates in post-Soviet cinema, that cinema nevertheless shows another gendered space—paradoxically, through violence, desperation, and castration, as well as through a strong female presence marked by sensitivity and depth, which erodes, however tentatively, the edges of the rigid male world of the symbolic order. The post-Soviet Russian screen exhibits synthetic characters that resist pigeonholes—an unusual blend of killers with ideals, aggressive yet castrated young men, and strong, yet tender and feminine, women. This blend simultaneously reflects and permits changes that challenge the traditional gender dynamics and the rule of the Symbolic Father.

In the Western world, faith in the Symbolic Father is also undergoing a crisis, perhaps more so than in Russia. In a replay of Nietzsche's famous pronouncement on metaphysics, scholars such as Žižek have even declared the Symbolic Father dead.[27] The absence of an uncontested masculine superiority and its consequent instability generate not only an aggressive, violent behavior rooted in uncertainty, but also men ready to adopt women's roles. Post-Soviet cinema therefore reflects the transitional period in Russia from a totalitarian regime to a weak economy and social chaos as one marked by an embattled, destabilized Russian patriarchy that may yet yield to a new, more complex order.

Notes

1. See the description of Russian film production during the early 1990s in Beumers, especially her introduction, 1–12.

2. Until 1986 the Soviet film industry annually produced twenty to thirty films, which sold over a million tickets each. In the 1990s no Russian film sold more than one hundred thousand tickets. During the 1990s Russians attended fewer movies than their Western counterparts, with economic factors certainly playing an important role in this decline. In 1998, thirty-six million tickets were sold in Russia, which is eighteen times fewer than in France. Despite this shrinkage, participants in the discussions mentioned below maintain the enduring power of Russian cinema today. See "Sekrety i obmany rossiiskogo kinokhita"; "Intelligentsiia za sotsializm?"; and "Rossiia. Posle Imperii," all of which are available at www.kinoart.ru.

3. Here the "Other" is used in the Lacanian understanding of the term as the Law, the underlying symbolic order (see Lacan, *Ecrits*). In psychoanalysis Lacan introduces the three orders of the Imaginary, the Symbolic, and the Real to discuss stages in human development as well as of levels of existence. The Symbolic, unlike the Imaginary, which is based on sense evidence and relations, exists as a network of social, cultural, and historical signs. The Symbolic is also referred to as the Other, which in the life of an individual may be represented by social, religious, political, or cultural norms and structures. To the first two registers, the Imaginary and the Symbolic, Lacan adds the Real. The Real is that about which one cannot speak; it is everything that escapes symbolization.

4. After this essay was written, Russian cinema produced three culturally significant films that call attention to the father figure and its role in family and society, and generally explore father-son relationships. To a certain degree they reflect Verhaeghe's idea (to be discussed) about today's Western latent desire to reinstall the authority of the Father. See Aleksandr Sokurov's *Father and Son* [*Otets i syn,* 2003], Andrei Zviagintsev's debut film, *The Return* [*Vozvrashchenie,* 2003], and Aleksei Popogrebskii and Boris Khlebnikov's *Koktebel'* (2003). At the same time, in Genadii Sidorov's *Little Old Ladies* [*Starukhi,* 2003], for example, Elena Stishova sees a departure from the construction of the male hero and a shift towards universal values experienced through a collective past. Stishova, n.p.

5. Readers interested in films by women should consult Roberts, also Horton and Brashinsky.

6. Although made and released during the Soviet period, *Taxi-Blues* adds to the discussion of Lungin's later film *Luna Park* and anticipates many traits of films made in the post-Soviet era.

7. The traditional patriarchal structure is understood here as a stable and secure male dominance and a female (moral and emotional) dependence and subordination.

8. Whatever one's view of gender patterns in present-day Russia, gender roles on the post-Soviet screen surprise one's understanding of the traditional patriarchal structure in various ways, beyond even the perceived blurring of male/female social boundaries, which various scholars have noted. Eliot Borenstein argues that "feminism is still largely a dirty word, and gender roles, assumed to be innate, are to be reinforced rather than questioned." Borenstein, "'About That'" 63. While this is undoubtedly true, there is also a growing concern over the feminization of men and the masculinization of women, noted by Helena Goscilo in *Dehexing Sex,* 10–11. Susan Larsen remarks, "The transformation of the victimized, and therefore virtuous, melodramatic heroine into the victimized, and therefore virtuous, melodramatic hero is a response to the identity crisis in which Russia finds itself after the collapse of Communist rule." Larsen, "Melodramatic Masculinity" 89. Goscilo offers an insightful gender analysis of Russian society based on popular magazines. She points out, "Amidst voluble feminist bashing and laments about a crisis in male identity, the 1990s have witnessed the emergence of several magazines patently intended to boost men's morale and supply guidelines for their image construction in the brave new world of market machismo." Goscilo, "Style and S(t)imulation," 27.

9. Ol'ga, the protagonist of Natal'ia Baranskaia's novella *A Week Like Any Other* [*Nedelia kak nedelia,* 1969], who is trapped among the pressures of familial duties, her professional life, and the Party, became emblematic of the "emancipated" Soviet woman's triple role. Women's passage from the domestic to the social sphere created acute problems, for they had to sustain their domestic roles as well as competitively construct their new profile as workers. Baranskaia's novella was the first literary text to reveal cracks in the ideological design of gender positions and to show, convincingly, how prescribed equality failed in the lives of ordinary people.

10. Here Rancour-Laferriere merely repeats what has become a truism of Slavic scholarship, but I cite his specific formulation because I take issue with his explanation about the cause of Soviet women's "double burden."

11. "They [women] were not forced by men to do what they did. In other words, women engaged in self-defeating behavior, behavior which is masochistic by definition." Rancour-Laferriere 163.

12. There are conflicting reports on women's choice to become wives and mothers (Rancour-Laferriere 179). A portion of the female population has cynically (or perhaps out of desperation) rejected the responsibilities of the Soviet era, and under the pressure of poverty, even turned to prostitution, drugs, and crime.

13. Freud's *Moses and Monotheism* constructs the myth of the primal father as follows: Once there was a primal father in total possession of all females, who was murdered by rebellious sons. His death, surprisingly, resulted in the establishment of matriarchy. With time, the fraternal clan reintroduced the father figure and created the cult of the father, and thus of patriarchal power. Freud 80–84, 130–32. Here, however, I follow Lacan's interpretation of Freud's myth as a metaphor for paternal power and organizational principle. Lacan 179–225.

14. Verhaeghe emphasizes only the latter effect, but I believe that the former also results from the collapse of the father. He notes, "The absence of the security-enhancing symbolic law regulating desire and enjoyment invests woman with all the ancient masculine fears, which results in a turnaround: today, we have woman-the-hunter and man-the-hunted" (139).

15. For a discussion of similar films in the West, see Sheen 74.

16. All translations from Russian are mine unless otherwise indicated.

17. From May 20 to July 2, 2000, NTV showed sixteen episodes based on eight of her novels. The novels enjoy popularity abroad and have been translated into many European languages, as well as airing on Italian TV in the form of a series. Readers of Marinina's novels can notice a difference in the filmic physical appearance of Kamenskaia: the actress, Elena Iakovleva, is more attractive than the literary original. This, however, does not affect the overall impression of the film's character as an independent and professionally successful woman. In this chapter, I employ several literary examples (Baranskaia, Petrushevskaia, Marinina) to support my observations. Although I am not prepared to argue that the Russian contemporary literary scene constructs similar gender roles, tendencies of a more active (leading) female presence in today's Russian literature are certainly noticeable, as in Boris Akunin's female detective series.

18. In the two more recent episodes, *When Gods Laugh* [*Kogda bogi smeiutsia*] (Moscow: EKSMO P, 2001), Kamenskaia undergoes a crisis. She begins to question her self-confidence and her youthful, rather boyish appearance (she often wears jeans and T-shirts). Perhaps under the influence of reactions to the earlier novels and serialized episodes, Kamenskaia here attempts to dress in a more traditionally feminine manner (but does not feel comfortable) and simultaneously realizes that she has always been protected by the men around her.

19. For anyone familiar with both the Russian language and the Rolling Stones, the name evokes testicles, a highly suitable association, since the heroine fights for her independence and attempts to appropriate imaginary power.

20. One can question the extent to which Russian men fulfilled their roles of husbands and fathers, but my argument centers only on the position Soviet ideology assigned to them and the demands it made on men, which differed from those made on women.

21. During glasnost and perestroika women's position began to change, as did women's representation in cinema. *Little Vera* [*Malen'kaia Vera*, 1988], one of the most popular films of the perestroika period, draws a stark portrayal of a young provincial woman caught up in the problems of the times. *Intergirl* [*Interdevochka*, 1989] offers a presentation of hard-currency prostitution and marriage to foreigners that genuinely attempts to explore the reasons for and consequences of this social phenomenon. For more on women's presentation in cinema during glasnost see Horton and Brashinsky 99–127, and Lawton 167–215.

22. Brigit Beumers calls Danila "the killer-hero": "He combines within himself the contradictions at the heart of the 'Russian Idea': self-assertion and self-effacement. . ." "To Moscow! To Moscow!" in *Russia on Reels*, 83. While I agree with Beumers's observation regarding Danila's internal contradictions, I attribute them to social changes and not to the Russian Idea.

23. The Duma Deputy Govorukhin worked on banning pornography and reintroducing the Soviet anthem. The director Govorukhin has changed little in the basic message of his films since his classic 1970s TV series, *The Meeting Place Cannot Be Changed* [*Mesto vstrechi izmenit' nel'zia*, 1979], in which Vladimir Vysotskii delivers a line that quickly entered everyday speech: "Thieves must be put in prison." *The Voroshilov Marksman,* a film about sin and retribution, offers even more radical lessons for offenders.

24. *Peculiarities of a Russian Bathhouse* [*Osobennosti russkoi bani*, 1999] and *Peculiarities of a Russian Bathhouse-2* (2000) are erotic comedies directed by Aleksei Rudakov. Only the main protagonist from Rogozhkin's films is present. The setting and pacing likewise differ, as the characters drink beer and talk about (and have) sex for two hours.

25. It won the *Kinotavr* Award (1995) and the Special Prize at the international festival *Karlovy Vary* in the Czech Republic (1995). The success was marked by controversy: some despised the film as kitsch and others called Rogozhkin a "Russo-

phobe," criticizing his portrayal of Russians as nothing but alcoholics. The film, however, became a box-office hit.

26. Three of the Russian films released in the new century mark this shift in the genre system: *Come Look at Me* [*Prikhodi na menia posmotret'*, 2000] styles itself as an alternative *Irony of Fate . . .* [*Ironiia sud'by . . .*, 1975]; Palev Lungin's film *The Wedding* [*Svad'ba*, 2001] explores issues of friendship, love, and marriage; and Vladimir Menshov's *The Envy of Gods* [*Zavist' bogov*, 2000] presents the sexual awakening of a Soviet woman in the early 1980s and her failure to find happiness with her French lover because the authorities deport him.

27. Slavoj Žižek in *Tarrying With The Negative* declares "the collapse of the Big Other," 200–239. See also Verhaeghe 131–57.

References

Abdullaeva, Zara. Symposium. "Rossiia posle imperii." *Iskusstvo kino* 4 (2000). <www.kinoart.ru/2000/4/23.html>

Arbatova, Mariia. "Kto prishel na smenu Goshe?" *Novyi ekran,* no.1/2, Feb.–Mar. 2003: 37–41.

Attwood, Lynne. *The New Soviet Man and Woman: Sex Role Socialization in the USSR.* Bloomington: Indiana UP, 1990.

———. "Sex and the Cinema." *Sex and Russian Society.* Ed. Igor Kon and James Riordan. Bloomington: Indiana UP, 1993. 65–88.

Baranskaia, Natal'ia. *A Week Like Any Other* [*Nedelia kak nedelia,* 1969]. Trans. Pieta Monk. Seattle: Seal Press, 1989.

Beumers, Birgit, ed. *Russia on Reels.* London: I. B. Tauris, 1999.

Borenstein, Eliot. "'About That': Deploying and Deploring Sex in Post-Soviet Russia." *Studies in Twentieth-Century Literature* 24 (2000): 51–85. Guest ed. Helena Goscilo. Special Issue on Russian Culture of the 1990s.

———. *Men without Women: Masculinity and Revolution in Russian Fiction, 1917–1929.* Durham: Duke UP, 2000.

Brat [*Brother*]. Dir. Aleksei Balabanov. Perf. Sergei Bodrov, Jr., Viktor Sukhorukov, Svetlana Pismichenko, Maria Zhukova. STV, "InterCinema-Art," "Prem'er," DVD Group Company. Russia, 1997.

Brennan, Teresa. "History after Lacan." *Economy and Society* 3 (1990): 277–313.

Butler, Judith. *Bodies that Matter.* London: Routledge, 1993.

Degot, E., A. Arkhangelskii, Zhorzh Niva, et al. Symposium. "Intelligentsiia—za sotsializm?" *Iskusstvo kino* 3 (2000). <www.kinoart.ru/2000/3/31.html>

Dondurei, D., O. Aronson, E. Stishova, et al. Discussion. "Sekrety i obmany rossiiskogo kinokhita." *Iskusstvo kino* 3 (1999). <www.kinoart.ru/1999/3/1.html>

Dondurei, D., N. Mikhalkov, Vl. Ryzhkov, et al. Symposium. "Intelligentsiia—za sotsializm?" *Iskusstvo kino* 2 (2000). <www.kinoart.ru/2000/2/33.html>

Epstein, Mikhail. *After the Future: The Paradoxes of Postmodernism and Contemporary Russian Culture.* Amherst: U Massachusetts P, 1995.

Erofeev, Venedikt. *Moskva-Petushki* [*Moscow to the End of the Line,* 1968]. Trans. H. Williams Tjalsma. Evanston: Northwestern UP, 1994.

Erofeev, Viktor. *Muzhchiny.* Moscow: ZebraE, 2002.

Freud, Sigmund. *The Standard Edition of the Complete Psychological Works.* Vol. 23. Ed. J. Strachey. London: Hogarth Press, 1953.

Goscilo, Helena. *Dehexing Sex: Russian Womanhood During and After Glasnost.* Ann Arbor: U Michigan P, 1996.

———. "The Gendered Trinity of Russian Cultural Rhetoric Today — or The Glyph of the H[i]eroine." *Soviet Hieroglyphics.* Ed. Nancy Condee. Bloomington: Indiana UP, 1995. 68–93.

———. "Mother as Mothra: Totalizing Narrative and Nurture in Petrushevskaia." *A Plot of Her Own.* Ed. Sona Stephan Hoisington. Evanston: Northwestern UP, 1995. 102–14.

———. "Style and S(t)imulation." *Studies in Twentieth Century Literature* 24 (2000): 15–51.

Horton, Andrew, and Michael Brashinsky. *The Zero Hour. Glasnost' and Soviet Cinema in Transition.* Princeton: Princeton UP, 1992. 99–127.

Interdevochka [Intergirl]. Dir. Petr Todorovski. Perf. Elena Iakovleva, Tomas Laustiola, Anastasia Nemoliaeva, Irina Rozanova. Russia and France, 1989.

Ironiia sud'by... [Irony of Fate...]. Dir. El'dar Riazanov. Perf. Andrei Miagkov, Barbara Bryl'ska, Iurii Iakovlev, Aleksandr Shirvindt. Soviet Union, 1975.

Karakhan, L., A. Balabanov, A. Khvan et al."Rossiia posle imperii." *Iskusstvo kino* 4 (2000). <www.kinoart.ru/2000/4/23.html>

Koktebel'. Dir. Aleksei Popogrebskii and Boris Khlebnikov. Perf. Gleb Puskepalis, Igor' Chernevich. "Gel'vars," Cinema Vision, Celluloid Dreams (France), 2003.

Krug vtoroi [The Second Circle]. Dir. Aleksandr Sokurov. Perf. Petr Aleksandrov, Nadezhda Rodnova, Tamara Timofeeva, Aleksandr Bystriakov. Soviet Union, 1990.

Lacan, Jacques. *Ecrits. A Selection.* New York, London: W. W. Norton, 1977.

Larsen, Susan. "In Search of an Audience: The New Russian Cinema of Reconciliation." *Consuming Russia.* Ed. Adele Barker. Durham: Duke UP, 1999: 192–217.

———. "Melodramatic Masculinity, National Identity, and the Stalinist Past in Post-Soviet Cinema." *Studies in Twentieth Century Literature* 24 (2000): 85–121. Guest ed. Helena Goscilo. Special Issue on Russian Culture of the 1990s.

Lawton, Anna. *Kinoglasnost: Soviet Cinema in Our Time.* Cambridge: Cambridge UP, 1992.

Luna Park. Dir. Pavel Lungin. Perf. Andrei Gutin, Oleg Borisov, Natal'ia Egorova, Nonna Mordiukova, Mikhail Golubovich. Dom Video, 1992.

Makarov. Dir. Vladimir Khotinenko. Perf. Sergei Makovetskii, Elena Maiorova, Irina Metlitskaia, Vladimir Il'in, Sergei Parshin. "Karmen," InterCinema-Art, Dom Video, 1993.

Malen'kaia Vera [Little Vera]. Dir. Vasilii Pichul. Perf. Natal'ia Negoda, Andrei Sokolov, Iurii Nazarov, Liudmila Zaitseva. Soviet Union, 1988.

Mama. Dir. Denis Evstigneev. Perf. Nonna Mordiukova, Oleg Menshikov, Vladimir Mashkov, Evgenii Mironov, Mikhail Krylov, Aleksei Kravchenko, Andrei Panin, Maksim Sukhanov. "Most-Sinematograf," NTV-Profit, "Piramida," 1999.

Marinina, Aleksandra. *Kogda bogi smeiutsia.* Moscow: EKSMO P, 2001.

Mat' [Mother]. Dir. Vsevolod Pudovkin. Perf. Vera Baranovskaia, Nikolai Batalov, Ivan Koval'-Samborskii, Anna Zemtsova. Soviet Union, 1926.

McCuaig, Kerry. "Effects of Perestroika and Glasnost' on Women." *Canadian Women's Studies* 10.4 (Winter 1989): 11–14.

Mesto vstrechi izmenit' nel'zia. Dir. Stanislav Govorukhin. Perf. Vladimir Vysotskii, Vladimir Konkin, Sergei Iurskii, Viktor Pavlov, Natal'ia Fateeva. Soviet Union, 1979.

Moskva slezam ne verit [Moscow Does Not Believe in Tears]. Dir. Vladimir Menshov. Perf. Vera Alentova, Irina Muraveva, Aleksei Batalov, Raisa Riazanova, Aleksandr Fatiushin, Boris Smorchkov. Soviet Union, 1979.

Musulmanin [The Muslim]. Dir. Vladimir Khotinenko. Perf. Evgenii Mironov, Nina Usatova, Aleksandr Baluev, Evdokiia Germanova, Aleksandr Peskov. V.V.S., InterCinema-Art, Lazer-Video, SEF, TV-6 Moskva, "Partner," 1995.

Nepomnyashchy, Catherine. "Markets, Mirrors and Mayhem: Aleksandra Marinina and the Rise of the New Russian *Detektiv.*" *Consuming Russia.* Ed. Adele Barker. Durham: Duke UP, 1999: 161–92.

Osobennosti bannoi politiki ili bania 2 [*Peculiarities of Bathhouse Politics or Bathhouse 2*]. Dir. Aleksei Rudakov. Perf. Viktor Bychkov, Sergei Gusinskii, Pavel Stepanov, Ol'ga Tolstetskaia. Pyramide Home Video, "DVD Servis," 2000.

Osobennosti natsional'noi okhoty [*Peculiarities of the National Hunt in Fall*]. Dir. Aleksandr Rogozhkin. Perf. Ville Haapasalo, Viktor Bychkov, Sergei Russkin, Aleksei Buldakov, Semen Strugachev, Sergei Kupriianov, Sergei Gusinskii, Igor' Sergeev. "Lenfilm," "Lenfilm-Video," "Standart Magnetik," Twister, 1995.

Osobennosti natsional'noi okhoty v zimnii period [*Peculiarities of the National Hunt in Winter*]. Dir. Aleksandr Rogozhkin. Perf. Semen Strugachev, Viktor Bychkov, Aleksei Buldakov, Andrei Fedortsov, Sergei Gusinskii, Irina Osnovina. West Video, 2000.

Osobennosti natsional'noi rybalki [*Peculiarities of National Fishing*]. Dir. Aleksandr Rogozhkin. Perf. Aleksei Buldakov, Viktor Bychkov, Semen Strugachev, Andrei Krasko. STV, InterCinema-Art, "Prem'er," DVD Group, 1998.

Osobennosti russkoi bani [*Peculiarities of a Russian Bathhouse*]. Dir. Aleksei Rudakov. Perf. Viktor Bychkov, Aleksandr Piatkov, Viacheslav Kulakov, Oksana Stashenko. "Piramida," "DVD Servis," 1999.

Otets i syn [*Father and Son*]. Dir. Aleksandr Sokurov. Perf. Andrei Shchetinin, Aleksei Neimyshev, Aleksandr Razbash, Fedor Lavrov, Marina Zasukhina. InterCinama-Art, Gemini Films (France), 2003.

Passport. Dir. Georgii Daneliia. Perf. Gerard Darmon, Natal'ia Gundareva, Oleg Iankovskii, Armen Dzhigarkhanian. Soviet Union, France, Austria, 1990.

Prikhodi na menia posmotret' [*Come Look at Me*]. Dir. Oleg Iankovskii. Perf. Oleg Iankovskii, Irina Kupchenko, Ekaterina Vasil'eva. "Most-Sinematograf," NTV-Profit, Pyramide Home Video, 2000.

Pro urodov i liudei [*Of Freaks and Men*]. (Russia 1998). Dir. Aleksei Balabanov. Perf. Sergei Makovetskii, Dinara Drukarova, Anzhelika Nevolina, Viktor Sukhorukov, Alesha De, Chingiz Tsydendambaev, Igor' Shibanov, Vadim Prokhorov. InterCinema-Art, STV, "Prem'er," 1998.

Rancour-Laferriere, Daniel. *The Slave Soul of Russia.* New York: New York UP, 1995.

Roberts, Graham. "The Meaning of Death: Kira Muratova's Cinema of the Absurd." *Russia on Reels.* Ed. Birgit Beumers. London: I. B. Tauris, 1999. 144–61.

Salecl, Renata. *(Per)versions of Love and Hate.* London: Verso, 2000.

———. *The Spoils of Freedom: Psychoanalysis and Feminism after the Fall of Communism.* London: Routledge, 1994.

Sheen, Erica. "Serial Killings." *Journal of Gender Studies* 1.1 (1991): 71–76.

Sluzhebnyi roman [*Office Affair*]. Dir. El'dar Riazanov. Perf. Andrei Miagkov, Alisa Freindlikh, Svetlana Nemoliaeva, Oleg Basilashvili. Soviet Union, 1977.

Smert' i nemnogo liubvi [*Death and a Little Love*]. Episode from *Kamenskaia* TV miniseries. Dir. Iuri Moroz. Perf. Elena Iakovleva, Sergei Nikonenko, Dmitrii Nagiev, Sergei Garmash, Il'ia Drevnov, Boris Nevzorov, Dmitrii Kharatian. Pyramide Home Video, NTV-kino, Video Film, 2000.

Starukhi [*Little Old Ladies*]. Dir. Gennadii Sidorov. Perf. Valentina Berezutskaia, Galina Smirnova, Zoia Norkina, Tamara Klimova, Branislava Zakharova, Anastasiia Liubimova, Sergei Makarov. "Tsentral Partnership," "Gel'vars cinema," "CP Classica," 2003.

Stishova, Elena. "Krizis srednego vozrosta: Sochi-2003." *Kinoart,* 10 (2003). <www.kinoart.ru/magazine/10-2003/review/stishova0310/>.

Strana glukhikh [*The Land of the Deaf*]. Dir. Valerii Todorovskii. Perf. Chulpan Khamatova, Dina Korzun, Maksim Sukhanov. Celluloid Dreams (France), Soiuz Video, "Film Pro," 1998.

Svad'ba [*The Wedding*]. Dir. Pavel Lungin. Perf. Marat Basharov, Mariia Mironova, Andrei Panin, Natal'ia Koliakanova, Aleksand Semchev. Bird Limited U.K., "Movement of Tomorrow's Day," "Prem'er," Pyramide Distr. (France), Venture Film (Germany), 2001.

Taxi-Blues. Dir. Pavel Lungin. Perf. Petr Mamonov, Petr Zaichenko, Vladimir Kashpur, Natalia Koliakanova. Soviet Union, France, 1990.

Tsyrkun, Nina. "Tinkling Symbols: Fragmented Society—Fragmented Cinema?" *Russia on Reels*. Ed. Birgit Beumers. London: I. B. Tauris, 1999. 57–66.

Urizchenko, Varvara. "Staraia skazka o 'novykh.'" *Nezavisimaia gazeta* 7 Dec., 2000. <www.ng.ru/culture/2000-12-07/7_skazka.html>.

Verhaeghe, Paul. "The Collapse of the Function of the Father and its Effect on Gender Roles." *Sexuation*. Ed. Renata Salecl. Durham: Duke UP, 2000. 131–57.

Voroshilovskii strelok. [*The Voroshilov Marksman*]. Dir. Stanislav Govorukhin. Perf. Mikhail Ul'ianov, Anna Siniakina, Il'ia Drevnov, Aleksei Makarov. Pyramide Home Video, DVD Serviz, 1999.

Vozvrashchenie [*The Return*]. Dir. Andrei Zviagintsev. Perf. Vladimir Garin, Ivan Dobronravov, Konstantin Lavronenko, Natal'ia Vdovina, Galina Petrova. InterCinema-Art, Lucky Red (Italy), Ocean Films (France), 2003.

Zavist' bogov [*The Envy of Gods*]. Dir. Vladimir Menshov. Screenplay: Marina Mareeva, Vladimir Menshov. "Panorama," "Soiuz-video," 2000.

Žižek, Slavoj. *The Metastases of Enjoyment: Six Essays on Woman and Causality*. London: Verso, 1994.

———. *Tarrying With The Negative*. Durham: Duke UP, 1993. 200–239.

TEN | Raising a Pink Flag The Reconstruction of Russian Gay Identity in the Shadow of Russian Nationalism

LUC BEAUDOIN

In New York City, as in the Russian Federation itself, perhaps the most notorious gay male writer is Yaroslav Mogutin. His most recent work, *Tale with a German* [*Roman s Nemtsem*, also translated as *German Entanglement*] was published at the end of 2000, after his self-published *SS: Superhuman Supertexts: A Superbook about Sex, Violence, and Death* [*SS: Sverkhchelovecheskie Superteksty: superkniga o sekse, nasilii, i smerti*], which appeared earlier in 2000 in a small printing, with many copies adorned with various stickers such as "pinko commie fag," "anal filth," "homofascism," etc.[1] Mogutin's primary notoriety in American gay circles, however, is as the Russian partner in a binational, Russian-American gay couple who attempted to legally marry in Moscow on April 12, 1994. It is striking that Mogutin and his boyfriend, Robert Filippini, would try Russia before the United States; for although both countries prohibit same-sex marriages, the former Soviet Union was (and continues to be in the post-Soviet era) a notoriously homophobic cultural and societal milieu.[2]

In 1994, the Stalinist-era article 121 prohibiting male homosexuality had only just been repealed.[3] Mogutin, a postmodernist and anarchic self-styled sex criminal, does not provide much in the way of postmodernist or anarchist reasoning for choosing Moscow over New York. He does, however, imply a connection between his own demonstrative sexuality and the construction of his post-nationalist identity; in an interview with *The Guide* in 1999, he remarked:

> The truth is, the whole gay mythology is based on totalitarian aesthetics, with its cult of the naked male body and "true male camaraderie" or whatever you want to call it. Tom of Finland used Nazi symbolism and uniforms to help create the grotesque carnival of SM subculture. The examples of homoerotic totalitarian and fascist art are countless, and so are the examples of queer art fetishizing fascism. (Mogutin 19)[4]

In this interview, as in his works, Mogutin implicitly recalls the role nationalism and sexuality have to play in the construction of gay identity. He does not refrain from reiterating his claim that (homo)sexuality is radically trangressive and anti-societal, as such possessing the power to unmask the pretensions of a dominant society and to undermine its conventions, which he sees as hopelessly corrupt and rooted in the (anti-)cult of the hypocritical individual.

Mogutin's own performance art aims an unflattering mirror at the audience. The audience is, of course, the society that has "bought into" the materialistic cult of consumer sex. Mogutin lashes out at the concept of buying into a sexuality:

> My idea of being queer is totally different from singing in the gay chorus or marching down Fifth Avenue in a crowd of thousands of topless cartoon-like clones with totally manufactured, waxed bodies. If I grew up in today's Chelsea, I would probably end up being a hardcore gaybasher in order to protest and attack this scary world of the unified look, unified morality, and lifestyle. We need more Andrew Cunanans, more queer terrorists, more "faggot-individualists" like Ginsberg, queer literary outlaws like Burroughs, more bad-ass fags to prove that the pioneering spirit of rebellion isn't yet entirely smothered by the Great American Consumerism. Or is it? (17)

Mogutin's anger follows in a well-worn trail walked by the likes of the Marquis de Sade, Jean Genet, Allen Ginsberg, and Larry Kramer. What is remarkable is that the angry gay man is not someone for whom native Russians have traditionally felt any sort of affinity.

The colonialist conquering of gay Russia is occurring on video: for the titillation of American gay men, supposed Russian conscripts—the military of the former Cold War enemy—have rough sex laced with a startling inattention to condoms and to any sort of romance (Beaudoin).[5] This is, in effect, little different from the classic James Bond representation of Soviet women as either sex kittens or probable man-hating lesbians (who, in fact, are mostly ripe for seduction by the victorious Bond). In such situations, the enemy is fetishized into a consumable sexual object of gendered identity enabling that consumption.

In her book *Imperial Leather,* Anne McClintock rejects the Freudian/Lacanian notion that fetishism is rooted in castration anxiety, claiming, rather, that "fetishes can be seen as the displacement onto an object (or person) of contradictions that the individual cannot resolve at a personal level" (184). As such, the fetishizing of Russian soldiers into gay porn stars cannot be seen as a task of emasculation and objectification in a strictly psychoanalytic sense (although there is evidently a great deal of that present, as well). On another level, it is perhaps representative of the unconcluded victory over the Soviet Union—an enfeebled economic victory that has left the Russian Federation a curiously hybrid first-/second-/third-world anomaly in the Security Council of the United Nations.

Such an outlook is certainly the converse of what was true just after the Bolshevik Revolution of 1917. While the nascent Soviet state trumpeted sexual equality and great fanfare accompanied the re-creation of a new, modern legal code that enshrined gender equality, forever turning its back on the perceived injustices of the Imperial period, certain gendered relations were left unspoken.[6] This atmosphere, if it did not encourage open homosexuality, at least did not discourage it, as long at it remained fairly inconsequential to the predominant power structure. Indeed, Mikhail Kuzmin's diary of the time is a striking testimony to this sexual openness; written as a literary document and treated by Kuzmin as such, it does not avoid his gay love affairs (Kuzmin).[7] As testimony to a disjuncture from the prevailing system of entitlements it is just as eloquent: Kuzmin lived in a state of artistic poverty most of his life. Material poverty at the time was but a distraction, and was one price to pay for being on the cutting edge of social norms. In fact, as Igor' Kon (arguably Russia's most famous sexologist) claims, the Silver Age was a time when homosexuality became fashionable in the Russian capitals: "In the beginning of the twentieth century same-sex love became fashionable in the circles of the artistic elite. [Aleksandr Benua recalled,] 'From our friends who remained in the city I discovered that in our close circle there had indeed occurred, you might say, a remarkable transformation connected to a certain kind of emancipation'" (294).[8]

In fact, Russians could not get enough homosexuality. Psychoanalysis became popular in Russia around the turn of the century, and Vasilii Rozanov conjoined questions of Russia's spiritual rebirth with sexology in his *People of Lunar Light: A Metaphysics of Christianity* [*Liudi lunnogo sveta: metafizika khristianstva* (Saint Petersburg: A. S. Surovin-Novoe Vremia, 1913)]. It was in this context that the Soviet state chose to ignore same-sex desire: homosexuality was relegated to the realms of the psychological and the metaphysical. Utterly self-involved, in the creation of the new Soviet man and woman it was useless. As Sarah Ashwin observes in her introduction to a recent study, gender was defined as a "triangular set of relations in which the primary relationship of individual men and women was to the state rather than to each other" (1–2). Although at first blush this might seem to be an opening for homosexual desire, it is in fact a gendered prison wrought by socioeconomic nationalism of the highest order: men are expected to fulfill their masculine roles in service to the country, and women—their feminine roles, especially in the realm of reproduction.

It was not until the 1930s, after all, that homosexuality was reintroduced into the legal code, with a violence that was breathtaking. The seeds had been sown among the roots of the Bolshevik Revolution, when respected writers such as Maksim Gor'kii wrote about Kuzmin: "They're old-fashioned slaves, people who *can't help* confusing freedom with homosexuality. For them, for example, 'personal liberation' is in some peculiar way confused with crawling from one cesspool into another and at times is reduced to freedom for the penis and nothing more."[9]

Ultimately, then, the fervent exploration of same-sex desire, reduced to "freedom for the penis," was doomed after the Silver Age because of its perceived uselessness to the greater cause of building the state. An ironic twist occurred sixty years later, during the revolutionary upheavals that culminated in Russia's independence: the now-defunct gay magazine *Tema* [*Theme*] provided the besieged government of Boris Yeltsin with a fax machine and copier during the darkest moments of the abortive putsch of 1991. Since 1991, the free flow of information has defined the nascent gay rights movement in the Russian Federation—a movement more concerned with its self-identification than with a strict pursuit of sexual equality. This asymmetric construct of sexual duties to and within the state governing structure has its roots in the Silver Age as well.[10] The Silver Age, then, serves as the primary paradigm for much of what is taking place in Russia today, from the etiquette schools for the newly wealthy, to the resurgence of mystical Russian erotica. There has been an explosion of interest, at least in the major economic centers, in mysticism, be it the teachings of Gurdjieff, yoga, macrobiotics, or tantric sex. This trend, too, has its roots not only in the enforced secularization of the USSR, but also in the mystico-erotic orientation of Russian Modernism.

One of the primary manifestations of this renewed questioning is the popularity of Rozanov, who, though unabashedly anti-Semitic,[11] indeed has undergone a renaissance in the new Russia. In his *People of Lunar Light,* a milestone in sex studies, Rozanov provides a primitive Kinsey scale of erotic attraction (although his is based on the ideal of a sexless homosexual). Fascination with the confluence of sexuality, psychology, and the state was at its peak in late-Tsarist Russia. A nonhomosexual example is the clinical notoriety of Leopold von Sacher-Masoch, whose *Venus in Furs* [*Venus im Pelz,* 1870] was a *succès de scandale* in the Russian Empire: Anton Chekhov was interested in his case for his doctoral dissertation.[12] *Venus in Furs* achieved popularity in the Empire between 1870 and 1900, after which it was more or less forgotten until the 1990s, when it regained its former popularity (along with Freud and sexology in general). The impact of *Venus in Furs,* however, as an example of the medicalization of sexual discourse, remained significant throughout the Silver Age. Psychiatry was a flowering art devoted to the nascent field of sexology, gleefully spewing forth manuals about masturbation, homosexuality (at the time commonly called "inversion"), and various so-called sexual perversions. Much of what was written could also commonly be found in Western Europe. Indeed, Lu Andreas-Salome, traveling around Western European capitals, helped to provide a connection between Western and Imperial psychoanalysis (Etkind). This enthusiasm for sexology and psychology contributed to the fascination with which the trial of Oscar Wilde, one of the most significant events in the codification of sexuality as a field of study (dissection and analysis), was followed in the Russian capitals.

At this confluence of sexual science and morality lay the defining *Zeitgeist* of the Russian Silver Age: asexual experimentation that pervaded the essentials of the Symbolist Beautiful Lady/prostitute, sexual experimentation, and the mechanized fantasy-nightmares of the Futurists. Women were cruel in their beauty and unavailability, the only recourse being their aesthetic objectification in a kind of self-defeating masculine possession. Viacheslav Ivanov, host of the famous Tower salon in Saint Petersburg along with his wife, Lidiia Zinov'eva-Annibal, called the sexually charged atmosphere of their 1905 gatherings a kind of "eros of impossibility" (*eros nevozmozhnogo*) (Etkind 58). Novels such as Evdokiia Nagrodskaia's *Wrath of Dionysis* [*Gnev Dionisa*, 1910] were wildly popular, appearing in ten editions in six years. Richard von Krafft-Ebing, the author of one of the first medical studies of gay sexuality, *Psychopathia Sexualis* (first published in Germany in 1872, and quickly translated into all major European languages, including Russian), was referred to as a sexual degenerate in book reviews of these novels about sexual morality. In Krafft-Ebing's work, as in Oscar Wilde's trial, the real issue at hand was the artistic element in perverse (homosexual or masochistic) sex. In *Venus in Furs,* the act of painting is the ultimate act of sexual possession, as it is in Nagrodskaia's *Wrath of Dionysis* and Zinov'eva-Annibal's novella *Thirty-three Abominations* [*Tridtsat' tri uroda,* 1907]. A more general form of artistic possession is found in two other novels of the time: Mikhail Kuzmin's *Wings* [*Kryl'ia,* 1907] and Anastasiia Verbitskaia's *The Keys to Happiness* [*Kliuchi schast'ia,* published between 1908 and 1913].

The intermixing of male masochism, gay identity, and Russian identity as presented in these seminal works of the Russian Silver Age, particularly the connection between homosexuality and cultural dominance, inform Mogutin's recent comments. The idea of a natural bisexuality as cited in Rozanov, however, was not always viewed in a positive sense. Otto Weininger used his own theories, developed a decade before Rozanov's, to extol a comparison between the bisexuality of the masses and the virile heterosexuality of the Aryan race.[13] During the 1970s, the drawings of Tom of Finland played eloquently, in an ironic mode, on the Nazi strength of the "typical" (homosexual) male, serving the homophobic fantasies of many gay men as fetishized in their phallic power, coded as leather, uniforms, broad shoulders, and narrow waists (Bordo 98).[14] Fascist hypermasculinity is itself an expression of the male body as phallus (as, for instance, in the pictures that Mogutin uses to adorn his books).[15]

In contrast to the hypermasculinized physicality that represents the state of gay male identity in the United States today, the gendered construction of Russian gay men is somewhat more fluid, drawing from the masochistic well of sexualized suffering.[16] Chronologically, the re-creation of a gay identity in the Russian Federation coincided with the official rediscovery by the public consciousness of the Russian Silver Age. More importantly, however, queers in Russia have sought a uniquely Russian (as opposed to American, for example) definition of gayness in precedents supplied by the Silver

Age—the last open flowering of queerdom before the Soviet era. The iconic status of Silver Age personalities was maintained throughout the Soviet period by reverent gay men and lesbians; hence the importance of delineating the gay experience in (and through) Russian Modernism. While late- and post-Soviet Russian letters proceeded with their own *sui generis,* end-of-the-century take on the decadence of the Silver Age (such as the sexually violent stories and novels of Viktor Erofeev), public fascination with that last period of artistic experimentation in Russia has fed a growing strain of Russian nationalism.

A search on the Russian Internet for anything gay brings up <gay.ru>, an Internet portal for Russian gay men. A source of information on contemporary Russian gay culture, the site is also a compendium of Russia's gay heritage. Scholarly and biographical articles on a range of writers and artists are archived here, allowing any young, gay Russian a chance to explore a gay cultural history. At the same time, however, a gay sensibility is imported into Russia from the West, providing an American gay overlay to a nascent Russian gay consciousness. *Afisha,* a Moscow entertainment weekly, regularly carries articles about art exhibitions, performance art, theater, dance, and other cultural events, including listings of gay and lesbian dance clubs and male strip shows. In a recent issue there was a review of an exhibition of transvestite photography by Vladislav Mamyshev-Monro (his own repertoire ranges from Marilyn Monroe to Catherine the Great via Hitler, Jesus, Napoleon, and Joan of Arc, among others [*Afisha* 73]). Despite their overtly sexualized nature, the fact that these media outlets choose to mention and review gay-, lesbian-, and queer-themed items brings the Russian queer experience into the mainstream, if only on the level of entertainment, and if only to distract the audience and titillate its sense of accepting liberalism. In North America, by contrast, gay-flavored events and listings are usually carried only in gay-specific media, adding to their segregation and intensifying their distinctly sexualized nature as separate, while paradoxically reaffirming the gay consumerist model (similar to the creation at the <Orbitz.com> Web site of a separate gay travel subsection).

Until recently, the search for a Russian gay identity has been rooted in the experience of the Russian Silver Age, which was the last flowering of open gay self-expression until the early 1990s. Finding gayness in something so "typically Russian" as poetry, art, and dance was ultimately a way of claiming a just place in the mainstream of Russian society. The result was to be an intermingling reminiscent of that in Scandinavia, following a European, rather than American, model of sexual politics. David Tuller, in his *Cracks in the Iron Closet,* writes with amazement at the ability of his Russian friends to defy categorization into gay, straight, and in-between. Laurie Essig's personal odyssey, *Queer in Russia,* on the other hand, charts the divisions and evasions of Russia's nascent gay and lesbian movement(s), though by necessity she seems to have socialized primarily with the

Moscow and Saint Petersburg gay and lesbian elite—a handful of very openly gay public figures.[17] Essig maintains that fixed sexual identity is, in fact, an import from the West, not a notion native to Russian soil (126–35).[18] Arguing for the expression of a Russian queer subjectivity without a queer identity, she writes:

> In Russia, to publicly engage in lesboerotic desires, whether symbolically or literally, is not an act for those who lack courage. What subjects of homosexual desire do lack, however, are the need to publicly identify as well as an identity in common. Queers may call themselves all sorts of things, including straight. To insist that all those who sleep with persons of the same sex take on the same identity, or any identity, is to miss that what they really share is desire, a desire in part constructed on the absence of a common identity (e.g., a "natural" desiring an "active lesbian"). Those who share common desires can act in highly public ways without ever contemplating a common identity.
>
> Indeed, this subjectivity without identity is exactly the part of Russian queerdom that is thriving, just as surely as Western models of identity politics have stagnated. (81–82)

Essig discusses these local subjectivities, some of which revolve around the republication of significant gay Russian Silver Age works, such as Mikhail Kuzmin's *Wings* (Essig 93). There has been an undercurrent of Russian gay identity, however, which has bubbled to the surface, particularly among newly consumerist gay male Russians, primarily in Moscow.

Saint Petersburgers, on the other hand, have a tradition of looking back to their cultural history somewhat nostalgically. It is fitting, then, that Saint Petersburg should have its very own gay historical travel guidebook: K. K. Rotikov's *The Other Petersburg* [*Drugoi Peterburg*, 2000] takes the reader, as the author baldly claims, through the homosexual history of the city that, he intimates, is laid out like a phallus (7). Judging by the press quotations cited in the inside pages of the guide, the Russian press by now is fully cognizant of the difference and otherness of male homosexuals (7).[19] Additionally, L. S. Klein has published a mammoth volume on male homosexuality, *The Other Love: Human Nature and Homosexuality* [*Drugaia liubov': Priroda cheloveka i gomoseksual'nost'*, 2000], attempting to cover its every aspect in a kind of wide-ranging cultural history that is imbued with personal recollections and erotic anecdotes. Saint Petersburg also witnessed the 1997 low-budget publication of *Love Without Borders* [*Liubov' bez granits*], which provided the Russian reader with an overview of gay world literature (chiefly Western) from antiquity to the present (Dumenkov), as well as two issues of the literary journal *Gay Slavs* [*Gay Slaviane*] in 1994 and 1997—a journal that covered not only gay and lesbian writers of the Silver Age but also the contemporary writers they inspired.

The noticeable difference between gay male attitudes in Moscow and Saint Petersburg may have to do with the economic situations in both cities as much as with their intellectual pretensions (or lack thereof). Certainly, Saint Petersburg has its gay bathhouses and dance clubs, but these cater to a generation to a degree homogenized by a neo-capitalist gay experience. Surprisingly, few gay young men are willing to part with some of the traditions of compulsory heterosexuality, treating women as delicate creatures to be pampered and idolized—objectifying their status in society, as opposed to giving them equal status. This phenomenon perhaps partially explains the lack of Russian gay pornography (gay pornography by extension supposedly having the same gendered complications—the objectification of women—as does heterosexual erotica produced primarily for straight male consumption). Women portrayed in traditional gay pornography serve as foils for an all-male fanstasy world where they are, ultimately, irrelevant.[20] As if they fear being too closely identified with the inevitability of gay sexual desire, the Russian gay media are strikingly sexually clean—in some ways chaste, at least in comparison with the West. In heterosexual male erotica there is a more open tolerance of the dominance and submission of sex, although its complications are rooted in the paradoxical attitude of Russian men and women towards each other. Eliot Borenstein characterizes heterosexual men's pornography as follows:

> In the West, celebrity interviews and short stories by writers of mainstream fiction allow the reader of *Playboy* to claim that he subscribes to the magazine for the articles rather than the pictures. In Russia, however, this process of legitimization is inevitably entangled with questions of gender and national identity. Without a doubt, even a cursory glance confirms the almost ritualistic objectification and subordination of women, but when the men who produce these works and images reflect on their work, it is the Russian male whom they present as weak and embattled. In the textual and visual two-dimensional world of the Russian pornographic magazine, Russian men see themselves as fighting back against national and sexual humiliation. (Borenstein, "Masculinity" 606)

It is no surprise, then, that the mainstream urban Russian heterosexual male's view of homosexuality is that of a passing fashion, informed by Western decadence and doomed to run its course "by the year 2015" (Borenstein, "Masculinity" 611). The Russian perspective on the American "culture wars" is substantially more smug than that of the more embattled American male. Ultimately, the difference lies in the nature of the homosexual community in each country: the United States has been the harbinger of gay identity, if not of gay rights, for at least the past forty years. Most gay art, gay pornography, and gay culture are produced and consumed in America, consistent with the massive output of American mainstream culture. In the proportionally smaller universe of gay male cultural consumption, however, the influence of American values (and of the German "European-American" cultural industry) is immense.

The Russian experience may be compared not only with the American, but also with the German. The latter shares some elements of the politically repressed but culturally dynamic Russian sense of gay identity and the sexually charged American manufacture of a consumerist gay community. In general the cross-pollination of gay male cultural values and national identity has been a unidirectional force in shaping German gay consciousness, as evidenced by the influence of Tom of Finland and the creation of a gay identity centered on gay male sexual consumerism. Yet Germany had a cutting edge gay cultural tradition from the late 1800s until the early 1930s, much like the Russian Empire's small but significant gay cultural consciousness before the early 1920s. Both countries then suffered periods when the nascent gay movement was destroyed historically, physically, and psychologically. The inability of the gay movement (in contradistinction to the lesbian contingent in the feminist movement) to step outside and not threaten the prevailing sex-gender system is undoubtedly at the root of Soviet and Nazi hostility.[21]

Prior to the imposition of Soviet and Nazi rule, the medicalization of homosexuality provided a forum and basis for the demand of equal rights. Central to the argument was the notion that homosexuality is innate and not a matter of voluntary choice. Certainly, this argument was the basis of the German gay rights movement[22] and of Rozanov's theories of girl-boys. One may make a similar argument, of course, for the progress of the gay rights movement in the United States, Canada, and Western Europe since the Stonewall riots. Dennis Altman, in his engrossing pre-AIDS analysis of the gay rights movement in the United States, clearly identifies the association between sexual and political identity:

> . . . the acceptance of group diversity in America has always existed within very severe limits. Indeed, groups are allowed to maintain their identity within American society only to the extent that they are prepared to subscribe to the dominant values of the society; to go outside these values is to be denounced as un-American. It was not by accident that in the fifties McCarthyism linked homosexuality with communism as a threat to "the American way"; this rhetoric is revived in the attacks of the Moral Majority today. (Altman ix)

Later in his discussion, Altman investigates the links between American gay identity and consumer capitalism, implicitly connecting sexual orientation with one of the cornerstones of American society (Altman, ch. 3). He argues that AIDS contributed to a strengthening of this identity, as witnessed by later books and magazines that celebrate gay consumerist urges or indicate ways that the gay movement can more fully assimilate into the North American value system.[23]

The Soviet Union, of course, never afforded its gay citizens the luxury of a consumerist sexual identification. The resulting perceived lack of sexual self-definition within the gendered power structure of the state has produced a rather curious situation. Gay identification in the Soviet Union was more class oriented than sexual: for example, gay men in the arts or the educated classes were comparatively open, though conveniently heterosexual when necessary. In the military or in the working class, sexual contacts between men were quite commonplace but would never have been considered gay.[24] This situation is not substantially different from the state of affairs in the West. However, the lack of a gay paradigm until the 1990s has prompted more than a few Western observers (David Tuller and Laurie Essig among them) to claim that Russian gay identity is beyond the merely sexual, and hence resists categorization characteristic of Western societies.[25] Though in its own way defensible, such a view remains ultimately flawed; its closest analogy would be the situation in the Russian Silver Age or in pre-Nazi Germany. The problem is that the anthropological observer tends to be a contemporary American gay man or lesbian. In this regard, it is striking to read the comments uttered by contemporary Russian youth and recorded by Elena Omel'chenko, a researcher at Ulianovsk State University. She concludes a brief section on attitudes towards homosexuality with these comments:

> All . . . spoke in favour of state regulation with regard to what constitutes appropriate and inappropriate sexuality. In their opinion, models and patterns of behaviour need to be presented in order to educate people. At present, these models come from the West, whereas Russia needs its own models, ones which would take account of the specific nature of the Russian character and spirit, and its tradition of warmth and emotion. The most striking example of a Western model is, according to our respondents, homosexuality, which they do not believe occurs naturally in Russian society. (Omel'chenko 162)

Common to all the respondents cited was disgust and a lack of acceptance of homosexuals as humans.[26] An evident link exists between such pervasive attitudes and the emergence of a cult of hypermasculine sexual consumerism among the New Russians, who cavort with thugs and prostitutes, and ease their way with fistfuls of cash.[27] That this economy of sexual exchange tends to leave out sexual minorities is as much a function of current Russian economic disparities as of the desire to destroy most of the Soviet cultural heritage (though under the leadership of Vladimir Putin, the Kremlin's attitude toward the Soviet past has become palpably more positive, if not revisionist). Viktor Erofeev, in the foreword to his edited collection of contemporary Russian short stories, *Russian Flowers of Evil* [*Russkie tsvety zla*, 1997], claims that current Russian literature is a natural offshoot, a weed, that resulted from the withered and failed bloom of idealized Soviet culture (8). The literature that he describes and includes in his collection frequently contains scenes of (homo)sexual humiliation and mutilation. As a response to the loss of a masculinity constructed in the totalitarian dreams of the Soviet Union, and as an analogy to the state of current heterosexual male Russian pornography (and the coincident invisibility of its gay male equivalent), this literature serves a purpose beyond that of shocking the reader with the heretofore unsaid.

It is no surprise, then, that the nascent gay consciousness in the Russian Federation has turned to the Silver Age in order to claim its historical and national relevance. Much as the single most influential gay male voice in Russia throughout the chaos of the First World War and the 1917 Revolutions was arguably that of Kuzmin, so today, in keeping with time-honored Russian traditions, it is poets, writers, and artists who most audibly articulate the aspirations of the gay community throughout the nation. That this cultural identification should recur while the role of the arts and letters in defining a Russian national consciousness has been sidelined is perhaps mostly a chronological irony, albeit not without significant ramifications. Very few gay writers of the Soviet era—a historical period much closer to home for most Russians, and hence much more threatening—have been recovered, although the voice of Evgenii Kharitonov stands out as a notable exception (Chernetsky 320). The Silver Age manifestations of open gay culture lie beyond the semiotic framework of Russian cultural norms. Saint Petersburger Valerii Mikhailovskii's Male Ballet (*Muzhskoi balet*) and its Moscow offshoots are among the most visible of these mainstream expressions of gay cultural sexuality, though at least initially the company distanced itself from its almost exclusively gay roots, mining theatrical tradition for a more heterosexual justification (Scholl 310).

Much as during the Silver Age, gay men (and lesbians) have turned to artistic expression to re-create and justify their identities.[28] While the academic and scientific establishments have studied homosexuality as a science, the mainstream press (with the exception of liberal newspapers and journals such as Moscow's *Afisha, Ezhnedel'nyi zhurnal,* and *Geo*[29]) has studiously maintained a largely neutral to negative stance, and nongay writers (among them Viktor Erofeev and Vladimir Sorokin) have occasionally used homosexuality as a type of male masochistic extreme to titillate readers. The gay community appears unable to incorporate itself into the current consumerist, gendered, nationalistic structure of the Russian Federation, other than as entertainment venues for the heterosexual nouveaux riches. Gay men and lesbians do not form a consumerist or political class in Russia and have marginalized themselves as a minority in various forms of artistic expression, the most prominent example being the Male Ballet. The troupe has adopted self-deprecating irony and professional self-victimization as tactics in the pursuit of a "greater goal": achieving a modicum of acceptance among the educated classes. Meanwhile, the Soviet idealized model of gender equality has largely disintegrated, replaced with the hypermasculinized culture of sexual consumption.

Not all of the signs that define a gay identity in the West translate successfully into the semiotic system of Russian culture. Tattoos, for example, have been representative of gay male urban hip in the West for over a decade. In Russia, however, tattoos have an entirely different referent and elicit a morbid fascination on account of their association with labor camps and gulags. Nancy Condee elaborates on the significance of tattoos in Russian prison culture:

> A third subset of tattoos signaled sexual preference. Setting aside the subject of punitive tattoos—that is, the forced branding by a fellow prisoner—sexual preference was declared with a bunny (a man who loves women), a butterfly (not a prostitute, just likes to fool around), a boar (butch) . . . , or a violin bow (fem). A pair of eyes tattooed on a man's stomach or groin meant "active gay." This was, however, a rare prison tattoo, insofar as "gay" was largely indistinguishable from "rapable." (Condee 347)

Whereas in Western gay culture tattoos can certainly be used to subvert a dominant cultural paradigm, today they are primarily a means of exerting control over the body. In this respect they are in a category together with body shaving, piercings, and religious adherence to low-carbohydrate diets and workout regimens. The perfected body is a cultural triumph (implicitly, over HIV) and is celebrated in the "dance and drugs scene" of circuit parties.

It is clear that the Russian and Western gay communities, despite their connection through pre-Nazi Germany, have diverged significantly in the past century. The import of American gay pornography and sexual consumerist standards has given rise to gay establishments, bathhouses, and discos, as in most major European cities. Such venues, however, continue to be enclaves with a far more hostile Russian mainstream, which views these businesses as Western imports and associates them with all the gaudy locales frequented by those with financial means.[30] The impulse to destroy is tied to the discomfort of sexual expectation, and it evidently motivates straight writers such as Erofeev (fighting both the discomfort of public homosexuality and the tacit participation it demands of society as a whole), and gay male writers such as Mogutin (who struggles from the opposite side—opposing the inevitable mainstreaming that a public gayness seems to require). This destructive impulse is fed by a need to rebel against the strictures imposed by the economic system, the government, and norms of sexual behavior.

The gendered construction of Russian gay identity is a paradoxical fusion of Russian literary history, American pornography and sexual mass-marketing, and the current growth of Russian consumer capitalism. As such, it is still an unquantifiable entity, clinging to its past in a seemingly vain attempt at justification on terms that can only indicate its existence by arguing its lack of sexualized coherence. Ultimately, when the masculinization of Russian culture is tempered, it is likely that the country's gay and lesbian communities will once again find their voices and their place at the table, wearing their gendered cloak in the nationalist fashion show with pride.

Notes

1. The author's copy has stickers on the cover and on the text itself. Rumor has it that thirty copies of the book were to include Mogutin's sperm and blood.

2. Although a new couple, Denis Gogolev and Mikhail Morozov, attempted to marry in the Russian Orthodox Church in Nizhnyi Novogorod in early September 2003. The marriage was not recognized, and the priest, apparently, was bribed to perform the service. See Mydans.

3. Indeed, the Russian Duma is considering legislation that would once again outlaw male homosexuality, and, for the first time, lesbianism (Braterskii and Mikhailov).

4. Although Tom of Finland may be the best-known example of fascist-inspired gay art in American gay circles today, Rainer Werner Fassbinder's 1982 film version of Jean Genet's *Querelle* was certainly one of the most influential. In contemporary Russia, Georgii Gur'ianov, known in the West as the artist who designed the Amsterdam 1998 Gay Games poster, also eroticizes the fascist ideal of the muscular, powerful man with a strong, square jaw. Eliot Borenstein, in his book *Men Without Women,* acknowledges the surface similarities between Soviet and fascist homoeroticism (although he points out that the aims of the two totalitarian systems were ultimately quite incompatible). See Borenstein, *Men Without Women* 35. Borenstein's introduction and first chapters provide an insightful discussion of the homoerotic and homosocial currents in early revolutionary Russia.

5. The most popular video series is "Military Zone," now in its sixth installment.

6. See Laura Engelstein, *The Keys to Happiness: Sex and the Search for Modernity in Fin-de-Siècle Russia* (Ithaca: Cornell UP, 1992), for a discussion on the progressive nature of sexuality and gender issues in Modernist Russia.

7. Kuzmin was easily the most open of the many gay writers of the Silver Age, a fact that contributed to his disappearance from official Soviet literary history until the late 1980s.

8. My translation; throughout, unless otherwise indicated, all translations are mine.

9. Cited in Karlinsky 355. The original Russian text is in *Literaturnoe nasledstvo 72,* 288. Gor'kii likewise claimed that European fascism and bourgeois values naturally ruined youth through homosexuality. See M. Gor'kii 238.

10. Dan Healey maintains that same-sex male relations continued well into the nineteenth century, despite a legal code prohibiting sodomy. By the 1870s, Saint Petersburg, arguably the capital of the Russian Silver Age, had been redrawn into a type of homosexual geography, with cruising grounds ranging from Nevskii Prospect to the Mariinskii Ballet on Wednesday nights. The bathhouse likewise became a fixture of gay male life. Moscow witnessed similar developments (even today the sidewalk between the Bolshoi Theater and the closest metro station is called the "avenue of love" ["*alleia liubvi*"; see V. E. Kozlovskii 39]. These developments occurred in open view, were known to commentators and satirists, remained basically unpunished by government authorities, and frequently provided a same-sex parallel to services such as government-sactioned brothels. Lesbians were less visible and formed more private social spheres. See Healey, chapters 1 and 2.

11. For a comprehensive analysis and discussion of the connections among sex, anti-Semitism, and philosophy, see Engelstein, chapter 8.

12. In fact, Chekhov was interested in sexuality from a medical point of view, commenting quite extensively, for example, on the practice of homosexuality in prisons on Sakhalin Island. See Chekhov.

13. See Weininger, especially 301–30, where the author equates weakness, intermediate sexuality, and Judaism.

14. Roger Horrocks carries this argument to the arena of pornography: "But what is the meaning of the erect penis in porn? Simply enough, one could answer that it serves to reassure the male viewer that male performance, male conquest, male dominance have no inhibition placed on them, are triumphantly celebrated. In this view, the penis is identified with by men: it is the *subject* of the text. However, one could also argue that the penis is desired by men, is the object of desire" (122).

15. See, for example, Mogutin's *SS: Superhuman Supertexts*.

16. The representation of Russian gay identity in the world of Western (particularly American) fantasy, however, is still hypersexualized (see Beaudoin). For a comprehesive study of suffering and masochism as a persistent trait throughout Russian culture, see Rancour-Laferriere.

17. Essig attempts to balance her coverage of important gay politicos by examining some of the more public expressions of queer sexuality, such as cruising toilets and discos.

18. Ultimately, the converse of a lack of sexual politics is the hostile reaction still encountered in Russia (particularly outside of Moscow and Saint Petersburg) by anyone who self-identifies as gay or lesbian. Whereas physical affection between members of the same sex arguably defines American and Western homosexuality, it is not a clear marker in Russia or most Slavic cultures.

19. Reactions to the notion of raising homosexuals as a special race range from the enthusiastic to the negative.

20. Camille Paglia makes the comparison in a slightly different fashion: "Gay men are guardians of the masculine impulse. To have anonymous sex in a dark alleyway is to pay homage to the dream of male freedom. The unknown stranger is a wandering pagan god. The altar, as in prehistory, is anywhere you kneel. Similarly, straight men who visit prostitutes are valiantly striving to keep sex free from emotion, duty, family—in other words, from society, religion, and procreative Mother Nature" (24–25).

21. See Teresa de Lauretis, *The Technology of Gender,* where she writes, "If gender representations are social positions which carry different meanings, then for someone to be represented and to represent oneself as male or female implies the assumption of the whole of those meaning effects" (5).

22. See Jones, particularly chapter 3.

23. See Kirk and Madsen; Browning. See also any copy of gay and lesbian magazines such as *The Advocate, Genre,* and *Out.* The late 1990s, however, have given birth to more decentralized notions of gay identity through cyberspace, allowing gay teenagers to self-identify at ever earlier ages. Egan 110–17, 128–33.

24. Most stories about sexual adventures in the military are the lore of long conversations with Russian gay men. Recent essays, however, have documented sexual contacts between men as early as the late Imperial period. See, for example, Smith.

25. There are, however, notable exceptions. See Healey; Schulter.

26. Similarly, the work of A. I. Belkin attempted to cure homosexuals so that they could reintegrate into Soviet society's mandated sex roles. See Attwood 116.

27. See Meshcherkina; also Borenstein, "Masculinity" 605–21.

28. Or, as in the West, lesbianism is used for commercial purposes. The popular group T.a.t.u. uses open lesbianism as a media signature.

29. *Geo's* December 2001 issue is devoted to sex. Homosexuality is treated as part of a burgeoning new sexual continuum in Russian society.

30. Like Gor'kii more than half a century earlier, the Russian government recently mixed Western decadence with disease and corruption in considering a bill that would outlaw male (and, for the first time, female) homosexuality with mandatory imprisonment (Braterskii and Mikhailov). The connection between Westernized capitalism and homosexuality is often more implicit than explicit. An interview in the *Saint-Petersburg Times* prior to the Saint-Petersburg Goodwill Games in 1994 highlighted the fears of a middle-aged woman, Valentina Vorob'eva, who worried that the influx of predatory foreigners would infect the city's children with venereal disease. The conflation of foreign (capitalist), pederast (sexual deviant), and disease is telling.

References

Afisha 21, 16–29 Oct. 2000: 73.

Altman, Dennis. *The Homosexualization of America, the Americanization of the Homosexual*. New York: St. Martin's Press, 1982.

Ashwin, Sarah, ed. *Gender, State and Society in Soviet and Post-Soviet Russia*. London: Routledge, 2000.

Attwood, Lynne. *The New Soviet Man and Woman: Sex-Role Socialization in the USSR*. Bloomington: Indiana UP, 1990.

Beaudoin, Luc. "Masculine Utopia in Russian Pornography." *Eros and Pornography in Russian Culture*. Ed. Marcus Levitt and A. L. Toporkov. Moscow: Ladomir, 1999. 622–38.

Bordo, Susan. *The Male Body: A New Look at Men in Public and in Private*. New York: Farrar, Straus & Giroux, 1999.

Borenstein, Eliot. "Masculinity and Nationalism in Contemporary Russian 'Men's Magazines.'" *Eros and Pornography in Russian Culture*. Ed. Marcus Levitt and A. L. Toporkov. Moscow: Ladomir, 1999. 605–21.

———. *Men Without Women: Masculinity and Revolution in Russian Fiction, 1917–1929*. Durham, Duke UP, 2000.

Braterskii, Aleksandr, and Aleksandr Mikhailov. *"Deputaty khotiat sazhat' gomosekualistov." Izvestiia*. 23 Apr. 2002.

Browning, Frank. *The Culture of Desire: Paradox and Perversity in Gay Lives Today*. New York: Vintage, 1994.

Chekhov, Anton Pavlovich. *Ostrov Sakhalin*. (Saint Petersburg: Izdanie A. S. Surovina, 1895).

Chernetsky, Vitaly. "After the House Arrest: Russian Gay Poetry." *Crossing Centuries: The New Generation in Russian Poetry*. Ed. John High et al. Jersey City: Talisman House, 2000. 315–23.

Condee, Nancy. "Body Graphics: Tattooing the Fall of Communism." *Consuming Russia: Popular Culture, Sex, and Society Since Gorbachev*. Ed. Adele Marie Barker. Durham: Duke UP, 1999. 339–61.

de Lauretis, Teresa. *The Technology of Gender*. Bloomington: Indiana UP, 1987.

Dumenkov, V. N. comp. *Liubov' bez granits: Antologiia shedevrov mirovoi literatury*. Saint Petersburg: "KET." 1997.

Egan, Jennifer. "Lonely Gay Teen Seeking Same." *New York Times Magazine*. 10 Dec. 2000: 110–17, 128–33.

Engelstein, Laura. *The Keys to Happiness: Sex and the Search for Modernity in Fin-de-Siècle Russia*. Ithaca: Cornell UP, 1992.

Erofeev, Viktor. *Russkie tsvety zla*. Moscow: Podkova, 1997.

Essig, Laurie. *Queer in Russia: A Story of Sex, Self, and the Other*. Durham: Duke UP, 1999.

Etkind, Aleksandr. *Eros nevozmozhnogo: Istoriia psikhoanaliza v Rossii*. Saint Petersburg: Meduza, 1993.

Gay, Slaviane [*Gay, Slavs*]. 1993; 1994.

Geo. Dec. 2001.

Gor'kii, M. *Sobranie sochinenii v tridtsati tomakh.* Vol. 27. Moscow: Khudozhestvennaia literatura, 1953.

Healey, Dan. *Homosexual Desire in Revolutionary Russia: The Regulation of Sexual and Gender Dissent.* Chicago: U Chicago P, 2001.

Horrocks, Roger. *Male Myths and Icons: Masculinity in Popular Culture.* New York: St. Martin's Press, 1995.

Jones, James W. *"We of the Third Sex": Literary Representations of Homosexuality in Wilhelmine Germany.* New York: Peter Lang, 1990.

Karlinsky, Simon. "Russia's Gay Literature and Culture: The Impact of the October Revolution." *Hidden from History: Reclaiming the Gay and Lesbian Past.* Ed. Martin Duberman and Martha Vicinus. New York: Meridan, 1989. 347–64.

Kirk, Marshall, and Hunter Madsen. *After the Ball: How America Will Conquer Its Fear and Hatred of Gays in the '90s.* New York: Plume, 1990.

Klein, L. S. *Drugaia liubov': Priroda cheloveka i gomoseksual'nost'.* Saint Petersburg: Folio-Press, 2000.

Kon, I. S. *Lunnyi Svet na zare: Liki i maski odnopoloi liubvi.* Moscow: Olimp, 1998.

Kozlovskii, V. E. *Argo russkoi gomoseksual'noi subkul'tury: materialy k izucheniiu.* Benson: Chalidze, 1986.

Kuzmin, M. *Dnevnik 1905–1907.* Saint Petersburg: Izdatel'stvo Ivana Limbakha, 2000.

Literaturnoe nasledstvo. Ed. ANSSSR. Moscow: Nauka, 1965.

McClintock, Anne. *Imperial Leather: Race, Gender and Sexuality in the Colonial Contest.* New York: Routledge, 1995.

Meshcherkina, Elena. "New Russian Men: Masculinity Regained?" *Gender, State and Society in Soviet and Post-Soviet Russia.* London: Routledge, 2000. 105–17.

Mogutin, Yaroslav. *SS: Sverkhchelovecheskie superteksty: Superkniga o sekse, nasilii, i smerti.* New York: Self-published, 2000.

Mydans, Seth. "Nizhny Novgorod Journal: Men Marry, With and Without a Church Blessing." *New York Times.* 9 Sept. 2003.

Omel'chenko, Elena. "'My Body, My Friend?' Provincial Youth Between the Sexual and Gender Revolutions." *Gender, State and Society in Soviet and Post-Soviet Russia.* 137–67.

Paglia, Camille. *Sex, Art, and American Culture.* New York: Vintage, 1992.

Rancour-Laferriere, Daniel. *The Slave Soul of Russia: Moral Masochism and the Cult of Suffering.* New York: New York UP, 1995.

Rotikov, K. K. *Drugoi Peterburg.* Saint Petersburg: Liga Plius, 2000.

Scholl, Tim. "Queer Performance: 'Male' Ballet." *Consuming Russia: Popular Culture, Sex, and Society Since Gorbachev.* Ed. Adele Marie Barker. Durham: Duke UP, 1999. 303–17.

Schulter, Daniel P. *Gay Life in the Former USSR: Fraternity Without Community.* New York: Routledge, 2002.

Smith, S. A. "Masculinity in Transition: Peasant Migrants to Late-Imperial St. Petersburg." *Russian Masculinities in History and Culture.* Ed. Barbara Evans Clements, Rebecca Friedman, and Dan Healey. New York: Palgrave, 2002. 94–112.

Tuller, David. *Cracks in the Iron Closet: Travels in Gay and Lesbian Russia.* Boston: Faber and Faber, 1996.

von Sacher-Masoch, Leopold. *Venus in Furs* [*Venus im Pelz*]. Frankfurt, 1870.

Vorobeva, Valentina. Interview. *Saint-Petersburg Times.* By Evgenii Pogorelov. 1 Aug. 1994: 4.

Weininger, Otto. *Sex and Character.* London: Heinemann, 1906.

Index

References to illustrations appear in italics. Literary works are generally listed by author, films by director, and songs and television series by title.

Contributors

Suzanne Ament teaches Russian and world history at Radford University. Her research focuses on the role of music in Russian society. Much of that music she herself performs as both vocalist and guitarist. Last year her article, "Russian Bard Music in Transition: A Case Study: Ivashchenko and Vasil'ev," appeared in *Journal of Popular Culture.*

Luc Beaudoin (Associate Professor of Russian at the University of Denver) has published on Russian Romantic poetry, including his monograph, *Resetting the Margins: Russian Romantic Verse Tales and the Idealized Woman* (1997). He has also written on queer studies in the Russian context and currently is completing a book on Russian gay poetics, while embarking on a study of the gay male gaze in contemporary Russian media.

Eliot Borenstein is Associate Professor of Russian and Slavic Studies and Director of the Morse Academic Plan at New York University. He is the author of *Men Without Women: Masculinity and Revolution in Russian Fiction, 1917–1929* (Duke 2000). His published research has focused on Russian modernism, postmodernism, and post-Soviet mass culture. He is currently completing a book entitled *Made in Russia (tm): Popular Culture and Moral Panic after 1991* and writing a second volume called *Catastrophe of the Week: Apocalyptic Entertainment in Post-Soviet Russia.*

Helena Goscilo (UCIS Research Professor/Professor of Slavic at the University of Pittsburgh) writes primarily on gender and culture in Russia from the eighteenth to the twenty-first century. She has authored and edited more than a dozen volumes, among them *Fruits of Her Plume* (1993), *Dehexing Sex: Russian Womanhood during and after Glasnost* (1996), *TNT: The Explosive World of Tatyana Tolstaya's Fiction* (1996), *Russian Culture in the 1990s* (2000), and *Politicizing Magic: An Anthology of Russian and Soviet Fairy Tales* (with M. Balina and M. Lipovetsky, Northwestern UP, 2005). Her current projects include an *Encyclopedia of Contemporary Russian Culture* (with T. Smorodinskaya and K. Evans-Romaine, Routledge 2006), a cultural study of the New Russians (with Nadezhda Azhgikhina), and *Fade From Red: Screening the Ex-Enemy During the Nineties,* which analyzes celluloid images of former Cold War antagonists in American and Russian film of the last fifteen years.

Yana Hashamova (Assistant Professor of Slavic, Film, Comparative Studies, and Women's Studies at The Ohio State University) has published in the areas of Russian film, Russian and West European drama, comparative literature and the arts, critical theory and gender studies, and Bulgarian theater and culture. Her articles have appeared in journals such as *Canadian Slavonic Papers, Elementa, The Communication Review,* and *Consumption, Markets & Culture.*

Elizabeth Jones Hemenway is Assistant Professor of History at Xavier University of Louisiana. Her research interests include the dynamics of gender and narrative in the context of revolution. She currently is working on a manuscript titled *Family, Conflict, and Continuity: Constructing Narratives of Revolution in Russia, 1905–1930,* which should be completed by spring 2006.

Lilya Kaganovsky is Assistant Professor of Slavic, Comparative Literature, and Cinema Studies at the University of Illinois, Urbana-Champaign. Her publications include "How the Soviet Man Was (Un)Made," *Slavic Review* (Fall 2004); and "Visual Pleasure in Stalinist Cinema: Ivan Pyr'ev's *The Party Card,*" in Christina Kiaer and Eric Naiman, eds., *Everyday Life in Early Soviet Russia* (Indiana UP, 2005). Her current project focuses on questions of male subjectivity in Stalinist literature and film.

Andrea Lanoux is Associate Professor in the Department of Slavic Studies at Connecticut College. Her book *Od narodu do kanonu [From Nation to Canon]* (Warsaw 2003) examines the formation of the Russian and Polish Romantic literary canons between 1815 and 1865. She has also published on Russian and Polish women's writing, Adam Mickiewicz, and Tolstoy's *Anna Karenina.*

Elena Prokhorova is Visiting Assistant Professor in the Department of Modern Languages and Literatures at the University of Richmond. She specializes in late Soviet and post-Soviet culture, film, and the media. Her recent publications include articles in *SEEJ* and *Slavic Review* on serial television and national identity. Among her current projects is an article on Nikita Mikhalkov's film *At Home Among Strangers, A Stranger At Home* (Wallflower Press) and a study of Sergei Mikhalkov's poetry and plays for children.

Michele Rivkin-Fish (Associate Professor of Anthropology at the University of Kentucky) has published on sex education, health development, and the politics of demographic analysis in Russia. Her monograph, *Women's Health in Post-Soviet Russia: The Politics of Intervention* (Indiana UP, 2005), examines the cultural and political dimensions of global and local efforts to improve Russian women's health in the 1990s. Her current work explores issues ranging from the re-creation of kinship in Russia and Poland under capitalism to the politics of addressing ethnic diversity in post-Soviet societies.

Valentina Zaitseva (Lecturer at the University of Washington at Seattle) teaches Russian, investigates the interaction between language and communication, and is the author of *The Speaker's Perspective in Grammar and Lexicon: The Case of Russian* (1995). She contributed a chapter, "Referential Knowledge in Discourse: Interpretation of {I, YOU} in Male and Female Speech," to the first monograph on gender in Slavic languages, edited by M. Mills (1999), and two book-length chapters on Russian literature for the award-winning volume edited by E. Boyle and G. Gerhart, *The Russian Context: The Culture Behind the Language* (2004). Her other published work (over a dozen articles in professional journals) concerns discourse theory, semantics, and pragmatics of Russian.